The Nationalities Question in the Soviet Union

edited by
GRAHAM SMITH

LONGMAN
London and New York

Longman Group UK Limited,

Longman House, Burnt Mill, Harlow,
Essex CM20 2JE, England
and Associated Companies throughout the world.

*Published in the United States of America
by Longman Inc., New York*

© Longman Group UK Limited 1990

First published 1990

British Library Cataloguing In Publication Data

The Nationalities question in the Soviet Union
1. Soviet Union, Nationalities. Political aspects
I. Smith, Graham
323.147

ISBN 0-582-03953-3
ISBN 0-582-03955-X pbk

Library of Congress Cataloging-in-Publication Data

The Nationalities question in the Soviet Union/edited by Graham Smith.

p. cm.

Includes bibliographical references.
ISBN 0-582-03953-3 : £28.00. — ISBN 0-582-03955-X (pbk.) : £14.95
1. Soviet Union—Politics and government—1985– 2. Nationalism–
–Soviet Union. 3. Perestroïka. I. Smith, Graham, 1953–
DK288.N37 1990
320.947—dc20   90–34756
CIP

The cover illustration is adapted from an idea seen in a cartoon in *PWA*, a Polish *samizdat* magazine, issue number 40, 2nd December 1988.

Set in 11/12 Garamond

Printed and bound in Great Britain
at the Bath Press, Avon

Contents

Preface

The idea for this book originated during the spring of 1988 when it was clear that Gorbachev's reforms were in the process of opening up a Pandora's box of ethnic problems which hitherto had remained largely hidden beneath the surface of Soviet politics. Since February 1988, when the Nagorno-Karabakh Soviet took the unprecedented step of calling for their region's transfer to the neighbouring Soviet republic of Armenia, the paroxysm of ethnic and nationalist unrest has continued unabated, embracing the traditionally assertive nationalities, like the Baltic peoples and Georgians, as well as the hitherto most loyal, such as the Belorussians and Moldavians.

Such developments, more or less overnight, have made an important but comparatively neglected area of Soviet studies – that of the nationalities question – not only topical but also in need of reappraisal. The aim of this book is therefore to provide a systematic analysis of the Soviet Union's major nationalities in the light of the new circumstances in which they now find themselves. The dramatic changes affecting the world's largest multi-ethnic society are clearly complex and multi-faceted. By bringing together a large group of contributors with expertise on particular nationalities it is hoped that this book will illustrate to the reader the often strikingly different ways in which the nationalities have been affected by and responded to *perestroika* and *glasnost'*.

According to official sources, there are 140 nationalities in the Soviet Union. Although this book only deals with twenty of them, in total they constitute over nine-tenths of the Soviet population. They include the fifteen union republic nationalities which make up the top tier of the federal structure, together with the Volga Tatars, Buryats and Yakut of the Russian republic, and the Crimean Tatars and Jews (Figure 1).

The book is structured as follows. Chapter One provides an historical overview of Soviet nationalities policy, thus enabling Gorbachev's policies to be located within an appropriate context. Due to their special position within Soviet society and politics, the Russians are singled out for particular treatment in the second chapter. The remaining chapters on the minority nationalities are divided into six parts, largely by regional – administrative groupings, with each part being prefaced by a brief introduction. An appendix of statistical tables on the nationalities is also included for general reference, and wherever possible, includes preliminary data published from the 1989 Soviet census.

In order to ensure continuity and the book's overall coherence, each contributor has followed a similar format. Chapters begin by briefly locating the nationality within an historical, geopolitical and cultural context. Next, the nationality is dealt with as part of the Soviet Union, paying particular attention to socio-economic, cultural and political developments, and to relations with Moscow. Each chapter then focuses on analysing developments since Gorbachev came to power, with particular attention being paid to such common themes as the impact of the reforms on national cultures and local economies, the role of native leaders in relation to such changes, issues pertinent to fuelling ethnic and territorial demands, and the emergence of new nationalist organisations and other forms of ethno-cultural resurgence. Needless to say, events continue to move fast in the Soviet Union not least due to the nationalities question. Every attempt has therefore been made to provide as up-to-date and analytically useful an examination as possible.

The major acknowledgement which an editor of a volume such as this needs to make is to the contributors. All of them responded with enthusiasm to the project, and I am particularly grateful for their willingness to follow editorial guidelines, which, we hope, provide the coherence in approach and balance in coverage that was intended. I should also like to thank Longman's editor, Chris Harrison, for his encouragement, interest and support and for his willingness to allow the project to expand beyond the initially intended coverage. To Maria Constantinou I am grateful for her secretarial help and to Ian Agnew for his cartographic work.

GRAHAM SMITH
Sidney Sussex College, Cambridge

May 1990

List of Maps

List of Contributors

Shirin Akiner, School of Oriental and African Studies, University of London.

Annette Bohr, Research Section, Radio Free Europe/Radio Liberty, Munich.

Marie Broxup, Society for Central Asian Studies, London.

Ralph Clem, Department of International Relations, Florida International University.

Simon Crisp, St Catherine's College, Oxford.

Simon Dixon, Department of Modern History, University of Glasgow.

Tamara Dragadze, School of Oriental and African Studies, University of London.

Peter Duncan, School of Slavonic and East European Studies, University of London.

Jonathan Eyal, Royal United Services Institute for Defence Studies, London.

Yoram Gorlizki, St Antony's College, Oxford.

Edmund Herzig, Department of Middle Eastern Studies, University of Manchester.

Caroline Humphrey, Department of Social Anthropology, University of Cambridge.

Riina Kionka, Research Section, Radio Free Europe/Radio Liberty, Munich.

Edward Lazzerini, Department of History, University of New Orleans.

Robert Parsons, BBC Russian World Service, London.

John Payne, Department of Linguistics, University of Manchester.

Graham Smith, Department of Geography, University of Cambridge.

Ingvar Svanberg, Centre for Multi-ethnic Research, Uppsala University.

V. Stanley Vardys, Department of Political Science, University of Oklahoma.

Piers Vitebsky, Scott Polar Research Institute, University of Cambridge.

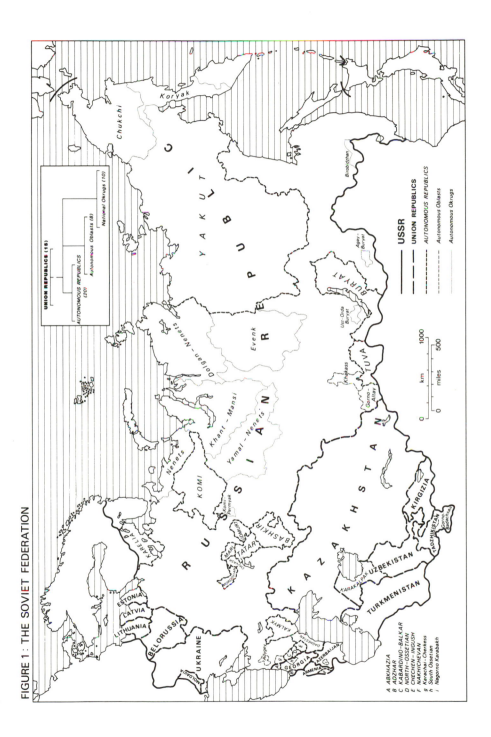

FIGURE 1: THE SOVIET FEDERATION

CHAPTER ONE

Nationalities Policy from Lenin to Gorbachev

Graham Smith

Alexis de Tocqueville's remark that the most dangerous time for a bad government is when it starts to reform itself has a particular applicability to the Soviet Union. Following Mikhail Gorbachev's election to First Party Secretary in March 1985, the Soviet Union has undergone major social, economic and political upheavals activated by a reform-minded leadership willing to engage in the country's systemic transformation. This 'revolution from above' has also fuelled a scale of ethnic unrest hitherto unparalleled in Soviet history as the nationalities within the world's largest multi-ethnic society seize upon the opportunities opened up by *glasnost'* (openness) and promises of democratisation to put forward their demands for greater national self-determination. It is, however, not only the traditionally assertive nationalities which have been drawn into the arena of ethnic politics, like the Georgians, Estonians and Latvians, but also those nationalities, like the Belorussians, Moldavians and Armenians, who up until recently were considered to be amongst the most loyal. Nationalisms have also emerged to take various Janus-like forms, resurrecting long-held national beliefs and prejudices rooted in the collective imagination and projected on to the reality of past and current inequities. Indeed, the growing disjuncture between nationality demands, as reflected in the scale and level of violence, demonstrations and strikes, and the centre's ability to convince the nationalities of the validity of its policies, is so great that a number of Sovietologists consider the nationalities question as posing probably the greatest challenge to the success of Gorbachev's reforms.[1]

As a necessary introduction to the subsequent systematic treatment of the Soviet Union's major nationalities, this chapter examines the nature of the nationalities question by focusing on the evolution of nationalities policy from Lenin to Gorbachev. In particular, it will be argued that, although still grounded within a Marxist-Leninist tradition, of necessity present-day nationality thinking has undergone a belated re-evaluation. Whether, however, this is sufficient to appease the complex demands which reflect the multi-ethnic character of the Soviet federation is still very much in question.

LENIN AND NATIONAL SELF-DETERMINATION

Classical Marxism had little to say about the national question and offered no advice on the issue of national self-determination. It did, however, bequeath both a vision of historical progress and methodology from which a theoretical and practical position on the nation was developed.[2] That both Marx and Engels should treat the national question as peripheral and ethnic divisions as purely contingent to social and economic development is in part due to their interpretation of capitalism as facilitating the dissolution of national differences. While the growth of nations – considered as essentially bourgeois phenomena – was viewed as inseparable from the rise of modern capitalism, for the politically important working class, nationality differences were seen to be gradually losing their meaning and would not outlive capitalism. Concerned with the universal and necessary properties of all capitalist societies, cultural differences between societies tended to be treated as 'complicating factors' that were both methodological and programmatic distractions from ensuring the establishment of socialism. Consequently, nations tended to be treated as either re-actionary or progressive, depending on their social location within the world economic order. From their writings also sprang a bias in favour of large state formations, for as Engels insisted, one les-son to be drawn from capitalism's development were the favourable conditions that large territorial organisations could provide for social and economic development. This, it was held, was in contradistinction to federalism which, in perpetuating regional division and isolation, preserved traditional values and economic backwardness.[3] It would seem, however, that neither Marx nor Engels envisaged either lin-guistic universalism or a world in which there would be no role for nations.

The right of nations to national self-determination was, however, adopted and incorporated into the Programme of the Second Interna-tional at its 1896 London Congress, but it was not until a few years later, at the 1903 Congress of the Russian Social Democratic Workers' Party (RSDWP), that the Leninist notion of national self-determination began to take shape. Particularly influential in formulating Leninist policy was the counter-reformist position adopted by the Austro-Marxists, Otto Bauer and Karl Renner.[4] Like many socialists in the turn of the century empires of eastern Central Europe, the multi-ethnic character and growing political salience of ethnic divisions made the role of nations in the establishment of socialism and their future position in a socialist society a far more problematic affair than in the established nation-states of Western Europe. If the economic logic of both capitalism and socialism led to large state formations, then in eastern Central Europe this implied that the boundaries of existing polities would constitute the basis for further integration. Moreover, there was also the problem of those nationality groupings living outside their national territories. For Bauer and Renner territory was not to be a prerequisite feature of the nation; rather, the nation was deemed to be a product of a common history, as 'an aggregate of people bound up into a community of fate' and as 'a cultural community no longer tied to the soil'.[5] Consequently, nations should be granted cultural autonomy without regard to the compactness of their geographical settlement. In offering each nation the right to educational and cultural autonomy within the overall framework of a multi-ethnic federal state, a practical vision was presented where support of the nationality groupings was essential to the building of socialism. Inspired by such proposals, representatives of the Jewish Bund, who had founded their own working-class organisation in 1879, and whose appeal to a diaspora nationality employed Yiddish as the language of the *shtetl*, called on the Congress to acknowledge ethnic interests in structuring a nationalities policy and in the right of nations to set up and run their own party organisations.

It was precisely this formulation of national self-determination which was interpreted by Lenin as politically retrogressive and divisive. Lenin saw a centralised party as essential to securing socialism, and later was to extend the centralised principle to the state. In an attempt to rebut the Austro-Marxist proposals polemically, Lenin requested Stalin to formulate a position on the national question, which was to set the basic guidelines for subsequent generations of Soviet policy-makers and thinkers.

In his *Marxism and the National and Colonial Questions*, Stalin provided a restrictive yet vague enough conception of nationhood to allow for political manoeuvrability. He took the nation to be 'an historically constituted, stable community of people, formed on the basis of a common language, territory, economic life, and psychological make-up, manifested in a common culture'.[6] For Lenin, however, what actually constituted a nation was of trivial importance compared with securing within the boundaries of the Russian empire the mobilisation and unity of the emerging industrial working class against tsarist autocracy, for above all else the nationality problem was viewed as a problem of securing political power. It is therefore precisely due to such a concern with providing the optimal conditions for mobilisation against capitalism and other retrogressive forces that his interpretation of national self-determination was developed. In forwarding the right of nations to self-determination, which he saw as linked exclusively with the right to political secession, Lenin was adopting a political strategy for resolving Russia's national question. By granting Russia's minority nations the right to statehood he was in effect acknowledging national sensibilities, for according to this logic, if nations were not given this right, then, amongst peoples whose national consciousness was emerging as a political force, it would encourage a combative nationalism which would run counter to the establishment of socialism in Russia.[7] But although endorsing the right of nations to secession, for Lenin this did not mean that *any* separatist movement should be supported. In an oft-quoted analogy, Lenin noted that 'the right of divorce is not an invitation for all wives to leave their husbands'.[8] Such a viewpoint was therefore wholly consistent with the resolution passed at the April 1917 conference of the Russian Communist Party, which reasserted the right of 'all nations forming part of Russia' to 'free separation and the creation of an independent state'.[9] Moreover, Lenin believed that even if small nations did seize the opportunity to declare themselves states, they would soon realise the benefits of being part of a larger territorial unit and would opt for reincorporation. For Lenin the ethnic constitution of such a polity included proposals to divide the country into 'autonomous and self-governing territorial units according – among other things – to nationality; freedom and equality of languages, and the protection of the cultural and educational rights of minorities'.[10] With socialism's establishment, such a programme also envisaged the *sblizhenie* ('coming together') and eventual *sliyanie* ('merger') of the proletariat of different nations.

THE SOVIET FEDERATION

After 1917, Lenin's position on federation underwent a complete change: from regarding 'the right to federation' as 'meaningless'[11] to an acceptance of it as the most suitable form of organisation for a multi-ethnic state. In the 1918 constitution, the Party had decided upon a federal form of state organisation and in 1919 was proposing 'a federated union of states, organised in a soviet manner', 'as one of the transitional forms on the road to complete unity'.[12] The extent to which such a federation could be realised following the Bolshevik Revolution of October 1917 and the freeing of 'the prison of the peoples' from the shackles of a territorially disintegrating empire was, however, another matter. Between 1918 and 1920, Bolshevik support outside the ethnically Russian heartland was restricted to large urban centres, while in most parts of the ethnic periphery anti-Soviet forces predominated. The 1918 Treaty of Brest-Litovsk had paved the way for independence for Finland, Poland, Estonia, Latvia and Lithuania, which meant that primarily for geostrategic reasons, these borderland states were beyond the remit of possible Bolshevik control. In the Ukraine, Central Asia and in Transcaucasia, however, Bolshevik interests remained alive, even although sovereign statehood had also been proclaimed throughout these regions in 1918. Different positions were also being publicly formulated among leading Bolsheviks in both Moscow and the provinces as to the exact form which relations between these states should take. Rakovsky and the Georgian Bolsheviks, Mdivani and Makharadze, favoured a loose political arrangement by treaty, in which socialist states would remain sovereign entities, thus rejecting the founding of an integral Soviet federation. At the other end of the spectrum, Stalin had put forward the notion of 'autonomisation', which in effect meant withdrawing state sovereignty from the independent socialist republics and providing them with only limited autonomous status. His conception of the right of nations to self-determination had also undergone refinement, for now the right to its exercise was restricted to the working population only. Lenin was clearly uneasy about the blanket way in which Stalin employed the notion of 'proletarian self-determination', and at the 8th All-Russia Congress in March 1919 pointed out that such a formulation often exaggerated existing intra-national class differences and unity, pointing out that the right to national self-determination must also apply to socially less-developed peoples, like the Bashkirs.[13] By 1922, Stalin, along with Kamenev and Manuilsky, were arguing for a unitary form of territorial organisation in which the non-Russian nationalities would become autonomous republics within a Russian-dominated Soviet federation.[14] This, however, was rejected by Lenin on the grounds that it would provide a privileged status to Russians and would further fuel Russian chauvinism.

A middle road was adopted by Lenin in what is euphemistically referred to as the federal compromise, but it was a combination of the outcome of the Civil War and Stalin's notion of 'proletarian self-determination' which sealed the nature of this 'compromise'. In the case of Georgia, independent statehood, under a successfully led Menshevik government (1918–20), was overthrown by the Red Army, a decision made by Lenin apparently as a result of Stalin and Ordzhonikidze purposely misinforming the General Secretary of local political circumstances.[15] The right of secession was in effect replaced by the right to unite, for it was in the interests of the workers to remain part of a larger proletarian state in which secession could not occur that was contrary to the interests of the workers. Constitutionally (as spelt out in the Union Treaty of December 1922),[16] the larger non-Russian nationality groupings were offered equality of union republic status within a Soviet federation which would honour their right to secession and would grant their major nationalities considerable cultural and administrative autonomy. In return for these guarantees, the nationalities would give up their present form of state sovereignty and become part of a socialist federation of states.

With incorporation into the Soviet federation, the national oppression of the nationalities was deemed to have been automatically eliminated; they were now acknowledged as free to develop towards fulfilment of their national aspirations. The policy of promoting the equality of nations, however, was bound up with a conception of nationhood in which the status of territorial homeland was fundamental, for it was on this basis that the more important national groups were given the most meaningful administrative, constitutional and legal expressions of nationhood in the form of union republic status. It was these indigenous peoples in particular who benefited from the new policy of *Korinezatsiya* (meaning 'nativisation'), introduced in 1923, and designed to promote the training and development of native personnel, rather than Russian or Russified elements. Other policies were designed to promote the local language, education and culture, and generally to de-Russify the non-Russian cities. As part of Party policy, the Russian language was officially discriminated against in the Ukraine and Belorussia, while in the Central Asian republics, with their non-literary languages, encouragement was given to develop titular alphabets and linguistic structures.[17] Moscow also began purposely to link the economic development of the less-developed regions, which by and large were the non-Russian borderlands, with nationalities policy, and considerable strides were made, particularly in the most backward region of Central Asia, in providing the beginnings of a modern urban-industrial economy and in improving the economic well-being and education of its indigenous peoples. As elsewhere, the migration of Russian specialists and workers into the non-Russian republics was also encouraged.

Never far from the surface of this attempt to incorporate a cultural pluralism into Soviet state-building was what Lenin had referred to as his fear of 'Great Russian chauvinism'.[18] The support and cooperation of the non-Russians in the building of socialism could only proceed, he argued, through suppressing Russian nationalism. Yet for Stalin, no doubt concerned about the level of indigenisation that was occurring in the non-Russian republics, which he probably interpreted as contrary to ensuring the effective implementation of his far-reaching economic policies, it was minority nationalisms which posed the greater threat. Nationalism was considered as a reason for opposition to collectivisation in the Ukraine and the purging of Ukrainian personnel presented as necessary in stamping out centrifugal tendencies. In referring to the non-Russian nationalities, he noted in a 1934 speech that 'survivals of capitalism in the minds of men are much more long-lived in the realm of the national question than in any other area'.[19] The Russification of the non-Russian republics began, which included the Russification of the native languages, and by the late 1930s the Russian language was being vigorously promoted in schools, as were the number of Russian schools in the provinces. It was, however, during the Second World War that the promotion of Russian and the Russian people as 'the elder brother' reached new heights, with Russian patriotic symbolism permeating Soviet propagandistic and ideological statements. For Stalin, it therefore did not seem inappropriate, as part of the 1945 victory celebrations, to propose 'a toast to our Soviet people, and in particular to the health of the Russian people . . . the leading nation of all nations belonging to the Soviet Union', because the Russian people had 'earned in this war general recognition as the guiding force of the Soviet Union among all the peoples of our country.'[20]

KHRUSHCHEV AND THE 1961 PARTY CONGRESS

In 1956, at the historic 20th Party Congress, the new General Secretary, Nikita Khrushchev, publicly rebuked Stalin and Stalinist practices. He exposed and denounced the forced mass resettlement of some of those nationalities – namely, the Balkars, Chechens, Ingush, Karachai and Kalmyks – who had been moved during the Second World War from their homelands for geostrategic reasons, and fully rehabilitated and restored their nationality rights. (Putting right previous wrongs did not, however, extend to the other deported nationalities, the Crimean Tatars, Meskhetians and Volga Germans.)[21] Accusations of Stalin deviating from Lenin's nationality policy were followed by a clear endorsement by the Congress of committing the Party to the flourishing (*ratsvet*) of nations. Other policies also seemed to bode well for nationality development, particularly within the arena of economic policy. Nationalities policy was linked to improving the socio-economic development of the non-Russian republics, with a commitment to bringing the least developed up to the level of the more advanced. In 1957, in an attempt to improve economic management, a degree of autonomy was granted to the regions through the setting up of regional economic councils (or *sovnarkhozy*), resulting in granting of substantial powers to various regions within the larger republics and to the smaller nationality republics.

Yet while Khrushchev continued in subsequent major speeches to reiterate the Party's commitment to the flourishing of nations, it was also increasingly evident that this was to occur concomitantly with encouraging their 'coming together' (*sblizhenie*). Within the arena of nationality education in particular, there was widespread concern in the non-Russian republics that the 1958–59 educational reforms would further promote the Russian language, to the detriment of the native tongue. The reforms favoured Russian as a medium of instruction in native schools while exempting Russians from learning local languages. This paved the way for the promotion of Russian language teaching, with particularly negative effects for the languages of the more minor, non-union republic-based nationalities.[22] Whereas almost half of the non-Russian population claimed a knowledge of Russian by the 1979 census, only 3.5 per cent of Russians could claim a similar knowledge of another Soviet language,[23] in spite of the high proportion (a fifth of all Russians) living outside their namesake republic.[24] That Khrushchev should choose increasingly to emphasise and step up assimilative aspects to nationality development probably had much to do with the emergence during the late 1950s of what Moscow labelled as 'localism' (*mestnichestvo*) and 'national narrow-mindedness', for the opportunities opened up by the newly founded economic autonomy of the nationality republics had resulted in the promotion of local interests. In those republics deemed to have gone too far, local leaders were purged.

It was, however, at the 22nd Party Congress in 1961 that Khrushchev spoke of his commitment to the dialectics of nationality development, so providing the basis for an official policy which was to remain largely unchallenged for the next twenty-five years. Separate national cultures were to 'flourish' alongside their 'drawing together' until their final 'merger' (*sliyanie*) was realised.[25] Despite Khrushchev's optimism about achieving full Communism in the foreseeable future, he did not envisage that reaching this end-stage of historical development was concomitant with *sliyanie*. Paraphrasing Lenin, he noted that 'state and national differences will exist long after the victory of socialism in all countries'.[26] So, while supporting the notion of *sliyanie*, he considered it to be a long way off, preferring in the short term the more politically pragmatic commitment to achieving the unity (*edinstvo*) of nations. His usage of this term should not be interpreted as interchangeable with *sliyanie*, but rather, as Rutland rightly notes, as a purely political notion meaning no more than the 'brotherly alliance' of Soviet nations ensured by the efforts of the Communist Party of the Soviet Union (CPSU). Furthermore, 'it does not imply any social policies that threaten their nationhood; on the contrary, "unity" logically entails the continued existence of nations, rather than their abolition'.[27] Yet when Khrushchev insensitively referred to the administrative divisions that formally described the national territorial homelands as 'losing their former significance',[28] he was not only being consistent with Lenin's vision of the federation's transitional nature, but probably also with the viewpoint current at the time that the logic of planning for modern economic conditions was counter to the continuation of nationality-based administrative divisions.[29] It is unlikely, however, that Khrushchev envisaged the current state of *rapprochement* as sufficiently developed to abolish the federation.

THE SOVIET PEOPLE AND 'DEVELOPED SOCIALISM'

The whole tenor of the Brezhnev administration differed from that of its predecessor. In contrast to Khrushchev, who had attempted to enact far-reaching economic and administrative reforms, and who had committed the regime to achieving rapid economic growth, the Brezhnev leadership pursued an increasingly cautious and conservative approach, more pragmatic and less idealistic in character. The return to centralised ministerial control over the economy by the mid-1960s ended further experimentation with the sort of institutional reforms which had previously threatened to undermine central authority. Western analysts interpreted the abandonment of such reforms and Brezhnev's emphasis on 'harmonious development'[30] as the price the regime was willing to pay for ensuring social stability.[31] Relations between Moscow and the nationality republics began to take on an increasingly corporatist character.[32]

In return for maintaining ethno-territorial stability and meeting more realistically set production targets, Moscow was prepared to allow republic political elites both greater flexibility in native appointments to local positions and some *de facto* administrative leeway. Brezhnev's policy of putting greater trust in native and local cadres certainly made party and state life in the republics less turbulent and more comfortable. The Brezhnev regime also made clear its continuing commitment to ethno-regional equalisation, to full employment (often at considerable economic cost), and to improving standards of living, all of which contributed to a general rise in the material well-being of the regions during the 1960s and 1970s. While occasions did arise when republic leaders were deemed by Moscow to have gone too far in putting republic interests first, such outbursts were the exception. Those who expressed nationalist views exceeding the bounds permitted by Moscow were subject to dismissal and repression.

The more cautious and socially pragmatic thrust to the Brezhnev administration was reflected in official policy towards the national question. The central tenets of the 1961 Congress, however, although subject to refinement and to the notable dropping from major policy speeches of the commitment to *sliyanie*, remained essentially intact. While never included in the Party programme at that Congress Khrushchev had referred to the emergence of a new historical community, that of the Soviet people (*Sovetskii narod*). At the 1971 Party Congress, Brezhnev expanded upon and made great play of the emergence of this 'new human community sharing a common territory, state, economic system, culture, the goal of building communism and a common language'.[33] Within the arena of nationality relations, the concept of *Sovetskii narod* in effect emerged as a synonym for the newly self-designated era of 'developed socialism', of how far the party and state had progressed in the flourishing and coming together of the nationalities, but also a shorthand reminder of the progress which society had still to make along the road of *sblizhenie*. As Brezhnev made evident on the fiftieth anniversary speech marking the foundation of the Soviet state: 'nationality relations, even in a society of developed socialism, are a reality which is constantly developing and putting forth new problems and tasks'.[34] He also made it clear that the further 'coming together' of nations was an objective process, and that the Party was against forcing integration.

Official policy throughout the 1970s and early 1980s continued to accept tacitly the existence of a multi-ethnic society of culturally distinct yet integrated nationalities.[35] This was also extended to include statehood, an issue which was resurrected during the years leading up to the formulation of the 1977 Soviet constitution. Those favouring the abolition of nationality-based administrative divisions contended that the *rapprochement* between nations had proceeded sufficiently far to make the notion of federation obsolete.[36] Brezhnev, however, made it clear that he was against any proposals advocating either the federation's abolition of curtailment or the constitutional right (as included in the 1924 and 1936 constitutions) of union republics to territorial secession. 'We should,' he noted, 'be taking a dangerous course if we were artificially to accelerate this objective process of *rapprochement* between nations'.[37]

At his last Party Congress in 1981, Brezhnev reiterated the success of *Sovetskii narod* and of a multi-ethnic state more united than ever. Again he noted with concern those tendencies designed artificially to speed up *sblizhenie* and obliterate national identities. But although the Soviet people were united more than ever, for the General Secretary this did not imply 'that all the problems of the relations between the nationalities have been resolved. The dynamics of the development of a large multi-ethnic state like ours gives rise to many problems requiring the party's tactful attention.'[38] It was, however, the socio-economic development and the further contribution of the republics to 'developed socialism' which he singled out for particular comment. While declaring that 'there are no backward ethnic outskirts today', he did make it clear that one of the Party's objectives was 'to increase the material and cultural potential of each republic', which would, at the same time, 'make the maximum use of this potential for the balanced development of the country as a whole'. Their 'coming together in every field', he went on to argue, would be speeded up through the intensive social and economic development of each republic. Like his predecessors, he also reminded his audience of the role played by the 'disinterested assistance of the Russian people' in the socio-economic development of the republics.[39]

Certainly by the early 1980s the increasing stagnation of the Soviet economy was beginning to be widely felt throughout the republics, with the gap in living standards also growing between the more advanced, like

Russia proper and the Baltic, and the less developed.[40] The corporatist character of centre-union republic relations was also being further undermined by new challenges from Moscow to the regions. By the late 1970s, the Brezhnev regime was calling for the promotion of the Russian language in the non-Russian republics through increasing the teaching of Russian from kindergartens to universities.[41] And at the 1981 Party Congress, spurred on by growing concern in Moscow for the scale of indigenisation of cadre appointments at the republic level, Brezhnev raised the delicate issue of non-Russian representation in the non-Russian republics. 'In recent years,' he noted, 'there has been a considerable growth in some republics in the number of citizens from the non-indigenous nationalities. These have their own specific needs in terms of language, culture and everyday life. The central committees of the Communist Parties of the republics and the territorial and regional committees should go deeper into these matters and opportunely suggest ways of meeting these needs.'[42] In a speech the following year, Candidate Politburo Member Boris Ponomarev hinted that affirmative action policies might have gone too far, reminding his audience that every republic should 'serve the interests of all labouring peoples regardless of whether they belong to the titular nationality'.[43] The problem of encouraging particularly the movement of specialist labour into areas of growing shortages was also becoming a major issue to which the demographers, Litvinova and Urlanis, attributed affirmative action policies and the rootedness to place which they encouraged, as a contributor: 'this policy [of preferential treatment] was justified during the initial post-war revolutionary years, but it should be changed in the light of current conditions'.[44]

Yuri Andropov, who succeeded Brezhnev in 1982, also reiterated concern about cadre policy and that past nativisation policies had gone too far. Although supporting the need for fairer representation of all nationalities within the union republics, he rejected the notion of formal quotas, for 'an arithmetic approach to the solutions of such problems is inappropriate'.[45] However, he appeared to take a more integrationist approach by stating that the goal of nationalities policy was 'not only the *sblizhenie* of nations, but also their *sliyanie*'.[46] But as Olcott rightly argues, the reintroduction of *sliyanie* after a decade of omission from major policy speeches should not be interpreted as indicative of an active commitment to the fusion of nations; rather, the firm line adopted had more to do with Andropov reasserting the role of the General Secretary as a leading authority on the nationalities question,[47] for in other respects he adopted a more conciliatory line. He reiterated his commitment to federalism, to 'the free development of each republic and each nationality within the boundary of the fraternal union'. He also made it clear that national differences would exist for a long time, 'much longer than class differences'.[48]

GORBACHEV AND THE NATIONAL QUESTION

Despite Gorbachev's willingness to set the pace and to tackle systemically the problems of the ailing Soviet economy and overhaul the state-censored society which he inherited in March 1985, the new leadership continued to treat the nationalities question as of relative insignificance. In contrast to the other major social and economic problems which the administration inherited, it was only when the reform programme triggered off growing ethnic discontent that the leadership was prepared to take the nationalities question on board the reformist agenda. In his honeymoon first year as General Secretary, on the few occasions that he spoke on the nationalities question, Gorbachev merely restated Brezhnev's policy. In the summer of 1985, on the occasion of the celebrations commemorating the fortieth anniversary of the Soviet victory in the Second World War, he referred to the continuing flourishing and *rapprochement* of nations, which continued to manifest itself in the deeply felt sense of belonging to 'a single family – the Soviet people'.[49] He also emphasised the role played by the Russian people in the final victory over fascism, as well as of Stalin's contribution, but the general tenor of his speech 'was presented in class and anti-imperialist rather than nationalist terms'.[50] But his insensitivity to the multi-ethnic nature of Soviet society was particularly evident on a visit to Kiev on 25 June 1985, in which on two occasions he referred to the Soviet Union as Russia.[51]

Although Gorbachev was the first Soviet leader since Lenin without any career background in a non-Russian republic, he was not without experience of the national question. A Russian by nationality, he was born and brought up in Stavropol *krai*, an area of the North Caucasus within the Russian republic (RSFSR). After a spell at Moscow State University during the early 1950s, he returned to his native homeland, where he spent all his early career before returning to the capital city in 1978 to take up a promoted post. In late 1943, when Gorbachev was twelve years old, Stalin had ordered the wholesale forced deportation of two national minorities of Stavropol *krai*, the Karachai and Cherkess. Gorbachev was probably too young to comprehend what had happened, but by the late 1950s, when Khrushchev had allowed these peoples to return to their native homelands, he was already First Secretary of the Stavropol town *Komsomol*, and a member of the *Kraikom Komosomol Bureau*. He must therefore have carried some responsibility both for overseeing the reinstatement of the Karachai-Cherkess Autonomous *Oblast* and for finding employment and housing for these peoples.[52] Later in his career, Gorbachev also made a number of statements on the national question before becoming General Secretary, but as Motyl points out, such pronouncements 'are notable only for their dullness, clichés and naïve optimism'.[53]

It was not until the 27th Party Congress, in February 1986, that

Gorbachev made his clearest statement, although it was brief, on the national question. In most respects, there was little departure from the Brezhnevite line: no reference was made to *sliyanie* of nations while much was again made of a united Soviet people, *Sovetskii narod*, 'cemented by the same economic interests, ideology and political goals'.[54] He did, however, note that such achievements 'must not create the impression that there are no problems in the national processes. Contradictions are inherent in any kind of development, and are unavoidable in this sphere as well.'[55] He also went on to acknowledge the problematic nature which made up these contradictory tendencies, which included 'national isolationism, localism and parasitism', and to speak of 'attempts to isolate oneself from the objective process by which national cultures interact and come closer together (*sblizhenie*)'.[56] But while acknowledging that there existed a problematic side to ethnic relations, other than placing faith in vague references to *sblizhenie*, no concrete proposals were forthcoming. Indeed, as in earlier speeches, when he had stressed the importance of prioritising those aspects of the economy which promised the greatest and most immediate return,[57] at the 27th Party Congress the onus was also on prioritising investment in those sectors and regions of the economy commensurate with economic modernisation and intensive development. Expensive, large-scale projects, particularly important to the development of peripheral regions, were either to be abandoned or given lower priority. In playing down the more balanced development among different regions of the USSR, which his predecessors had been careful to stress and had identified as an important aspect of nationalities policy,[58] Gorbachev chose to emphasise the importance of the 'republics' contribution to 'the development of an integrated national economic complex' which 'should match their [republic] grown economic and spiritual potential'.[59] Although he also advocated greater power for republic and local interests, like his programme for economic modernisation and socio-economic acceleration (*uskorenie*), no attempt was made to link such policy shifts to the nationalities question.

As the tempo and scale of nationalist unrest quickened, so the Gorbachev regime began to revise its attitude towards the nationalities. The Kazakh riots of mid-December 1986 in Alma Ata were the first major blow from the ethnic periphery to the reform programme. The riots were triggered off by the replacement of a Kazakh First Party Secretary with a Russian, which broke with the hitherto universal practice of appointing a native to such a post. Bringing in an outsider in order to reassert control over a republic economically crippled by elite corruption and mismanagement may have made rational sense, but for many Kazakhs, numerically outnumbered and feeling socially vulnerable and economically deprived in their own homeland, it showed the new regime as being totally insensitive to national sensibilities. From that point onwards, and as incidences of ethnic unrest on a scale hitherto unknown to Soviet society quickly unfolded across the country, the illusion of a society having secured cultural coexistence and moving steadily towards *rapprochement* was shattered. Following ethnic demonstrations throughout 1987, by the Crimean Tatars, Baltic peoples and the Ukrainians, in February 1988 the epicentre of ethnic unrest unexpectedly switched to Transcaucasia. The ethnically Armenian-dominated enclave of Nagorno-Karabakh, administered as part of Azerbaijan, passed a resolution calling for their territory's transfer to Armenia. The demonstrations, riots and bloodshed which followed prompted Gorbachev to declare publicly that the nationalities question was now a vital political issue on the Kremlin's agenda.[60]

After the Kazakh riots, Moscow was willing to concede that past mistakes had been made in nationalities policy, and a Central Committee Plenum, meeting in January 1987, acknowledged that the root causes of ethnic unrest were not just unique to Kazakhstan.[61] Social scientists were also singled out for creating too rosy a picture of national relations and were accused of creating a growing gap between their scientific research and reality. As the nationalities expert, Bagramov, admitted, 'in practice, the sphere of national relations had been treated as if everything were harmonious . . . and that which did not fit into this harmony was simply dismissed and stigmatised as a manifestation of bourgeois nationalism'.[62] Gorbachev's response to the events in Alma Ata was to call for 'greater internationalist education', particularly amongst the young, but he also gave the stern warning that 'those who would like to play on nationalist or chauvinist prejudices should entertain no illusion and expect no loosening up'.[63] In a speech in Tallinn, the capital of Estonia, in February 1987, Gorbachev adopted a more conciliatory tone but without departing from Brezhnevite thinking: 'The flourishing of nations and nationalities has been ensured by Leninist nationalities policy. Of course there were shortcomings and mistakes in that Great Course, as well as aggravations [of the situation], and we are aware of them and do not overlook or forget them.'[64]

Rather than formulating a coherent nationalities policy, Gorbachev's handling of the nationalities question has been to respond to each new ethnic crisis as it has arisen, in which there has been a tendency to treat each as a distraction from the central tasks of economic restructuring, *glasnost'* and democratisation, by which the solution to ethnic unrest could be largely resolved. In its crisis management, Moscow has tended to favour short-term, piecemeal measures – in particular, instances linked to some economic and cultural programme – as a means of appeasing some of the more problematic of ethnic demands, as in the case of the Kazakhs, Crimean Tatars and the peoples of Nagorno-Karabakh. Indeed, the regime was slow to acknowledge officially that such measures were not sufficient to resolve ethnic conflict.[65] At the special 19th Party Conference in June 1988, it was, however, announced that a Special Party Plenum would be held in the near future to re-examine nationalities policy. Little comfort, however, was offered by Gorbachev at the Conference to those nationalities with either extra-territorial claims or with aspirations of elevating the administrative status of their homelands, for he made plain his commitment to 'the existing state structures of our union'.[66] The Special Conference did, however, go some way to incorporating the demands of those nationalities represented on the federal map into the overall reformist schema of greater economic decentralisation and democratisation. Yet no consistent policy response has occurred whenever demands from or events in the nationality republics seemed to be getting out of Moscow's control. The November 1988 constitutional crisis in Estonia, for example, precipitated by proposed changes to the Soviet constitution, which were seen in the republic as a challenge to their constitutionally guaranteed sovereignty, resulted in Moscow going some way to accommodating their demands. In Georgia in April 1989, however, inter-ethnic tensions between Georgians and Abkhazians resulted in the use of force in order to normalise the situation.

BACK TO THE FUTURE

While muddling through in its handling of a multiplicity of complex and very different nationality problems, none the less official reconsideration of the nationalities question has taken place. This, however, has not meant rethinking afresh the nationalities question but rather the undertaking of 'a radical renewal of nationalities policy',[67] grounded in Lenin's works and in his general conception of a multi-ethnic society based on true equality and friendship between nations. In seeking ideological justification for their position on the nationalities question, reformists, as in their dealings with many other aspects of *perestroika*, are discussing nationalities policy against the background of the early 1920s and in relation to the ideals originally set down in the Soviet constitution. Thus an 1989 article in *Kommunist* refers to Lenin's notion of national self-determination as a declaration still to be implemented, for it was 'the command-administrative system' which is held to be responsible for the demise of national self-determination and for the cause of nationality unrest.[68] The Stalinist and post-Stalinist period and the failure of successive regimes to implement a proper nationalities policy is represented as a futile diversion from the path laid down by Lenin. As Gorbachev noted in his speech of 1 July 1989, the sources underlying current ethnic tensions emanate from a variety of distortions and acts of lawlessness in the past, the result of which was indifference towards ethnic interests, the failure to resolve many socio-economic problems of the republics and autonomous territories, deformations in the development of the languages and cultures of the country's people, the deteriorating of the demographic situation, and many other negative consequences.[69]

Reformulation of nationalities policy is therefore to occur within the framework of Lenin's conception of a Soviet federation, in effect, to 'restore ... the original Leninist principles of a Soviet federation, a union of republics possessing real sovereignty in all spheres of state life'.[70] As Gorbachev reminded the Soviet people in his July 1989 speech, *perestroika* means 'fully implementing in practice the principles on which Lenin based the union of Soviet republics'.[71] The proposals put forward by the CPSU Platform on Nationalities, which were endorsed by the Special Plenum on the Nationalities in September 1989, reflect the views of Gorbachev as enunciated in his speech of 1 July 1989.[72] The Plenum agreed to reconstruct nationalities policy along the following lines, as recommended by the Platform.[73]

1   To transform radically the Soviet federation by 'investing it (constituent parts) with real political and economic content, which is to include republic financial autonomy and self-financing (*khozraschet*). Nationality republics, however, are not to have party organisations separate from the CPSU, and nor are other forms of social organisation to be constructed on nationality grounds. None the less, greater autonomy for the republic Communist Parties is proposed, which would include more organisational and financial autonomy, and greater control over cadre appointments.

2   The union republics are to be allowed to establish relations with foreign states and international organisations and are to be responsible for ensuring the country's defence, but the armed forces are to continue to be organised on an inter-ethnic basis.

3   With regard to citizenship rights, it is made plain that citizenship is closely bound up with the sovereignty of the republic but that Soviet citizens must feel at home anywhere in the country. 'Privileges of some citizens, and the infringement of the rights of other Soviet citizens are inadmissible on national, religious and linguistic grounds, or on the grounds of length of residence.'

4   Given that the Russian republic does not possess the administrative and party infrastructure of other union republics, it is recommended that additional bodies be established for it, including creating a bicameral Supreme Soviet for the Republic.

5   The rights of the autonomous republics should be substantially expanded as well as the legal status of more minor nationality-administrative units. But provision should be made for ensuring that 'the territory of an autonomous oblast or okrug cannot be altered' without the consent of the union republic Supreme Soviet.

6   Those nationalities expelled by Stalin from their homelands are to be fully rehabilitated.

7 Affirmative action policies are to be designed to ensure the necessary socio-territorial representation of nationalities to cadre positions within the republics and in the selection of deputies for the Soviet parliament.

8 Whether the language of the nationality of a namesake union or autonomous republic is to become the state language is to be left up to the republic.

Through the 'renovation of the Soviet federation', the emphasis is on protecting the state's unity, with both self-determination and sovereignty being discussed solely within existing international borders. Rather than focusing on the *sblizhenie* of nations, the emphasis is placed on the strengthening of friendship and cooperation between nations which the reconstituted nature of centre-union republic arrangements will help ensure. In essence, what is being proposed is based on the newly stated formula, 'Without a strong union there are no strong republics, without strong republics, there is no strong Union.' Although these proposals recommend the most radical reshaping of the Soviet federation since Lenin, the centralised role of the Party remains, which Lenin envisaged as fundamental to the building of socialism. This vision of a multi-ethnic society based on a federation of more equal nations but which stops short of the federalisation of the Party itself has already been challenged following the Lithuanian Party's unilateral decision in December 1989 to separate from the CPSU. Four months later, on 11th March 1990, the Lithuanian parliament became the first to declare its independence from the USSR. In responding to events in that republic and to the increasingly radical stance on political sovereignty elsewhere, notably in Estonia, Latvia, Georgia and Azerbaijan, the Supreme Soviet passed an April 1990 law providing for a waiting period of up to five years for a union republic to secede from the Federation in what is likely to be an unsuccessful strategy to hold the country together. History may prove Lenin right in viewing the Soviet federation as a transitional form but not in the way he envisaged.

NOTES

1. See, for example, A. Motyl, 'The Sobering of Gorbachev: nationality, restructuring and the West' in S. Bialer (ed.) *Inside Gorbachev's Russia: Politics, Society and Nationality* (Boulder CO, Westview Press 1989), pp. 149–73; and G. E. Smith 'Gorbachev's greatest challenge: perestroika and the national question' *Political Geography Quarterly* vol. 8, no. 1 (1989), pp. 7–20. Earlier views on the problematic nature of the national question are contained in the following: H. Carrere d'Encausse *Decline of Empire: The Soviet Socialist Republics in Revolt* (New York, Newsweek Books 1979); R. Karklins *Ethnic Relations in the USSR: The Perspective from Below* (Boston, Allen & Unwin 1986); G. Lapidus 'Ethnonationalism and Political Stability: The Soviet Case' *World Politics* vol. 36, no. 4 (July

1984), pp. 555–80; T. Rakowska-Harmstone 'The nationalities question' in R. Wesson (ed.) *The Soviet Union: Looking to the 1980s* (New York, Hoover Institute 1980), pp. 129–53.

2. For one of the most comprehensive analyses of the development and practice of nationalities policy in socialist societies, see W. Connor *The National Question in Marxist-Leninist Theory and Strategy* (Princeton NJ, Princeton University Press 1984).

3. F. Engels 'The movements of 1847' in K. Marx and F. Engels *Collected Works* vol. 6 (Moscow, Progress Publishers 1979).

4. H. B. Davis (ed.) *The National Question: Selected Writings* (New York, Monthly Review Press).

5. Quoted by E. H. Carr *The Bolshevik Revolution, 1917–1923* vol. 1 (London, Macmillan), p. 421.

6. J. V. Stalin *Marxism and the National Question* in *Collected Works* vol. 2 (Moscow 1952–55), p. 307.

7. Carr, op. cit. pp. 260–62.

8. V. I. Lenin *Sochineniya* 4th ed, vol. 23 (Moscow, Institute Marksizm-Leninizm 1941–57), pp. 61–2.

9. As quoted in Carr, op. cit. p. 262.

10. Lenin, op. cit. vol. 20, p. 432.

11. Ibid., p. 411.

12. J. Peters 'Stalin's nationality policy: an interpretation' (Unpublished Ph.D. thesis, University of Pennsylvania 1964), p. 146.

13. Lenin, op. cit. vol. 29, pp. 150–51.

14. R. Szporluk 'Nationalities and the Russian problem in the USSR: an historical outline' *Journal of International Affairs* vol. 27, no. 1 (1973), pp. 22–40.

15. Peters, op. cit. pp. 168–69.

16. For a discussion of the 1922 Treaty and 1924 Constitution, see S. Bloembergen 'The union republics: how much autonomy?' *Problems of Communism* vol. 16, no. 5 (1967), pp. 27–35.

17. I. Kreindler (ed.) *Sociolinguistic Perspectives on Soviet National Languages* (Berlin, Mouton de Gruyter 1985).

18. Lenin, op. cit. vol. 23, p. 335.

19. Peters, op. cit. p. 288.

20. Quoted by F. Barghoorn, *Soviet Russian Nationalism* (New York, Oxford University Press 1956), p. 27.

21. I. Kreindler 'The Soviet deported nationalities: a summary and an update' *Soviet Studies* vol. 38, no. 3 (1986), pp. 387–405.

22. B. Silver, 'The status of national minority languages in Soviet education: an assessment of recent changes' *Soviet Studies* vol. 26, no. 1 (1974), pp. 28–40.

23. Calculated from *Vestnik Statistiki* no. 7 (1980), p. 43; no. 8 (1980), pp. 64–70; no. 9 (1980), pp. 61–70; no. 10 (1980), pp. 67–73; and no. 11 (1980), pp. 60–4.

24. Yu. Arutunyan, V. *et al. Sotsial' no-kul 'turnyi oblik Sovetskikh Natsii (po materialam etnosotsiologischeskogo issledovaniya)* (Moscow, Nauka 1986), p. 32.

25. *XX11 s"ezd kommunisticheskoi Partii Sovetskogo Soyuza. Stenograficheskii otchet* (Moscow 1961).

26. Ibid., p. 216.
27. P. Rutland 'The "nationality problem" and the Soviet state' in N. Harding (ed.) *The State in Socialist Society* (London, Macmillan 1984), pp. 150–78.
28. See Note 25.
29. See, for example, the article by Alampiev and Kistanov in *Literaturnaya gazeta*, 28 May 1961.
30. *Pravda* 7 Nov. 1964.
31. See, for example, S. Bialer *The Soviet Paradox: External Expansion, Internal Decline* (London, I.B. Tauris Co Ltd 1986); V. Zaslavsky *The Neo-Stalinist State* (Brighton, Harvester Press 1982).
32. G. Smith 'The Soviet federation: from corporatist to crisis politics' in M. Chisholm and D. Smith (eds) *Shared Space: Divided Space: Essays on Conflict and Territorial Organisation* (London, Unwin Hyman 1990) pp.84–105.
33. *Materialy XXIV se"zda KPSS* (Moscow, Izadel'stvo Politicheskoi Literatury 1971), p. 76.
34. *Pravda* 22 Dec. 1972, p. 3.
35. Olcott, op. cit. p. 105.
36. For example, S. E. Ebzeeva 'Sovetskaya federatsiya na etape zrelogo sotsializma' *Sovetskoe Gosudarstvo i Pravo* 7 (1982), pp. 10–14.
37. *Pravda* 5 Oct. 1977.
38. *Pravda* 24 Feb. 1981.
39. *XXVI s"ezd kommunisticheskoi partii Sovetskogo Soyuza. Stenograficheskii otchet* (Moscow 1981), Part I, pp. 70–5.
40. See, for example, E. Jones and F. Grupp 'Modernisation and ethnic equalisation in the USSR' *Soviet Studies* vol. 36, pp. 159–84.
41. R. Solchanyk, 'Russian language and Soviet politics' *Soviet Studies*, vol. 34 (1982), pp. 23–42.
42. See Note 39.
43. Quoted by Lapidus, op. cit. pp. 568–69.
44. Litvinova and Urlanis 'Demograficheskaya politika v SSSR' *Sovetskoe Gosudarstvo i Pravo* 3, pp. 38–46.
45. Yu. Andropov, 'Shest' desyat let SSR', *Kommunist* no. 1 (1983), p. 8.
46. Ibid., p. 5.
47. Olcott, op. cit. p. 103.
48. Andropov, op. cit. p. 6.
49. M. Gorbachev *Ibrannye rechi i stat'i* (Moscow Izdatel'stvo Politicheskoi Literatury 1985), p. 52.
50. P. Duncan 'The Party and Russian nationalism in the USSR: from Brezhnev to Gorbachev' in P. Potichenyi (ed.) *The Soviet Union: Party and Society* (Cambridge University Press 1988), p. 240.
51. Y. Bilinsky, 'Nationality policy and Gorbachev's first year', *Orbis* (Summer 1986), p. 341.
52. Z. Medvedev *Gorbachev* (Oxford, Basil Blackwell 1988), pp. 31–2.
53. Motyl, op. cit. p. 156.
54. M. Gorbachev, *Politicheskii doklad tsentral'nogo komiteta KPSS XXVII Sëzdu Kommunisticheskoi Partii Sovetskogo Soyuza* (Moscow, Izdatel'stvo Politicheskoi Literatury 1986), p. 101.
55. Ibid., p. 101.

56. Loc. cit.
57. *Pravda* 12 June 1985.
58. See, for example, D. Bahry *Outside Moscow: Power, Politics and Budgetary Policy in the Soviet Republics* (New York, Columbia University Press 1987), pp. 30–1.
59. Gorbachev (1986), op. cit. p. 101.
60. *Pravda* 18 Feb. 1988.
61. *Pravda* 28 Jan. 1987.
62. *Pravda* 14 Aug. 1987.
63. *Pravda* 28 Jan. 1987.
64. *Tass* 21 Feb. 1987.
65. Gorbachev clearly acknowledged this in his speech of 1 July 1989 (*Soviet News* 5 July 1989).
66. *Pravda* 29 June 1988.
67. *Pravda* 17 Aug. 1989.
68. *Kommunist* no. 9 (1989).
69. Gorbachev's television speech, the text of which is reproduced in *Soviet News* 5 July 1989, p. 218.
70. *Tass* 14 March 1989.
71. See Note 69.
72. Ibid.
73. *Pravda* 17 Aug. 1989.

CHAPTER TWO

The Russians: the Dominant Nationality

Simon Dixon

In 1862, in a classic critique of the theory of modern nationality, Lord Acton denounced it for reducing 'practically to a subject condition all other nationalities that may be within the boundary' of the 'dominant body which claims all the rights of the community'.[1] In the minds of many, both outside and inside the Soviet Union, the Russians today dominate in precisely the way that Acton found so distasteful. But that is not how Russians see themselves. They may accept the idea, found in the earliest nationalist texts by Herder and Fichte, that one nationality can only dominate by virtue of a struggle with others, since so many of their ideas – even those which are claimed as purely Russian – are rooted in German thought. But they see their role in that struggle as defensive and reactive rather than offensive and predatory. So, whilst Russians evidently do dominate the USSR territorially (since the Russian republic (RSFSR) occupies more than 80 per cent of the state's total area) culturally (through the controversial use of Russian as the Soviet *lingua franca*) and more precariously in demographic terms (the relative decline of the Russian population since 1923 now having reduced them from 72 per cent to just over half the total Soviet population), Russians themselves are inclined to think first of the advantages gained by others at their own expense.[2] This view is more than a trite excuse for self-assertiveness. It has a long history in which the aggressors are believed to have come both from abroad and from within.

In the Russian memory the successful defence of Russian integrity against Nazi Germany in the 'Great Patriotic War' (1941–45) is only the last in a litany of bitterly fought campaigns against foreign incursion: against the Mongol hordes in the fourteenth century (notably at the battle of Kulikovo, whose sexcentenary was celebrated by Russian nationalists in 1980); against the Poles, the Swedes and the Turks in the early modern period; and against Napoleon in 1812. In the aftermath of all these victories, the dominant Russian self-image has been sacrificial rather than triumphalist. The spiritual qualities of moral goodness and patience, together with physical courage, are held to have

21

overcome evil and cunning. The Russians do not allow themselves to forget their past suffering. They constantly relive the sacrifices of the last world war: in fiction (notably in the novels of Yurii Bondarev, a prominent nationalist); in ceremonial and ritual; and most importantly in life, as a consequence of a crippled economy incapable of producing even basic foodstuffs above a level defended by posters warning that bread is 'a national treasure' to be conserved.

Alongside this external menace, the Russians perceive an internal threat, potentially the more subversive, in the minds of some, for being insidious. It takes two very different forms. The first is the internationalist doctrine of Marxism-Leninism, which suffuses the education of every Soviet citizen. Although many of them joke about it, few forget it. Not only does it reinforce xenophobic fears of imperialist aggression, but it also implicitly undermines Russian identity. Secondly, the Russians are nervous of competition from other ethnic groups within the Soviet Union. Up to a point, such fears are understandable. To take only two examples, literacy rates in the Protestant Baltic lands were vastly superior to those of Orthodox Russians from the moment they joined the empire, and in the twentieth century the previously backward Muslims of Central Asia have made rapid educational progress – an important indicator of ethnic consciousness and anti-Russian sentiment. But when such fears are transposed into fanciful conspiracy theories (often with an anti-Semitic slant) they become both dangerous and distasteful.

It is hard to overstate the degree to which Russians are capable of exaggerating their own vulnerability. Vladimir Osipov warned in 1972, in his short-lived dissident journal *Veche (Rumour)*, that 'the Russian nation could disappear'.[3] In 1986, novelist Vasilii Belov echoed Osipov's apocalyptic fear, complaining of 'the prospect of the slow, gradual disappearance of a nation, of its complete fusion with other nations'.[4] One need not take this rhetoric literally to believe that a key to understanding contemporary Russian nationalist sentiment lies in recognising its defensive tone and its consequent hole-in-corner attempts to salvage what it sees as a threatened, damaged and decaying Russia from the ravages of the modern world. This attitude surfaces in different ways and various moods, from the passive to the aggressive. It may be found in its most concentrated form in the publicistic writings of nationalist activists. But it is also evident, and potentially more menacing for Gorbachev and political stability as a whole, in a widespread perception that in the simple essentials of everyday life, Russians are worse off than their 'younger brothers' among the other nationalities in the Soviet Union.[5]

THE RUSSIANS BEFORE THE REVOLUTION

The core of the Russia which Peter the Great declared an empire in 1721 was formed by the unification of several medieval principalities under Muscovite hegemony. The advance into Siberia in the sixteenth and seventeenth centuries did little to disturb the ethnic balance of a population whose self-identity owed much to its religion, Russian Orthodoxy. But from the mid-seventeenth century, Russia expanded into areas populated neither by Russians nor by Orthodox. In 1654, the Ukraine brought with it a pronounced Latin and Catholic influence. The Great Northern War against Sweden (1700–21) won the German Protestant Baltic lands in the north-west. To the south, successive victories against the Muslim Ottoman Turks culminated in 1783 with the annexation of the Crimea, while in the west three partitions of Poland brought not only more Catholics but a significant number of Jews. Further expansion into Central Asia in the 1860s and 1870s incorporated still more Muslims.

During the eighteenth century, when national consciousness was less significant than rational uniformity in affairs of state, successive Russian tsars were prepared to grant privileges to local elites in these newly acquired territories to ensure their smooth assimilation into a centrally administered empire. But in the nineteenth century, the rise of modern nationalism encouraged Russians no longer to be content simply with administrative assimilation: many now demanded cultural penetration as well. Despite periodic bursts of Russification, that penetration was never achieved. The state began in the 1830s by supporting aggressive Russification. In the religious sphere, for example, the Ukrainian Uniates were forcibly 'reunited' with Orthodoxy in 1839, many Baltic peasants were converted *en masse* in the 1840s, and a renewed attempt was made to convert the Muslim Tatars. But the tsarist regime's enthusiasm for such assertive action faded when it provoked civil unrest. The government reverted in the 1860s and 1870s to an uneasy placation of local elites, though its policies were harsh on those without political influence. Only a relatively short period of intensive Russification in the 1880s punctuated what to fervent Russians seemed to be policies designed to benefit only their non-Russian rivals – people who occupied parts of the empire which seemed then, and have never ceased to seem, like foreign territory to Russians.

Their sense of frustration was all the greater since their theories of Russian nationalism claimed that Russian civilisation was superior to others. Of course, thinkers argued in ways that were far from identical, and to summarise them is to violate the texture of individual nuance. But despite their differences of emphasis, most Russian nationalists debated within an intellectual context in which three themes may be identified. The first is an allegiance to Russian Orthodoxy, whose thinkers developed theories justifying its unique spiritual authority and apostolic authenticity parallel to the secular claims made on behalf of Russian nationalism. The nature of this allegiance varied: whilst some nationalists were sincere believers, subscribing to sophisticated religious philosophies, others simply wanted the church to act as an agent of social control. The second is a deep interest in Russia's medieval past and especially in the Muscovite period, which many nationalists believed was unsullied by the foreign influences introduced by Peter the Great. The third is a belief in the Russian peasantry as a moral force for good, exemplified by its communal lifestyle and self-government. These three themes – Orthodoxy, the Russian past and the peasantry – united by a common stress on ethics and morals, have remained prominent in nationalist writings ever since.[6]

THE RUSSIANS IN THE SOVIET UNION

Under the Soviet regime, the fortunes of Russian nationalism have waxed and waned in counterpoint to those of Marxism-Leninism.[7] In the immediate aftermath of the revolution of October 1917, the old Russian civilisation seemed bound to crumble in the face of Leninist 'proletarian internationalism'. Ironically, Russian domination of the new socialist state was rescued by a most unlikely guardian angel, the Georgian Josif Stalin. Like another non-Russian, the Pole Feliks Dzerzhinsky who headed the Cheka, Stalin, as Commissar for the Nationalities, proved to be more Russian than the Russians in Lenin's government. Stalin wanted the constitution of the Soviet Union to reflect Russia's pre-eminence in the revolutionary movement, and he got his way: in the end, the Constitution of 1924 was, in Geoffrey Hosking's pithy phrase, 'Leninist in form, but Stalinist in content'.[8]

Even so, and despite the further triumph of Stalin's doctrine of 'Socialism in One Country' over Trotsky's 'Permanent Revolution' in the 1920s, Russian nationalism took a back seat to local national cultures during his first years in power. Not until 1934 did Stalin – facing the spectre of fascism abroad and social dislocation at home, following his campaign of forced industrialisation – encourage a return to the values of Russian nationalism. From 1934, patriotic Russian symbols reappeared. The reputations of Alexander Nevsky and especially of Peter the Great were reassessed. Whereas elements of the negative view of Petrine society propagated in the 1920s by M.N. Pokrovskii survived, positive evaluations of Peter's energy (especially in diplomacy and military affairs) now appeared alongside them in the history books, though his interest in the West was played down. Historical parallels were important. Stalin encouraged an identification of himself with Ivan IV and awarded film-director Sergei Eisenstein a Stalin Prize for the first part of his *Ivan the Terrible*, released in 1945.[9] The Russian Orthodox church, split by schism in the 1920s, had to wait for rehabilitation until the outbreak of war in 1941. Then, in return for supporting the war effort, presenting Stalin in Christ-like terms, and portraying the Russians as God's chosen people, the Russian church was allowed some respite from persecution. In 1943 it was granted a council, and in a repetition of the events of 1839, the 'reunification' (forcible incorporation) of the Uniate church with Orthodoxy was brought about in 1946.[10]

The immediate post-war years saw the zenith of the crudest possible Russian chauvinism, predicated on the existence of supposedly 'cosmopolitan' (the code-word for Jewish) and masonic conspiracies against the Soviet state. But the Russian element in Zhdanov's cultural policy, and that of his successors, was subordinate to an overall revival of Marxist-Leninist orthodoxy. Though the church maintained a precarious peace with the state until it was assaulted by Khrushchev's militantly anti-religious campaign, the years of the onset of the Cold War were relatively bleak for most Russian nationalists. Ironically, it was Khrushchev, himself antipathetic to nationalist causes, whose policies were largely responsible for their revival. Not only did his denunciation of Stalin in 1956 implicitly challenge the infallibility of Marxism-Leninism, but the search for alternatives was also further encouraged by the 'thaw' in censorship policy that allowed the publication of critical writings. Above all, the physical destruction of many churches opened up the possibility for nationalist sympathies to be channelled through conservationist outlets. Indeed, the conservationist movement has remained an important strand of Russian nationalist activity ever since, particularly in the form of the All-Russian Society for the Protection of Historical and Cultural Monuments (*VOOPIK*), founded in 1965.

However, conservationism was not the only significant element in the Russian revival of the 1960s. John Dunlop identifies a spectrum of Russian nationalist views which has continued to develop to this day. This spectrum now includes a wide variety of opinion, from the relatively moderate 'Russian patriots', many of them Orthodox believers, who have no truck with crude chauvinism but are staunch defenders of Russian culture, through a central group who take a more alarmist view of the plight of Russian values, to the so-called National Bolsheviks on the far right, most of them militantly anti-religious, linked to the military and to Gorbachev's conservative political rival, Yegor Ligachev, who is not himself a Russian nationalist.[11] The tide turned against the nationalists in the 1970s and early 1980s, and many, especially those who emphasised the religious component of nationalism, were driven underground, publishing their work in *samizdat*. But the official publication of the much-admired 'village prose' writers served to keep nationalist issues in the public mind – linking them to moral problems of the family, the community and so on – so that when the intellectual climate changed under Gorbachev, this spectrum of nationalist views re-emerged, fully fledged.

RUSSIAN NATIONALISM UNDER GORBACHEV

In the new atmosphere introduced by Gorbachev's policy of *glasnost'*, three journals, all published in Moscow, stand out as bastions of a broadly conservative nationalist position. *Nash sovremennik* (in the centre of the nationalist spectrum) and *Moskva* (on the right), both journals of the prestigious Writers' Union of the Russian republic, and *Molodaya gvardiya* (right), published by the Komsomol, were all prominent in the Russian nationalist revival in the 1960s, and they have continued to support and proselytise it under Gorbachev. Although it is true that broadly reformist journals (notably *Novyi mir* – which touches the liberal end of the nationalist spectrum and has now republished Solzhenitsyn – and *Druzhba narodov* – which published Anatolii Rybakov's fictional unmasking of the Stalin era, *Deti Arbata* (Children of the Arbat), much criticised in the nationalist press) have far outstripped the nationalist journals in their subscription rates, individual nationalist writers nevertheless still attract a big readership. Consider, for example, the 'village prose' writer Vasilii Belov, whose *Vse vperedi* (*Everything lies ahead*), originally published in *Nash sovremennik* in 1986, was issued separately in an addition of 2,700,000 the following year, and the even greater (though far less intellectual) appeal of Valentin Pikul', whose chauvinist historical novels fetch some of the highest prices on the black market for books.[12]

It would be wrong to think that *perestroika* and Russian nationalism have nothing in common. Some of the ideas dearest to the nationalists (though not necessarily to them alone) have been propounded by Gorbachev himself, even though they find little favour with his radical supporters. Prominent among them is his trumpeting of the values of sober family life – an inheritance from the Andropov days – in phrases which might have been taken from the pages of nationalist journals (and for that matter from pre-revolutionary temperance pamphlets). Contemporary nationalists have been glad to support Gorbachev's temperance campaign and his fight against moral decay. But evidence that this decay is rampant – for example, in the form of rising crime rates – has made nationalists intemperate in their rejection of liberal social values. Valentin Rasputin, for example, has attacked *Vzgliad*, one of the radicals' flagship television programmes, for defending homosexuals and interviewing prostitutes and has given intellectual backing to the campaign against decadence by Yegor Ligachev.[13]

Linked to this concern for domestic morality is a re-examination of the Soviet state's attitude to the Russian Orthodox church. As Igor Romanov, director of the Centre of Scientific Atheism, explained in 1988: 'as atheists we have begun to pay greater attention to the moral approach to life'.[14] The religious revival has gone far beyond this tepid admission of curiosity. Aware of the recent attraction of religion for the younger generation, Gorbachev, in his biggest departure from

Khrushchev's programme, is now openly considering the political and social benefits to be gained from allowing the churches greater flexibility of action. The commentary of a 1988 Soviet documentary, *The Temple*, was notable not only for portraying Orthodox clergy in a sympathetic light as disciplined, moral individuals, but also for asserting baldly that 'atheism is harmful' – a remarkable admission when one remembers that it was only in 1982 that Vladimir Soloukhin, whose work implies that the decline of the church goes some way to account for moral dissipation, was forced publicly to reaffirm his atheism.[15] In line with this relaxation, a number of monasteries have been returned to the church, and the celebrations of the Orthodox millennium in June 1988, notable for their Great Russian, anti-Ukrainian bias, were given a high profile. In return, senior churchmen have been only too anxious to profess their patriotism.

It is too early to say what will be the result. Much will depend on the nature of the promised new legislation on the rights of religious communities.[16] But it is unlikely that the regime's dalliance with the church will offer much comfort to Orthodox believers in the long term. The regime's aim is not specifically religious but is to inculcate a sense of strictly earthly morality. Although it has so far seemed advantageous to exploit the 'integrative role'[17] of the Russian Orthodox church among Ukrainians and Belorussians (at the expense of both Ukrainian Uniates and Ukrainian Orthodox), the demographic balance of the Soviet Union will make it difficult for Russian Orthodoxy consistently to be offered greater privileges than rival religions, especially Islam. Gorbachev may decide, as did the tsarist regime that shared his initial hopes, that these rivals are more reliable teachers of discipline than the Orthodox themselves.[18] If he does, it is hard to believe that he will show the Russian church much more respect than the later tsars did. Significantly, statistics for 1988 show a marked increase in the number of new parishes of *all* denominations, whilst the Orthodox have yet to recoup the losses of the 1970s and early 1980s.[19]

The third prominent issue on which nationalist and reformist sentiment have to some extent coalesced is the environment, and there is now an openly acknowledged Green movement outside the Party in the Soviet Union which has widespread support in the Russian republic.[20] In 1986, leading figures from all parts of the nationalist spectrum objected to a proposed irrigation project that would have diverted a number of Russian rivers south into the Ukraine, Moldavia, and especially Kazakhstan and Central Asia. Nationalists' opposition centred on the potential for ecological damage in Western Siberia, particularly in the Ob'-Irtysh basin, where fish habitats would have been destroyed had the scheme gone ahead. Their united voice, though by no means the only influence at work, must be given at least some of the credit for the abandonment of the project in August of that year. Certainly it played a large part in bringing the project to the attention of the public. And the river project was only the largest in a series of incidents concerned with the environment.[21] Throughout 1986–88, the Soviet press reported spontaneous meetings of workers in various parts of the Russian republic to protest against pollution by chemical plants and the construction of power stations. Such demonstrations reflected disaffection not so much with the policies as with the bureaucracy of both local and central government (a target shared by reformists). The injection of a specifically nationalist element into these protests may be detected not only when particular cultural or historical monuments are threatened, but also when a religious view of nature as God's handiwork is offended by man's trespassing beyond the boundaries of his place in God's scheme.[22]

If it is not surprising that so astute a politician as Gorbachev should have taken advantage of the strength of Russian nationalist sentiment on these issues to support his own initiatives, it was scarcely to be expected that he and the nationalists would agree on everything. As we shall see, the more extremist nationalists have been alarmed by the reformists' apparent liberalism and sympathy for things Western, and have not been afraid to voice their disquiet in virulent terms. But more interesting than these sharp conflicts are the grey areas in which nationalists face some awkward dilemmas. Amongst these more ambivalent issues, the most significant is the assessment of Russia's cultural and historical heritage.

Here, too, moderate nationalists have gained prominence under Gorbachev. Not only have they assumed a high profile in the Writers' Union of the Russian republic, but the veteran Academician D.S. Likhachev, the doyen of Russian medieval literary scholarship, has become a guru figure in the cultural affairs of the country as a whole. On close terms with Raisa Gorbacheva, he has led the new Soviet Cultural Foundation since its inception in 1986, making a number of controversial statements in defence of the national heritage, notably in the aftermath of the disastrous fire at the Library of the Academy of Sciences (BAN) in Leningrad in 1988. Likhachev represents that part of the nationalist spectrum least inclined to denigrate other nations, consciously opposing (inoffensive) patriotism to (aggressive) nationalism.[23] Indeed, the Cultural Foundation may have been intended as a consciously internationalist counterweight to stridently nationalist unofficial associations. Perhaps as a consequence of its modesty, the Cultural Foundation has been slow to make an impact. The first issues of its new journal, *Nashe nasledie (Our Heritage)*, published from September 1988, focused on Russian culture of the Silver Age at the turn of the century,[24] sharing the concern of other nationalist writers to rehabilitate the work of the religious philosopher P.A. Florenskii.[25] Scholarly projects, such as the fundamental Russian encyclopaedia promised for the year 2000, planned on a scale grand enough to take into account the life of Russians abroad, will naturally take years to come to fruition.[26] In the meantime, the Cultural Foundation's efforts are bound to seem lacklustre by comparison with the devastating revelations to be found elsewhere in the Soviet press.

The greatest public impact of *glasnost'* has come in the reinterpretation of history. For the Soviet Union, a state whose very existence is justified by a determinist historical doctrine, the meaning attached to the past is crucial in defining the identity of the present. The official version of the past has long borne so little resemblance to reality as to be a travesty of the truth. Since so many have been kept ignorant for so long, and so disturbing is the evidence as it emerges, to confront the past squarely is a traumatic experience for Soviets and not least for the Russians.[27] The emphasis of reinterpretation has so far been on the Soviet period, especially on Stalinism. Its essence is brilliantly captured by Alec Nove: 'The Rehabilitation of History – or the History of Rehabilitation'.[28] The reformist critique of the orthodox Soviet line centres on the rejection of Stalin's collectivisation of agriculture in 1928–29 as a ghastly mistake, which, consciously or unconsciously (and there is at last a debate about its motivation) caused many thousands, perhaps millions of deaths (again, the statistics are disputed) by starvation during the famine of 1930–32. The corollary is the rehabilitation of the mixed market approach associated with the New Economic Policy and identified with Stalin's rival, Bukharin, discredited (and executed) following the great purge trial of March 1938, the climax of Stalin's terror.[29]

Shocking revelations about the Stalinist regime have created a conundrum for Russian nationalists. The moderates and most of those in the centre are, of course, no friends of the collectivisation campaign, which they hold responsible for destroying the small-scale, rural nexus of a peasant society whose mores they idealise, even though they do not place the same emphasis on the commune itself as their nineteenth-century predecessors, the Slavophiles. But for those on the far right who preach the virtues of a strong, centralised state, recent revelations are a mixed blessing. Even Sergei Vikulov, editor of *Nash sovremennik*, and by no means on the most extreme wing of Russian nationalism, argued against the widespread publication of new material even before the flood of hitherto concealed or unknown sources began to appear in mid-1987. Clearly, it is no coincidence that *Moskva* has been serialising the work of N.M. Karamzin (1766–1826) – whose history of Russia idealised the role of autocracy – and of S.M. Solov'ev, the founder of the so-called 'state school' of nineteenth-century historiography.[30] Since Soviet scholarship on all periods has for so long laboured in a chauvinist straitjacket, particularly damaging to the study of the cosmopolitan eighteenth century, it is little wonder that Russian nationalist publicists have been less than eager to see radical change in the history books. By contrast, professional historians with a sense of integrity, though slow to enter the debate behind more adventurous literary figures, have begun to denounce chauvinist distortion of the sources on a wide range of subjects, especially as practised by the ageing Stalinist medievalist, Academician B.A. Rybakov, still the patron of a vain search for ancient (pagan) Russian roots among civilisations which had not the remotest connection with the Slavs.[31] Clearly, the impact of *glasnost'* on Russian history is only just beginning.

In order to publicise their views on those issues where they oppose reform, Russian nationalists have followed a widespread trend by forming unofficial associations. Characteristically, their purpose is often to defend Russian interests against what they believe to be rival aggression. November 1988 saw the appearance in Moscow of the *Tovarishchestvo russkikh khudozhnikov* (Association of Russian Artists), coordinated by Rasputin, Belov, Vikulov and Ivanov to combat separatist minority nationalist tendencies by proselytising Russian culture. The *Fond slavianskoi pis'mennosti i slavianskikh kul'tur*, founded in March 1989 to cement the relationship between Russians, Belorrusians and Ukrainians, also has a strong Russian nationalist slant. Significantly for a group aiming in some ways to perform a function similar to that of the Russian Orthodox church, clergy have become involved.[32] A Leningrad group explicitly concerned with the church's social role has published the *Nevskii dukhovnyi vestnik (Nevskii Spiritual Messenger)* claiming descent from the *Sankt-Peterburgskii dukhovnyi vestnik*, the journal of a pre-revolutionary society which united zealous laymen with the more evangelical Orthodox priests in the capital in a campaign to rechristianise the population. The modern version, however, shows a greater sympathy for the extremist element in contemporary Russian nationalism.[33]

This is the element associated with the most notorious of unofficial Russian groups, the *Pamyat'* association. There is still little hard information on its activities. Several conflicting explanations of its origins are in circulation.[34] The most widely held places them in meetings of a literary-historical society at the Aviation Ministry in Moscow in the early 1980s, though some claim less savoury antecedents as far back as the 1960s, and the group has since been obliged to move its base several times. On 9 October 1988, *Leningradskaya pravda* claimed that the group had branches in thirty cities of the Soviet Union, but its best-known activities have been in Moscow and Leningrad. Although the opinions of its membership probably vary, the views of its principal spokesmen, expressed with increasing unambivalence, proclaim it as an anti-Semitic and anti-liberal group wanting to resurrect post-war denunciations of Zionist and masonic conspiracies. Of all the menaces facing the Russians, these are surely the most imaginary. But it would be wrong to underestimate the intensity of the belief in them of a few zealots (particularly when the message is preached by men such as Dmitrii Vasil'ev, a charismatic figure who makes an impression on some of the more gullible people who meet him) or to ignore the fact that a latent anti-Semitism undoubtedly exists in Russian society in a way that bears comparison with racial prejudice in Britain.

Prominent reformists had meetings disrupted by *Pamyat'* members during their campaign for election to the new Council of People's Deputies in spring 1989. Vitalii Korotich, editor of *Ogonek*, was accused by a heckler of being the 'foreman of the scum of restructuring', and of being an 'alcoholiser of Russia'.[35] The sociologist Tatyana Zaslavskaya, whose 1983 report on the dismal state of the Soviet economy made her first *persona non grata* with the KGB and later a key Gorbachev aide, had a rally organised against her at which her Jewish origins were stressed.[36] Zaslavskaya and her mentor, the economist Abel Aganbegyan, whose Novosibirsk think-tank incubated many of the ideas on which *perestroika* depends, are easy prey for the nationalist press. Their privileged existence as academicians enjoying superior accommodation and access to special facilities leaves them vulnerable to accusations that they advocate price rises with no conception of the effect they will have on ordinary people's lives.[37] In taking such a stand, nationalists can pose in the guise of a crude populism which may attract more support for its attacks on the establishment than nationalist or anti-Semitic slogans ever could. A still more obvious target for their abuse is Aleksandr Yakovlev, the principal ideologist of reform and a Politburo member close to Gorbachev, whose 'exile' as ambassador to Canada in 1972 was the price he paid for an attack on Russian nationalism in an article explicitly denounced as Russophobic by a *Pamyat'* broadsheet in December 1987.[38] Increasingly under fire in other parts of the bureaucracy, out-and-out reformers like Yakovlev have found a congenial berth only in foreign affairs, symbolic of their link with what many believe to be Gorbachev's only reliable constituency, the Western democracies.

The regime's reactions to *Pamyat'* have been ambivalent. It is certainly taken seriously. Historians were annoyed by a ban, now lifted, on work on the history of Freemasonry, imposed by veteran Academician I.I. Mints, apparently out of fear of *Pamyat'*.[39] There is clear reformist distaste at the highest level. In a 1988 interview in the USA, Fedor Burlatskii, a close adviser and speechwriter for Gorbachev, stated categorically that he would not cooperate with *Pamyat'*.[40] And yet, in some parts of the *nomenklatura*, there is covert sympathy for the group's views, or, perhaps more accurately, for its opposition to reform as it is now conceived. Such sympathy seems particularly strong in the Leningrad Party, where officials of the *Obkom* attended regular *Pamyat'* meetings in the Rumiantsev gardens in 1988. Korotich has warned against the view of *Pamyat'* as 'an organisation of nice kindly folks whose sole wish is to preserve historical monuments', suggesting that behind its contemptible leadership stand 'fellows armed with brass knuckles' and 'dangerous' elements, 'harmful' to Gorbachev and *perestroika*.[41] Although Pamyat's leadership continues to deny any association with violence, it is revealing, in this context, to recall a letter reproduced in *Znamya* in October 1988. Sent by 'revolutionary fighters' from *Pamyat*', it promises the reformist journal's editor 'INEVITABLE RETRIBUTION!', and assures him that 'we will get even with you!'[42] The impression is of a regime that has nothing in common with *Pamyat*', but must nevertheless tolerate its existence.

PROSPECTS

In the decade before the advent of Gorbachev, opponents of Russian nationalism such as the emigré Alexander Yanov warned of the dangers of the triumph of a Russian form of fascism, whilst Western sympathisers such as John Dunlop implied that a less offensive version might provide a new direction for the regime to follow. As Peter Duncan has remarked, neither of these possibilities came to pass, and it may be suggested that neither seems likely to do so in the near future.[43] Rumours of Alexander Solzhenitsyn's return to Russia persist, as do suggestions that he might act as the focus of a nationalist movement. But Solzhenitsyn himself has remained aloof from any nationalist programme,[44] and even were he to adopt one, it could surely only be one among many since, as we have seen, the term 'Russian nationalism' is best understood as shorthand for a wide spectrum of views – from latent patriotism to neo-fascist action – rather than as a specific doctrine. In fact, although in the first months of *glasnost'* nationalists from different parts of that spectrum spoke and acted in concert, their differences have since emerged to the extent that they publicly contradict and oppose one another. In these circumstances, it is difficult to believe that a coherent, specifically 'Russian nationalist' threat to Gorbachev will emerge.[45]

However, as attention swings from the intellectual and cultural preoccupations of *glasnost'* towards the more grimly political and economic focus of *perestroika*, so the role of the Russians in Gorbachev's USSR will change. Whereas in the non-Russian republics ethnic national consciousness is a major focus of mass grievance in itself, in Russia it is far surpassed by economic problems of the most basic kind, especially food supply. For all the renewed cultural vitality of the Soviet press, Gorbachev has made precious little headway in economic matters. If *glasnost'* has worked, *perestroika* has not. In the summer of 1989, Gorbachev faced the first politically significant mass protests against shortage in Russia when the Siberian miners went on strike demanding more sausage-meat. This emotional cry was soon manipulated by conservatives to articulate other demands.

In September 1989 more than 100 delegates from all over the RSFSR held an inaugural congress of the United Front of Russian Workers in Sverdlovsk, declaring the need to defend fellow Russians in other republics of the USSR. Some index of the potential for instability that such incidents create is given by the fact that open discontent among poorly paid and badly housed railway workers – vital for maintaining food supply and communication between Moscow and the trouble-spots in non-Russian republics – prompted Gorbachev to impose a radical fifteen-month ban on all strikes from October 1989, despite attempts by the newly self-assertive Supreme Soviet to dilute the measure to apply only to service industries in problem areas outside the Russian republic. It is in these areas that Russian workers' nationalism will be at its most militant, since it is in these areas that Russians feel most vulnerable as they watch with trepidation the reassertion of other national traditions and in some cases hear separatist demands. Already in 1989, the Russians in Latvia, the most Russified of all the Baltic republics, are uniting under the umbrella of the (officially tolerated) Interfront organisation to protest at attempts to force their children to learn Latvian in school. The revival of the native language in Moldavia has caused similar resentment. In some of the southern republics, notably Kazakhstan, Russians now face similar discrimination, and some even fear violent retribution.

Since Russian nationalists have no better solution than Gorbachev to the economic predicament of the Soviet Union, a principal menace of Russian nationalism to Gorbachev will remain the way in which it can be exploited by conservatives in the Party who cannot themselves be properly classified as nationalists, but who want to counter reformist 'democratisation' of politics with the virtues of a strong, centralised state. This is the use classically formulated by the neo-Stalinist Nina Andreeva in her notorious, Ligachev-inspired letter to *Sovietskaya Rossiya* on 13 March 1988, which explicitly denounced Russian nationalists, but implicitly assumed Russian hegemony in the Soviet Union. So far, the democratised Party elections have not provided any real success for the extremist Russian nationalists. No candidate openly associated with *Pamyat'* was elected to the Council of People's Deputies in spring 1989. But the body might well be taken over by the conservatives, were there to be a backlash against reform.

However, it is not only the conservatives who are capable of harnessing Russian national sentiment to their own cause. Striving to undermine Gorbachev's political authority by discrediting his economic reforms, the radicals have also realised the potential power of populism in Russian clothing. And in the summer of 1990, it is the radicals who are in the ascendant. Even before his election to the post of president of the Russian republic in May 1990, Boris Yel'tsin was openly exploiting Russian feelings of insecurity. His task was made easier by an increasingly severe food shortage and panic buying in Moscow. Since his election, he has fanned the flames of a resurgent Russian consciousness. In June 1990, in a clear challenge to the Soviet constitution, the Russians have declared the sovereignty of their own republic – a defiant response to the Baltic republics' campaign for independence.

In spite of their worst fears, the Russian nation that the Russians are anxious to defend is not fundamentally threatened by Gorbachev: the top echelons of his administration contain a higher proportion of Russians than ever before, and he recognises the power of Russian hegemony as a social cement in the Soviet Union. But Gorbachev will certainly have to take into account the strength of Russian sentiment: however irrational it may seem to an outsider, many Russians feel as powerfully now as they have felt for the last two centuries that their civilisation is threatened. They cannot be ignored. Alain Besançon argues that the Soviet Union is held together by a balance of tensions between the centrifugal force of non-Russian nationalism and the centripetal force of Russian nationalism.[46] If he is right, it is becoming an increasingly difficult balance for Gorbachev to hold. The economic, social and political potential of the non-Russian peoples forces him to take their grievances seriously and dictates the restraint of overt Russian nationalism lest it offend them. Yet such a policy appears prejudicial to Russian interests, forcing Russians in turn into more extreme statements and actions. It is always rash to make predictions, and never more so than about a man who has already confounded so many previous forecasts, but whilst basic public order problems force him to focus in the short term on the overtly separatist movements in the non-Russian republics, in the longer term Gorbachev will surely need to keep the needs of millions of discontented Russians firmly in his sights. They will not be easily satisfied.

NOTES

1. Lord Acton 'Nationality' in his *Essays on Freedom and Power*, G. Himmelfarb (ed.) (London, Thames & Hudson 1956), p. 168.
2. B. Harasymiw *Political Elite Recruitment in the Soviet Union* (London, Macmillan 1984), pp. 119–21, extends the overall demographic point to membership of the Communist Party.
3. Quoted in M. Heller and A. Nekrich, *Utopia in Power: The History of the Soviet Union from 1917 to the Present* (London, Hutchinson 1986), p. 667. See also P. Duncan 'The fate of Russian nationalism: the *Samizdat* journal *Veche* revisited' *Religion in Communist Lands* 16, no. 1 (1988) 36–53.
4. Quoted by B. Nahaylo, 'Change in Russian views on the nationality problem?' *Radio Liberty Research Bulletin* 456/88, p. 2.
5. Valentin Rasputin has articulated this view: see N. Hyams 'Russian nationalism' in G. Schöpflin (ed.) *The Soviet Union and Eastern Europe* (London, Muler, Blond & White 1986), pp. 232–43, at p. 243. He surveys the pre-Gorbachev period.

6. On the eighteenth century, H. Rogger *National Consciousness in Eighteenth-Century Russia* (Cambridge MA, Harvard University Press 1960). On the nineteenth century, E. C. Thaden *Conservative Nationalism in Nineteenth-Century Russia* (Seattle, University of Washington Press 1964); N. Riasanovsky *Nicholas I and Official Nationality, 1825–1855* (Berkeley, University of California Press 1969); A. Walicki *The Slavophile Controversy: History of a Conservative Utopia in Nineteenth-Century Russian Thought* trans. H. Andrews-Rusiecka (Oxford, Oxford University Press 1975).

7. This section draws on J. B. Dunlop *The Faces of Contemporary Russian Nationalism* (Princeton NJ, Princeton University Press 1983), esp. pp. 3–62; G. Hosking *A History of the Soviet Union* (London, Collins 1985), esp. chaps 4, 9, 14; and R. Pipes *The Formation of the Soviet Union* rev. edn (Cambridge MA, Harvard University Press 1964).

8. Hosking *Soviet Union*, p. 118.

9. N. V. Riasanovsky *The Image of Peter the Great in Russian History and Thought* (Oxford, Oxford University Press 1985), pp. 255–90; M. Perrie *The Image of Ivan the Terrible in Russian Folklore* (Cambridge, Cambridge University Press 1987), pp. 15–27. On Pokrovskii, see especially J. Barber *Soviet Historians in Crisis, 1928–1932* (London, Macmillan 1981).

10. D. Pospielovsky *The Russian Church under the Soviet Regime, 1917–1982* 2 vols (New York, St Vladimir's Seminary Press 1984) sees the subject from a Russian point of view, critical of the leftist schism and unsympathetic to Ukrainians. I am grateful for having seen a draft version of P. Duncan's valuable paper, 'Orthodoxy and Russian nationalism in the USSR, 1917–1988'.

11. Dunlop *Contemporary Russian Nationalism*, chap. 10; *idem The New Russian Nationalism* (New York, Praeger 1985); *idem* 'The contemporary Russian nationalist specrum' *Radio Liberty Research Bulletin*, special ed, *Russian Nationalism Today* 19 Dec. 1988. See also D. Pospielovsky 'The neo-Slavophile trend and its relation to the contemporary religious revival in the USSR' in P. Ramet (ed.) *Religion and Nationalism in Soviet and East European Politics* (Durham NC, Duke University Press 1984), pp. 41–58.

12. See J. Graffy on the literary press in J. Graffy and G. A. Hosking (eds) *Culture and the Media in the USSR Today* (London, Macmillan 1989); and G.D.G. Murrell 'When the desert blooms: cultural developments under Gorbachev', *Survey* 30, no. 3 (Oct. 1988), pp. 59–78, esp. p. 76.

13. On the conservatives, see P. Reddaway 'The threat to Gorbachev' *New York Review of Books* 17 Aug. 1989.

14. BBC 'Everyman' programme 'Christians in an atheist world' 12 June 1988.

15. 'The Temple' (*Khram*), as shown on BBC2, 9 Oct. 1988.

16. See J. Anderson 'Drafting a Soviet law on freedom of conscience' *Soviet Jewish Affairs* 19 no. 1 (1989), pp. 19–33, for further references and a different view.

17. The phrase is used by B. Bociurkiw 'Institutional religion and nationality in the Soviet Union' in *Soviet Nationalities in Strategic Perspective*, S.

Enders Wimbush (ed.) (London, Croom Helm 1985), pp. 181–206, at p. 186.

18. See, for example, N.A. Weissman 'Rural crime in tsarist Russia: the question of hooliganism 1905–1914' *Slavic Review* 37, no. 2 (1978), pp. 228–45.

19. O. Antic 'Increase in number of Orthodox parishes' Radio Liberty *Report on the USSR* vol. 1, no. 2 (13 Jan. 1989), pp. 2–3. Of course, the 'National Bolshevik' wing of the Russian nationalist movement has no sympathy for a religious revival.

20. The biggest group concentrated in the Russian republic is the Social-Ecological Union, which consciously advocates political change to achieve its ends. It should be distinguished from the Ecological Society of the Soviet Union, which has links with *Pamyat'*. See *The Economist* 4–10 Nov. 1989, pp. 27–34.

21. See P. Sinnot 'Water diversion politics' *Radio Liberty Research Bulletin* 374.88; A. Sheehy and S. Voronitsyn 'Ecological protest in the USSR, 1986–88', ibid. 191/88; and the background in C. E. Ziegler *Environmental Policy in the USSR* (London, Frances Pinter 1987). The point is not that Russian nationalists are unique in their concern for the environment but that their concern is a vital part of their identity.

22. Russian writers' treatment of nature is sensitively analysed by G. Hosking, *Beyond Socialist Realism: Soviet Fiction since Ivan Denisovich* (London, Granada 1980), esp. chap. 3. W. Kasack *Dictionary of Russian Literature since 1917* (New York, Columbia University Press 1988) is a magnificent guide to further reading.

23. On Likhachev, see Dunlop 'Contemporary spectrum', pp. 4–6.

24. V. Tolz '*Nashe nasledie* – the Journal of the Soviet Cultural Foundation' Radio Liberty *Report on the USSR* 1, no. 3, 20 Jan. 1989.

25. See, for example, V. Desiatnikov 'Pod svodami lavry' *Moskva* (1989) no. 1, pp. 173–79, and L.P. Voronkova 'Mirovozzrenie P.A. Florenskago' *Vestnik Moskovskogo Universiteta* Seriia 7, Filosofiia (1989), no. 1, pp. 70–81.

26. *BBC Summary of World Broadcasts* SU/03451 B/8, 6 Jan. 1989.

27. Geoffrey Hosking made the recovery of collective memory a key theme of his 1988 Reith Lectures for the BBC, 'The rediscovery of politics'. See *The Listener* 120 (1988), nos. 3088–93. It is no coincidence that the most extreme Russian movement, *Pamyat'*, takes as its name the Russian word for memory.

28. A. Nove *Glasnost' in Action: Cultural Renaissance in Russia* (Boston, Unwin Hyman 1989), heading to chap. 3.

29. R.W. Davies *Soviet History in the Gorbachev Revolution* (London, Macmillan 1989) is the fullest guide to the debate, which has already begun implicitly to question the sanctity of Lenin. See also the interview with Yurii Afanas'ev, reformist director of the State Historical Archive Institute since late 1986, in 'Filling in the blank spots in Soviet history' *History Today* 39 (March 1989), pp. 12–17.

30. For one of the more sophisticated nationalist attempts to negotiate the difficulties, see V. Kozhinov 'Samaia bol'shaia opasnost'', *Nash sovremennik* (1989) no. 1, pp. 141–75.

31. A full translation of a round-table discussion in *Voprosy istorii* (1988)

no. 3, is in *Soviet Studies in History: A Journal of Translations* 27, no. 4 (spring 1989), pp. 6–98. See especially pp. 24, 49–50, 66–7.

32. J.B. Dunlop 'Two noteworthy Russian nationalist initiatives' in Radio Liberty, *Report on the USSR* vol. 1, no. 21 (26 May 1989). The research project headed by Geoffrey Hosking and Peter Duncan at SSEES, University of London, will help to reveal the submerged part of the iceberg whose tip is hinted at here.

33. Radio Free Europe/Radio Liberty *Materiala Samizdata*, vyp. 27/88, and my article 'The church's social role in St Petersburg, 1880–1914' in G.A. Hosking (ed.) *God's Servants: Church, Nation and State in Russia and Ukraine* (London, Macmillan forthcoming).

34. The most detailed account so far (by a very unsympathetic commentator) is J. Wishnevsky 'The origins of *Pamyat*'' *Survey* 30, no. 3 (1988), pp. 79–91.

35. *BBC Summary of World Broadcasts* SU/0366 B/3, 24 Jan. 1989.

36. 'Women in politics' BBC2 documentary, 23 July 1989.

37. See, for example, letter in *Nash sovremennik* (1989) no. 4, pp. 187–8, in response to articles on *perestroika* and price reform in *ibid.* 1988, no. 7, pp. 144–68.

38. Radio Free Europe/Radio Liberty *Materialy Samizdata*, vyp. 5/88, p. 5. English translation in *Soviet Jewish Affairs* 18, no. 1 (1988), pp. 60–71.

39. Round table discussion (see note 31), p. 67.

40. *New York Review of Books* 2 June 1988, p. 7.

41. M. Mihajlov 'A talk with *Ogonek's* Chief Editor, Vitalii Korotich' Radio Liberty *Report on the USSR* 3 March 1989, pp. 29–37, at pp. 32–4.

42. *Znamya* (1988) no. 10, pp. 233–4.

43. P.J.S. Duncan 'The party and Russian nationalism in the USSR: from Brezhnev to Gorbachev' in P.J. Potichnyj (ed.) *The Soviet Union: Party and Society* (Cambridge, Cambridge University Press 1987), pp. 229–44, esp. p. 235.

44. Interview in *Time International* 24 July 1989, pp. 54–8.

45. The alternative case is argued by J. Wishnevsky '*Nash sovremennik* provides focus for "opposition party"' Radio Liberty *Report on the USSR* 1 no. 3, 20 Jan. 1989.

46. A. Besançon 'Nationalism and Bolshevism in the USSR', in R. Conquest (ed.) *The Last Empire: Nationality and the Soviet Future* (Stanford CA, Hoover Institution Press 1986), pp. 1–13.

PART I

The Baltic Republics

The Baltic republics of Estonia, Latvia and Lithuania, with a combined population of 8.8 million, are amongst the youngest and smallest of the union republics. They are also unique within the Soviet federation in having enjoyed a period of independent statehood between the world wars, but their national sovereignties came to an abrupt end following the signing of the Molotov–Ribbentrop Pact between Nazi Germany and the Soviet Union on 23 August 1939, which paved the way for their incorporation into the Soviet Union. Although sharing important historical experiences, culturally they are very different. Each possesses its own language and literary traditions, Lithuanians their Catholic religion, Estonians Lutheranism, while Latvians comprise a mix of both.

Besides being culturally the most westward-orientated of the nationality republics, the region is also the most urbanised, with their peoples enjoying a standard of living higher than that of Russia proper. It is the Baltic republics, with their democratic traditions and greater receptivity to experimentation with new economic, technical and democratic ideas which have been at the cutting edge of the reform programme and which the Gorbachev regime sees as crucial to the success of *perestroika*. The new climate of openness also facilitated the formation of the first grassroots popular movements in the Soviet Union, which have become increasingly radical and nationalistic in their demands and which have played a pivotal role, along with the reformist wings of the local Communist Parties, in questioning the legitimacy of the Soviet federation in its present form. There is little doubt that of all the union republics it is the Baltic states which have emerged to become Gorbachev's greatest challenge to the unity of the Soviet Union.

CHAPTER THREE

Estonians

Riina Kionka

Despite its relatively small size and the disadvantageous geographic position of their homeland, the Estonian people have prevailed for centuries under difficult conditions. Estonians have been under several varieties of foreign rule for over 700 years, and emerged from the mid-1980s to be pacesetters in challenging the continuation of rule from Moscow.

Geographical positioning of the Estonians at the far eastern reaches of the Baltic Sea, neatly sandwiched between the Great Slavic nations of the East and the Germanic nations of the West, has left the territory of Estonia precariously vulnerable to outside influence. That same geostrategic positioning allows Estonia – especially in modern times, with varying degrees of success – to function as a go-between, a kind of conduit, between East and West. The tiny population, having hovered around 1 million in modern times, allows for easy domination by others. And because political and economic domination usually goes hand in hand with cultural domination, the spectre of assimilation, forced or otherwise, has always lurked nearby for the Estonians, be it by Germans, Swedes, Poles or, most recently, Russians.

BACKGROUND

The Estonians have lived in the territory now known as Estonia for some 5,000 years. Little is known about Estonians in prehistoric times. The Estonian language belongs to the Finno-Ugric language group, which embraces such modern languages as Finnish and Hungarian. The origins of the Finno-Ugric peoples is unclear, but archaeological, linguistic and anthropological evidence points to a westward migration from the middle Volga region between the Kama and Oka rivers.[1] Most twentieth-century Finnish, Hungarian and Estonian scholars agree that the Finno-Ugric peoples first lived in the forest zone of

Eastern Europe just west of the Ural Mountains. Around the third millennium BC they began migrating in a succession of small waves towards the west. One major branch went north to the eastern littoral of the Baltic Sea; the other headed further west into what became modern Hungary.

Agriculture dominated the economy, but the level of technology the Estonians reached before the Middle Ages is unclear. Farmsteads were organised by village, and were almost never individual. Estonian family structure in prehistoric times was most likely similar to other nomadic and early agricultural societies, in that extended families, or clans, were the norm. These male-dominated clans were economically self-sufficient units. In the last centuries before German conquest, Estonian society still displayed few differences in wealth or social power, excepting a class of slaves of increasing importance as a source of cheap labour as the nomadic way of life came to an end. On the eve of the Middle Ages most Estonians were small landholders with a measure of societal decision-making that came from owning land and bearing weapons. Politically the Estonians were decentralised, with administrative and political subdivisions emerging on the local level only in the first centuries after the birth of Christ. Estonia was fundamentally independent, with Kievan Russia in the east and the Vikings in the west collecting tribute only occasionally under military duress. Until the German conquest, beginning at the end of the twelfth century, Estonia was not ruled by outsiders.

By the end of the twelfth century, incursions from the west had begun, and with them began the long pattern of foreign domination made attractive by Estonia's convenient location. Estonia was one of the last dark corners of medieval Europe to be Christianised. The German crusading order, the Sword Brethren, were the first outsiders to establish a modicum of control, along with Danish help, over northern Estonia at the beginning of the thirteenth century.[2] Under German–Danish conquest, Estonians were Christianised, colonised and gradually enserfed. In the words of one scholar, 'the social dichotomy of lord and peasant was enhanced by an ethnic one as well'.[3]

The Swedes and Russians also became involved at times in the conquest of northern Estonia. In 1236, as a reaction to a serious defeat at the hands of the Lithuanians and Semigallians, the Sword Brethren allied with the military monastic Order of the Teutonic Knights and became known as the Livonian branch of the Teutonic Knights. In 1346 the Danes, finding upkeep of the distant colony too costly, sold their part of Estonia to the Livonian Order of the Teutonic Knights. The Germans ruled Estonia until the Livonian Wars in the middle of the sixteenth century hastened the already advanced demise of German power. Northern Estonia submitted to Swedish authority

41

in 1561, and southern Estonia (Livonia) became part of Lithuania's Duchy of Kurland. Sweden and Lithuania filled the power vacuum until the Russian push to the Baltic Sea in the Great Northern War. The Treaty of Nystad of 1721 imposed Russian rule in the territory that became modern Estonia – finally with southern Estonia (Livonia) and northern Estonia united. The Baltic German nobility under Russian rule regained many powers over the native peasants that had been lost under Swedish rule, and consequently showed considerable loyalty to Imperial Russia.[4]

The Baltic Provinces were the first in the Russian empire in which serfdom was, by 1819, abolished. By the mid-1800s peasants were able to hold small plots of land, and the abolition of compulsory guild membership spurred Estonian peasants to move to cities. These moves created the economic foundation for the Estonian national cultural awakening that had lain dormant during some 600 years of foreign rule. During the last two decades of the nineteenth century especially, the tsarist administration attempted to assimilate culturally, or Russify, the Estonians. Despite these efforts, Estonia was caught in the current of national awakening (ärkamisaeg) that began sweeping through Europe in the middle of the nineteenth century. This first took a cultural form: a movement sprang up to adopt the use of Estonian as the language of instruction in schools; all-Estonian song festivals were held regularly and became, after a time, expressions of national feeling rather than of loyalty to the tsar; and a national literature in Estonian developed.[5] More importantly, the same activists who agitated for a modern national culture began to focus on establishing a modern national state. Another pattern that would later become central to political developments – the use of culture as politics – emerged.

The possibility for the expression of growing political demands for self-determination presented itself as the 1905 Revolution swept through Estonia. Estonians called for freedom of the press and assembly and for universal franchise, and in November an all-Estonian assembly called for national autonomy. Although Estonian gains were minimal, the 1905 uprisings were brutally suppressed, yet the tense stability that reigned between 1905 and 1917 allowed Estonians to advance the aspiration of national statehood.

A window of opportunity presented itself in the collapse of the German empire in the First World War, and the Russian revolution and subsequent civil war. Russia's Provisional Government granted national autonomy to Estonia, but the internecine struggle mirroring the one in Petrograd continued in Estonia. An autonomous Estonian government (*Maapäev*) was formed but was quickly forced underground by opposing political forces. In the face of the impending German invasion, the Committee of Elders of the underground *Maapäev* announced the Republic of Estonia on 24 February 1918, one day before German troops occupied Tallinn. After the German armistice and subsequent troop withdrawal from Estonia in November 1918, fighting broke out between Bolshevik troops and Estonian partisans. After some fifteen months, the Republic of Estonia and Soviet Russia signed the Peace of Tartu – the Soviet Union's first foreign peace treaty – on 2 February 1920. According to the terms of that treaty, Soviet Russia renounced in perpetuity all rights to the territory of Estonia. The Tartu Peace Treaty was to become a cornerstone in Estonia's struggle under Gorbachev to reinstate Estonia's independence some seventy years later.

Independence lasted twenty-two years.[6] During that time, Estonia underwent a number of economic, social and political reforms necessary to come to terms with its new status as a sovereign state. Economically and socially, the most important step was land reform in 1919. As a result of the sweeping legislation, the large estate holdings belonging to the Baltic nobility were redistributed among peasants and especially among volunteers in the war of independence. Loss of markets in the east led to considerable hardship compounded by the Great Depression before Estonia developed an export-based economy and domestic industries such as oil-shale extraction. Estonia's principal markets became Scandinavia and Western Europe, with some exports to the United States and the Soviet Union.

During independence Estonia also operated under a liberal democratic constitution modelled on the Swiss, Weimar, French and American constitutions. Estonia's first attempt at liberal democracy proved unstable under considerable economic pressures. From 1934 to 1938, partly to guard pre-emptively against a coup from far rightist parties, President Konstantin Päts governed the country by presidential decree. After 1938 a constitutional regime was re-established, which functioned until Soviet annexation in the summer of 1940.

The independence period was one of great cultural advance. Estonian language schools were established, and artistic life of all kinds flourished. One of the more notable cultural acts of the independence period, unique in Western Europe at the time of its passage in 1925, was a guarantee of cultural autonomy to minority groups comprising at least 3,000 persons.

The imminent demise of independence was signalled by the signing of the Molotov–Ribbentrop Non-aggression Pact on 23 August 1939. That agreement's secret clause provided for the Soviet take-over of Estonia, Latvia and part of Finland, and, later, Lithuania, in return for Nazi Germany's assuming control over most of Poland. After some diplomatic jockeying, the Soviet Union staged fraudulent elections in June 1940, the Estonian Soviet Socialist Republic was proclaimed on 21 July 1940, and the newly formed Estonian Socialist republic was formally accepted into the Soviet Union on 6 August 1940.[7]

ESTONIANS AS PART OF THE SOVIET UNION

The year of Soviet rule that followed was accompanied by the expropriation of property, the Sovietisation of cultural life and the installation of Stalinist communism in political life.[8] Deportations also quickly followed, beginning on the night of 14 June 1941. That night more than 10,000 people, a majority of whom were women, children and the elderly, were taken from their homes and sent to Siberia in cattle cars.[9] Thus, when Nazi Germany attacked the Soviet Union on 22 June 1941, the invading troops were received in a relatively warm fashion by Estonians.

Most Estonians did not yet know that German plans for the Baltic included annexation to the Third Reich, expulsion of two-thirds of the population and assimilation of the rest with ethnic Germans. The two and a half years of Nazi German occupation gave ample evidence to conclude that German intentions were not much more generous than were Soviet intentions. Nevertheless, few Estonians welcomed the Red Army's push west through the Baltic, starting at Narva in January 1944. Some 10 per cent of the population fled to the West between 1940 and 1944, most in the last months of 1944 before Soviet troops pushed through for the last time. By late September, Soviet forces expelled the last German troops from Estonia, heralding a second phase of Soviet rule.[10]

Post-war Sovietisation of life in Estonia continued in 1944 where it had left off in 1941. First and foremost, this meant integrating Estonian agriculture and industry into the All-Union economy. Forced collectivisation did not begin in earnest until 1947, and proceeded slowly until late March 1949. On 25–26 March some 8 to 12 per cent of the rural Estonian population, with estimates ranging from 20,000 to 80,000 people, was deported to labour camps in various parts of the Soviet Union.[11] Within the next month over 56 per cent of Estonian farms were collectivised, over 20 per cent in the first two weeks of April 1949 alone, and the collective farm quickly emerged to become the main form of economic and social organisation in the countryside.

As in the agricultural sphere, Estonia's industry was also quickly integrated into Stalin's highly centralised economy. Despite the fact that between the wars Estonia's industrial speciality was in light manufacturing and foodstuffs, post-war investment in heavy industry far outweighed that in other industrial branches. Moscow focused on those industries in Estonia that had locally available raw materials, such as oil-shale mining for electricity production and the chemical sector, especially phosphorites. Yet one notable characteristic of Estonia's post-Stalin economy is the republic's role as a laboratory for economic experiments. Under Khrushchev and Brezhnev, there was considerable experimentation in industrial management techniques that were implemented sooner and with more success in Estonia than in other regions of the Soviet economy. For instance, in the mid-1960s central authorities began giving greater power to local managers, including the powers to offer incentives for increased workers' productivity and to dispose of profits. By 1969, 84 per cent of the overall Soviet industrial output came from enterprises using this system; in Estonia that percentage reached 96 per cent.[12]

However, the more tightly enmeshed in the Soviet economy Estonia became, the less control republic authorities had over production plans, output disposition or management of local industries. For instance, although Estonia, along with the rest of the Soviet Union, participated in Khrushchev's 1957-65 *sovnarkhoz* experiment to increase regional control over industry, over 75 per cent of Estonia's industrial output, both before and after this temporary reform, was controlled by central authorities.[13] By the mid-1980s the percentage of central control over republic industrial output exceeded 90 per cent.[14]

Post-war political integration into the Soviet Union paralleled economic integration. The Estonian republic underwent several administrative reorganisations during the Stalin years to bring it into accordance with the prevailing Soviet model.

After the war the Estonian Communist Party (ECP) had been gradually transformed from a group of 133 members in spring 1940 into the pre-eminent organisation in the republic. The early post-war years saw a rapid increase in Party membership. Most of these new members were Russified-Estonians who had spent most of their lives in the Soviet Union, were assimilated as Russians, and returned to Estonia to make careers only after the Soviet annexation. Not surprisingly, Estonians were reluctant to join the ECP and thus take part in the Sovietisation of their own country. This is reflected in the decreasing ethnic Estonian share of the total Party membership, from some 90 per cent in 1941 to 48 per cent in 1946 to 41 per cent in 1952.[15] The abrupt drop in the Estonian share of Party membership by the early 1950s reflects the CPSU's purge of 'bourgeois nationalists' from the ECP in 1950-51. Compared to Stalin's CPSU purges of the 1930s and 1940s, the ECP purge was less bloody, and probably reflected Moscow's unease over an ECP heavily populated by ethnic Estonians with no Soviet training who might be inclined to think 'nationalistically'.

After Stalin's death, Party membership continued to increase absolutely, and its social base widened to include more ethnic Estonians, especially during the generally greater optimism of the early 1960s. By the mid-1960s the proportion of ethnic Estonians in the ECP stabilised at around 50 per cent. On the eve of *perestroika*, the ECP claimed about 100,000 members, less than half of them ethnic Estonians, and took in about 1.6 per cent of the republic's population. The upper echelons of the Party, however, continued to be dominated by Russians and Russified-Estonians.

Dissent, as the term is understood today, was largely eliminated in the immediate post-war period by the effectiveness of Stalinist terror. However, another more potent form of protest against Sovietisation, that could hardly be called 'dissent', emerged. From the retreat of Nazi troops in 1944 until as late as 1955, a protracted anti-Soviet pro-independence guerrilla movement existed in the countryside. The movement drew its followers – called 'forest brethren' (*metsavennad*, a popular Estonian term for guerrillas) – from stranded Estonian soldiers who had been mobilised into the Nazi German army, from those seeking to avoid arrest by Soviet security forces or mobilisation into the Soviet army at the war's end, and from those seeking revenge for the mass deportations of both 1941 and 1949. The forest brethren worked in groups or alone, and used German and later Soviet equipment that had been left behind. In some areas the guerrillas had effective military control until the late 1940s: in others areas they could only protect themselves and the local population from acts of violence. At the high point of guerrilla strength in 1946-48 there were probably some 5,000 forest brethren. These men did not hope to bring down the Soviet regime by their actions, but evidently expected a restoration of Estonian independence with Allied help, and thus sought to ensure their own survival until such a time came.

More traditional forms of dissent in significant quantity did not appear until the late 1960s. Hopes for systemic reform accompanied the process of de-Stalinisation carried out through the late 1950s and early 1960s. When reform did not materialise and heightened expectations proved groundless, open dissent appeared. This 'quiet dissent' of the 1960s, mostly in the form of protest letters, centred on civil rights issues and was bolstered by the Soviet invasion of Czechoslovakia in August 1968.

By the 1970s national concerns, including concerns about ecological ruin, a consequence of the country's rapid industrialisation, had become the major theme of dissent in Estonia, and the dissenters came increasingly from the ranks of natural scientists and, later, students. A spate of protest letters in the 1970s was followed in each instance by an official crackdown. Despite the authorities' reactions, ranging from arrest and imprisonment to censure, the scope of dissent broadened and the area of concern widened to include worries over cultural autonomy.

By the late 1970s there was growing concern throughout most sectors of Estonian society about the threat of cultural Russification to the Estonian language and national identity. An official Moscow policy implemented in 1978 that sought to increase the role of the Russian language in non-Russian Soviet republics explains a great deal of the worry among Estonians. By 1981, for the first time in the republic's history, Russian was taught in the first grade of Estonian language schools, and was also introduced into Estonian pre-school teaching. Among Estonians, the catch-phrase encompassing this concern was 'Will the people disappear?' (*kas rahvas kaob?*). This widespread concern about cultural survival is responsible for the broadening of the social base of dissent in the late 1970s. In October 1980 some 2,000 secondary school students gathered in the streets of Tartu to protest against Russian rule and call for a free Estonia. Brutal use of police force to suppress this protest prompted forty established intellectuals, among them some leading Communists with impeccable credentials, to sign an open protest letter sent to Moscow and the republic authorities. This 'Letter of the Forty', as it came to be known, decried the increase in ethnic tensions in the republic, precipitated by Russian immigration, and spoke out against the increasing threat to the Estonian language and culture. Such concerns became particularly critical for Estonians due to their demographic position.

Before incorporation, the Estonian proportion of its territory's population was 88.2 per cent but by 1950 it had dropped to some 76 per cent. It is not surprising that the population of Estonia sank during the war and immediately afterwards to new lows. War losses, the 1941 deportation, and a brain drain of some 10 per cent of the population to the West, partially explain the sudden drop in the post-war years, as do territorial changes.[16]

This demographic trend of an ever-decreasing ethnic Estonian share of the total population continued after Stalin's death. According to official census data, by 1960 Estonians made up 74.1 per cent of the total population, in 1970 68.2 per cent, in 1980 64.5 per cent, and by 1989 only 61.5 per cent. There are a number of explanations for this phenomenon. Although from 1953 to 1961 natural increase outstripped net migration increase in the republic, this trend reversed itself after 1961 and has remained reversed. Since 1962 Estonia's birth-rate has been among the lowest in the Soviet Union.

The low birth-rate is only part of the explanation for the demographic situation. The massive influx of non-Estonians since 1945 is responsible for the precipitous drop in the ethnic Estonian share of the population. The heavy industrial projects developed or augmented in the Stalin era and later required a larger pool of labour than was locally available. Thus, non-Estonian workers came to the republic from other parts of the Soviet Union to staff these industrial projects. These workers, who were attracted by the republic's higher standard of living, paved the way for later waves of immigration. Most were Russians, but a significant minority comprised Ukrainians, Belorussians and other nationalities.

A positive aspect of the post-Stalin era for Estonia was a re-opening in the late 1950s of citizens' contacts with foreign countries. After Khrushchev denounced Stalin's 'two-camp theory' of international relations in favour of 'peaceful coexistence' in his 1956 'secret speech' to the 20th CPSU Congress, it became permissible, to a point, for Soviet citizens to have contacts with foreigners. This move had a tremendous impact on Estonia. For the first time since the Second World War, Estonians were allowed, theoretically, to have contact with their friends and family in the West. Ties were also reactivated with Finland. Contact with Finnish tourists lent Tallinn a cosmopolitan air in keeping with its Western atmosphere, and boosted a flourishing black market. Starting in the middle 1960s, Estonians began watching Finnish television beamed from nearby Helsinki. This electronic 'window on the West' afforded Estonians more information on current affairs and more access to Western culture and thought than any other group in the Soviet Union. This heightened media environment may have been pivotal in preparing Estonians for their vanguard role in extending *perestroika* under Gorbachev.

ESTONIANS UNDER GORBACHEV

(Although the exact meaning of Gorbachev's terms *perestroika* and *glasnost'* remain inexact, Estonains quickly discerned that the new policies could hold very interesting possibilities for the nation. These twin policies have had the effect, in Estonia, of catalysing a 'new awakening period' *(uus ärkamisaeg)* that was to lead, as did the first awakening period in late tsarist times, to striving for independent statehood.[17]

The wave of reform began in Estonia with the environmental movement. Vociferous criticism of Estonia's ecological devastation in 1985 was followed by a curious silence in 1986. Later it became clear that despite *glasnost'*, new censorship rules had been implemented in 1986 to quell discussion of pollution. The primary focus of concern was open-pit mining of some of the world's largest phosphorite reserves in the north-east of Estonia. Although the issue was an ecological one, it also hinged on demographic concerns. A plan to enlarge the phosphorite mining project would have included the in-migration of some 30,000 workers and dependants into Estonia, pushing Estonians into minority status in their own country. Thus, although the debate was environmental in form, it was actually national in content.[18]

The phosphorite mining project, along with a host of other highly polluting industrial projects, became the subject of bitter open criticism during 1987. By June 1988 a loose coalition of dissidents, rural inhabitants, workers and intellectuals (including Party intellectuals), all concerned about this double environmental/demographic threat, had successfully consolidated their efforts and succeeded in ending the ten year rule of ECP First Secretary Karl Vaino.

Karl Vaino's demise was a harbinger of the ECP's own gradual loss of influence in the late 1980s. In the early *perestroika* years, the ECP remained stable; the only significant personnel change was replacement of Aleksandr Kudriavtsev, its Second Secretary, a post traditionally reserved for non-Estonians, by another Russian, Georgii Alyoshin. The Party appeared strong at its 19th Congress in 1986. First Secretary Vaino devoted most of this first *glasnost'*-inspired speech to attacking national culture and Estonians' love of 'Western mass culture' (a clear reference to Finnish television). But by 1988 the ECP's weakness had become clear. In the highly changeable political environment of that year, the Party was unable to assume more than a passive role, and thereby was relegated to a reactive position. Vaino's removal in response to public dissatisfaction indicates how weak the Party had become.

Karl Vaino was replaced by the much more acceptable Vaino Väljas. A number of initial steps by Väljas, including praising the 1980 'Letter of the Forty', enhanced his own and the ECP's reputation, at least for a time. But the Party continued its downward spiral of influence in 1989 and 1990, and began to disintegrate. In November 1989, the Writers' Union Party Organisation voted to suspend its activity and the Estonian Komsomol disbanded. In February 1990 Estonia's Supreme Soviet eliminated paragraph 6 of the republic's constitution which had guaranteed the Party's leading role in society. The final blow came at the ECP's 20th Congress in March 1990 when it voted to break with the CPSU. The Party splintered into three branches, then consolidated into a pro-CPSU and an independent ECP.

As the ECP waned, other political movements, groupings and parties moved to fill the power vacuum. The first and most important of these was the Estonian Popular Front, established in April 1988 in response to appeals made at the Estonian Cultural Union's plenum two weeks earlier. Initially a grass-roots organisation, the Popular Front became a well-organised movement with its own platform, leadership and broad constituency. The Popular Front was followed by the Greens and the dissident-led Estonian National Independence Party, the latter the first to call for full independence in January 1988. By 1989 the political spectrum widened and new parties were formed and re-formed almost daily. Between November 1989 and February 1990 some twenty to thirty parties existed in a republic of 1.5 million people. This frenzied party proliferation stabilised in time for the Supreme Soviet elections of 18 March 1990, where sixteen parties endorsed candidates.[19]

A number of changes in the governance of the republic, brought about by political advances, played a major role in the late 1980s in forming a legal framework for political change. This involved the republic's Supreme Soviet being transformed into an authentic regional law-making body in which key nationally minded leaders, mostly but not exclusively ethnic Estonians, pushed through reformist legislation.

This was not always an easy task. Even though the Supreme Soviet, elected in 1985, was nearly 75 per cent ethnic Estonian, it had not traditionally been a medium of reform.

Nevertheless, this relatively conservative Supreme Soviet managed to pass a number of laws. Notable among them is a package of laws that addresses the most sensitive ethnic concerns. The package includes the early declaration of sovereignty (November 1988); a law on economic independence (May 1989) that was subsequently confirmed by the USSR Supreme Soviet (November 1989); a language law which made Estonian the official language of the republic (January 1989); and local and republic election laws stipulating residency requirements for voting and candidacy (August and November 1989).

On 18 March 1990, Estonians elected a new Supreme Soviet in the most democratic elections for a republic-level organ since incorporation into the USSR. Following laws making service in the Soviet military voluntary and creating an alternative service (March and April 1990), the new Supreme Soviet quickly established its tenor by declaring the beginning of a transition period to full independence on 30 March 1990. It also chose Popular Front leader Edgar Savisaar as Estonia's first non-Communist Prime Minister. Savisaar in turn chose a moderate cabinet comprising very few Communists.

Despite the Estonian Supreme Soviet's apparent responsiveness to new conditions, an alternative legislature developed in Estonia in 1990. In February 1990 a body known as the Congress of Estonia was elected in completely unsanctioned, unofficial elections. The Congress was organised by a group called the Estonian Citizens' Committees. The Citizens' Committees, acting as an informal body much like the Committees of Correspondence in the American Revolution, registered citizens of the inter-war Republic of Estonia and their descendants with the goal of forming a legally competent citizens' forum. The Congress of Estonia's point of departure is that Estonia remains an occupied country because as Estonia was forcibly annexed by the Soviet Union, the inter-war republic continues to exist *de jure*. Only citizens of that republic and their descendants, argues the Congress, can decide the future of Estonia. The Congress organisers encouraged all non-Estonians who could not claim citizenship to apply for citizenship – and some 60,000 have done so. The Congress, which met for its initial session in March 1990, shows every sign of becoming a complementary, not competing, political force in relation to the Supreme Soviet.[20]

Reaction to Estonia's interpretation of *perestroika* and *glasnost'* among its 600,000 non-Estonians (about 38.5 per cent of the population) has been mixed.[21] In 1988 two groups were formed among non-Estonians in response to the rise of the Popular Front. The International Front and the United Council of Work Collectives have nearly identical constituencies, and together form 'Intermovement'. Intermovement, a conservative Russian nationalist organisation, is opposed to Estonian-style reform and independence. It was established, ostensibly, to protect the interests of non-Estonians and to further an 'internationalist' (as opposed to a 'nationalist') orientation. Intermovement has organised mass demonstrations opposing the republic's Supreme Soviet nationality laws, and has asked Moscow directly to intervene on behalf of non-Estonians in the republic's move towards independence.

Although not all non-Estonians support full independence they are divided in their goals for the republic. According to opinion polls, in March 1990 some 18 per cent of Russian speakers supported the idea of a fully independent Estonia, up from 7 per cent in September 1989. More significant is the shift that has occurred in their opinions of the status quo. While a majority of the Russian speakers supported preserving the status quo in 1989, by September of the same year the majority favoured Estonia forming part of a Soviet confederation. Clearly, only a small group of non-Estonians were opposed to full independence in early 1990. Furthermore, polls show that less than one-fifth of the republic's ethnic minorities back the conservative Intermovement.[22]

CONCLUSIONS

Concern over the cultural survival of the Estonian people had, by the beginning of the Gorbachev era, reached a critical point. *Glasnost'* allowed Estonians to voice those concerns. Although these complaints were first couched in environmental terms, they quickly became the grist of straightforward political national feelings. In this regard, the two decades of independent statehood were pivotal. Past independence provided a national symbol for mobilisation around the separatist cause; it had also furnished Estonian society with a experience of democracy which, in combination with its 'electronic window on the West', helps us to understand the republic's vanguard role in the first years of Gorbachev's administration in extending reform far beyond what the Soviet leadership ever intended.

ACKNOWLEDGEMENTS

I would like to thank Paul A. Goble and Toomas Hendrik Ilves for helpful comments on earlier versions of this chapter.

NOTES

1. See Toivo Raun *Estonia and the Estonians* (Stanford, CA, Hoover Institution Press 1987); and Evald Uustalu *The History of the Estonian People* (London, Boreas Publishing 1952).
2. Estonia's capital city derives its modern name Tallinn from the Estonian equivalent of 'Danish citadel', from the Danes having enlarged the Estonian fortress during their domination of Tallinn and north-eastern Estonia.
3. Raun *Estonia and the Estonians*, p. 19.
4. See Edward Thaden *et al., Russification in the Baltic Provinces and Finland, 1855-1914* (Princeton, NJ, Princeton University Press 1981).
5. Arvo Mägi *Estonian Literature* (Stockholm, Baltic Humanitarian Association 1968).
6. Georg von Rauch, *The Baltic States: Years of Independence 1917-1940* (Berkeley, University of California Press 1974).
7. William Hough 'The annexation of the Baltic states and its effect on the development of law prohibiting forcible seizure of territory,' *The New York Law School Journal of International and Comparative Law*, 6(2), 1985.
8. For a contemporary appraisal of Estonian history from the Stone Age to the present, see Mart Laar, Lauri Vahtre and Heiki Valk *Kodu Lugu I & II* (Tallinn, Loomingu Raamatukogu 1989).
9. Laar *et al., Kodu Lugu II*, p. 54.
10. For a detailed review of the war years, see Raun *Estonia and the Estonians*; and Romuald Misiunas and Rein Taagepera *The Baltic States: Years of Dependence 1940-1980* (Berkeley, University of California Press 1983).
11. Parming suggests that 80,000 were deported, Taagepera puts the number at 50,000–60,000, and Laar *et al.* estimate that nearly 21,000 were deported in late March 1949. Tõnu Parming, 'Population changes and processes' in Parming and Järvesoo (eds) *A Case Study of a Soviet Republic: the Estonian SSR* (Boulder, CO, Westview 1978); Misinunas and Taagepera *Estonia and the Estonians*; Laar *et al., Kodu Lugu.*
12. Raun *Estonia and the Estonians*, p. 198.
13. Elmar Järvesoo 'The postwar economic transformation', in Parming and Järvesoo *A Case Study of a Soviet Republic;* Raun *Estonia and the Estonians.*
14. For a comparison of the effects of Soviet rule on the economies of two comparable societies – Estonia and Finland – see Sirje Sinilind *Viro ja Venäjä* (Helsinki, Alea-Kirja 1985).
15. Raun, *Estonia and the Estonians*, pp. 190-93.
16. In 1945 Estonia lost territories in the north-east and south-east amounting to some 5% of the total inter-war area and possibly encompassing some 70,000 residents. The Narva area in the north-east was joined with the RSFSR, and the Petseri area in the south-east, largely populated by Estonians of the Orthodox faith, was given to the Pihkva Oblast. These alterations in territory and population, ostensibly made 'for ethnic reasons', also help explain the initial increase in the Estonian share of the total in the immediate post-war years.
17. For a descriptive chronological account of events, see Rein Taagepera

'Estonia's road to independence', *Problems of Communism* 38 (6), 1989.

18. Toomas Ilves 'Environmental problems in Estonia', Baltic Area Situation Report, *Radio Free Europe Research*, 6, 1985; and Riina Kionka 'Ecological concern in Estonia,' Baltic Area Situation Report, *Radio Free Europe Research*, 5, 1986.
19. See Riina Kionka 'Estonia, Political Parties in Eastern Europe', *Radio Free Europe Research*, 1990.
20. See Riina Kionka 'The Estonian Citizens' Committees: an opposition movement of a different complexion', *Report on the USSR*, 1, (6), 1990; and 'The Congress of Estonia', *Report on the USSR*, 2 (12), 1990.
21. Of the 602,393 non-Estonians living in the republic in 1989, some 30.3% were Russians, 3.1% were Ukrainians, 1.8% were Belorussians, and the rest belonged to other nationalities. Estonians comprised 61.5% of the population according to the 1989 census (Rahva Hääl, 19 September 1989).
22. Päevaleht 10 and 21 March 1990.

CHAPTER FOUR

Latvians

Graham Smith

The history of the Latvian people is inextricably bound up with their location at the interface of European and Russian cultural influences and with neighbouring geopolitical Great Power struggles to establish supremacy over their homeland. During this century Latvians succeeded in achieving national self-determination from Russia in November 1918, only to be followed two decades later by loss of independent statehood. A brief period of Soviet rule (1940–41) was followed by four years of German occupation until in 1944 Latvia was again incorporated into the Soviet Union. As part of the Soviet federation, the Latvian union republic has become one of the most urbanised and multi-ethnic regions in the USSR. By 1989, Latvians made up 50.7 per cent of the republic's 2.7 million population.[1]

THE MAKING OF THE LATVIANS

From the early Middle Ages onwards, successive invasions, wars and treaties have ensured the division, partition and colonisation of this small country.[2] In the early thirteenth century, Western-central Latvia was invaded and brought into the Christian Order of Western Europe by the 'Bretheren of the Sword'. The region's conquest was completed by the German Teutonic Knights in 1290 with the enserfment of the Latvian peasantry and the establishment of the Livonian State. In 1561, following the partition of Livonia, south-western Latvia became the hereditary Duchy of Kurland, a successful trading entity under the suzerainty of the Polish monarchy. The rest of Livonia became first a dependency of the Polish Commonwealth, followed by a period under Swedish rule (1629–1721), and finally, by 1721, following the Treaty of Nystadt, the region was annexed by Russia. Eastern Latvia, known as Latgalia, remained part of the Polish Commonwealth until 1773 when it also was annexed by Russia, with Kurland's incorporation following in 1795. Throughout the nineteenth century, the descendants of the

Teutonic Order, the Baltic German nobility (*Ritterschaften*) of western central Latvia (Kurland and southern Lifland), continued to enjoy a special relationship with St Petersburg which gave them considerable economic and cultural autonomy. In contrast, in Latgalia, administered as part of Vitebsk province, the largely Catholic Latvian population remained subservient to a Polish and Russian nobility, developing rural institutions similar to those found in Russia proper. It was not, however, until the latter half of the nineteenth century that a Latvian national consciousness was to develop, which was later to spark off demands for political autonomy, culminating in the establishment of an independent Latvia.

For Latvians, the formation and development of a national conscious-ness is inextricably bound up with these two crucial periods in their pre-Soviet history. The formation of this sense of nationhood paralleled the region's nineteenth-century transition from feudalism to capitalism. From 1804 onwards, a series of local decrees began the gradual process of weakening the hold of the *Ritterschaften* over peasant society, and in 1849 a law granted a legal basis for the creation of peasant-owned farms. Further laws of 1865 and 1866 were to end the exclusive rights of nobles to hold estates. Not only did these changes permit the establishment of a class of Latvian small-scale landed property owners (who by the early 1900s owned around 40 per cent of the land), but also, with the beginnings of the region's industrialisation from the 1860s onwards, the migration of Latvians to the towns, particularly into Riga, resulted in the emergence of an indigenous middle class and industrial proletariat. During this period, the urban share of the region's population increased from 178,800 (or 14.8 per cent) in 1863 to 939,000 (or 38.0 per cent) by the eve of World War One.[3]

Until the 1860s, there was little sense of a Latvian national identity. Both serfdom and institutional controls to migration and social mo-bility limited the boundaries of the peasants' intellectual and social geography.[4] Influenced by the Romantic movement's conception of the *Volk* and of a Lutheran religion which held that preaching should be conducted in a people's mother tongue, the Baltic German clergy and literati took a benevolent interest in the distinctive language and culture of the Latvian peasantry, particularly in their oral traditions, such as their folk-songs (*dainas*) and folk-tales, and in promoting the Latvian language. Such attitudes were to ensure that early in the nineteenth century the Latvian tongue became a literary language for a people who, by the time of the 1897 tsarist census, could rightfully claim near universal literacy. It was, however, the newly emergent Latvian intelligentsia who were to become the social bearers of Latvian nationalism. In the 1860s, the Young Latvian Movement was formed amongst their number, the aim of which was to promote the indigenous language and to counteract and publicise the socio-economic oppression of Latvians, in town and country alike, by the Baltic Germans. It was this organisation which was influential in formulating the ideas behind *Jaunā Strāva* ('New Current'), an organisation set up in the 1890s, which was to give birth to a range of political viewpoints organised along both class and national lines. Attempts by the Russian empire from the 1880s onwards to culturally Russify the region, although initially directed against weakening the privileged position of the Baltic Germans, probably did much in a crucial period in Latvian nation-building to ensure that enmity towards a Russian-dominated state became a feature of the nationalist struggle.

By 1901, *Jaunā Strāva* had evolved into the Latvian Social Democratic Party (LSDP). In advocating greater territorial autonomy for Latvia, the LSDP was conscious of the plight of the region's growing number of minorities, including the cultural particularity of Latgalia. They advocated the transformation of the empire into a federation of democratic states (to include Latvia), and following the Austro-Marxists, the adoption of a policy of cultural autonomy for its extra-territorial ethnic communities. In 1903, however, the LSDP split into two, with a newly formed Latvian Social Democratic Workers' Party (LSDWP) eventually allying itself with Lenin's Russian Social Democratic Workers' Party, and adopting an internationalist policy. The other political offshoot of the LSDP, the Latvian Social Democratic Union (LSDU), continued to champion national interests and Latvia's national self-determination.[5] There is, however, evidence to suggest that, in comparison with the Ukrainians and Estonians, the Latvians were slower to adopt a platform of national separatism, and even as late as 30 July 1917, at the so-called Riga 'autonomy' conference, also attended by some Bolsheviks, agreement to set up a Latvian National Assembly was unsuccessful.[6] Rather, it was not until October 1917, as a result of the efforts of the newly formed Riga Democratic Bloc, which included representatives of all political factions except the Bolshevik wing of the LSDWP, that a resolution was passed demanding the establishment of a fully independent and neutral Latvia.[7] Independence was briefly punctuated by the Red Army's invasion in 1919 and the establishment of a Latvian Soviet republic, but with support from the Western allies it was quickly overthrown by Latvian nationalist troops.[8]

Having obtained independent statehood, in which the Latvians were an absolute majority (making up 75.5 per cent of the 1,960,502 population by 1935),[9] a second important phase in nation-building began. The Latvian language was recognised as the state's official tongue, and with statehood, all the symbols and trappings of successful nationhood were introduced. Cultural autonomy was also granted to the country's sizeable minorities, which included the Baltic Germans, Jews, Russians and Poles.[10] The electoral system, introduced into the Latvian constitution in 1922, also protected minority interests. Based on a complex system of proportional representation, with any five persons being able to register as a political party, it resulted in the representation of a large number of political groupings in the 100-strong Latvian parliament, the Saeima, with political parties reflecting the dominant ethnic, regional, religious and urban/rural divisions in society. It was, however, the Agrarian Bloc, centred on its largest party, the Latvian Peasant Union (LPU), which dominated Latvian politics during the inter-war years, and which was pivotal in supporting the interests of the socially dominant, rural Latvian population. Agrarian reform ensured the reallocation of land in favour of peasant smallholders, with the individual peasant farmstead (*mājas*) becoming an economic basis and a social symbol of Latvian statehood. Agriculture and rural-related industries received priority, with Latvia becoming a major exporter of agricultural commodities to the West. A series of shortlived coalition governments unable to govern over a politically fragmented Saeima, in combination with a national economy heavily dependent on Western countries now firmly locked into recession, paved the way for the establishment of authoritarian rule in 1934 under Karlis Ulmanis.[11] In emphasising 'national unity as the foundation of the state', Ulmanis nationalised large sections of industry on the pretext that the largely minority-owned trade and industry sector should be under Latvian control.[12] The educational and cultural rights of minorities were also curtailed. Following the Molotov–Ribbentrop Pact of 23 August 1939, Latvia was to share the same fate as its Baltic neighbours, coming under Soviet hegemony.

LATVIA AS PART OF THE SOVIET UNION

As part of Stalin's USSR, the Latvian union republic was subjected to a scale of social and economic reorganisation which rapidly transformed its economy from agriculture to heavy industry, its overwhelmingly ethnically Latvian population into a more multi-ethnic polity, and its predominantly peasant social structure into a fully urbanised class of industrial workers.[13] However, while dislodging Latvians from their traditional roles, there is little evidence to suggest that their national consciousness became simply a passive recipient of structural change: it continued to have a proactive capacity to modify and occasionally to resist these changes, most starkly so up until the early 1950s in armed guerrilla resistance to Soviet rule.

In their sense of nationhood, the Latvians, unlike most other peoples of the Soviet Union, could draw upon a rich variety of pre-Soviet national symbols, including the democratic years of statehood from which to judge contemporary reality and an established, century-long, national culture which was adapted to the new social conditions demanded and produced by Soviet modernity. Such an established set of cultural traditions and values became bound up with dissident politics, occasionally entered the public arena of federal politics (most notably during the late 1950s and from the mid-1980s onwards), and was manifested in the reconstituted but never entirely recast national literature and song festivals, as well as finding expression in official Soviet rituals and ceremonies.

The primary objective of the Stalinist state was to 'ensure the transformation of Latvia from an agrarian country into a highly developed industrial-agrarian republic'.[14] Despite its lack of a raw material or energy base (except hydroelectric power and peat), within the first two post-war five year plans (1946–55), the republic had been transformed into a centre for metal and machine working and associated heavy industries. By 1960, industrial output had increased to ten times the 1940 level, while the output for metal-building and machine-working and the chemical industry increased, respectively, by a staggering sixty and fifty times.[15] In contrast, by 1960, agricultural output had barely reached the 1940 level.[16]

The republic's rapid industrialisation, it has been concluded, was essentially motivated to ensure the mass immigration of Russian labour and to facilitate cultural assimilation and political stability. Yet it would seem that the availability of a skilled labour force in a region which by the early twentieth century had already developed a manufacturing base in combination with the beneficial linkage effects of coastal proximity and an already established east–west rail network is as likely to have favoured the adoption of such a strategy, with Slav immigration being more a consequence than the motivating force.[17] From the mid 1950s onwards, however, it was immigration from other republics, notably from Russia proper, which overtook the countryside as the main source of supplemental urban labour and which contributed greatly to transforming Latvia from a predominantly pre-war rural society into a country of urban dwellers by the late 1950s.

In contrast, the Latvian countryside did not undergo substantial reorganisation until nearly four years after incorporation. This was partly due to its being perceived as less immediately amenable to structural reorganisation than the city, not least because of the strength of traditional affiliations with nationalism in a countryside which Stalin had regarded as 'the guardian of nationality'.[18] By 1948, however, collectivisation began, but by January 1949 only 10 per cent of peasant households were collectivised. By introducing the well-experimented, draconian techniques of Stalinism, which included mass deportations, 98.4 per cent of peasant households had been incorporated into collective farms by the end of 1951.[19] Officially, it was the richer class of Latvian smallholders – deemed to be the backbone of support for 'bourgeois nationalism' – who were blamed for opposing and holding up the process of collectivisation. Yet, in spite of collectivisation, the *mājas*, deemed a 'burdensome heritage of the past' and a major obstacle to the modernisation of the countryside, remained a feature of the rural landscape and an embarrassing symbol to the Soviet authorities, certainly up until the Gorbachev period, of what was once small-scale Latvian agriculture.[20]

Systemic change was facilitated by a republic party and state apparatus disproportionately made up of 'Russified Latvians' (the so-called *latovichi*); that is, by those Latvians and their descendants who had spent the inter-war years in the Soviet Union and whose only connection with the Latvian nationality was through their passport status. However, with Khrushchev's mid-1950s policy of economic decentralisation, which resulted in the setting up of a Latvian *sovnarkhoz* (or economic council), it was clear that a sizeable section of the republic's Party elite saw in the republic's newly acquired economic powers the means to redress Moscow's standardising policies. At the forefront were members of the Riga Institute of Economics, who argued that the aims of the national economy should be

to develop Latvia's industrial structure and specialisation so that the most rational and economical use of all Latvian natural and labour resources would maximise the Latvian contribution to the development of the USSR's economy as well as the living standards of Latvia.[21]

Preference was to be given to the development of agriculture and consumer industries over outside raw material- and labour-dependent heavy industries.

Prioritising local interests was not, however, limited to the economy; demands were also being made for the promotion of the Latvian language and for Russian migrants to learn Latvian. As one prominent Party official suggested, 'The level of party work would be raised significantly if communists would conduct talks among workers in the language native to the workers.'[22] Action was also taken to increase the number of compulsory hours for the study of Latvian in the republic's schools.

Economic decentralisation therefore provided a way of promoting a particular set of policies more in keeping with the pre-1940 national economy, which was also compatible with economising on immigration. Political consequences, however, followed, which went far further than in any other Soviet republic. Those within the top echelons of public life, which Moscow labelled 'the nationalist group',[23] were duly removed from power. Among those dismissed were Eduards Berklāvs, Vice-chairman of the Latvian Council of Ministers, and Pauls Dzērve, head of Riga's Institute of Economics. Following the purges, the newly appointed First Party Secretary, Arvīds Pelše (1959–66), who replaced Jānis Kalnbērziņš (1940–59), singled out the contested issue of immigration for particular comment:

Some of our comrades, fearing without any basis that our Latvian republic might lose its national identity, wanted to stop the objectively natural process of population shifts. In their speeches they repeatedly maintain, for instance, that the mechanical increase of the population of Riga should be avoided. This attitude is both harmful and politically dangerous. By cultivating national isolationism they identify with bourgeois nationalism, impairing the interests of the peoples of the Soviet Union and endanger also the interests of the Latvian nation.[24]

The return to centralised ministerial control marked an end to experimentation with radical, decentralising reform, but the *sovnarkhoz* episode did illustrate how the diffusion of republic economic authority could so easily rekindle territorial and national interests. Throughout the 1960s and 1970s Latvia's political leadership resumed its administration over an economy whose balance and pattern of activity had been primarily determined by Stalin. None the less, considerable strides were made in the development of the electronics and communications industries; compared with the first two decades, agriculture also began to prosper, all of which ensured for the republic's economy a disproportionate role in overall Soviet economic performance. It continued to be a leading net financier to other parts of the Soviet Union, as measured in terms of the small proportion of turnover tax which it was allowed to retain for internal consumption.[25] The republic's standard of living also improved immeasurably, with a per capita income generally higher than in Russia proper and second only to Estonia.[26] By 1988, over 28 per cent of Latvia's population earned 200 roubles or more per month, bettered only by Estonia, and which compared with the All-Union average of 17.2 per cent.[27]

Although Latvia's economic growth targets assigned to industry were amongst the lowest of any republic during the 1970s and early 1980s, the pattern and tempo of industrial development continued to have profound consequences for the labour supply and for the republic's ethno-demographic composition. Centrally determined sectoral priorities and outmoded practices continued to ensure an insatiable demand for outside labour in spite of limits being set to the overall size of enterprise work forces and in spite of earmarking the capital city, Riga, for limited industrial growth. Largely oblivious of attempts to manage the labour supply, All-Union ministries and their plant managers continued to increase the size of their labour force, to the extent that such practices were publicly condemned by First Party Secretary Augusts Voss (1966–84).[28]

It was immigration, primarily from the Russian republic, which continued to account for the major part of population growth where the attractions of higher living standards and Western lifestyles motivated much migration. It accounted for over two-thirds of Latvia's demographic increase throughout the 1970s.[29] By the early 1980s, in part due to lower rates of planned industrial growth for the republic, immigration did slow down, but from the mid-1980s again increased.[30] Labour shortages have also been exacerbated by the republic's low birth-rate, which, by 1980, had reached the all-time low of 14 per thousand population.[31] With a level of natural increase only slightly recovered from the 1980 level of 1.3 per thousand, there remains concern about the republic being able to reproduce its increasingly ageing population naturally. Consequently, from Latvians constituting 62 per cent of the population in 1959, they now (1989 census) make up a bare majority within their own homeland (50.7 per cent).

It is the social consequences of Russian immigration in combination with those policies which challenge the institutional supports enjoyed by the native language and culture which many Latvians fear will further erode the benefits of being Latvian in their native homeland. Yet there is little evidence to suggest during the Brezhnev years that cultural assimilation was occurring. In terms of declared native language, for Latvians probably the most important criterion of nationhood, in 1979, 97.8 per cent of the titular nationality affirmed Latvian as their native language, compared with 98.4 per cent in 1959.[32] The vast majority of Latvians continued to have the opportunity to attend either native or mixed-language (as opposed to Russian) schools, while provision for the native language in the media and institutional support for it as the medium of Latvian culture ensured that the indigenous language remained pivotal to the Latvian way of life. Although knowledge of Russian continued as a precondition for entrance into higher and specialised education, urbanised Latvians have not needed to assimilate into the Russian language and culture in order to gain position and status in the republic.[33] Latvians are well represented in administration, economic management and in the professions. Moreover, their over-representation in the 'creative' professions in comparison with most other Soviet nationalities has no doubt played an important part in preserving and promoting the native culture.

These opportunities also reflect the significance of republic status in providing employment for those with a vested interest in the production and reproduction of the native culture. Such social opportunities for the indigenous population are also more broadly reflected in the benefits which accrue to being officially designated as 'Latvian' within the Latvian republic. Terenteva's study showed that, when having to choose the nationality of either a Latvian or Russian parent, sixteen-year-olds preferred the titular nationality.[34] A combination, therefore, of sense of attachment to being Latvian and the material and status privileges which republic designation brings, has also meant that few Latvians either adopt Russian cultural attributes or leave their homeland (over 93 per cent of Latvians in the USSR reside in their native republic, which makes them one of the most rooted of the major nationalities).[35]

None the less, both institutional and migrational pressures continued to facilitate the spread of the Russian language, so challenging the dominance of the native language and culture. Knowledge of Russian increased: in 1970, 45.3 per cent of Latvians declared a knowledge of Russian compared with 58.3 per cent by 1979.[36] Of equal concern, however, has been the reluctance of incoming Russians to learn the indigenous language (by 1979 only 19 per cent knew Latvian, and in 1970 18 per cent).[37] Moscow's renewed emphasis from the late 1970s in expanding the teaching of Russian in schools and universities came as yet further evidence, particularly to the intelligentsia, of the threatened position of the Latvian language, although the republic's then Minister of Education warmly supported such measures on the grounds that it was promoting the language of internationalism.[38] First Party Secretary Augusts Voss, however, adopted a more cautious approach. At an All-Union scientific conference in Riga in June 1982, he spoke of the need to promote bilingualism in Party work, noting that the attention given to promoting the Russian language should not deflect from the need to ensure the promotion of the indigenous tongue.[39]

Throughout the Brezhnev years organised dissent tended to couch its appeal in the collectivist language of the nation, in which demands for individual freedoms were presented as being bound up with the national right to self-determination. Russification, in particular, was singled out as the greatest threat to the nation, in which the preferred solution to policies of Soviet statism was the re-establishment of a Latvian state. Dissident groups, however, tended to have a limited lifespan. But dissent did not remain exclusively outside the Party. The most widely publicised dissent came from a document signed by seventeen alienated Latvian Communists which was sent to sister organisations in the West and which provided details of the republic's systematic Russification, including, it was noted, that of the political leadership.[40] Although national dissent throughout the Brezhnev years was more evident in Latvia than in most other republics, compared with its two Baltic neighbours, it remained more subdued. Latvia possessed neither the strong mobilising and organisational role that religion played in Lithuanian dissent nor a republic leadership, as in Estonia, willing, on occasion, to take a firmer stance in support of local interests.

LATVIA IN THE GORBACHEV PERIOD

The opening up of Latvian society (*glasnost'*) provided the first real acid test since 1959 of how easily an ethnic consciousness could find its way into the political arena of public life. Even before Gorbachev's rolling agenda of reforms got under way, anti-Russian demonstrations and riots took place in Riga, on 9 and 15 May 1985. Further demonstrations followed in late December 1986. It was, however, 1987 which was to mark a year of public displays of defiance against past Soviet practices and current policies on a scale hitherto unknown in the republic's post-war history. The dominant strains of these demonstrations were around a series of symbolically important key dates and events in Latvia's history, focusing, on the one hand, around successive, cumulative woundings to the nation (for example, commemorating the anniversaries of the 'Secret Protocol' (23 August) and Stalin's deportations (14 June)), and, on the other hand, celebrations of events associated with Latvian statehood (such as the proclamation of Latvia's independence on 18 November). Both the demonstrations on 14 June and 23 August, not least because of their scale, received considerable coverage in both the republic and national press but were largely dismissed as provoked by 'Western and emigré interference', while the historical actions of the Soviet state in 1939 and 1941 were defended.[41] The local press, however, did go so far as to concede that some current grievances were justifiable – notably, ignorance amongst elements of the republic's Russian community of the titular language and culture – and acknowledged that this had contributed to fuelling tensions. Furthermore, it was admitted that as a legacy of Stalinism, 'blank spots' in Latvia's 'tragic history' existed but which it was claimed were only too readily taken advantage of and exploited by Latvian nationalists.[42]

There is little doubt, given the nature of Gorbachev's programme of economic restructuring and later his plans for the democratisation of society, that Latvia (along with the other two Baltic republics) was considered as likely to be the most receptive to such systemic changes. Gorbachev's five-day 'meet the people' visit to Latvia and Estonia in February 1987, which included visits to experiments where cooperatives, private enterprises and new work practices were already successfully in place, must have underlined this for the General Secretary. Given these developments and Latvia's political and cultural history, to convince its people of the need for and benefits of *perestroika* and democratisation was hardly likely to be a difficult task. Indeed, on his return to Moscow, Gorbachev drew upon what he had witnessed in Latvia and Estonia – in what became labelled his 'revolution of expectations' speech – to warn of the dangers of expecting too much of a speedy social and material return from the reform programme.[43] There were already clear signs, despite the Latvian leadership's endorsement of *perestroika*, that the gap was growing both within the republic and with Moscow over the remit and tempo of reform.

It was Latvia's intelligentsia – Gorbachev's natural constituency of support in the republic but also the traditional bearers of Latvian nationalism – which seized upon the opportunities opened up by *glasnost'* and by the setting up of Estonia's Popular Front in May 1988, to recast and to revitalise the agenda for reform in the republic.[44] They were led by the Writers' Union, and its chairman, Janis Peters, whose call for the republic's autonomy had already received coverage in the national press.[45] At the Plenum of the Writers' Union on 1–2 June 1988, the local party and government came in for particular criticism over their handling of *perestroika*. In the same month, Latvia's Cultural Unions passed a resolution, later submitted to the CPSU June Conference, calling, among other things, for Latvian to be made the state language, the republic to be represented in certain international organisations, publication of the secret Molotov–Ribbentrop protocol, and steps to be taken to prevent ecological catastrophe caused by accelerated industrialisation.[46] The authorities were quick to respond, and on 1 July the Presidium of the Latvian SSR Supreme Soviet acknowledged the need to establish a pro-*perestroika* movement in the republic.[47] By 19 July, events had moved so quickly that the newspaper of the Young Communist League, *Padomju Jaunatne*, also joined in condemning both the government and Party of Latvia over their handling of *perestroika*.[48] The paper demanded that the authorities give priority to securing the economy's restructuring and democratisation, which included economic sovereignty and statehood, and introducing concrete measures to safeguard Latvia's environment. In response to the summer of demands, a movement in support of *perestroika*, the Latvian People's Front, was formed.

Moscow opted to accommodate such developments. The visit of Gorbachev's emissary, Politburo member Alexandr Yakovlev, to Latvia in August 1988 provided an opportunity for Gorbachev to be briefed on developments in the republic and for both the fledgeling People's Front and Latvia's leadership to get a response from Moscow of the parameters for manoeuvrability. In a candid speech to representatives of Latvia's intelligentsia, Yakovlev warned of confrontationism of the intelligentisia and mass media against the local party apparatus, and against ideas of redefining the notion of republic citizenship based on 'selectiveness, exclusion or isolationism'.[49] Although emphasising unity and patience, in paraphrasing Lenin, he seemed to leave the republic in little doubt of what a reconstituted relationship between Latvia and Moscow could mean in the foreseeable future: 'a state in the form of a union must have a common defence and foreign policy. All the rest ... ought to be the prerogative of the republics'.[50]

With the setting up of the People's Front, a wide range of previously fragmented environmental, human rights, religious and nationalist groupings were brought together and united with radicals from within the Latvian Communist Party. This included representatives of the Latvian National Independence Movement (set up in June 1988 and headed by the leader of the so-called 'nationalist group' of 1959, Eduards Berklāvs), the Environmental Protection Club (which had been set up in 1984 and has been active in campaigning against untreated sewage and industrial wastes in the seaside resort of Jurmala, the building of a hydroelectric power station on the Daugava river and the proposed Riga subway system), members of the human rights organisation Helsinki-86, and the religious group Rebirth and Renewal (formed in 1987 from amongst the Latvian Lutheran clergy).[51] At the Front's inaugural congress, held in Riga on 8–9 October 1988, in which calls for Latvia's economic sovereignty and statehood were adopted,[52] its overwhelmingly Latvian membership stood at 120,000, a third of whom were Party members. By the end of 1988, the People's Front had emerged to become a truly mass organisation, with a membership of around 250,000.[53]

In contrast with the other two Baltic republics, no major purge of the republic leadership followed, probably because of the speed with which Latvia's leadership responded positively to demands for the formation of a popular movement and by the way in which it had avoided challenging head-on the Popular Front (as in Lithuania) or political controversy (as with Estonia's First Party Secretary over the phosphorite affair). The promotion of the First Party Secretary, Boris Pugo (1984–88), to Chairman of the CPSU Central Committee Party Control Committee on 30 September and his replacement by Jan Vagris, previously Chairman of the Presidium of Latvia's Supreme Soviet, who in turn was replaced by Anatolii Gorbunovs, also made the republic's transition to accommodating the People's Front a far less traumatic affair. Once in place, the republic's leadership has tended to follow Estonia's lead in initiating far-reaching socio-economic reforms, although, given the multi-ethnic composition of the republic and the proportionately higher representation of Russians in Latvia's Supreme Soviet and Party, has necessarily dictated a more cautious approach. On 29 September 1988, the Latvian language was designated the state language of the republic, and the symbols of national independence, the flag and national anthem, could be flown and sung in public. In May 1989, the Latvian Communist Party also gave its backing to a law making the Latvian language (rather than Russian) the language of business and government, which was later endorsed by Latvia's Supreme Soviet. And in June 1989, a decree was issued reversing decades of claims that the mass deportations of 14 June 1941 were justified.

It is within the economic arena that the Latvian Party and government leadership have been prepared and found it easiest to go furthest, often adding the republic's own character to *perestroika*. Plans are well advanced to move towards total economic self-management, a mixed economy and a republic fiscal policy, as outlined in the law on economic independence, which reformists in Moscow see as an important experiment in giving a more realistic meaning to the Soviet Federation.[54] Much has also been made in the republic's press of having to redress the imbalances within the economy and in particular of the 'unjustified priority development of industrial production over agricultural production'.[55] In attempting to redress this imbalance, reminiscent of 1958–59, agriculture and rural development are not only to receive a higher investment priority, but, as a result of legislation passed by Latvia's Supreme Soviet on 6 May 1989, the countryside is to be reorganised along more private and cooperative lines, a policy in keeping with recreating a country of small farmers. The peasantry are to be allowed to lease land for an indefinite period of time and are to be provided with bank credit for housing and other construction needs. Re-emphasising the importance of rural development to Latvia's future may also further the recent trend towards counter-urbanisation in the republic, particularly if large-scale industry is to be given low priority. Investment in 1970s seaboard development in combination with proximity to European markets also bodes well for the republic to take advantage of Moscow's call to open up the Soviet Union to foreign trade and to establishing Joint Venture Schemes, something which the Inter-Latvia Organisation, formed in June 1987, is currently coordinating. Much interest within official republic circles has also been shown for making Latvia part of a Special Economic Zone to attract foreign capital, possibly along Chinese lines.[56]

It cannot be doubted that the Popular Front has emerged to play an important *de facto* policy-shaping role in ensuring that the Latvian republic remains at the cutting edge of Gorbachev's reforms. But the more ethnic politics become an issue, the greater the difficulty the Popular Front has had in appealing to an audience beyond the titular nationality. Although consistently arguing that its concerns are with championing the economic and social well-being of a territorial rather than just an ethnic constituency, it has been particularly the position taken by the Front in its handling of the issues of citizenship and sovereignty which are of concern to non-Latvians, particularly the Russian community. On the hotly contested issue of citizenship, the republic's native political leadership has also discussed the need to redefine a citizen's electoral rights, with length of residency in the republic as a possible qualifying criterion. If enacted, it has been estimated that a ten-year residency qualification in order to participate in elections for the republic's Supreme Soviet would disenfranchise 3 per cent of the republic's population, while the five-year proposal for the right to vote in local Soviet elections would deprive 1.5 per cent.[57] The overwhelming majority would be recently arrived Russian migrants.

It was precisely because of the Front's inability to appeal to a broader constituency that a second, officially backed movement in support of *perestroika* was set up towards the end of 1988.[58] Although calling itself the International Front (or 'Inter-Front'), its 300,000 estimated membership[59] is drawn largely from Latvia's 821,000-strong Russian community (which today makes up a third of the republic's population), with only about a tenth of members being Latvian.[60] Although supporting the broad aims of the People's Front, it has shown itself to be less than enthusiastic about full economic sovereignty, and keen to ensure that the interests of Latvia's Russian community, in particular, are safeguarded. No doubt designed to act as a counterweight to ensure more balanced representation of views within the republic in order to prevent the further alienation from *perestroika* of the Russian community, the republic's authorities have permitted the political establishment of probably the most socially divisive cleavage.

The establishment of Inter-Front has been particularly important in enabling its large Russian managerial and administrative membership to publicise their own vested interests with regard to such questions as the New Language Law, which will require up to 100,000 of their number to know Latvian.[61] These movements therefore represent the increasing polarisation at all levels within the republic, as ethnic issues become inescapably bound up with the whole programme of *perestroika*.

It is, however, the issue of Latvia's sovereignty outside the Soviet federation which has crept onto the agenda of the Popular Front and from which the Party political leadership, in attempting to strike a balance between Moscow and its constituents, has been pushed into a compromising role. The increasingly radical stance taken by members of the Popular Front, in which support for re-establishing a Latvian republic within a Soviet federation has given way to supporting full Latvian sovereignty, has no doubt been fuelled both by their triumphs as well as frustrations at the way affairs are being handled by the authorities in both Riga and Moscow. The Front's position is that the republic's electorate should choose 'through parliamentary means' the form and mechanism of political power.[62] On this issue at least, the People's Front has moved towards the position adopted by the more radical, 8,000-member-strong, Latvian National Independence Movement which is committed to the cause of Latvia's peaceful separation from the USSR.[63]

Despite its proportionately smaller ethnic constituency than that of its Baltic neighbours, the Latvian Popular Front won handsomely in the 18 March 1990 elections to the republic's Supreme Soviet. The following month, on 8th April, the local Communist Party followed Lithuania's example and split with the CPSU, but unlike its southern neighbour, its pro-Moscow faction constituted a majority. Cautious of embarking upon the style of confrontational politics adopted by Lithuania in its March decision to declare itself independent of the Soviet Union, and tempered by greater opposition within the republic towards national separatism, on May 4th the Latvian parliament, in proclaiming an independent republic, was careful to state that such a proclamation was part of an envisaged transitional stage towards full independent statehood.[64] The reformist wing of the Party thus remains in an uneasy position in seeking to strike a compromise with other political and ethnic factions over the issue of territorial sovereignty.

CONCLUSIONS

As Latvia moves towards full economic sovereignty, it has proved itself, like its Baltic neighbours, to be at the forefront of the *perestroika* experiment, while *glasnost'* has furnished the opportunity for Latvians to reassess the political status of their homeland within the Soviet Union. Striking at the very heart of this reappraisal is the issue of Latvia's loss of statehood and incorporation into the Soviet Union, which until recently, as in Estonia and Lithuania, was officially interpreted as having commanded widespread popular support. With Moscow now accepting the need to investigate the circumstances surrounding annexation,[65] most notably the 1939 Molotov–Ribbentrop Secret Protocol, the legitimacy of nearly five decades of Soviet rule in the republic has been publicly brought into question. And this necessarily means, particularly for the People's Front and for the large Latvian emigré community living in the West, resurrecting the issue of full political independence. Given, however, the near minority status of Latvians in their republic, this necessarily entails the Popular Front gaining the support of Latvia's other minorities (Poles, Jews, Ukrainians and Belorussians). Although supporting their cultural demands, there is considerable concern amongst these minority groups of the Popular Front's more radical stance on the issue of full sovereignty.[66] Past ethno-regional divisions within the republic have also reemerged as Latgalians, and in particular the majority Russian community centred on Latgalia's largest city, Daugavpils, voice their concern at what they see as the way in which Riga-based politicians of all complexions have been insensitive to local interests. In addition to calls for local autonomy for Latgalia, the region's Russian population has demanded that Latgalia should be exempt from recent language legislation which undermines the role of Russian in a region where it predominates as the spoken language. Both demography and polarisation within the Party means that, compared with its Baltic neighbours, national self-determination remains a more complex affair.[67]

NOTES

The author wishes to thank the British Academy for its financial support.

1. *Dzimtenes Balss* 11 May 1989.
2. For general histories and geographies of Latvia, see A. Bilmanis *A History of Latvia* (Washington DC, 1951); A. Drizula *Istoriya Latviiskoi SSR* (Riga 1971); J. Rutkis *Latvia: Country and People* (Stockholm Latvian National Foundation 1967).
3. Rutkis, *Latvia*, p. 292.
4. A. Plakans 'The Latvians' in E. C. Thaden (ed.) *Russification in the Baltic Provinces and Finland, 1855–1914* (Princeton, NJ, Princeton University Press 1981), pp. 207–86.
5. U. Germanis 'The idea of an independent Latvia and its development in 1917' in A. Sprudzs and A. Rusis *Res Baltica* (Leyden 1968), pp. 27–87.

6. A. Ezergailis 'The Latvian "autonomy" conference of 30 July 1917' *Journal of Baltic Studies* vol. 8, no. 2, pp. 162–71.
7. Germanis 'The idea of an independent Latvia'.
8. S. Page 'Social and national currents in Latvia, 1860–1917' *American Slavonic and East European Review* vol. 9 (1949), pp. 25–36.
9. G. E. Smith 'Soziale und geographische veranderungen in der bevolk-erungsstruktur von Estland, Lettland und Litauen 1918–40' *Acta Baltica* vol. 19/20 (1979/80), pp. 118–81.
10. See, for example, G. Von Rauch *The Baltic States: The Years of Independence, 1917–1940* (London, G. Hurst & Co. 1974).
11. J. Rogainis 'The emergence of an authoritarian regime in Latvia, 1932–34' *Lituanus* vol. 17, no. 3 (1971), pp. 61–85.
12. Ibid.
13. For accounts of socio-economic and political developments since 1944, see E. Allworth (ed.) *Nationality Group Survival in Multi-ethnic States: Shifting Support Patterns in the Soviet Baltic Region* (New York, Praeger 1977); J. Dreifelds 'Latvian national demands and group consciousness since 1959', and J. Penikis 'Latvian nationalism: preface to a dissenting view' in J. Simmonds (ed.) *Nationalism in the USSR and Eastern Europe in the Era of Brezhnev and Kosygin* (Detroit, University of Detroit Press 1977), pp. 136–56 and pp. 157–61; G. E. Smith, 'The impact of modernisation on the Latvian Soviet republic' *Co-existence* vol. 16 (1979), pp. 45–64; G. E. Smith, 'Die probleme des nationalismus in den drei baltischen sowjet republiken Estland, Lettland und Litauen' *Acta Baltica* vol. 21, pp. 143–77.
14. I. K. Lebedev *Bol'sheviki Latvii v bor'be za razvitie promyshlennosti* (Moscow 1949), p. 12.
15. Tsentral'noe statisticheskoe Upravlenie pri Sovete Ministrov Latviiskoi SSR, *Narodnoe Khozyaistvo Latviiskoi SSR v 1976 godu* (Riga, Liesma 1977).
16. Ibid.
17. T. Parming 'Population processes and the nationality issue in the Soviet Baltic' *Soviet Studies* vol. 32, no. 3 (1980), pp. 398–414.
18. J. Stalin *Marxism and the National and Colonial Question* (London 1936), p. 110.
19. K. Ya. Strazdin *et al. Istoriya Latviiskoi SSR* (Riga 1952–58), vol. 3, pp. 549–52.
20. L. Terent'eva *Kolkhoznoe krest'yanstvo Latvii* (Moscow, Izdatel'stvo 1960).
21. *Padomju Latvijas Komunists* no. 1 (Jan. 1960), p. 11.
22. *Sovetskaya Latviya* 26 Jan. 1958.
23. *Sovetskaya Latviya* 18 Nov. 1961.
24. *Padomju Latvijas Komunists* no. 9 (Sept. 1959), pp. 7–14.
25. D. Bahry *Outside Moscow: Power, Politics and Budgetary Policy in the Soviet Republics* (New York, Columbia University Press 1987), p. 56.
26. See, for example, A. Bohnet and N. Penkaitis 'A comparison of living standards and consumption patterns between the RSFSR and the Baltic republics' *Journal of Baltic Studies* vol. 19, no. 1 (1988), pp. 33–48.
27. A. Kovalev 'Kto i pochemu za chertoi bednosti' *Ekonomischeskaya gazeta* vol. 25, p. 11.

28. *Pravda* 27 Feb. 1981.
29. P. Zvidrinysh *et al. Naselenie Sovetskoi Latvii* (Riga, Zinatne 1986), p. 33, provides the following five-yearly figures on net migration and its percentage contribution to the republic's population growth: 1951–55: 16,900, 26%; 1956–60: 58,000, 47%; 1961–65: 78,000, 58%; 1966–70: 66,300, 63%; 1971–75: 63,900, 65%; 1976–80: 40,000, 71%; and 1981–84: 40,800, 62%.
30. For 1987 it has been estimated that net migration reached 18,800. See *Literaturnaya Gazeta* 19 July 1989, p. 10.
31. Latvijas PSR Centrala statisikas parvalde *Latvijas PSR tautas saimnieciba 1985 gada* (Riga, Avots 1986), p. 23.
32. Yu. V. Arutunyan *et al. Sotsial'no-Kul'turnyi oblik Sovetskikh natsii (po materialam etnosotsiologischeskogo issledovaniya* (Moscow, Nauka 1986).
33. Yu. V. Arutunyan *et al., ibid.*, p. 66; M. Kulichenko *et al. Natsional'nye otnosheniya v razvitom sotsialesticheskom obshchestve* (Moscow, Mysl' 1977), p. 97.
34. L Terent'eva 'Kz divautu gimenes jauniesi izskir savu tautibu' *Zinatne un Tekhnika* no. 8 (Aug. 1970), p. 12.
35. Arutunyan, op. cit., p. 32.
36. *Vestnik Statistiki* no. 10 (1980), p. 72.
37. Ibid., p. 72.
38. *Sovetskaya Latviya* 6 June 1979.
39. *Sovetskaya Latviya* 29 June 1982.
40. 'Letter by Seventeen Latvian Communists' in G. Saunders (ed.) *Samizdat* (New York 1974), pp. 427–40.
41. *Komsomolskaya Pravda* 26 Aug. 1987.
42. *Sovetskaya Latviya* 30 Aug. 1987.
43. *Tass* 25 Feb. 1987.
44. For accounts of developments over the summer of 1988 leading to the formation of Latvia's Popular Front, see D. Bungs 'The national awakening in Latvia' *Radio Free Europe*, RAD/175, 1988; J. Dreifelds 'Latvian national rebirth' *Problems of Communism* vol. 38, (1989) pp. 77–94; and O. Rozitis 'The rise of Latvian nationalism' *Swiss Review of World Affairs* (Feb. 1989), pp. 24–6.
45. *Pravda* 16 Sept. 1987; *Literaturnaya Gazeta* 18 Nov. 1987.
46. *Literatura Maksla* 10 June 1988.
47. *Cina* 3 July 1988.
48. *Padomju Jaunatne* 19 July 1988.
49. *Sovetskaya Latviya* 12 Aug. 1988.
50. Ibid.
51. For an account of Rebirth and Renewal, see M. Sapiets '"Rebirth and Renewal" in the Latvian Lutheran Church' *Religion in Communist Lands* vol. 16, no. 3 (1988), pp. 237–49.
52. The draft programme of the People's Front appeared in *Sovetskaya Moldodezh* 8 Sept. 1988.
53. *Literaturnaya gazeta* 19 July 1989, p. 10.
54. The details of this law are laid out in *Sovetskaya Latviya* 7 July 1989, p. 2.
55. A. Kalninsh, head of the Latvian Komsomol Report Group on Latvia's

Socio-economic development to the year 2000 *Sovetskaya Molodezh* 7 Sept. 1988.

56. See, for example, the interview with the Chairman of Latvia's State Planning Committee, in *Izvestiya* 4 Aug. 1989, p. 2.
57. *Izvestiya* 1 Aug. 1989, p. 3.
58. *Pravda* 14 Dec. 1988.
59. *Literaturnaya gazeta* 19 July 1989, p. 10.
60. Ibid.
61. Ibid.
62. *Padomju Latvija* 2 June 1989.
63. 'Baltic – Congress of the Latvian National Independence Movement, 18–19 February 1989' *RFE Latvian Service* Munich (Feb. 1989).
64. *Sovetskaya Latviya* 5 May 1990.
65. *Pravda* 22 May 1989.
66. Dreifelds, op. cit. (1989), p. 91.
67. M. Bumanis 'Die KP Lettlands und die nationale Frage im Zeichen der "Umgestaltung"' *Berichte des Bundesinstituts für ostwissenschaftliche und internationale Studien*, vol. 10 (1989).

CHAPTER FIVE

Lithuanians

V. Stanley Vardys

THE PEOPLE AND THEIR HISTORY

The Lithuanians are the larger of the two surviving branches of the Baltic family of nations which for almost two and a half thousand years inhabited most of the eastern littoral of the Baltic sea.[1] In 1989 over 95 per cent of the 3,068,296 Lithuanians in the Soviet Union lived in the Lithuanian SSR.[2] The republic covers an area smaller than once inhabited by the Lithuanian people, but its territory of 65,200 square metres is slightly larger than that of the other Baltic republics. Of Lithuania's 3,690,000 population (1989) 80 per cent are Lithuanian.[3] Of the total number of Lithuanians in the Soviet Union, an estimated 100,000 live beyond the republic's boundaries, primarily in the Kaliningrad region and Latvia, but also in Belorussia, Ukraine, Estonia, Uzbekistan, Azerbaijan and former places of deportation such as the Komi autonomous republic. Some 30,000 Lithuanians compactly inhabit the Suwalki–Sejny (Suvalkai-Seinai) district of Poland, adjacent to Lithuania's southern borders. An additional two-thirds of a million people of Lithuanian ancestry are found overseas, primarily in the United States and Canada, but also in Australia and Latin America.

The Lithuanians speak an ancient Baltic tongue considered important to the study of Indo-European linguistics. The language is not Slavic and uses the Latin alphabet. The first Lithuanian book, a Lutheran catechism, was published in 1549. However, most Lithuanians are Catholics by belief or by tradition.[4] There exist only small communities of Lutherans and Calvinists. Some Lithuanians belong to younger Protestant sects but virtually none to Russian Orthodoxy.

Lithuanian tribes were first united into a nation in 1231.[5] The founder of the state was Grand Duke Mindaugas, who some years afterwards accepted Latin Christianity and in 1253 was crowned king. However, in 1263 Mindaugas was assassinated and the country returned to paganism. Under a shrewd leadership by Mindaugas' successors, especially Gediminas, Algirdas and Vytautas, the Lithuanian state expanded between the Baltic and Black seas, conquering or diplomatically gaining control over Russian principalities, some of which sought to escape Mongol rule. In 1387, Grand Duke Jogaila accepted the crown of Poland and established a personal union between the two states. One result of this dramatic Lithuanian shift from Russian expansion to union with Poland was the permanent introduction of Latin Christianity between 1387 and 1413, the last nation in Europe to be Christianised.

The attempts of Grand Duke Vytautas, Jogaila's successor in Lithuania, to sever the ties of personal union by obtaining the kingly crown failed because of Polish resistance and his unexpected death. Afterwards, the union with Poland was gradually institutionalised, and in 1569 Lithuania was merged into a single state albeit with autonomy, which in time reduced ethnic Lithuania to a provincial status. Lithuanian nobles and gentry became considerably Polonised. To a large degree, however, this process was facilitated by the neglect of Lithuanian rulers in the thirteenth to sixteenth centuries to create a political and cultural infrastructure in the idiom of the Lithuanian language. This failure remains one of the unexplained mysteries in the development of the Lithuanian state and nation.

After the union of Lublin, Lithuania shared the fate of Poland. At the final partition of Poland in 1795 Lithuania was annexed by the Russian empire. In addition to Polonisation, the region now experienced intensive Russification. The tsars sought both to eliminate Polish influence and to convert the village population to Russian Orthodoxy. Their method, in the main, was to suppress the Catholic church – considered a carrier of Polish influence and an enemy of Russian Orthodoxy, especially after the insurrections of 1831 and 1863 – and to promote Russian schooling and Cyrillic print among the Lithuanians.[6] However, during the second half of the nineteenth century church leadership was in the hands of Lithuanian bishops, foremost among them Bishop Motiejus Valančius, who resisted tsarist persecution and promoted needed literacy by printing religious and secular volumes abroad in Latin print. From the German-ruled East Prussia publications were smuggled in as contraband for use in clandestine Lithuanian schools. From the 1880s, educated sons of farmers earlier freed from servitude either under Napoleon or Tsar Alexander II articulated the goals of Lithuanian national awakening, and in 1905 Lithuanians were the first nationality in the empire to demand autonomy. It was not granted, but in 1918 – formally on 16 February 1918 – Lithuania emerged as an independent democratic republic from the ruins of the tsarist empire and the control of the collapsed German Kaiserreich. The fledgeling state further survived Lenin's campaign to establish a Lithuanian-Belorussian Soviet republic and also Pilsudski's attempts to regain it for the resurgent Poland. Lenin had the Soviet republic proclaimed at the very end of 1918, but it died with the fortunes of the Red Army which was forced to leave the Vilnius region in the summer of 1919. At the end of 1920

Pilsudski was able to gain, through manipulated military action, the region of Vilnius but had to accept the independence of the remaining larger part of Lithuania.[7]

Independent Lithuania established a democratic system on the model of the Weimar republic which stressed the omnipotence of the legislature. The laws provided for elections based on proportional representation, thus encouraging a multi-party system and a need for party coalitions to create an effective executive. At the end of 1926 the democratic system was overthrown by a military *coup d'état* which brought to power Antanas Smetona, one of the founders of the independent Lithuanian state.[8] In two years the new president began to rule alone, without the legislature. Smetona's authoritarian regime, supported by the Nationalist Party he nursed to prominence, lasted until Soviet occupation in 1940, though already in 1938 foreign policy failures forced the establishment of coalition government and gradual democratisation. During the independence period Lithuania restructured the economy, enacted and quickly implemented a radical land reform, created an educational system, including institutions of higher education, initiated social services and promoted the development of literature and the arts. Its overwhelmingly agricultural economy was oriented towards producing exports needed by West European nations such as Germany and Great Britain. Relations with the Soviet Union were good but commercial ties rather weak.

In 1940 Lithuania fell victim to the Molotov–Ribbentrop Pact of 23 August, 1939, amended on 28 September, 1939.[9] The Soviets won Hitler's approval of the introduction of Soviet army garrisons and eventual occupation. Soviet army bases were established in October 1939 according to a mutual assistance pact between Lithuania and the Soviet Union, by which the Soviets turned over to Lithuania the city of Vilnius which had been ruled by Poland but claimed by Lithuania as its capital. On 14 June, 1940, Lithuania submitted to a Soviet ultimatum, and on 15–17 June was occupied by Soviet forces, allegedly to secure proper implementation of the 10 October 1939 pact by the Lithuanian government.

During the summer of 1940 the Soviets manipulated the political process to legitimise their occupation and incorporation into the Soviet Union which formally followed on 3 August, 1940. President Smetona fled the country. Prime Minister Merkys was deported. A people's government, dominated by the Communists, now released from prisons or surfacing from underground activity, followed the directions of the Kremlin's plenipotentiary Vladimir Dekonozov, who stage-managed elections to the People's Diet on 14 June (extended to 15 July) and then the meeting of the Diet on 21 July. Without any warning to the country, the Diet passed a resolution asking for Lithuania's admission to the Soviet Union as a union republic.

During the following four months the country was sovietised:

economy and real estate property were nationalised; although Soviet law was introduced by the end of the year, however, forcible
collectivisation was not begun. The first year of Soviet occupation cost
Lithuania over 50,000 casualties, among them over 34,000 deportees
captured and exiled to the Soviet Union a week before the start of
the German–Soviet war on 22 June, 1941. On 23 June, Lithuanians
revolted against the Soviets and established a Provisional Government
which declared restoration of Lithuanian independence.[10] However, the
expected relief did not come. The Nazis suppressed this government
and introduced a *Zivilverwaltung*. Lithuania became a part of Ostland.
Economic exploitation, political and cultural suppression, forcible use
of human resources and outright massacre again caused enormous
casualties – an estimated 210,000 people, among them 165,000 Jews
or approximately 75 per cent of the total Jewish population.[11] An
anti-Nazi resistance coalition was organised to obstruct the policies
of occupation authorities. All Lithuanian political groups, except the
Communists, belonged to this coalition, seeking independence both
from the Germans as well as from the Soviets. The Communists,
managed from Moscow, organised their own partisan groups. The
nationalist coalition foresaw Germany's defeat but also refused to
accept the permanence of the Western alliance with the Soviets. The
expected collapse of this alliance, resulting in Western opposition to
Soviet rule in Lithuania, was projected to open an opportunity for the
restoration of the country's independence.

LITHUANIA AS PART OF THE SOVIET UNION

Remembering the cruelty of the first year of Soviet rule, 1940–41, an
overwhelming majority of the Lithuanian population did not perceive
the return of the Red Army as liberation. Though some thousands
of refugees of the total of an estimated 20,000[12] who were evacuated
to the Soviet interior in 1941 returned with the victorious Soviet
divisions, some 70,000 Lithuanians,[13] among them an extremely large
percentage of professionals and other skilled population groups fled to
the West. A strong and widely supported partisan movement for eight
years (1944–52) fought the reimposition of the Soviet system, costing
Lithuania between 40,000 and 60,000 casualties.[14] Even larger population losses were incurred by the deportations to Soviet labour camps
or exile. Deportations were carried out in waves between 1946–52. An
estimated 350,000 men, women and children were uprooted in this
manner.[15] Many of them perished. During this period the Soviets
also brutalised the oldest and most influential Lithuanian institution,
the Catholic church.[16] One of its bishops, Vincentas Borisevičius, was
executed, three others were arrested and imprisoned, one-third of the

clergy were deported, churches were seized, and a state-sponsored atheist indoctrination was turned into a tool of discrimination and harassment of the believers. At the same time, the Soviets destroyed another basic institution of Lithuanian society: namely, private farming. By the end of 1952, virtually all farms were forcibly collectivised. As elsewhere, collectivisation ruined agriculture. It took Lithuania until the late 1950s to reach the levels of pre-war production,[17] though in another twenty-five years the republic claimed to have doubled agricultural production.

While collectivisation and disappearance of the homesteads and villages strongly affected the essentially peasant-oriented Lithuanian society, the country's radical transformation came through industrial-isation which was begun after Stalin's death. It had enormous effects on the economy, social structure, culture and politics. As a result of intensive industrial activity which outpaced the Soviet average, in the 1980s industry already accounted for about 60 per cent of the total social product. The share of industrial workers in the economy was quintupled, to approximately 40 per cent, from the pre-war 8 per cent.[18] This resulted in a huge increase in industrial production and, of course, in a quick growth of cities. The percentage of the urban population grew from 23 per cent at the time of Soviet annexation to 68 per cent in 1989.[19]

The Soviet model of industrialisation reoriented the country's interna-tional position. It tied Lithuania down to Russia's economy. For the most part, the Soviets developed labour-intensive industries for which Lithuania had no raw materials. These needed to be imported from Russia and the other republics. For energy, Lithuania relied partly on its own hydroelectric and the highly unpopular atomic power, but it had to import oil from Russia and coal from both Russia and Poland, and natural gas from the Ukraine. Lithuania has its own modest oil deposits, but these are not exploited, partly for commercial, partly for ecological and partly for political reasons. Lithuanian industries now produce fertiliser, petroleum and other chemical products, metal-cutting lathes, construction materials, TV sets, refrigerators, paper, furniture, bicycles, vacuum cleaners, hosiery and textiles. Food-processing industries – founded before the war but neglectd until the end of the 1950s – now process meat, dairy, fish, fruit and other produce.

Just as for raw materials, Lithuania became dependent on the Soviet hinterland for its markets. Fifty per cent of Lithuanian production, including agricultural products, is exported to the Russian republic, another 21 per cent goes to the Ukraine and Belorussia, and only 9 per cent to Estonia and Latvia.[20] Only 7 per cent of its industrial production is exported to foreign countries.[21] This includes TV sets made for West German and British distributors.

As in the other Baltic republics, the management of Lithuanian industries is centralised in Moscow. A Lithuanian party leader revealed that Moscow controls an unbelievable 89 per cent of the republic's industries.[22] Differently from Estonia and Latvia, quick industrial development did not markedly affect Lithuania's demography. The percentage of the ethnic Lithuanian population remained a constant 80 per cent. The percentage of Russians quadrupled but stayed under 10 per cent (9.3 per cent in 1989). Similarly, whereas in Estonia and Latvia the ruling Communist parties attracted larger and larger numbers of Russians from the increasing immigration, in Lithuania the Party became gradually more Lithuanian.

In October 1940 when the Lithuanian Communist Party was merged into the all-union Communist organisation, about one-half of its membership was non-Lithuanian. Lithuanians remained hostile and refused to join for yet another decade after the war. But when the suppression of the Hungarian Revolution and later the resolution of the Cuban crisis made it clear that the Soviet system was here to stay, attitudes toward the Party changed. Membership was now considered a ladder for personal career advancement which could also help to protect Lithuanian interests. The Party's perennial First Secretary, Antanas Snieċkus, an idealistic hardliner in his youth, after Stalin's death used his powers for lobbying to promote republic needs in Moscow, and protected his own people in their educational and cultural pursuits. By 1968, Lithuanian membership in the Party reached 66.3 per cent.[23] In early 1989, it was 70.7 per cent.[24] The Party's total membership, including candidate members, rose to 209,510. The Lithuanian[25] percentage is below its share of the ethnic Lithuanian population in the republic, but it is substantial. The Russian percentage in the Party is twice its share in population (17.1 per cent),[26] but the Russians are concentrated in Vilnius and Klaipeda organisations.

This dominant Lithuanian position in the Party as well as in the population has given *perestroika* reformists strength and confidence and made the national colouring of the reform movement in Lithuania inescapable. However, even though the Party gradually became more and more Lithuanian, it could not prevent or contain the republic's Russification. Moscow controlled the economy, and central organisations directed Lithuania's cultural and social life, Lithuanian history and traditions were falsified or altogether rejected as a factor of socialisation; Russian bilingualism was pushed to the point of Russian language teaching in kindergartens; Lithuanian was ousted from economic, governmental and Party communications. Since 1975, Ph.D. dissertations could no longer be written in Lithuanian. With Snieċkus' death in 1974, there ended, for example, the recording of Central Committee meetings in Lithuanian, despite the fact that an absolute majority of its membership was Lithuanian. For most of the post-war period, minutes had been taken in both Lithuanian and Russian. The intellectuals, artists and educators chafed under Russian cultural hegemony.

What have been the social consequences of such rapid and radical changes bureaucratically imposed on the Lithuanian society? Only some can be listed here. First, the needs of an expansionist economy have fuelled an impressive development of educational institutions, scientific cadres (though still below some Soviet averages) and research facilities, as well as of communications media. The number of college students and medical doctors per 10,000 population, for example, has reached levels higher than those in Western European countries. Second, the same expansionists, bureaucratically developed industrialisation and even 'modern' agricultural techniques have poisoned the soil, the lakes, the air; ecologically, Soviet-type industrialisation has been a disaster aggravated by the fear of the Ignalina atomic station, intended to be the largest in the Soviet Union, which is fuelled by the Chernobyl model of nuclear reactors.

Signs of social disorganisation also abound. Some of it is generally a consequence of industrialisation and the growth of cities. Much of it has specifically Soviet origins. The Lithuanian economic system suffers from the same political schizophrenia and corruption as other Soviet economies. The 'second' economy has become huge, *blat* very popular, bribes and use of alcohol widespread. It is estimated that Lithuania has 200,000 chronic alcoholics and takes one of the first places in Europe as regards users of alcohol.[27] The Lithuanian divorce rate of 35 per cent – it has increased twenty times between 1950 and 1984 – follows Estonia's, which is the highest in the Soviet Union.[28]

This brief review of the main characteristics of Soviet rule in Lithuania would be incomplete without mentioning that destruction of armed and unarmed opposition in the early 1950s did not signify popular acceptance of Russian rule or a single party system. Opposition reappeared in the form of dissent found primarily in deviations from norms which regulated cultural life.[29] Sporadically in the late 1950s and 1960s and quite regularly since 1968, dissent has spread to religion, and to cultural and also political fields. Dissent activities embraced the elder as well as the younger Soviet educated generations. The Lithuanian dissent movement in an organised form appeared as a movement for religious freedom, sponsored by Catholic activists pushed to the wall by the regime's attempts to seize complete control over the Catholic church and to choke off recruitment and education of new priests. In the 1960s, only twenty-five new seminarians were allowed annually to be admitted to prepare for the priesthood. In 1972, these activists started a movement for religious and human rights by beginning the publication of *The Chronicle of the Catholic Church of Lithuania* which periodically appeared underground for the next sixteen years. At the same time, groups of young Lithuanians raised the question of Lithuania's right to independence. Romas Kalanta, a nineteen-year-old high-school student, on 14 May, 1972, burned himself to death 'for the freedom Lithuania'.[30] *Samizdat* publications spread through the country, giving Lithuania the distinction of the Soviet republic with the highest per capita *samizdat* production.

These dissidents both from religious and nationalist movements, on 23 August, 1987, in a public demonstration denouncing the Molotov-Ribbentrop Pact of 1939, challenged the government to live up to the realisation of *glasnost'* and sparked the flame that within a year became a wildfire of national liberation.

THE GOALS AND POLITICS OF REFORM IN LITHUANIA

Appreciation of Lithuania's experiences as an independent nation and a Soviet republic is indispensable for understanding why Lithuanian *perestroika* quickly turned into a movement of national liberation. Although Soviet rule had left an imprint on political culture, under the impetus of Gorbachev's *glasnost'*, the acquired loyalties proved to be very superficial. The sublimated traditional patriotism, frustrations, and opposition to Communist rule now could be publicly articulated, and, unexpectedly for Moscow, overwhelmed Gorbachev's goals and expectations.

Glasnost' came to Lithuania some months later than to Latvia and Estonia, but the reform process ran a parallel course and was driven by the twin forces of nationalism and democracy.[31] Cautious and conservative Lithuanian Communist leaders at first attempted to disregard and then to contain manifestations of *glasnost'*. The regime of First Secretary Petras Griškevičius endured the demonstration of 23 August, 1987 with clenched teeth, but afterwards sought revenge against its organisers. Matters did not improve under Ringaudas Songaila, who inherited Griškevičius' mantle on 1 December, 1987, after the latter's death two weeks earlier. Songaila used army and police troops to prevent the celebration of the seventieth anniversary of Lithuanian independence on 16 February, 1988. He also attempted to turn the occasion into a propaganda campaign against the United States, specifically targeting President Ronald Reagan who had issued a proclamation reaffirming US non-recognition of Soviet annexation of the Baltic states. Songaila's reaction inflamed the Lithuanian intelligentsia, which had already been growing impatient with the Lithuanian Communist Party's negative attitude towards Gorbachev's *glasnost'* in intellectual and public affairs. Moscow was already speaking out. Why not Vilnius? According to Arvydas Juozaitis, one of the sponsors and leaders of the Lithuanian Perestroika Movement (*Sąjūdis*), 'the desecration of the commemoration of the February 16 anniversary was the last drop that overfilled the cup of patience'.[32] Small groups of intellectuals and writers began to consult among themselves. On 20 April, Juozaitis read a paper on 'Lithuania and political culture' at a public meeting of the Lithuanian Artists' Union in which he discussed the question of sovereignty. This was the first time of which we are aware that the legitimacy of Soviet rule was publicly and not so subtly questioned by an intellectual who did not belong to familiar dissident circles. Scholars, especially the economists in the Academy of Sciences, were much worried about the economy, and eager to join the Estonian initiative of planning for the republic's economic self-management. *Perestroika* seemed to be aiming in that direction. The republic's state planning committee also was interested in it. Concern that Songaila was insufficiently committed to *perestroika* and that the pace of reform in Lithuania was too slow led many Party intellectuals from the Academy and the universities to combine forces with writers and artists and also with non-party colleagues, like Juozaitis, to establish on 3 June, 1988, the Lithuanian Movement for Reconstruction (*Lietuvos Persitvarkymo Sąjūdis*). It was born, so to speak, in the womb of the Academy of Sciences, where committees had already been formed to prepare plans for new economic management and a new constitution for Lithuania. At a meeting held in one of the Academy's halls, the sponsors established an 'Initiative Group', composed of thirty-six members, half of them Communists and half not, which quickly succeeded in forging an alliance between the intellectuals on the one hand and the broad strata of population on the other – a feat never achieved in Russian society – and in short order overwhelmed Lithuania's political scene. The Party leadership did not like the coalition of Party and non-Party intellectuals. The Initiative Group did not trust the Party leadership. Songaila had been happier without the new movement, but he could not find a way of getting rid of it or of controlling it.

During the summer of 1988 *Sąjūdis*' Initiative Group and its allies – ecologists, rock musicians and sportsmen among them – organised a number of events attended by tens or even hundreds of thousands of participants to enhance its position in the republic. Among the numerous demonstrations, the ecological meeting in Kaunas attracted half a million people and the anniversary of the Molotov-Ribbentrop Pact on 23 August in Vilnius was commemorated by a crowd estimated between 200,000 and 250,000. Ability to engage mass support by exploiting the issues of the wretched state of the environment, the danger of nuclear contamination by the Ignalina atomic power plant, the plight of deportees of 1941 and 1946–52, Russification, suppression of national culture, of the Catholic church and the national symbols, propelled *Sąjūdis* to the dominant political position in the republic. Party leaders Songaila and Nikolay Mitkin, the latter a Moscow appointee from the central Party apparatus, accepted the establishment of *Sąjūdis* only grudgingly, denied it the use of the media, and unsuccessfully sought to contain its influence. Gorbachev at first saw in the stirring of the Lithuanian masses an ally for *perestroika* and sent Politburo member Alexandr Yakovlev to nudge the Lithuanian party leaders into cooperation with the new movement. Moscow apparently hoped to harness Lithuanian nationalism for the purposes of *perestroika*. Songaila and Mitkin, however, bungled the assignment: on 28 September Songaila sent troops against the demonstrators in Vilnius, triggering demands for his resignation. Two days before *Sąjūdis* met for its founding congress, Songaila was replaced by Algirdas Brazauskas, a fifty-six-year-old reform-minded moderate, a civil engineer by profession who until then had served as Party Secretary in charge of industrial development. Mitkin disappeared from the scene in another month, to be succeeded by Vladimir Beryozov, a Russian born in Lithuania and of course fluent in the language.

In June the new movement did not demand reforms more radical than suggested by Gorbachev or expected to be approved by the convening 19th All-Union Party Conference – though from the very beginning *Sąjūdis* engaged in the struggle to restore the rights of Lithuanian language, culture and history. Radicalisation of the movement's goals, however, was demanded by the nationally awakened masses and also pushed by the Lithuanian Freedom League (*Lietuvos Laisves Lyqa*), an organisation composed of former dissidents and their supporters. The league demanded the annulment of the Molotov–Ribbentrop Pact and an uncompromising re-establishment of independence. It also frontally opposed Communist rule. In time *Sąjūdis* appropriated these goals, but instead of boycotts and confrontation, the movement advocated and never deviated from tactics of peaceful change and parliamentary process.

The movement held its founding congress on 22–23 October, 1988, attended by 1,127 delegates who represented 1,000 groups. It was a solemn and emotional occasion, the first such gathering in almost fifty years. At the time of the meeting, the movement already supported Lithuania's economic self-management, freedom of religion and other human and civil rights, strong environmental policies, restoration of Lithuanian traditions and symbols, military service in Lithuania and even Lithuanian divisions. Independence was not yet on the agenda. The very idea sounded provocative. Generally, the movement sought vaguely defined sovereignty.

In concrete terms, *Sąjūdis* aimed at insuring the republic's sovereign autonomy by a declaration of supremacy of Lithuanian over Muscovite laws. This meant, in addition to the declaration of sovereignty, a revision of Article 70 of the republic's constitution. A consensus on the question seemed to have been reached between *Sąjūdis* and the Communist Party. There also was an agreement with the Estonians, who adopted a similar constitutional change on 17 November. But the Lithuanian leadership caved in under Moscow's pressure. The Party reneged, and on 18 November the republic's Supreme Soviet refused to change the constitution invalidating Moscow's laws unless approved by the Lithuanian legislature. The proposal was not rejected. It simply was not allowed to be put on the agenda.

To placate the disappointed Movement for *perestroika* and the masses of population who watched the Supreme Soviet proceedings on TV, the Supreme Soviet declared Lithuanian to be the official language of the republic and further revised the Constitution to restore the old Lithuanian flag, flown between 1918 and 1940, to official status as flag of the Lithuanian SSR and to make the old anthem the official anthem of the republic. This, however, was not enough to redeem disappointed expectations. The triggered political storm brought Party leader Brazauskas to television to ask for calm and patience on the road to 'sovereignty'. A letter from Cardinal Vincentas Sladkevičius, apparently solicited by the party leadership and published on the first page of Party daily *Tiesa*, also asked for the tenacity and wisdom needed to push further for 'unstoppable' changes. The *Sąjūdis* leadership was also shaken up: disagreements on tactics arose. They were resolved by closing the ranks for firm action exemplified by the election of the movement's president, a position until now considered unnecessary. Professor Vytautas Landsbergis, a professor of musicology at the Vilnius Conservatory whose outward softness and modesty disguised inner shrewdness and determination, became the choice for the newly created executive.

The Party, it must be said, had tried tactically to respond to popular pressures. In October, just before the founding meeting of *Sąjūdis*, a decree adopted by the Presidium of the Supreme Soviet provided rehabilitation and financial compensation of deportees. Some prominent church buildings, including the cathedral of Vilnius, were returned to church use. To soothe the hurt national feelings and to outflank *Sąjūdis*, the party even rehabilitated the long-maligned 'bourgeois' Lithuanian state: this was declared as a 'progressive' step in the nation's search for self-government. The anniversary of the 'bourgeois' declaration of independence in February 1918 – suppressed by the police in 1988 – was now made a legal holiday. For the first time, the celebration of religious holy days, such as All Souls Day and Christmas, was allowed, and in 1989 these were declared legal holidays. Bishop Julijonas Steponavičius, in 1961 removed and exiled from Vilnius diocese, was reinstated. Lithuania's system of education was ordered to be reorganised into a 'national' instead of 'Soviet' school system. Russian language teaching was eliminated from kindergarten and the first grades. The movement of support for Gorbachev's *perestroika* quickly turned into a struggle for democracy and independence.

These moves, especially the establishment of Lithuanian as the official language, frightened the more conservative strata of Russian and Polish minorities, already made uncomfortable by the emotional summer demonstrations and Lithuanian flag-waving. An organisation calling itself Vienybe-Yedinstvo-Jedność was started after the founding congress of *Sąjūdis* to represent the interests of Russian and Polish minorities. At the founding congress in May of 1989 the leadership of the new organisation was dominated by Russian extremists who later collaborated with some Russian *apparatchiks* and managers to create a Committee for the Defence of Soviet rule in Lithuania. These groups, with the support of the management of some factories, organised politically motivated but unsuccessful work stoppages to press especially for the abolition of the law granting official status to the Lithuanian language.[33]

In May 1989, the Poles (7 per cent of the population or 260,000 in the republic) organised their own association to collaborate with Yedinstvo. The organisation demanded territorial autonomy, the establishment of a university with Polish as the language of instruction, more Polish schools in addition to the ninety-two that already existed, and more positions in the government. Two districts, Vilnius and Šalčininkai, with a Polish majority, declared territorial autonomy.

The Lithuanians responded by, on the one hand, refusing to recognise this autonomy and by attempting to satisfy some Polish demands, on the other. In the summer of 1989, Communist Party leader Brazauskas went to Warsaw to sign an agreement with Jaruzelski providing for Polish-Lithuanian cooperation and exchanges. The government took up concrete Polish complaints, and both the government and *Sąjūdis* engaged in a dialogue with the Poles to encourage social peace. These efforts were supported by the leadership of *Solidarność* in Poland.[34]

Other Lithuanian minorities, the most prominent and articulate among them the small Jewish group (0.3 per cent of the population), supported the Movement for Restructuring and the new policies of the republic's government. So did the Catholic church, though it avoided the role of conspicuous participant.

The Lithuanians have accused Moscow of fomenting difficulties with the Russian and Polish minorities in the republic. Minority complaints, however, caused the republic's Supreme Soviet on 23 November, 1989, to adopt a 'law on national minorities' which guarantees 'freedom of their development', and a virtual cultural autonomy.[35] This includes the right to state support of cultural and educational activities, native language schools, press, organisations, relations with compatriots beyond republic boundaries, religious services in native languages, government employment and representation, and the preparation of needed teaching staffs and cultural workers at home or abroad. This last point is specifically important to the Polish minority.

Participation of these new actors on the political stage – Yedinstvo, the Polish association, smaller minorities, the Lithuanian Freedom League, the Catholic church, and finally some additional smaller groups – could not obscure, however, the fact that the main political competition involved the Communist Party and the Movement for Restructuring. Neither trusted the other. Time and again Party conservatives sought to bridle *Sąjūdis*, but they were not successful. Skirmishes between the two contenders for influence usually led to consensus sufficient for common action. Competition, though fierce, was eased by two political realities: first, the fact that most Party intellectuals were either in *Sąjūdis* or supported many of its proposals; and second, that for some mutually exclusive and some similar reasons the two forces agreed on a number of crucially important issues. One such issue was the republic's economic self-management. The plan was agreed among the governments of the three Baltic republics already on 21–22 September, 1988. It provided for republic ownership of land and natural resources, powers of taxation, control over fiscal policies and currency, foreign investment and trade. The model foresaw that relations with Moscow in defence and foreign relations, or other matters, would be regulated by contracts.

The two competitors, furthermore, generally shared a critical attitude towards Gorbachev's proposed amendments to the Soviet Constitution and the draft of the new electoral law. *Sąjūdis* took special initiative in opposing Gorbachev's proposals, including the collection of 1,800,000 signatures on a petition demanding that the consideration of proposed amendments be postponed. As a former president of the Lithuanian Writers' Union said, this petition – representing some 75 per cent of the republic's adult population – represented a popular referendum on Lithuania's independence from Moscow. The Communist-dominated Supreme Soviet kept a distance from this initiative, but in its session of 18 November adopted virtually the same demands, couching them in a language which showed deference to Moscow.

But the two competitors clearly were at odds over the question of political sovereignty and independence. The Party at first advocated 'real federation' within the Soviet Union, but since the idea was not popular with the voters, tried to obfuscate the differences between federation and independence by hiding them under a slogan, 'Lithuania without sovereignty is Lithuania without a future'. However, every time the Party leadership sought to conceal its moderation by the use of patriotic-sounding generalities, *Sąjūdis* spoke an increasingly radical language. In the winter election campaign for the new Congress of Deputies in Moscow, *Sąjūdis* already virtually ran on a platform of independence.

The Communist Party was thoroughly thrashed in the elections of 26 March. Of the seats for forty-two popularly elected deputies, *Sąjūdis* won thirty-six. In addition, the Movement for Restructuring won supporters among the sixteen deputies elected by various organisations.

The Party swallowed the humiliating defeat by deciding that it was more important for its survival as a political force to listen to the voice of the voters than to the orders from Moscow. This change led to the historical Supreme Soviet meeting of 18 May, 1989, at which the republic declared its sovereignty – the statement reads like a declaration of national independence – and the supremacy of Lithuanian law as it was intended on 18 November, 1918. A law on economic self-management, as earlier proposed, was also adopted.

From then on, the influence of *Sąjūdis* on the government and the Party did not falter. Stung by the electoral defeat which spelled its possible political ruin, the Party itself now decided to pull in a similarly radical direction as the Movement for *Perestroika*. The introduction of democratic accounting to the voters thus generated steam to run the republic's political engine in the direction of independence. This led to a string of statements and laws creating an expanding distance between Moscow and Vilnius. Among those at the fore was the challenge to the legitimacy of Soviet rule in Lithuania and the other two Baltic states.

Like the dissidents of the 1970s,[36] *Sąjūdis* held the view, shared by Communist Party historians, that Soviet rule in Lithuania and the other Baltic states resulted from a breach of international law perpetrated by Stalin and Hitler in their non-aggression pact of 23 August, 1939. It was maintained that the pact, especially its secret protocols, had facilitated the Soviet takeover. Moscow's recognition of this fact could open the doors for a restoration of independent statehood to Lithuania, Latvia and Estonia. Consequently, together with the other Baltic deputies, Lithuanian representatives in Moscow's newly elected Congress of Deputies sought and secured Gorbachev's blessing for the establishment of a parliamentary commission to investigate the history of the pact, collect the documents and appraise the Baltic status in the newly reviewed historical perspective. But the commission procrastinated. A report was prepared, but by 1 December, 1989, three of its important members, Georgii Arbatov, Falin and the group's chairman Alexandr Yakovlev still refused to sign it. Yakovlev gave an interview to *Pravda* in which he disapproved of secret protocols but defended the pact, insisting that it served national Soviet interests and had nothing to do with the current condition of the Baltic states.[37] As if in response to Yakovlev's conclusion, the Lithuanians in the summer of 1989 collected 1,500,000 signatures for a petition asking the Kremlin to publish the pact documents and nullify its results.[38] The Lithuanian Supreme Soviet went even further. Its special commission chaired by the President of the Lithuanian Academy of Sciences, Juras Požéla, declared that the decision of the People's Diet of 21 July, 1941, to establish Soviet power and to ask for admission to the Soviet Union, was null and void because the Diet had overstepped its powers: it was never authorised by the voters to consider such action.[39] Though on narrow grounds, the decision of the People's Diet was considered unconstitutional, thus making illegitimate the very establishment of Soviet rule in Lithuania.

On 23 August, 1989, the Lithuanians, together with the Estonians and Latvians, expressed their rejection of the pact and its consequences by forming a human chain all the way from Tallinn to Vilnius to commemorate the conspiracy which spelled the death of their independence.[40] More than a million people joined hands in this 'Baltic Way', as the demonstration was labelled.

Moscow was deeply hurt by this massive but peaceful demonstration which symbolised Baltic rejection of Soviet rule. The Politburo exploded. In a page-long statement published in *Pravda* it denounced diverse Baltic initiatives and almost directly threatened the survival of the Baltic nations.[41]

However, none of the Baltic peoples were intimidated. The parliament of the Lithuanian *Sąjūdis* reaffirmed its commitment to independence. Lithuania's Communist Party showed remorse but was not very contrite. Its conservative wing attacked *Sąjūdis* at the September session of the Lithuanian Supreme Soviet, which was postponed and advanced four times in a tug of war between *Sąjūdis* and Party *apparatchiks* expressing defiance and deference to Moscow, but the conservatives did not have enough strength to stop the process of law-making designed to advance political reform and to put more distance between Vilnius and Moscow. On 3 November, the fourteenth session of the Supreme Soviet changed Article 50 of the Lithuanian Constitution, which had put a wall of separation between church and state and institutionalised discrimination against believers. The new Article 50 guaranteed equal rights to believers and non-believers, approved 'peaceful' teaching of religion, and conferred on the Catholic church and other denominations the status of legal person and the right to manage freely their own internal affairs.[42] Although state educational institutions were declared to be secular, private schools were not forbidden, and the revised article provided for state–church cooperation for the purpose of 'fostering society's morality'. At the same time the Supreme Soviet adopted two important laws: the law on citizenship and that on referendum. The first law established separate Lithuanian citizenship, but stated that, 'since Lithuania has not yet regained full state sovereignty, Lithuanian citizens can use the passports of the Soviet Union'.[43] The law on referendum aimed at creating legal conditions for direct decision-making by the people on relations with Moscow.[44] On 7 December, by a vote of 237 to 1, the Supreme Soviet changed Article 6 of the Constitution which abolished the Communist Party's monopoly of leadership and legalised a multi-party system.[45] Thus, Lithuania joined Hungary and other Eastern European countries which had abolished Communist monopoly of power in response to popular pressures and in the interests of Communist self-preservation.

But this was not the last action of defiance of the Kremlin and even of General Secretary Gorbachev himself. For months the Communist Party had been furiously debating the question whether to break away from the All-Union Party organisation. A special Party conference was called for 19 December to decide the question. On 20 December it voted to break away from Moscow. It also adopted a new programme which condemned past Communist behaviour, disassociated itself from Stalinist crimes and declared support for independent statehood, multi-party democracy and socialist society which bears undeniable similarities to Western social democracy.[46] The Party's new statutes,[47] similarly, guarantee its members 'freedom of conscience' and even religious affiliation, and provide for responsibility of Party leaders to the lower Party organisations, which are given a limited veto power over some decisions. It also omits any mention of democratic centralism.

The Kremlin had both angrily insisted and pleaded with the Lithuanians not to go so far. Leaders of all three Baltic Communist parties were called to Moscow after the issuance of the Politburo's 26 August statement.[48] Later, when it became clear that the Lithuanian Party was determined to proceed with its emancipation from the all-union organisation, on 16 November the entire Lithuanian Politburo was 'hauled over the coals' by Moscow's Politburo and a letter of denunciation and warning followed them home.[49] It demanded that the scheduled Lithuanian Party conference should not take place. In the meantime, on 27 November Moscow's Supreme Soviet adopted a law granting economic self-management to Lithuania, Latvia and Estonia.[50] It was passed with Gorbachev's support against a strong opposition spearheaded by central planning and government leaders. Although the Balts did not get all they wanted, passage of the law showed Moscow's willingness to compromise and Gorbachev's interest in soothing Baltic feelings.

However, the adoption of this law did not diminish the Lithuanian appetite for more independence. When the Politburo's admonition did not help to quell the Lithuanian Party rebellion, Gorbachev sent to the Lithuanian Party membership a long personal letter eloquently and persuasively pleading with them not to seek restoration of separate Lithuanian statehood nor to leave the all-union party organisation. 'The restoration of an independent state outside borders of the USSR,' Gorbachev wrote, 'the establishment of a republic Communist party independent from the CPSU based on the prospects of the restoration of statehood will bring to naught the economic and cultural progress achieved under Soviet rule.'[51] In addition, Gorbachev sent to Lithuania Vadim Medvedev, party secretary in charge of ideology.[52] Medvedev was received politely, even warmly, but at most only received assurances that the Lithuanian Party would maintain close relations with Moscow. Lithuanian Party leader Algirdas Brazauskas insisted that the contemplated change was needed to save the Party's position as a political force in the republic. The separation, he said, was necessary in view of approaching Supreme Soviet and local Soviets' elections.[53] After returning from Lithuania, Medvedev told Western reporters that Moscow would not oppose the Lithuanian Party's decision.[54]

The 20th Lithuanian Party Congress met as scheduled on 19-22 December 1989, and declared itself free of subordination to the all-union party organisation, the first republic Party to do so in seventy years of Soviet history. Of the 855 delegates, however, 160 decided to remain loyal to the CPSU. On the 11th January, Gorbachev visited the republic in an unsuccessful attempt to dissuade the breakaway Lithuanian Communists from embarking upon the separatist path.[55] In the following month's Supreme Soviet elections, the first post war multiparty elections in the republic, *Sąjūdis* won an overwhelming victory of seats. The new pro-independence parliament, mindful of its mandate and the internal situation of the Soviet Union, proved to be impatient. By March 10th, *Sąjūdis* replaced Algirdas Brazauskas, with Vytautas Lansbergis, the leader of *Sąjūdis*[56]. Despite his radical stance, Brazauskas fell victim to the unpopularity of his Party and to the publically unacceptable position of having a Communist for President in the new democratically-elected parliament. On March 11, the parliament declared 'the restoration of the exercise of sovereign powers of the Lithuanian state' which had been annulled in 1940. Declaring into existence an independent Lithuania,[57] the parliament also suspended the Soviet constitution and changed the country's name to the 'Republic of Lithuania'.

The Kremlin, as Gorbachev expressed it, became 'alarmed'. On March 15, a special session of the Congress of People's Deputies condemned the Lithuanian declaration as 'contrary to Articles 74 and 75 of the (Soviet) constitution and (therefore) invalid'.[58] On March 21st, Gorbachev ordered the KGB border army to 'enhance' the security of borders around Lithuania and that Lithuanians turn in their fire arms. Despite a show of strength by the Red Army in Vilnius, which involved seizing some Communist Party buildings, arresting 'refuseniks' (deserters from the Red Army) and taking over the printing presses of the largest republic newspapers, the *Sąjūdis* government refused to reinstate the Soviet constitution. On April 17th, three days after Gorbachev's telegram to the Lithuanian parliament which stated that an economic embargo would begin if the declaration of independence was not renounced, much needed energy supplies and other materials central to the republic's economic well-being, were suspended. Lithuania's request of recognition of independent statehood by western countries brought about only silence or equivocation, with the United States, concerned about securing the May 1990 Superpower summit, urging negotiations between Moscow and Lithuania and of stressing the need to 'peacefully' resolve the issue.

The Lithuanian restoration of independence means the destruction of a single, Communist party-orientated, dominated and controlled society. It also represents the first nail in the coffin of the Soviet empire which Gorbachev and the Kremlin can be expected to protect by virtually any means.

NOTES

1. See also Marija Gimbutas *The Balts* (New York, Frederick A. Praeger 1963).
2. See Ann Sheehy 'Russian share of Soviet population down to 50.8 per cent Radio Liberty, *Report on the USSR*, vol. 1, no. 42 (20 Oct., 1989) pp. 2 ff.
3. See *Tiesa* 29 April, 1989, p. 1. Cf. Ann Sheehy, 'Preliminary results of the All-Union Census published,' Radio Liberty, *Report on the USSR*, vol. 1, no. 20 (19 May, 1989); see also Ann Sheehy 'Russian share of Soviet population' op. cit. for estimates of Lithuanians beyond republic boundaries, cf. 'Lietuviai' in *Lietuviškoji tarybine enciklopedija* (Vilnius, Mintis 1980), vol. 6, p. 526. This source estimates that half a million Lithuanians live outside the Soviet Union.
4. Current statistics are not available. Existing estimates vary. In 1938, 80% of Lithuania's population was Catholic; this would indicate that about 95% of Lithuanians belonged to the Catholic church. In 1989, a survey conducted in Lithuania found that 70% of Lithuania's population identified themselves as 'believers' (*Komjaunimo tiesa* 17 Oct., 1989, p. 3). Ninety-five per cent supported the teaching of religion to school-age children either at school or in church. The percentage of Catholics was not determined. In 1969, a 'progressive' East German Catholic journal *Begegnung* estimated that 75% of the republic's population was Catholic. This would raise the percentage for Lithuanians over 80%/*Begegnung* no. 1 (1969), p. 12. The 1989 survey discovered that a portion of the surveyed sample identified themselves as 'believers' on the basis of 'tradition'.
5. The best Lithuanian source is Zenonas Ivinskis, *Lietuvos istorija*, vol. 1 (Rome, Lietuvos Katalikų Mokslo Akademija 1978); cf. Constantine R. Jurgela, *History of the Lithuanian Nation* (New York, Lithuanian Cultural Institute 1948).
6. A brief analysis is found in V. Stanley Vardys *The Catholic Church, Dissent and Nationality in Soviet Lithuania* (Boulder – New York, East European Quarterly, distributed by Columbia University Press 1978), pp. 2–18.
7. See Alfred E. Senn *The Emergence of Modern Lithuania* (New York, Columbia University Press 1959); Pranas Čepénas *Naujuju laiku Lietuvos istorija*, vol. II (Chicago 1976), pp. 571–672.
8. See V. Stanley Vardys 'The rise of authoritarian rule in the Baltic states in V. Stanley Vardys and Romuald J. Misiunas (eds) *The Baltic States in Peace and War, 1917–1945* (University Park and London, Pennsylvania State University Press 1978), pp. 65–80.
9. The most recent study of the Hitler–Stalin alliance is Anthony Read and David Fisher, *The Deadly Embrace* (New York–London, W. W. Norton 1988); a fascinating collection of various documents is found in the two volumes edited by J. Felshtinskii *SSSR–Germaniia 1939* and *SSSR–Germaniia 1939–1941*, both published in Vilnius, Lithuania, by Mokslas Publishers in 1989.
10. The best account is found in Zenonas Ivinskis 'Lithuania during the war: resistance against the Soviet and Nazi occupants' in V. Stanley Vardys

(ed.) *Lithuania under the Soviets* (New York, Frederick A. Praeger 1965), pp. 61–84.

11. Estimates of Nazi victims during the wartime occupation, 1941–44, do not always agree. Cf. Romuald J. Misiunas and Rein Taagepera *The Baltic States: Years of Dependence, 1940–1980* (Berkeley, University of California Press 1983), p. 275; Kazys Pakštas, *Lietuvių enciklopedija* (Boston 1968), vol. 15, p. 448; Adolfas Damušis, *Lietuvos gyventoju aukos ir nuostoliai* (Chicago, Lithuanian Research and Studies Center 1988), p. 16. For calculation of Holocaust victims Damušis relies on research by Dov Levin published in volume 16 of Yad Vashem (Israel) studies, p. 334.

12. *Lietuviškoji tarybinė enciklopedija* (Vilnius: Mokslas, 1980), vol. 6, p. 610. Of refugees to the Soviet Union, an estimated 16,000 were Jews (Dov Lenin, cited by Damušis, as in note 11).

13. After the war, more than 62,000 Lithuanian refugees found themselves in Western Europe. Additional thousands were overrun by the Red Army in East Germany and Poland. See *Lietuvių enciklopedija* (Boston 1955), vol. 5, p. 148.

14. See V. Stanley Vardys 'The partisan movement in postwar Lithuania' in V. Stanley Vardys *Lithuania under the Soviets* (New York, F. A. Praeger, 1965); also a volume in Lithuanian by Kestutis K. Girnius *Partizanu kovos Lietuvoje* (Chicago, II Laisve Fondas 1987).

15. Estimates vary. Soviet Lithuania's Ministry of the Interior claims that 120,926 were deported in 1941–52 (*Tiesa*, 16 April, 1989, p. 1). First Party Secretary Antanas Sniečkus is said to have reported to Moscow that during Stalin's rule the number of 'repressed' was 200,000. Western scholars and private researchers in Lithuania speak of figures between 260,000 (Misiunas and Taagepera, *The Baltic States*) and 410,000 (Damušis). These do not include those who were individually arrested or exiled. Much research will be needed to establish a firm figure.

16. See V. Stanley Vardys *The Catholic Church, Dissent and Nationality in Soviet Lithuania*, pp. 62–79.

17. See *Tiesa* 6 July, 1989, p. 3; Tsentral'noe statisticheskoe upravlenie SSSR *Narodnoe khozyaistvo SSR 1922–1982* (Moscow, Finansy i statistika 1982), pp. 74–5.

18. Tsentral'noe statisticheskoe upravlenie pri Sovete Ministrov Litovskoi SSR, *Narodnoe khozyaistvo Lituvskoi SSSR v 1980 godu*, p. 150.

19. *Tiesa* 19 April, 1989, p. 2.

20. *Tiesa* 25 Oct., 1989, p. 2.

21. Lecture by Professor Aleksandras Vasiliauskas of Vilnius University, in Chicago, 25 Nov., 1989.

22. *Tiesa* 7 April, 1989, p. 2.

23. *Mažoji lietuviskoji tarybine enciklopedija* (Vilnius, Mintis 1968), vol. 2, p. 386.

24. Saulius Girnius 'Lithuanian Communists deny Gorbachev's request' Radio Liberty, *Report on the USSR*, vol. 1, no. 44 (3 Nov., 1989), p. 30; *Ekspresinformacija* (Vilnius) Dec. 1989, p. 2.

25. Ibid.

26. Ibid.

27. *Tiesa* 23 Nov., 1989, p. 3.

28. Ibid.
29. See V. Stanley Vardys *The Catholic Church*; Thomas Remeikis *Opposition to Soviet Rule in Lithuania 1945–1980* (Chicago, Institute of Lithuanian Studies Press 1980).
30. For the story see Vardys *The Catholic Church*, pp. 173–78.
31. For a detailed description and analysis of the process, see V. Stanley Vardys 'Lithuanian national politics' *Problems of Communism*, (July–Aug. 1989), pp. 53–76.
32. Interview with Juozaitis *I Laisve* (Chicago, Oct., 1989), p. 58.
33. *Tiesa* 13 Sept., 1989, p. 2.
34. Cf. *Gimtasis kraštas* (Vilnius) 16–22 Nov., 1989, p. 2.
35. Text in *Tiesa* 26 Nov., 1989, p. 3.
36. See V. Stanley Vardys. 'Human rights issues in Estonia, Latvia, and Lithuania' *Journal of Baltic Studies*, vol. XII, no. 3 (Fall 1980), pp. 275–98.
37. *Pravda* 19 Aug., 1989, p. 1.
38. *Tiesa* 27 Sept., 1989, p. 1.
39. *Tiesa* 22 Aug., 1989, p. 2; the Supreme Soviet confirmed the report on 23 Sept., 1989.
40. See *Tiesa* 23 Aug., 1989, p. 1 ff.
41. Text in *Pravda* 26 Aug., 1989, p. 1.
42. Text in *Tiesa* 10 Nov., 1989, p. 2.
43. Text in ibid., pp. 1–2.
44. Text in *Tiesa* 12 Nov., 1989, p. 2.
45. *New York Times* 8 Dec., 1989, p. 1.
46. Text of draft in *Tiesa* 20 Oct., 1989, p. 2 ff.
47. Text of draft in *Tiesa* 29 Oct., 1989, p. 1 ff.
48. *Tiesa* 6 Oct., 1989, p. 1.
49. See *Tiesa* 18 Nov., 1989, p. 1.
50. Text in *Tiesa*, 2 Dec., 1989, p. 3. Professor Kazimiera Prunskiené, one of the leaders of *Sąjūdis* and eventual Prime Minister, claims that the new law will allow Lithuania to control 93% of industries (only eleven enterprises will be left to Moscow's management). The republic will have its currency but it will not be convertible; lecture in Toronto, see *Téviškés sžiburiai* (Toronto), 5 Dec., 1989, p. 9.
51. *Tiesa* 2 Dec., 1989, pp. 1–2.
52. *Tiesa* 30 Nov., 1989, p. 1.
53. *Tiesa* 2 Dec., 1989, p. 2.
54. This was reported by Associated Press from Moscow; see *The Sunday Oklahoman* 10 Dec., 1989, p. 1.
55. *Tiesa* 12–16 January, 1990.
56. *Tiesa* 12 March, 1990, p. 2.
57. For the facsimile of the text, see *Literatura ir manas* 17 March, 1990, p. 1.
58. For the translation of this document, see Information Bureau of the Supreme Council of the Republic of Lithuania, *Documents Pertaining to Relations Between the Republic of Lithuania and the Union of Soviet Socialist Republics*, Vilnius, 1990, p. 11.

PART II

The South-Western Borderlands

The three union republics of the south-western borderlands comprise Belorussia, Moldavia and the Ukraine, which together have a population of 66.2 million. The Ukrainians and Belorussians have most in common. They share with the Russians their Eastern Slav origins from which their languages are also derived. Their religion is grounded in Byzantine Christianity, while historical roots in the medieval state of Kiev-Rus are another important link with a common past.

Declared union republics as part of the 1922 Federal Treaty, both the Ukrainians and Belorussians, relative to the other non-Russian nationalities, have in a number of ways benefited from their common Eastern Slav origins. In contrast to the other non-Russian nationalities, they have enjoyed greater upward mobility beyond the boundaries of their namesake republics, and have advanced in significant numbers into the central elite and have served in important positions. Close cultural affinity, together with a large Russian presence in both republics, have also facilitated linguistic Russification, with the Ukrainians and Belorussians recording by far the highest proportion of Russified, non-native speakers amongst the union republic nationalities.

As Europe's largest stateless nation, and with a strong national consciousness, the Ukraine is of special significance to the nationalities question. Economically and in terms of resources, it is of far more importance to the Soviet Union than any other non-Russian republic, but, in part as a result of a conservative party leadership, has shown itself one of the slowest to embrace economic reform. The Catholic church in the Western Ukraine, a region annexed only after the Second World War, has been especially active in mobilising national feelings.

The third peoples of the region, the Moldavians, are ethno–linguistically and culturally indistinguishable from neighbouring Romanians. In 1924, the Soviet state created a Moldavian autonomous republic within the Ukrainian Union republic, ostensibly to counter Romania's annexation of Bessarabia six years earlier, an area lying west of the Dneister, whose sovereignty has long since been disputed between the two countries. Like the Baltic republics, Bessarabia was handed to Stalin by the secret 1939 protocol with Hitler, and annexed a year later. Elevated to union republic status, Moldavia now consists of much of Bessarabia along with the western portions of the original autonomous republic. It is the most rural and least developed of the European union republics.

CHAPTER SIX

Ukrainians

Peter J. S. Duncan

THE EMERGENCE OF THE UKRAINIANS

The Ukrainians have a special position in the Soviet Union. They are the second largest nationality, after the Russians, and the Ukrainian Soviet Socialist Republic is the second most populous republic, with a larger population (50.8 million) than any of the East European states. Furthermore, the Russians have closer historical links with the Ukrainians than with any other Soviet nationality. The Eastern Slavs who formed the state of Kiev-Rus in the ninth century are seen by Russian historians as the ancestors of the Russians, Ukrainians and Belorussians. In the tenth century the Kievan princes accepted Christianity from Byzantium. After the Tatar invasion of the thirteenth century, the southern and western parts, including what became the Ukraine, gradually fell under the control of Lithuania and then Poland.

The name 'Ukraina' means borderland, and the Ukraine for most of its history has lacked independent statehood. Its institutions have usually been imposed from outside, mainly from Poland or Russia, as the border between these two countries has shifted. In 1596, under the Union of Brest, the Polish government forced the Orthodox Christians of the Ukraine and Belorussia into union with Rome. This was done by establishing the Uniate, or Ukrainian Catholic, church, which maintained the Eastern rite but recognised papal supremacy. Ukrainian discontent led to the national revolution of 1648 against Poland and the Polish landlords, and then to the Treaty of Pereyaslavl of 1654. Under this the Ukrainian Cossack hetman Bohdan Khmel'nyts'kyi recognised the suzerainty of the Muscovite tsar in return for protection against Poland. In 1663, however, Muscovy divided the Ukraine with Poland, regaining control of the whole country (except Galicia in the west) by the partitions of Poland in the eighteenth century. Peter the Great began the process of abolishing the distinctive Ukrainian institutions, and of integrating the Ukraine into the Russian empire.

While the Russians looked on the Ukraine and Belorussia ('Little

Russia' and 'White Russia') as organically linked to Russia, differing from it only by the dialect of their inhabitants, the Ukrainians felt themselves to be different. The Ukrainian national revival came, as elsewhere in Eastern Europe, in the nineteenth century. The poet Taras Shevchenko (1814–61) created a Ukrainian literary language. Small, underground, nationalist groups called for Ukrainian autonomy, often in the context of a Slav federation. Indeed the influential publicist Mykola Kostomarov (1817–85) contrasted the individualism and federalism of the Ukrainians with the collectivism and centralism of the Russians. The tsarist empire reacted to the Ukrainian movement by banning the use of the Ukrainian language in the education system and in print, from 1876 up to the 1905 revolution. Only in Galicia was there a Ukrainian press over this period, allowed by the Habsburgs. After 1905, Nicholas II legalised the Ukrainian press, but the victory of reaction led to a return to Russification. This in turn encouraged the growth of the Ukrainian nationalist movement, up to 1914.

THE UKRAINIANS IN THE SOVIET UNION

Following the Bolshevik Revolution, a German-backed Ukrainian government, the Rada, declared the Ukraine independent. Between 1918 and 1921 Russians, Poles and Ukrainians, Red and White, fought over the Ukraine in a devastating civil war. The new Polish state gained the Western Ukraine, including the city of Lvov. The rest of the country became the Ukrainian SSR. Although formally independent, it was ruled by members of the Russian Communist Party (Bolsheviks), which was centrally controlled from Moscow. In 1922 the Communists brought form into line with substance and made the Ukraine, together with the Russian republic, Belorussia and Transcaucasia, one of the founder republics of the USSR.[1]

The wealth of the Ukraine traditionally lay in its agriculture, and later also in its raw materials. Its fertile black-earth lands had made it the bread-basket of tsarist Russia. Bolshevik support in the Ukraine, as in the other Russian borderlands, was weak in the peasantry and concentrated among the industrial workers, who were mainly of Russian nationality. From 1923, Moscow adopted a policy of nativisation (*korenizatsiya*), promoting leaders from the indigenous nationality, and developing the local language. This policy was nowhere taken further than in the Ukraine. Ukrainian Communists worked together with nationalist leaders, brought back from exile to promote 'Ukrainianisation'. The Ukrainian language became the language of politics, economics and most of the press. Rapid industrialisation created an ethnic Ukrainian working class; by 1930 over half the industrial workers in the Ukraine were Ukrainians. A further reflection of the growth of nationalist feeling was the formation of the Ukrainian Autocephalous Orthodox church in 1921, from within the Russian Orthodox church. The authorities forced this back into the Russian church in 1930 because of its Ukrainian nationalism.

Meanwhile, Stalin grew suspicious about the increasing tendency of the Ukrainian Communists, especially the education commissar Mykola Skrypnik, to act independently of Moscow's wishes. He forced the policy of collectivisation on the Ukraine and imposed excessively high demands for grain delivery from the republic to the centre. The result of these policies was the 1932–33 grain famine in which perhaps more than 7 million people died. Millions died in other parts of the Soviet Union as well, but in the Ukraine the famine appears to have been deliberately engineered to destroy Ukrainian nationalism and its peasant base.[2] The results of the 1937 census were suppressed as they revealed a catastrophic decline in the Ukrainian population. Another census was organised in 1939, but its results are not considered reliable.

The unsuccessful efforts of Skrypnik and the Ukrainian Communists to counter the famine led to Skrypnik's suicide in 1933. Stalin reimposed Moscow's control, purged the Ukrainian leadership on charges of 'bourgeois nationalism' and ended Ukrainianisation. The role of the Ukrainian language was reduced, and in 1938 Russian became a compulsory subject in schools in the Ukraine, as throughout the USSR. The history books were rewritten to reflect the Stalinist conception of history: the non-Russians had not been forcibly incorporated into the Russian empire but had voluntarily joined it. The nationally minded Ukrainian intellectual élite was destroyed in the purges by the end of the 1930s.[3] In 1938 alone, the whole of the Politburo and Secretariat of the Central Committee of the Communist Party of the Ukraine (CPU), with one exception, and the whole of the Ukrainian government were executed.[4]

In view of Stalin's treatment of the Ukraine, it is not surprising that there was some collaboration between Ukrainians and the Nazis, who occupied the republic during the Second World War. The great majority of Ukrainians fought on the Soviet side. In recognition of the destruction suffered during the war, the Ukraine and Belorussia were allowed to become founder members of the United Nations. Neither has ever put forward a view which was not identical with that of the Soviet Union. The moving west of the Soviet border after the war reunified the more nationalist Western Ukraine with the rest of the country. Attempting to weaken Ukrainian nationalism, Moscow ordered the Russian Orthodox church to absorb the Uniate church, which was strong in this area and itself linked with nationalism. This was accomplished with the aid of the secret police. Nevertheless, the Organization of Ukrainian Nationalists and the Ukrainian Insurgent Army waged an armed struggle for independence into the early 1950s.

The death of Stalin in 1953 and Khrushchev's denunciation of him in 1956 made possible the revival of Ukrainian political and cultural life. The top positions in the republic were again given to Ukrainians, and writers began to develop a new wave of literature in the Ukrainian language. At the same time, a new development appeared under Khrushchev which lasted up to the end of Brezhnev's rule: Ukrainians, and Russians from the Ukraine, came to occupy prominent positions in the USSR outside the Ukraine. This reflected two political factors. First, the CPU is the largest constituent unit within the CPSU (since there is no Party organisation for the RSFSR as a whole). Second, both Khrushchev and Brezhnev (although Russians) were closely associated with the Ukraine, and promoted people who had worked with them there to senior positions in Moscow. These included Nikolai Podgornyi, the head of the Soviet state from 1965 to 1977, and Nikolai Tikhonov, Soviet Prime Minister from 1980 to 1985.[5] If the Russians were the 'elder brother' among the Soviet nationalities, the Ukrainians were the 'junior elder brother'.

While in the 1980s many of the most prominent Ukrainians were replaced by Russians, it remained the case in both the Party apparatus and the Council of Ministers that the Ukrainians were the only non-Russian nationality to have significant representation. This situation gives ambitious Ukrainians the opportunity to aim to achieve high rank outside their republic in a way not easily open to non-Slavs. (In the army, Ukrainians are well represented among the permanent NCOs.) A precondition for this is their willingness to work entirely in the Russian language. Within the Ukraine, the CPU is one of the few republican parties where the Second Secretary (as well as the First Secretary) has normally come from within the republic, instead of being a representative of the centre.

The relationship between the Ukrainians and Russians and the development of Ukrainian national feeling has been fashioned by demographic factors. According to the 1979 census, of the 42.3 million Ukrainians in the Soviet Union, 36.5 million lived in the Ukrainian SSR, 3.7 million in the RSFSR, 0.9 million in Kazakhstan, 0.6 million in Moldavia, and the rest dispersed throughout the other Soviet republics. The population of the Ukraine was 49.6 million, of which 73.6 per cent were Ukrainians (down from 76.8 per cent in 1959), 21.1 per cent Russians, 1.3 per cent Jews and 4.0 per cent other nationalities. As a nation, the Ukrainians are now barely reproducing themselves.

The immigration of Russians (especially manual workers) and the emigration of Ukrainians (including skilled workers and specialists) to other parts of the Soviet Union has added to Ukrainian worries. The proportion of Ukrainians in the USSR speaking Ukrainian as the mother tongue fell from 87.7 per cent in 1959 to 82.8 per cent in 1979. Less than half the Ukrainians outside the republic, lacking native-language schools and largely deprived of a Ukrainian-language press, retained the language as a mother tongue. In the Ukraine, the proportion of

Ukrainians reporting Ukrainian as their mother tongue fell from 93.5 per cent in 1959 to 89.1 per cent in 1979. Russians and Russified Ukrainians are most strongly concentrated in the Crimea and in the cities of the Voroshilovgrad, Donetsk, Kharkov, Dnepropetrovsk and Zaporozhe provinces in the east of the republic.

The key feature of demographic change is urbanisation. In the mid-1960s the size of the urban population overtook the rural population, and reached 61 per cent of the whole population in 1979. This process was mainly a movement of ethnic Ukrainians from the countryside to the cities, where they formed 62.2 per cent of the urban population in 1970 (when the Russians formed 30.0 per cent). This has included a move from the rural provinces of the more nationalist Western Ukraine to the most industrially developed cities in the Eastern Ukraine. At the same time, with Russians in the Ukraine not under pressure to learn Ukrainian, but with nearly half of Ukrainians claiming bilingualism in 1979, the normal language of work in Ukrainian cities is Russian. In the capital Kiev, where the Russian population was just under a quarter of the total in 1979, the Russian language is used throughout the university except in philology. In the republic, Ukrainians are less likely than Russians to go to university or be found in white-collar jobs.[6]

The fall of Khrushchev was followed by the arrest and sentencing in 1965–66 of at least thirty of the most active defenders of the Ukrainian language. The new Moscow leadership seemed bent on increasing the role of Russian. The First Secretary of the CPU Central Committee, Petro Shelest, was under pressure from both Moscow and the political and cultural forces in the Ukraine which were resisting Russification. He apparently gave protection to some of the nationally minded intellectuals. He circulated Ivan Dzyuba's *samizdat* book, *Internationalism or Russification?* (1965), an attack on Russification couched in Leninist terms, to CPU provincial secretaries.[7] In 1966 he called for more works to be written in Ukrainian, and allowed leading writers such as Oles' Honchar and Vitalii Korotych to call for the publication of suppressed works. Shelest was unable to maintain his position, however. In the late 1960s, a human rights movement developed in the Ukraine, protesting against the repression of intellectuals. The *samizdat Ukrainian Herald (Ukrains'kyi visnyk)* appeared in 1970, chronicling dissent and the authorities' response. In 1972 Moscow acted on its fears of resurgent Ukrainian nationalism and replaced Shelest by the Ukrainian Prime Minister, Volodymyr Shcherbyts'kyi.

Shelest was accused of idealising the Ukrainian past and overestimating the Ukrainian contribution to the USSR in his 1970 book, *Ukraino, nasha radyans'ka* (O Ukraine, Our Soviet Land). Before Shelest's fall, a wave of arrests, labour-camp sentences and incarcerations in psychiatric hospitals was unleashed in the Ukraine, and this continued under Shcherbyts'kyi. There were at least a hundred victims, including the mathematician Leonid Plyushch, the writers Valentyn Moroz,

Vyacheslav Chornovil, the editor of the *Ukrainian Herald* and Dzyuba. The latter subsequently recanted and was released. Shcherbyts'kyi also purged the Party leadership of those considered to be supporters of Shelest's line. At Moscow's behest, the use of Russian was stepped up in the press, the schools and finally even the nursery schools. Numerous historical studies in the Ukrainian language which were in the pipeline were denied publication. Symbolically, whereas Shelest had addressed the CPU Congress in Ukrainian, Shcherbyts'kyi used the Russian language. The propaganda organs repeated themes about the historical friendship of the Russian, Ukrainian and Belorussian peoples – described as 'peoples of one blood' *(edinokrovnye)*. Ukrainians feared that Moscow seemed to be building up a Russian-speaking East Slav bloc of these nations, to resist centrifugal forces in the Soviet Union. In 1976 Mykola Rudenko and Oleksii Tykhyi established the Ukrainian Helsinki Group, to highlight violations of the Helsinki Final Act in the Ukraine. With the support of the Moscow Helsinki Group, they succeeded in drawing world-wide attention to Russification and repression in the Ukraine. Both the leaders were arrested and sent to labour camps the following year.[8]

It was probably in order to undercut the potential appeal of the Helsinki Group that Shcherbyts'kyi tried to come to terms with the Ukrainian intelligentsia in the late 1970s. Scholars were allowed to study more closely the pre-revolutionary history of the Ukraine, including the work of the Ukrainian populist Mykhailo Drahomanov.[9] But for those who stepped beyond the permitted lines, the political climate was not merciful. In the clampdown on dissent which began throughout the Soviet Union in 1979, and continued for the next five years, Ukrainians comprised a high proportion of the new labour-camp prisoners. In 1984 Tykhyi and two other Ukrainian activists died in the camps. In September 1985, soon after Gorbachev had come to power, Vasyl' Stus died after torture and illness in a special regime camp.

THE IMPACT OF GLASNOST' ON THE UKRAINE[10]

The single most important event in the life of the Ukrainians in the 1980s was the tragic explosion of a nuclear reactor at Chernobyl, near Kiev, in April 1986. Although only about thirty people died in the immediate aftermath of the explosion, the reluctance of the authorities to admit first to the event and then to the dangers from the leak of radiation caused unnecessary delay and then panic evacuation from the affected area. It would be impossible to estimate the total damage caused, in terms of the poisoning of the water supply, the effect on the soil in this important agricultural zone, and the future deaths from cancer. In the conditions of *glasnost'* emerging in Moscow, the disaster was widely reported by the Soviet media. This gave a fillip to feelings of concern about the environment and to a greening of politics throughout the Soviet Union. Nationally minded Russians and non-Russians, and especially Ukrainians, saw the model of industrial development and the political system which had allowed the disaster as threats to the ecological survival of their peoples.

The most striking feature of Ukrainian political life in this period was Shcherbyts'kyi's ability to remain in his post for so long, until his dismissal in September 1989. He and the Moldavian First Secretary were the only leaders of republican party organisations to survive for more than four years under Gorbachev. Moreover, he was the only full member of Brezhnev's Politburo (other than Gorbachev himself) to remain a member. His survival was not due to his zealous promotion of *perestroika*; there was virtually no change from above in Kiev. Although naturally Shcherbyts'kyi paid lip-service to Gorbachev's line, he made few concessions to the rising tide of demands emanating from the Ukrainian intelligentsia. These demands focused on the publication of banned works; an investigation into the 1932–33 famine; the defence of the Ukrainian language; opposition to the expansion of nuclear power; and permission for the formation of a Popular Front, along the lines of those existing in the Baltic republics.

The demands were articulated mainly by members of the Union of Writers of the Ukraine (UWU). As in other republics, the Ukrainian writers have assumed a responsibility to defend national interests which extends beyond purely cultural concerns. *Literaturna Ukraina*, the Ukrainian-language weekly newspaper of the UWU with a circulation of 60,000, has been the main vehicle of these demands. The emergence of a large number of unofficial 'informal groups', dealing with cultural, human rights and political problems, did not provoke a mass crackdown, but neither did it lead to an improvement in the situation of the banned Ukrainian religions. Indeed, by the time of the October 1988 Plenum of the CPU Central Committee, Shcherbyts'kyi seemed if anything less concerned about the state of Ukrainian culture than he had ten years earlier. He blamed extremists, nationalists and Uniates for taking advantage of 'socialist pluralism' and leading young people astray.

It is likely that Gorbachev planned to remove Shcherbyts'kyi, as he removed Brezhnev's other cronies from leading positions, but found him to be in a particularly strong position in the Party. There seems to have been no attempt to make him the scapegoat for Chernobyl. As well as his support in the Ukrainian bureaucracy, Shcherbyts'kyi may have had backing from the more conservative wing of the Moscow Politburo, led by Viktor Chebrikov and Egor Ligachev. Chebrikov, head of the KGB until October 1988 and then a Central Committee Secretary, had worked under Shcherbyts'kyi in Dnepropetrovsk. Another link is that Mykola Holushko, who became head of the Ukrainian KGB in 1987, had previously worked under Ligachev in Tomsk. In late 1987 and early 1988 Moscow newspapers ran two stories exposing corruption scandals within the Ukrainian KGB and the Ukrainian Party organisation itself. These were presumably included in order to discredit both Shcherbyts'kyi and the KGB.

By the middle of 1988, however, Gorbachev may well have decided to keep Shcherbyts'kyi in his post for the time being. The evidence of the aspirations of the Baltic peoples for autonomy and the outburst of conflict between Armenians and Azeris highlighted the dangers involved in loosening the reins in the non-Russian republics. A political explosion in the Ukraine could well mean the end of *perestroika*. Shcherbyts'kyi would not reform the Ukraine, but he had sixteen years experience of working with the KGB to maintain political stability.

Shcherbyts'kyi did not lack his critics within the Ukrainian elite, however. At the January 1988 CPU Central Committee plenum, for example, the First Secretaries of four provincial Party committees and the Kiev city Party committees specifically referred to the republican First Secretary's errors. He had failed to change his style of leadership or to allow the Ukrainian Council of Ministers more power to deal with the economy. At the October 1988 plenum, Shcherbyts'kyi put the blame for economic problems on the Ukrainian Prime Minister, Vitalii Masol. The problems do seem to be serious. In industry, the Ukraine's traditional coal and steel industries appear to be in general decline, which has not been sufficiently compensated for by the development of the new electronics industry. The situation is worse in agriculture: the production of some staple products has been falling. Shortages of some foods, especially meat and dairy products, has reduced food consumption to below the recommended levels. Special commissions have been established to improve supplies, with Masol himself in charge of that for the republic as a whole. Those within the Ukraine who would like to replace Shcherbyts'kyi have the open sympathy of Vitalii Korotych, now based in Moscow as editor of one of the flagships of *glasnost'*, *Ogonek*. In an interview with *La Vanguardia* (Barcelona, 28 August 1988), he called the Ukrainian situation 'anti-democratic' but warned of the problems Gorbachev would have if he moved against the Ukrainian leadership too soon.

In spite of the lack of change at the top in Kiev, the Ukrainian intelligentsia took the rise of *glasnost'* in Moscow as a signal to make demands on the local leadership. Pressure mounted for the truth to be told about the history of the Ukraine, in the pre-revolutionary and especially the Soviet period. In 1987 and 1988 *Ogonyok* published suggestions that the 1932–33 Ukrainian famine had been created artificially. After this *Literaturna Ukraina* (18 February 1988) published a long speech by the writer Oleksa Musienko. He portrayed the history of the Ukraine under Stalin and Brezhnev as one of crimes committed by Moscow against Ukrainians, including among these crimes the famine. At the

19th Conference of the CPSU in June 1988, Borys Oliinyk called for an inquiry into the famine in the context of Stalin's crimes and was applauded. The following month the UWU plenum heard calls for a monument to the victims to be built in Kiev. At the same meeting a speaker asked for the re-publishing of Mykhailo Hrushevs'kyi's history of the Ukraine, first published in 1928–30, and said that there was still no better history – in other words, one which did not reflect a Russian perspective.

Demands came also for the publishing of banned literary works. Oles' Honchar's novel *Sobor* (The Cathedral), which was criticised in 1968 for nationalism, was allowed to be republished in Russian and Ukrainian. The poet Vasyl Holoborod'ko was allowed to publish in 1986 after eighteen years' silence. Lina Kostenko, a poet who participated in the 1960s protest movement, received recognition in 1987 when she was awarded the Shevchenko State Prize for Literature. Several articles in 1988 asked for the rehabilitation of writers who had suffered repression under Brezhnev, including in particular Vasyl' Stus. The campaign was boosted by the Moscow *Literaturnaya gazeta* (22 June 1988), which listed Stus as among the major Ukrainian cultural figures who were still proscribed. These articles represented veiled criticism of Shcherbyts'kyi, who had run the Ukraine during much of the repression.

The major concern of the Ukrainian writers, however, was with the future status of the Ukrainian language. At the UWU Congress of June 1986, Honchar attacked those Ukrainians who held their own language in contempt, and he called for the defence of the 'linguistic environment'. Oliinyk at the USSR Writers' Congress in the same month was careful to blame not Moscow, but Ukrainians who behaved like Russian chauvinists in promoting the Russian language and thereby violating Leninist nationality policy. From then on, writers regularly expressed their concern at the fate of Ukrainian. They saw the problem as particularly acute in the education system: nearly half of all schoolchildren in the republic studied in Russian, and some knew no Ukrainian at all. Significant numbers of Ukrainian parents prefer to send their children to schools where the medium of instruction is Russian, in the belief that fluency in Russian will assist them in their careers.

In July 1987, the UWU plenum passed a resolution making a comprehensive series of demands on language. These included giving the Ukrainian language official status in the republic; the compulsory study of Ukrainian in all schools; increasing the use of the language in the media and in films; and making widespread its use in state and public organisations and workplaces. The following month the CPU Politburo passed a resolution calling for more attention to be given to the teaching of both the Ukrainian and the Russian languages, but making no significant concessions to the Ukrainian intellectuals.[11] Shcherbyts'kyi was prepared to go no further, and at the January and

October 1988 CPU Central Committee plenums he attacked writers for continuing to protest about the language situation. On the other hand, late in 1988 cultural centres for Ukrainians were opened in Moscow and Leningrad, and Radio Kiev expressed support for cultural rights for Ukrainians outside the republic.

Another issue which inflamed Ukrainian national feelings was the plan to expand the generation of nuclear power, in spite of the Chernobyl catastrophe. The Ukraine includes about 40 per cent of Soviet nuclear power capacity. In 1987 a protest movement against plans to build new sites and expand the Chernobyl facilities developed under the leadership of Honchar and other writers and scientists.[12] In April 1988 a demonstration of 500 people, organised by the unofficial Ukrainian Culturological Club, was prevented from marching through Kiev, but in June a petition against nuclear power was sent from the Ukraine to the 19th Party Conference, bearing 4,000 signatures. Since the nuclear power industry is run from Moscow, not Kiev, the issue pitted the Ukrainian intellectuals directly against the centre. With environmentalist feeling growing in Moscow, it began to seem that the Kremlin might not force the expansion of nuclear power in the Ukraine. The UWU, meanwhile, established an ecology commission to watch over environmental issues in the republic.

The amnesty of political prisoners in 1987, introduced by Gorbachev in the spirit of *glasnost'*, returned to the Ukraine most of the well-known dissidents who had been sentenced under Brezhnev. As in the Russian republic, a parallel phenomenon was the development of a wide variety of unofficial organisations known as 'informal groups', in which Brezhnev-era dissidents participated together with a younger generation of citizens.

The *Ukrainian Herald* resumed publication, again under the editorship of Chornovil. The first issue contained a major section on the Ukrainian Culturological Club. This informal group was formed in Kiev in summer 1987 and was concerned with language, environment and history, especially the famine. In March 1988 the Ukrainian Helsinki Union (UHU) was relaunched, and the *Herald* became its official organ. The UHU called for a new constitution for the USSR and the republics, with the aim of transforming the Soviet Union into a confederation of independent states. The Ukraine would have its own citizenship and immigration controls, and Ukrainian would be the official language. The Crimean Tatars, expelled by Stalin from the Crimea at the end of the Second World War, would be allowed back, and the Crimean autonomous republic would be re-established within the Ukraine.[13]

It would be impossible to list here even the largest of the informal groups and outline their activities. It was reported in May 1988 that Kiev alone had thirty different groups. Their concerns cover Ukrainian culture, politics, human rights, religion, the environment and world peace. They range from Ukrainian Catholic groups to those whose main concern is to promote *perestroika*. Naturally they vary tremendously in size and influence. In June 1988 the Native Language Society in Lvov organised a meeting about the 19th Party Conference. It was addressed by Chornovil and attended by 6,000–8,000 people. Five days later a follow-up meeting was not allowed to take place, although the numbers turning up had reportedly risen to 50,000. Placards supported the Ukrainian language and the legalisation of the Uniates.

During the summer, unions to support *perestroika* were established in Kiev, Odessa and Lvov – in the latter case at least, out of a coalition of informal groups. In view of the fact that these seek to back Gorbachev's policies, it is not surprising that their supporters sing the Internationale at demonstrations, along with Ukrainian patriotic songs. After three mass meetings in Lvov, the authorities moved from criticising the organisers through the press to large-scale arrests. Ivan Makar was arrested in August, and against the normal trend of the time, was held for several months for his part in arranging a demonstration. In October the Kiev Popular Union was allowed to hold a meeting, but the Shcherbyts'kyi leadership was making it clear that a Ukraine-wide Popular Front on the Baltic model would not be permitted. The demand for such an organisation could only be put forward in Moscow. In January 1989 Ivan Dzyuba (despite his earlier renunciation of his previous activities) called in *Moscow News* for a Ukrainian Popular Front to help fight the 'spiritual Chernobyl' threatening the republic.[14]

The situation began to change in February 1989, coinciding with the visit of Gorbachev to Kiev. On 16 February *Literaturna Ukraina* published the Draft Programme of the 'Popular Movement [*Rukh*] of the Ukraine for Perestroika'. This recognised the leading role of the Communist Party, but demanded that Ukrainian be given the status of the state language of the republic, and made other national demands. Shcherbyts'kyi's media reacted with hostility. In the elections to the Congress of People's Deputies in March–April 1989, many officials were elected without opposition being permitted, but some freely contested elections led to victories for radicals. In June the Donbass miners went on strike over industrial and social issues, weakening Shcherbyts'kyi's position. In September the Ukrainian leadership was finally forced to allow the *Rukh* to hold a Ukraine-wide founding conference, under the leadership of the writer Ivan Drach.

Shcherbyts'kyi was finally ousted in November 1989 and replaced as First Secretary by Vladimir Ivashko. The elections to the Ukrainian Supreme Soviet, held in March 1990, took place in considerably freer conditions than those of the previous year. The *Rukh* formed an electoral alliance with other opponents of the apparatus, known as the Democratic Bloc. This succeeded in winning about one quarter of the seats in the Supreme Soviet, and, as was to be expected, achieved its greatest support in the more nationalist Western Ukraine. The *Rukh* also made important gains in the local elections, sweeping the board in the Lvov City Soviet and also doing well in Kiev. Former dissidents who now led independent political movements found themselves in high elected office: Chornovil, for example, became Chairperson of the Lvov *Oblast'* Soviet, confronting the bitter resistance of the Communists. Environmental problems were a factor in the success of the democrats, with new revelations emerging about the damage inflicted by the Chernobyl radiation on the health of the population, the extent of the cover-up and the failure of the authorities to protect the victims.

The religious situation in the Ukraine is probably worse than anywhere else in the Soviet Union, with two major churches banned. The issue of religious freedom is of increasing importance to Ukrainian human rights activists. Since 1982 the Action Group for the Defence of the Rights of Believers and the Church in the Ukraine had been fighting for the Uniates, and publishing the *Chronicle of the Catholic Church in the Ukraine. Glasnost'* broadened the struggle. An added dimension was the reported apparition, on the first anniversary of Chernobyl in April 1987 and for some time afterwards, of the Virgin Mary, at a closed Uniate church in Hrushov, near Lvov.

Perhaps more important was that the emergence of *glasnost'* over-lapped with the millennium of the Christianisation of Kievan Rus, celebrated in summer 1988, stimulating interest among Ukrainians and Russians alike in their national histories. The Russian Orthodox church held the main celebration of the millennium in Moscow. In line with its imperial ideology, the Patriarchate celebrated it as a Russian occasion and showed little concern for Ukrainian feelings. Some Ukrainian Christians felt that Kiev should have been the focal point. In the period up to the millennium, demands increased from the informal groups and from leaders such as Chornovil for the legalisation of both the Uniates and the Ukrainian Autocephalous Orthodox church.

The Moscow Patriarchate was not sympathetic to these demands. Over half of its functioning churches were in the Ukraine, and it faced losing many of them to the Ukrainian churches if they were legalised. Outside the Ukraine, Andrei Sakharov and foreign politicians such as President Reagan backed the call for legalisation. Pope John Paul II, in solidarity with the Uniates, refused to attend the Moscow celebrations. Thousands of people took part in unofficial celebrations in the Western Ukraine, and the Ukrainian Culturological Club organised a small meeting in Kiev. Unlike in Lithuania and Armenia, religion in the Ukraine has historically been a divisive factor, the East being Orthodox and the West Uniate. If national feeling develops further, however, it is likely that the two denominations may come together in the common demand for legalisation. It is significant that the draft programme of the *Rukh* called for religious freedom. Late in 1989, Uniates seized control of many of the churches in the Western Ukraine. The Patriarchal representatives in Kiev protested to the local authorities, but to little effect. It appeared that during the negotiations surrounding Gorbachev's visit to the Pope, the Soviet government had given assurances to the Vatican that the situation of the Uniates would improve.

CONCLUSION

The Ukrainians have some of the benefits of *glasnost'*, but even less *perestroika* than the rest of the USSR. The intelligentsia, through the Union of Writers, was articulating a programme which harked back to the Ukrainianisation of the 1920s. It was faced with a leadership which had set itself against Ukrainianisation and was hostile to independent political and cultural activity. The whole population had been alerted by the Chernobyl tragedy to distrust the leaders in Kiev, and the supply of food was worsening.

The fate of the Ukrainians seemed inextricably linked with the fate of Gorbachev's reforms. If Moscow were to signal an end to *glasnost'*, hopes for evolutionary change in the Ukraine would be dashed for a decade. If *perestroika* were to develop in the Soviet Union, however, it would not be possible to exclude the Ukraine indefinitely. The question then would be whether the still conservative post-Shcherbyts'kyi Ukrainian leadership would be changed through pressure from Moscow or through moves from within the Ukraine itself. In either case, once the movement started, it would be difficult for Moscow to stop it. The sheer size of the Ukraine would make a Popular Front there a much greater threat to the stability of the USSR than the Baltic movements, if it went too far.

On the other hand, as far as one can tell, most Ukrainian opinion is not separatist. Unlike the Estonians and Latvians, the Ukrainians do not face being outnumbered in their own republic by immigration. Even the adoption of the Russian language does not seem to deprive them of their Ukrainian identity, although intermarriage with Russians may be a greater threat.

It seemed more likely that if Moscow and Kiev showed greater sensitivity to Ukrainian concerns in relation to language, culture, religion and the environment, Ukrainian aspirations could be accommodated within the Soviet Union. With the grandiose Siberian projects of the Brezhnev era going out of fashion, it seemed that Soviet investment priorities were shifting back to the European part of the USSR, where the infrastructure was better developed. Furthermore, the Ukraine was well placed geographically to benefit from the renewed emphasis on economic cooperation with Eastern Europe. If, however, a nationalist outburst provoked Moscow to a new series of repressions, then this would threaten the process of *perestroika* throughout the USSR.

NOTES

1. For a historical overview, see R. Szporluk 'The Ukraine and Russia' in R. Conquest (ed.) *The Last Empire: Nationality and the Soviet Future* (Stanford, CA, Hoover Institution Press 1986), pp. 151–82.

2. See R. Conquest *The Harvest of Sorrow: Soviet Collectivization and the Terror-Famine* (London, Hutchinson 1986).

3. J. E. Mace 'Famine and nationalism in Soviet Ukraine', *Problems of Communism*, 33, no. 3 (May–June 1984), pp. 37–50.

4. B. Krawchenko *Social Change and National Consciousness in Twentieth-Century Ukraine* (Basingstoke, Macmillan 1985), p. 150.

5. See S. Bialer *Stalin's Successors: Leadership, Stability and Change in the Soviet Union* (Cambridge, Cambridge University Press 1980), pp. 223–24, for a list of Ukrainians prominent in 1974.

6. *Vestnik statistiki* 1980, nos. 2 and 8; B. Krawchenko 'Ethno-demographic trends in Ukraine in the 1970s' in B. Krawchenko (ed.) *Ukraine after Shelest* (Edmonton, Canadian Institute of Ukrainian Studies, University of Alberta 1983), pp. 101–19; B. Lewytzkyj *Politics and Society in Soviet Ukraine 1953–1980* (Edmonton, Canadian Institute of Ukrainian Studies, University of Alberta 1984), ch. 6; R. Szporluk 'The Ukraine and the Ukrainians', in Z. Katz (ed.) *Handbook of Major Soviet Nationalities* (New York, Free Press 1975), pp. 31–4.

7. I. Dzyuba *Internationalism or Russification?* (New York, Monad 1974).

8. V. Chornovil *The Chornovil Papers* (New York, McGraw-Hill 1968); M. Hayward (ed.) *Ferment in the Ukraine* (Woodhaven, NY, Crisis Press 1973); K. C. Farmer *Ukrainian Nationalism in the Post-Stalin Era: Myth, Symbols and Ideology in Soviet Nationality Policy* (The Hague, Nijhoff 1980); R. Solchanyk 'Politics and the national question in the post-Shelest period' and B. Nahaylo 'Ukrainian dissent and opposition after Shelest' in Krawchenko *Ukraine after Shelest*, pp. 1–29 and 30–54; Lewytzkyj *Politics and Society, passim*.

9. Y. Bilinsky 'Shcherbyts'kyi, Ukraine and Kremlin politics' *Problems of Communism* 32, no. 4 (July–Aug. 1983), pp. 1–20.

10. English-language periodical sources for contemporary developments in the Ukraine include: *Radio Liberty Research Bulletin; Ukrainian Review; Soviet Ukrainian Affairs; Soviet Nationality Survey; USSR News Brief; News from Ukraine.*

11. For the proceedings of the UWU Plenum and the Politburo resolution, see *Soviet Ukrainian Affairs* 1 (3) (1987), pp. 8–27.

12. B. Nahaylo 'Mounting opposition in the Ukraine to nuclear energy program' *Radio Liberty Research Bulletin* RL Supplement 1/88 (16 Feb. 1988).

13. For documents of the UHU, see *Ukrainian Review* 36, (4) (Winter 1988), pp. 72–86.

14. I. Dzyuba, 'A time to gather stones' *Moscow News* 15 Jan. 1989.

CHAPTER SEVEN

Belorussians

Ralph S. Clem

The Belorussian people, who since medieval times have inhabited the region that bears their name today, are one of the largest ethnic groups in the multi-national Soviet state, yet also one of the least known.[1] To a large extent the relatively low visibility of Belorussians can be attributed to historical and geographical circumstances which combined to retard their coalescence into a modern nation. In the present century, however, despite the trauma of revolution and war, the Belorussians have undergone a profound ethnogenesis and have emerged as one of the major nationalities of the USSR, a process which to an appreciable – although perhaps unintended – extent resulted from the manner in which the Soviet government has dealt with the question of ethnicity. In coming years the Belorussians may find themselves in an even more advantageous situation, if the Gorbachev administration creates the conditions for further ethno-cultural growth and economic opportunity.

BACKGROUND

Belorussia's location has influenced its historical, political and social development, and not always positively. Bordered on the east by Russia, on the south by the Ukraine, on the west by Poland, and on the north by Lithuania and Latvia, Belorussia has been at one of the crossroads of European history and has suffered accordingly. Thus situated among more powerful and often aggressive neighbours, Belorussia is also positioned on one of the principal east – west transportation routes (Warsaw and Vilnius through Minsk to Smolensk and on to Moscow); Napoleon invaded Russia by this route in 1812, as did Guderian and his panzers in 1941.

The indigenous people of this region, the Belorussians, are descended from Slavic tribes which migrated into the area from Central Europe, apparently during the sixth century AD. By the ninth

109

century, principalities subordinate to the Kievan state (in what is now the Ukraine) had been established in Belorussia; internecine conflict among these was characteristic of the era. The Mongol invasion of the mid-thirteenth century destroyed Kiev, and in the power vacuum that followed Belorussia was annexed by the Grand Duchy of Lithuania to the north. Thus began a period of over 400 years during which Belorussia was dominated by Lithuania and – following their union in 1569 – by Poland. This separation of Belorussia from Slavic lands to the east (Russia) and south (Ukraine) began a long process of divergent linguistic and cultural development which ultimately led to the evolution of the Belorussians as a distinct ethnic group.[2]

With the rise of Russian hegemony to the east in the late eighteenth century, Belorussia found itself at the mercy of another expansionist neighbour. During the reign of Catherine the Great, a weakened Polish state was dismembered in a series of partitions (1772, 1793 and 1795), with Russia obtaining all of the Belorussian provinces. Incorporated into the Russia empire, Belorussia became an integral part of the tsarist state, and was subject to the influence of the Russianisation policies of the time.[3] From 1859 to 1906 Belorussian language publications and the use of Belorussian as the medium of instruction in schools were banned. As a consequence, Belorussian cultural activities were poorly developed in the last years of the *ancien régime*, although the poets Yanka Kapala, Yakov Kolas and others laid the foundation for a national literature, and at least one newspaper in the Belorussian language was in publication.[4] Furthermore, the social and agrarian economic order that had existed in Belorussia was largely intact; although Russians had assumed a greater role in the Belorussian provinces, Poles and Jews predominated in the cities, while ethnic Belorussians remained almost exclusively peasants.[5]

The evolution of modern Belorussian nationalism is closely linked to the unsettled political conditions in Eastern Europe and Russia in the early twentieth century, and to the ethnic stratification system which placed the indigenous Belorussians at the bottom of the socio-economic ladder and largely outside the small modernising sector of their homeland. Although it is clear that some indicators of a Belorussian ethnogenesis (for example, the beginnings of a national literature) were in evidence by the turn of the century, it was only in 1902 that a small political organisation was founded (the Belorussian Socialist Hromada) which espoused Belorussian autonomy.[6] During the chaos of the First World War, Russian Revolution and Civil War, and the Russo-Polish War of 1919–20, the Belorussian nationalists were overwhelmed by events, having found it impossible to establish a viable ethnic separatist movement in the face of military occupation by German, Polish and Red forces and the manoeuvring of larger political parties (especially the Russian Communists). Although a Belorussian nationalist council (the Rada) came into existence in the summer of 1917, it had little popular support and its declaration of independence in December 1917, was of no real importance.[7]

In a penetrating analysis of the antecedents of Belorussian nationalism, Stephen Guthier demonstrated that the socio-economic and demographic conditions in Belorussia during the late nineteenth and early twentieth centuries contributed to this lack of enthusiasm for the Belorussian nationalist cause.[8] Although a large number of people (5.7 million) identified themselves as speakers of the Belorussian language in the 1897 tsarist census (there was no question in this enumeration about ethnic affiliation), and despite the fact that Belorussian speakers composed a majority or plurality in several provinces and districts, the Belorussians were not well positioned for the development of a national consciousness of sufficient strength to withstand the external pressures occasioned by the troubled times.[9] Significantly, because virtually all (98 per cent) of Belorussians were rural or small-town dwellers, they were isolated from the politically dynamic urban environment. Furthermore, in their own homeland Belorussians were vastly under-represented in the skilled professions and intelligentsia (which typically provides the core of nationalist movements), and very few Belorussians could read and write (which cut off the majority from ethnic literature and newspapers). Finally, Belorussia itself lacked a political centre (or primate city) to act as a focal point for the nationalist cause.[10]

Out of the upheavals of the first quarter of this century, however, emerged a geographical entity which would at last provide a framework within which a Belorussian identity could coalesce. At the conclusion of the Russo-Polish War, the Treaty of Riga (1921) divided Belorussian lands between a newly independent Poland and the fledgeling Soviet state. In the following year, the establishment of the Union of Soviet Socialist Republics as a federation of ethno-territorial units brought into existence the Belorussian Soviet Socialist Republic (BSSR); in the next few years the territory of the BSSR was expanded to include almost all areas of ethnic Belorussian settlement in that part of Belorussia that remained within the USSR. The geographical denouement of the BSSR occurred in 1939 when the western part of Belorussia (which had been ceded to inter-war Poland) was annexed by the Soviet Union (and retained by it following the Second World War).

The period between the wars witnessed the gradual development of an indigenous socio-economic infrastructure in Belorussia, and not coincidentally, the growth of a Belorussian ethnic identity. The principal reason for the increased vitality of Belorussian nationalism was the existence of a legitimate ethno-territory and primate city (the capital, Minsk), coupled with official approval and even encouragement of minority ethnic consciousness in the USSR during the 1920s. For example, between 1927 and 1938 the number of books published in the Belorussian language increased from 1.3 to 12.3 million, and was accompanied by a rise in literacy.[11] Even though the 'nativisation' and 'flowering of nationalities' policies were later to be reversed in the Stalin era, the effect was to abet ethnic groups (such as the Belorussians) in their critical formative stage.

In demographic terms, the number of Belorussians grew comparatively little between the tsarist census of 1897 (5.7 million) and the first Soviet census, conducted in 1926 (6.1 million), although it should be noted that the figures for both dates are tainted by technical problems.[12] Ethnic Belorussians in the USSR were overwhelmingly concentrated in the BSSR territory (81.2 per cent in 1897 and 82.9 per cent in 1926), where they composed just over 71 per cent of the population in 1897, a figure that declined to about 66 per cent by 1926.[13] Jews were a major presence in Belorussia in 1897 and 1926, especially in urban areas (where they accounted for about half of the population, and Poles were also prominent in the region's population. Significantly, by 1926 the Belorussian share of the urban component of the BSSR almost doubled, reflecting the initial stage of the formation of a modernised Belorussian population. Nevertheless, the overall level of urbanisation for the Belorussians was still far below the national average, both because the BSSR itself was relatively unurbanised and due to the presence of large numbers of Jews, Poles and Russians in the cities of the republic. In terms of other socio-economic characteristics, Guthier points to a pronounced increase in literacy among Belorussians in the 1897–1926 period, as well as their further integration into the professions.[14]

The interval between the censuses of 1926 and 1939 is of considerable interest as regards the maturation of the Belorussian ethnic group, because during this time the processes of industrialisation and urbanisation were accelerated by the Soviet Five Year Plans, which in turn set in motion massive social change. Unfortunately, the results of the 1939 census were never published in sufficient detail to permit even a cursory analysis of the ethnic and socio-economic milieu of this critical period. The fragmentary data which are available indicate that the changes under-way in the 1920s continued through the remainder of the inter-war years, with further increases in the level of urbanisation among Belorussians and in literacy (especially in rural areas of the BSSR).[15]

DEMOGRAPHIC AND SOCIO-ECONOMIC TRENDS IN BELORUSSIA IN THE WAR AND POST-WAR ERA

Both the ravages of the Second World War and rapid post-war economic development were to alter the socio-economic and ethno-demographic landscape of Belorussia, the latter propelling the Belorussian people towards a more modernised status (with all that that implies for their future evolution as a nationality).

It is not possible to state with any precision the magnitude of population losses which occurred in Belorussia or among the Belorussian people during the Second World War. The entire territory of the BSSR was held by German forces for almost three years, and suffered considerably in both human and material terms from combat action and a protracted partisan campaign. It is feasible, however, to estimate the demographic impact of the war in absolute numbers and relative to other areas of the USSR. Soviet sources put the population of the BSSR in 1939 (in current borders) at 8.9 million, and give the 1951 population as only 7.8 million.[16] If one projects the 1939 population forward to 1951 at the growth rate which obtained between 1926 and 1939, then a shortfall of approximately 2.7 million persons results between the expected and observed figures. Looked at another way, the BSSR did not regain its 1939 population until 1969. Owing to the effects of the war, Belorussia lost a greater percentage of its population than any other region of the USSR; between 1939 and 1951, the population of Belorussia declined by 12.7 per cent, while that of the Ukraine dropped by 8 per cent and that of the entire USSR fell by 4.7 per cent.[17]

As a result of the severity and atrocities of the German occupation, as well as population movements which followed the realignment of international borders in Eastern Europe after the war, the ethnic composition of Belorussia was radically altered. First, the once large Jewish population was virtually annihilated by the Germans or, in lesser numbers, was evacuated to other areas of the Soviet Union.[18] Second, many Poles moved from western Belorussia (formerly part of interwar Poland) to Poland proper as the Soviet–Polish frontier was shifted to the west. Also, at the same time some ethnic Belorussians probably migrated from Poland and Lithuania to the BSSR. Finally, many more Russians moved into the BSSR in the post-war period to take up positions vacated by those that were eliminated or displaced and to serve as cadre for the recovery effort (and perhaps also to provide an ethnic Russian presence in an important non-Russian border region).

Consequently, by 1959 (the first post-war census in the USSR) the Belorussians composed a much larger share of the population of the BSSR than had been the case in the pre-war era. Conversely, the proportion of Jews and of Poles declined precipitously. These changes were even more pronounced in cities, where Belorussians increased from about a third to over two-thirds of the republic's urban population, with the Russians accounting for another fifth.

After 1959, as the pace of economic development quickened in Belorussia, the Belorussian people were drawn increasingly into the republic's modernised sector. The best evidence of this phenomenon is the continued growth of the urban population of the BSSR and of the

Belorussians themselves. In the first instance, the level of urbanisation in the BSSR rose at a rate higher than the national average from 1959 to 1970 and again from 1970 to 1979.[19] Likewise, the data for the Belorussian ethnic group indicate intensified urbanisation (in 1959, about a third of Belorussians were urban, whereas by 1979 over a half lived in cities) and further growth in their share of the BSSR's urban population.[20] Guthier attributed these trends to a strong demand for labour in the cities generated by rapid economic growth (industrial output expanded three-fold from 1959 to 1970) and the vacuum created by the loss of the urban Jewish population, a demand which attracted hundreds of thousands of ethnic Belorussians from the countryside.[21]

The development of Belorussia's economy also produced changes in the workforce and occupational characteristics of the Belorussian people. As recently as 1959, well over half of all Belorussians were collective farmers, a figure that declined to under a fifth by 1979. In comparison with Ukrainians and Russians, over this period the Belorussians overtook the former and closed the gap on the latter in terms of social class distribution.[22]

The final aspect of social change among the Belorussian people that we will examine is educational attainment. Although they have shown marked improvement in recent decades, the Belorussians have not fared as well as have many other nationalities. Despite ranking seventh among the fifteen union republic nationalities in the increase in level of schooling achieved from 1959 to 1979, the Belorussians remained in tenth place in educational attainment in 1979 (they were tied with the Uzbeks for ninth in 1959). Thus, although the Belorussians may have made progress in education, they only just kept pace with the rising national average and remained below it as of 1979. This situation is unlikely to change dramatically in coming years due to the chronic under-representation of Belorussians in higher education institutions. In the last year for which age-adjusted data were available (1970) for participation in higher education, the Belorussians ranked 14 out of 15 union republic nationalities, with only about half the rate for the highest ranking group (Georgians).[23] Interestingly, Belorussians were much better represented in specialised secondary schools in that year.

In summary, the period following the Second World War was one in which the BSSR and the Belorussian people underwent large-scale modernisation and social change. Of particular note were the rapid changes in urbanisation and social class composition for both the republic and the Belorussian ethnic group. In other aspects of socio-economic status, such as participation in the specialised work-force and education, the Belorussians have made major strides but have lagged behind other nationalities. The overall record is thus mixed, but certainly attests to the advancement of the Belorussians and their position in Soviet society.

ACCULTURATION AND ASSIMILATION OF BELORUSSIANS

Just as the maturation of a modern Belorussian nationality was tied to the existence of a political entity within which the group could modernise and develop the sustaining elements of a viable ethnic identity, the post-second World War era has also been one in which the Belorussians have become increasingly subject to the ethnically disruptive forces of rapid social change. Many analysts view the situation in the 1960s and later as another watershed for Belorussian nationalism, pointing to a steady – or possibly accelerating – erosion of ethnic cohesion (acculturation) among Belorussians since that time, an erosion which, if unchecked, will lead to the loss of individuals through ethnic re-identification (assimilation). Indeed, it appears from the available evidence (which is incomplete) that large numbers of Belorussians assimilated to the Russian nationality in the first half of this century.[24] More recently, the relatively strong propensity for Belorussians to acculturate and assimilate is extremely important demographically because losses from ethnic re-identification compound the already low rate of national population growth characteristic of the group.

It is generally believed that the linguistic and cultural affinity between Belorussians and Russians has facilitated the acculturation and possibly the assimilation of the former by the latter. Soviet census figures on native language adherence, often employed to study acculturation trends, indicate that Belorussians have the lowest level of native language loyalty among the fourteen non-Russian Union Republic nationalities, and also rank first in knowledge of Russian as a second language. Furthermore, the extensive social mobilisation experienced by Belorussians has – ironically – often resulted in their acculturation through the effects of urbanisation and migration to areas outside Belorussia; these two tendencies lead to greater inter-ethnic contacts and higher rates of marriage with non-Belorussians, both of which are linked to acculturation.[25] Acculturation is also typically more in evidence among younger Belorussians, which suggests that the phenomenon will progress as the generations change unless mounting nationalist sentiments create a renewal of ethnic consciousness, particularly among the youth of Belorussia.

BELORUSSIA IN THE 1980s: PROSPERITY AND DISCONTENT

The decade of the 1980s witnessed both a continuation of the rapid socio-economic modernisation of Belorussia and the emergence in that republic of an incipient nationalist movement, the latter being something of a surprise in light of what had been thought to be the relatively inert status of ethnic consciousness among Belorussians.

Belorussia has been one of the leading economic growth regions of the USSR since 1980. In terms of percentage increase in the total volume of industrial output, the BSSR ranked second among the fifteen republics from 1980 to 1985, and was also placed second in growth of the value of agricultural production over the same period.[26] Perhaps even more importantly, Belorussia led all republics in the increase in labour productivity in both industry and agriculture between 1980 and 1987, a significant fact given the current emphasis on productivity growth as a means of compensating for declining capital investment.[27] The strength of Belorussia's economy is due to several factors: the republic has received comparatively large amounts of capital investment; its industry mix (machinery, chemicals, textiles, electronics and computers) is favourable for a technologically modernizing economy; its central location *vis-à-vis* Eastern Europe and the densely populated and developed western and Baltic regions of the USSR; and an extensive transportation network (railroads and pipelines in particular), all serve to promote development in the BSSR.

These positive economic indicators have translated into beneficial trends for both wages and the standard of living in Belorussia; whereas formerly the republic was seriously disadvantaged in these respects, major gains have been made in the 1980s. For example, in 1960 Belorussia ranked fourteenth and fifteenth among the republics in blue-collar and white-collar wages in the urban and rural sectors; by 1987 its position had improved to eighth and seventh respectively.[28] In terms of living standards, Gertrude Schroeder indicates that Belorussia has made tremendous strides forward, moving from ninth place among the fifteen republics in real per capita consumption in 1960 to sixth place in 1985, with consumption in the BSSR above the national average for the first time.[29] Demographic evidence also attests to Belorussia's improved circumstances: according to the most recent figures, the BSSR has the third lowest infant mortality rate in the USSR.[30] Also, the republic has apparently changed from a negative to a positive migration balance in this decade, a reflection of the greater demand for labour created by the economic growth mentioned above, the low rate of increase in the indigenous workforce, and the general tendency for people to move to or remain in regions of relative prosperity.[31]

Somewhat paradoxically, as the economic situation in Belorussia improved into the late 1980s, the first evidence of a revitalised Belorussian nationalism came to light, manifesting itself in the same manner – albeit later – as had similar movements elsewhere in the USSR. Under the more permissive social and political environment engendered by the Gorbachev administration (that is, the politics of *glasnost'* and democratisation), informal (or 'patriotic') groups with varying agendas sprang up in Belorussia, espousing linguistic, cultural, historical, environmental and other concerns. Foremost among these organisations are *Talaka* (Mutual Aid) and *Tuteishyia* ('the Locals', a term used in tsarist times to refer to the inhabitants of Belorussia) which, together with smaller groups, seek to promote a revival of Belorussian language, literature and ethnic consciousness.[32] Individual groups typically adopt specific causes, ranging from the posting of signs in Belorussian in the Minsk metro to the termination of nuclear power station construction (Belorussia was severely affected by the Chernobyl reactor accident, with large areas contaminated by radioactivity and the expectation of serious health problems among the republic's population), but the issues raised have in common the theme of greater involvement of the Belorussian people in the affairs of their nationality homeland. One prominent example of how these unofficial clubs bring to the public eye matters of popular concern is the exposure of crimes of the Stalin era, most notably the uncovering of mass graves of as many as 30,000 victims of the NKVD in the Kurapaty woods; many of those killed were prominent Belorussian writers and intellectuals, whose demise is now portrayed as an atrocity against the Belorussian people.[33]

Though small in membership, these informal associations, composed mainly of young people and members of the intelligentsia, are exerting an increasing influence on the social and political life of the republic. Initially, the authorities took a strong stance against the proliferation of unofficial groups, and suppressed the first such club, *Spadcyna* ('Heritage') in December, 1986.[34] Subsequent attempts to stage public rallies in Belorussia were blocked or disrupted by the police or those presumed to be acting on their orders (at times violently). Likewise, when Belorussian independent youth organisations attempted to arrange a conference in Minsk in January 1989, officials restricted their use of facilities and otherwise obstructed their plans to the point that the organisers moved the meeting to Vilnius, where they were welcomed by the Lithuanian *Sąjūdis* popular movement.[35]

In this particular case, the authorities no doubt erred in forcing the issue, as the effect of their intransigence was to facilitate greater interaction between the Belorussian groups and those in more politically active Lithuania. In fact, Belorussian informal groups were represented for the first time at the fifth meeting of representatives of non-Russian national-democratic movements in Vilnius in late January 1989, an indication of the growing ties between popular front organisations in Belorussia and those in other republics.[36]

A significant occurrence in this unfolding drama took place in February 1989, when over 50,000 people attended a rally in Minsk organised by the Renewal Belorussian Popular Front for Perestroika, a confederation of informal organisations. On this occasion the event proceeded peacefully amid the display of the traditional Belorussian national flag and the nationalist 'Pahonya' symbol (a mounted knight). Although much smaller in size than similar demonstrations in the Baltic and Caucasian republics, the February rally proved that there was sufficient interest in the cause of Belorussian legitimacy to mobilise an appreciable number of people in what seems to have been a direct challenge to the political leadership of the republic.[37]

Criticism of the activities of informal groups appears in the official press in what appears to be an attempt to define limits to the 'progressive reformist' movement. For example, after the *Tuteishyia* group sponsored a 'literary evening' in Minsk in December 1987, at which the virtues of the Belorussian language in contemporary writing were extolled and demands were voiced for an expansion of publishing in that tongue, the event was criticised in the major establishment literary journal as too political in content.[38] In a lengthy and important piece which appeared in the main newspaper of the BSSR, the government's view of the Popular Front movement was articulated by a university professor, who seemed to be balancing the need to advocate 'restructuring' (*perestroika*) against the danger of overstepping the bounds of reform by advocating intolerable, extreme positions.[39] Thus, on the one hand the author characterised many members of the Belorussian informal groups as 'ardent patriots and sincere fighters for renewal and for the extrication of our country and the republic from the stage of stagnation' (that is, the Brezhnev era).[40] Further, 'their civic concern and activism are forcing local bureaucrats to bestir themselves and are injecting dynamism into political life'.[41] However, he reminded readers that 'the fate of restructuring is today decided not at street rallies and demonstrations, but at workplaces',[42] and 'that representatives of the ruling party, in addition to honour and decency, must also display political responsibility for restructuring and its results'.[43] With specific reference to the ethnic question, the author acknowledged the

Belorussian writers' contributions in awakening national consciousness and drawing attention to the state of the Belorussian language, their contributions to culture and the problems of environmental protection and historical and cultural monuments, and their growing attention to the Belorussian people's historical past.[44]

But, it is especially inappropriate, the article continues,

To refuse to perceive any positive shifts and changes in the republic, and . . . to seek to destabilize the situation and mould a people's consciousness, charged with national mistrust, suspicion, grievances and discontent with Belorussia's development within the community of fraternal peoples . . . and to whip up Russophobic sentiments in the republic.[45]

Finally, the author quotes the First Secretary of the Belorussian Communist Party, Ye. Ye. Sokolov, who is an ethnic Belorussian, as stating that

The most important thing is the [Popular Front's] platform. Is it consonant with the spirit and decisions of the 27th CPSU Congress and the 19th All-Union Conference? Are the efforts of the association's members directed toward implementing those decisions as swiftly as possible and preserving and augmenting the fundamental values of socialism? If so, we are in favour of such associations. But if the opportunities opened up by democratization and public activism are exploited to inflame unhealthy sentiments and destabilize the situation, the attitude toward this must be unequivocal.

This is nothing but parasitism on restructuring.[46] The message delivered through the official Belorussian press is intended to rein in the unofficial organisations, to deter them from moving beyond the confines of acceptable, constructive opposition. The problem here is that in Belorussia – as elsewhere in the USSR – these confines have expanded so rapidly that the ultimate boundaries are as yet unknown, that a game is being played according to rules which are being revised as the contest is in progress. The outcome of such a scenario must remain uncertain, and any attempt to predict it will certainly be overtaken by events.

CONCLUSIONS AND PROSPECTS

In the highly dynamic social, economic and political arenas in the USSR in the late 1980s, the pace of change and the scope of reform are such that an assessment of prospects, even over the short term, is problematic indeed. Yet, the experience of previous decades and an appreciation of the possibilities created by the Gorbachev initiatives allow for at least a guarded forecast concerning the future of Belorussia and the Belorussian people.

Probably the major concern as regards the vitality of Belorussian ethnic nationalism has been the question of acculturation-assimilation. Recently evidenced trends indicate that underlying socio-economic patterns which are related to that phenomenon are realigning in such a fashion as to retard the process of ethnic re-identification. Specifically, the reversal of migration flows from net movement out of Belorussia to net movement into the republic suggests that fewer Belorussians are leaving their homeland and thus will not be as susceptible to acculturating pressures. Second, the participation of Belorussian youth in the unofficial club movement may signal a growing tendency for many young people to adhere to their ethnic identity; it will be recalled that previously acculturation has been especially pervasive among younger generations.

The economic condition of Belorussia will probably continue to improve, as the republic is well suited for the type of modernisation envisaged by Gorbachev; promotion of high-technology industries and intensified economic interaction with Eastern Europe will clearly benefit Belorussia. Further economic growth would allow for greater social development of the Belorussians *in situ*, and a steadily increasing standard of living will narrow the gap with the Baltic republics and perhaps move the BSSR into a closer relationship with its neighbours to the north. Such a shift would place Belorussia within the relatively more developed sphere of the Soviet federation.

Finally, the enhanced autonomy of the union republics in economic, social and possibly political terms will no doubt strengthen Belorussian ethnic consciousness, as the importance of ethno-territories as the primary units of social development and economic management increases. Pressures generated by the unofficial 'patriotic' (that is, nationalist) organisations will be likely to push the republic leadership towards a more ethnocentric posture ('Belorussia for the Belorussians'); at this juncture it is difficult to know how far that might go, although at a minimum one could expect that greater attention will be paid to the ethnic Belorussian language, literature and media, and culture as the legitimate right of the indigenous people. This will in turn solidify ethnic consciousness among Belorussians and tie them more closely to the affairs of their nationality territory. In the case of Belorussians, a people who hitherto have not been known for the strength of their nationalist sentiments, it would seem that the changing situation in the USSR will lead to renewed ethnic awareness, much as occurred in the 1920s. Gorbachev and his policies may be ushering in the second era of Belorussian ethnogenesis.

NOTES

1. The term 'Belorussian' literally means 'White Russian', but should not be confused with the 'White' (i.e., counter-revolutionary) element of the Russian Civil War period. The Belorussian language belongs to the Slavonic group and is linguistically akin to Russian and Ukrainian. See Bernard Comrie *The Languages of the Soviet Union* (Cambridge, Cambridge University Press 1981), pp. 144–46.

2. Jan Zaprudnik 'Belorussia and the Belorussians' in Zev Katz (ed.) *Handbook of Major Soviet Nationalities* (New York, Free Press 1975), pp. 50–2.

3. Hugh Seton-Watson *The Russian Empire, 1801–1917* (Oxford, Oxford University Press 1967), pp. 45–6, 49–50, 191.

4. Zaprudnik 'Belorussia and the Belorussians', *The Russian Empire*, p. 609; Roman Szporluk 'West Ukraine and West Belorussia' *Soviet Studies* 31 (1) (Jan. 1979), pp. 89–90).

5. Steven L. Guthier 'The Belorussians: national identification and assimilation, 1897–1970' *Soviet Studies* 29 (1) (Jan. 1977), pp. 40–8.

6. Richard Pipes *The Formation of the Soviet Union* (New York, Atheneum 1968), pp. 11–12.

7. Pipes *Formation of the Soviet Union*, pp. 71–75. See also Nicholas Vakar *Belorussia: The Making of a Nation* (Cambridge, MA, Harvard University Press 1956), pp. 93–106.

8. Guthier 'The Belorussians', pp. 37–61; and *Soviet Studies* (2) (April 1977), pp. 270–83.
9. Robert A. Lewis, Richard H. Rowland and Ralph S. Clem *Nationality and Population Change in Russia and the USSR* (New York, Praeger 1976), p. 279.
10. Guthier, p. 43.
11. Ibid., Table 14, p. 59.
12. For a discussion of the enumeration procedures used, see Brian D. Silver 'The ethnic and language dimensions in Russian and Soviet censuses', in Ralph S. Clem (ed.) *Research Guide to the Russian and Soviet Censuses* (Ithaca, NY, Cornell University Press 1986), pp. 70–97. Population figures for 1897 and 1926 are from Lewis, Rowland and Clem op. cit., p. 279.
13. Ibid., p. 412.
14. Guthier, op. cit., pp. 54–5.
15. A. A. Isupov *Natsional'nyi Sostav Naseleniya SSSR* (Moscow, Statistika 1961), pp. 27–42; Guthier, op. cit., p. 60.
16. USSR, Tsentral'noe Statisticheskoe Upravlenie, *Naselenie SSSR, 1973* (Moscow, Statistika 1975), pp. 10–11.
17. Calculated from *Naselenie, 1973*, pp. 10–11.
18. Eugene M. Kulischer *Europe on the Move* (New York, Columbia University Press 1948), p. 109, mentions that large numbers of Jews migrated from Belorussia to other areas of the USSR prior to the German invasion and may have, depending on their destination, survived.
19. The figures for Belorussia are: 31% urban in 1959, 43% in 1970, and 55% in 1979.
20. By 1970 Belorussians accounted for 69% of Belorussia's urban population.
21. Guthier, pp. 272–74.
22. Yu. V. Arutyunyan and Yu. V. Bromlei *Sotsial'no – Kulturnyi Oblik Sovetskikh Natsii* (Moscow, Nauka 1986), p. 55.
23. Ellen Jones and Fred W. Grupp 'Measuring nationality trends in the Soviet Union: a research note' *Slavic Review* 41, (1) (Spring 1982), Table 2, p. 117.
24. A Soviet study concluded that about 60,000 Belorussians living outside the BSSR may have assimilated to Russian nationality between 1926 and 1959. See A. A. Rakov *Naselenie BSSR* (Minsk 1969), p. 91, cited in Guthier, pp. 276–77. See also Lewis, Rowland, and Clem *Nationality and Population Change*, p. 222.
25. Robert J. Kaiser 'National territoriality in multinational, multi-homeland states: a comparative study of the Soviet Union, Yugoslavia, and Czechoslovakia', Unpublished Ph.D. dissertation, Columbia University, New York, 1988, pp. 310–34 and Appendix E, p. 390.
26. USSR, TsSU *Narodnoe Khozyaistvo SSSR v 1985g* (Moscow, Finansy i Statistika 1986), pp. 104–5, 188.
27. USSR, Goskomstat *Trud v SSSR* (Moscow, Finansy i Statistika 1988), pp. 241, 244.
28. USSR *Trud v SSSR*, pp. 156–57.
29. Gertrude E. Schroeder 'Nationalities and the Soviet economy' in Lubomyr Hajda and Mark A. Beissinger (eds) *Nationalities in Soviet Politics and Society* (Boulder, CO, Westview, forthcoming).

30. The latest infant mortality data, for 1986, are in USSR, Goskomstat *Naselenie SSSR, 1987* (Moscow, Finansy i Statistika 1988), p. 345.
31. Projecting the BSSR's population forward based on birth and death rates in the republic indicates an apparent reversal of net migration from out to in around 1985. See Richard H. Rowland 'Union republic migration trends in the USSR during the 1980s' *Soviet Geography* 29 (9) (Nov. 1988), pp. 809–29.
32. Bohdan Nahaylo 'More signs of greater national assertiveness by Belorussians' Radio Liberty Report 22/88 18 Jan. 1988.
33. Bohdan Nahaylo 'Political demonstration in Minsk attests to Belorussian national assertiveness' Radio Liberty Report RL 481/87, 26 Nov. 1987.
34. Nahaylo 'Political demonstration', p. 5.
35. 'They didn't reach agreement' *Pravda* 17 Jan. 1989, p. 3, translated in *Current Digest of the Soviet Press* 41 (3) (15 Feb. 1989), pp. 26–7.
36. Bohdan Nahaylo 'Non-Russian national-democratic movements adopt charter and issue appeal to Russian intelligentsia' *Report on the USSR* 1 (8) (24 Feb. 1989), pp. 15–17.
37. Kathleen Mihalisko ' "Renewal" Belorussian Popular Front for Perestroika' *Report on the USSR* 1 (10) (10 March 1989), pp. 28–9. See also 'Belorussian "informal" groups gather in Minsk' *Krasnaya Zvezda* 22 Feb. 1989, p. 4, translated in *FBIS–Soviet Union Daily Report* 22 Feb. 1989, pp. 52–3.
38. Nahaylo 'More signs', p. 8.
39. 'What is hampering the unification of restructuring forces?' *Sovetskaya Belorussia* 18 Feb. 1989, p. 9, translated in *FBIS–Soviet Union Daily Report*, 9 March 1989, pp. 56–60.
40. Ibid., p. 59.
41. Ibid., p. 56.
42. Ibid., p. 59.
43. Ibid., p. 56.
44. Ibid., p. 56.
45. Ibid., p. 56.
46. Ibid., p. 59.

CHAPTER EIGHT

Moldavians

Jonathan Eyal

The area between the Pruth, Danube and Dniester rivers, the territory of Bessarabia, was part of historic Moldavia, one of the Danubian principalities overwhelmingly inhabited by Romanians. Moldavia was traditionally disputed by the Ottoman and Russian empires: for the tsars, it meant access to the Danube and to the Balkans; for Constantinople it entailed a last line of defence against the traditional enemy to the north. On one issue, however, tsar and sultan were agreed: the Romanian population should not be allowed to have its own nation-state. The fact that this state did finally come into existence in the second half of last century is due in no small measure to the ingenuity of Romanian nationalists, who were able to play off one neighbour against another and benefit from cessions of territory from all.

Bessarabia could not escape the Romanian struggle for independence and unity. Its acquisition by Russia in 1812 (when the Moldavian principality was still under nominal Ottoman suzerainty) was intended to be but the first step in a broad Russian plan to 'liberate' the Balkans.[1] Historical circumstances, however, dictated otherwise, and Bessarabia remained the only territory inhabited by Romanians under Russian control after Romania's independence, and the failure of the tzars either to occupy all Romanian lands or prevent the establishment of a Romanian nation-state lies at the heart of the Bessarabian problem to this day. Although the territory of current Soviet Moldavia does not correspond to the boundaries of historic Bessarabia, one factor remains unchanged: the majority of Moldavia's inhabitants are still Romanians. And, although Moscow's official parlance still refers to 'Moldavians', the inhabitants are Romanian.

To be sure, the ethnic characterisation of any group is always a hazardous undertaking, for it depends on a multitude of factors which may converge into a separate ethnic identity. Yet in the case of the Moldavians, there can be no doubt, for, according to any conceivable definition of a nation, they can only be considered Romanians: they share exactly the same language, practise the same faith and have the same history. At every conceivable opportunity (in the 1870s, in 1918 and in 1941) the inhabitants of Soviet Moldavia freely opted for union with Romania and considered themselves as Romanian. Furthermore – and despite persistent Russian or Soviet attempts to prove the contrary – Moldavians never sought nor achieved an independent existence as a state. For all Moldavians, there are only two historic experiences: either union with Romania or Russian rule. Soviet Moldavia is, therefore, the only republic in the USSR which has a nation-state outside the country's boundaries; it is a territory without its own, separate nation, a political notion rather than an ethnic reality.[2]

HISTORICAL BACKGROUND

Both Russian and Soviet policies have also been primarily influenced by this basic fact. Throughout the last century – and once it became clear that a Romanian national state would ultimately come into being – the Russian government encouraged the dilution of Bessarabia's Romanian character through the settlement of other ethnic groups. Jews who migrated to the province were granted exemption from military service and the usual discriminatory legislation which applied in other parts of the empire; Bulgarians and Gagauz (a Christian Turkic group) were granted land and financial inducements to settle in the strategically sensitive south of the province. The Orthodox church (whose initial loyalty was to Constantinople) was taken over by the Russian church, and Bessarabia's hugely profitable farms were distributed among the neighbouring Russian nobility which, by the turn of the century, dominated the cultural and political life of the province. This systematic policy of de-nationalisation had one consequence still evident in Soviet Moldavia today. The region's cities became dominated by other ethnic groups (usually Jews in the capital of Chisinau and in Cahul and Balti, sometimes Germans and more often Russians and Ukrainians), while the local Romanians remained confined to the villages. Most of the commercial activities were handled by Jews, most administration by Russians, and the largest share of higher education establishments was frequented by Germans and Jews. From representing roughly 80 per cent of the population in 1812, the Romanian share of Bessarabia's inhabitants sank to 56 per cent a century later. Nevertheless, nationalist stirrings did take place. During the 1905 Russian revolution, the first Romanian-language publications appeared and, concomitantly, the first indications that a Romanian intelligentsia still existed started to be felt. The truth was that, regardless of Russia's policies, Romanian culture continued to exist in neighbouring Romania, and the city of Iasi (the capital of historic Moldavia, only 50 kilometres from the border with Bessarabia) became a Mecca of Romanian culture.

The 1917 upheavals in Russia immediately sparked off a nationalist uprising in Bessarabia as well. However, due to the province's particular circumstances, the Bessarabian revolt was not led by intellectuals, but by peasants and soldiers defecting from the front, and initially assumed the character of a social revolution. For most of the soldiers and peasants who declared an independent 'Moldavian Republic' in 1918, unity with Romania was a poisoned chalice, for the neighbouring state was still ruled by a coalition of boyars and a royal court, a cabal of politicians who represented no one and who only a decade before had suppressed a peasant uprising with great bloodshed.

The revolutionary committees in Chisinau therefore established a parliament, the Sfatul Tarii. Yet this parliament quickly discovered that promises of social reform could not contain nationalist aspirations. Opposition of the local Russian nobility and church was only to be expected; the designs of the Ukrainian leaders (who also engaged at the same time in a fight for the independence of their own state) was not, and came as a great surprise. Torn between the territorial designs of neighbouring Ukraine, the threat of Bolshevik and White Guard forces – both of whom refused to accept Bessarabia's independence – and a state of internal anarchy from other unruly ethnic groups in the province, Sfatul Tarii ultimately asked for Romanian protection. This came in the shape of a massive deployment of troops and, after a short interval, Bessarabia's parliamentary assembly voted for union with Romania.

Much has been written about the significance of this union: official Soviet history claims that the union was 'illegal' since it was decreed by an 'unrepresentative' assembly; Romanians, on the other hand, have always claimed that the union was an 'expression of popular will'.[3] Both views are mistaken. In the atmosphere prevailing throughout Russia at the time, no 'national assembly' could be regarded as wholly representative of the popular will. At the time, it is equally clear that most Bessarabian Romanians accepted the union as legitimate and never questioned it.

Needless to say, difficulties arose: throughout the 1920s and 1930s Bessarabians accused other Romanians of failing to fulfil their initial promise to create a democratic state; Romanians in other provinces regarded the Bessarabians as uncouth and simple peasants who should not be taken seriously. Nevertheless, no one considered the Bessarabians as anything but Romanians.

The Soviet leaders always refused to recognise the union of Bessarabia with Romania, and Moscow's demands for the return of the province poisoned relations between the two states throughout the inter-war period.[4] Negotiations between the two neighbours were held at various locations in the 1920s and 1930s, but all of them failed and, on the eve of the Second World War, Bessarabia remained a contested land.[5] As part of the secret protocol attached to the Nazi–Soviet Pact of 1939,

Bessarabia was assigned to the Soviet sphere of influence[6] and, on 24 June 1940, a Soviet ultimatum was delivered to Romania demanding the immediate cession of the territory. Although Romania did recover Bessarabia again in 1941 (when it invaded the USSR on the coat-tails of the German armies), the province was lost again in 1944 and has remained ever since under Soviet control.

SOVIET POLICIES IN MOLDAVIA

Stalin's policies in Soviet Moldavia were ostensibly very similar to those implemented in other republics at the end of the Second World War. The negation of national culture and the destruction of any form of social organisation outside the Communist Party; the deportations, arrests, executions, deliberately induced famines and other acts of brutality were applied in Soviet Moldavia as well with a rigour which probably claimed the life of one Moldavian out of ten between 1945 and 1953.

However, some features of Soviet policies in the republic were unique, specifically tailored for Moldavia's particular circumstances. The most important was Soviet policy towards the definition of Moldavia's 'nation'. There is considerable evidence that immediately after the incorporation of Bessarabia into the USSR in 1940, the Soviet authorities toyed with the idea of incorporating the territory into the Ukraine; the Ukrainian Communist Party certainly argued that this would provide a solution to Moldavia's problems and many people in Moscow favoured it too. For reasons which are still unclear, Stalin decided otherwise and a Moldavian republic was formed. However, once this decision was taken, the question of the republic's ethnic make-up had to be faced as well and Stalin opted for nothing less than the creation of a separate 'Moldavian' nation. This appeared to promise several long-term advantages: first, it delineated the Moldavian republic from the Ukraine and thus justified the latter's independent existence. More importantly, the 'creation' of a separate Moldavian nation could also sever the connection with neighbouring Romania for good. Finally, the classification of Moldavians as a separate nation also answered another Stalinist policy: that of incorporating only entire nations into the USSR.[7]

As any ethnographer could have suggested, a new nation cannot be created overnight. But ethnographers were not much in demand in Stalin's USSR and, as long as sheer force was what kept the Moldavians under control, the manipulation of their ethnic identity was merely a feeble justification, rather than the rationale of Soviet policies. The nexus of this justification concentrated on the language, as the most perceptible ingredient of any nation. In order to differentiate the Romanian spoken in Moldavia from that spoken in Romania, the

Latin alphabet in which Romanian is written was supplanted by the Cyrillic. Indeed, according to the authorities, it was only the Cyrillic which was 'natural' to Moldavian[8], and literary figures who persisted in using the Latin alphabet were promptly punished for seeking to 'Romanise'[9] a language which they regarded as Slavic in origin.[10]

In cultural affairs, Moldavia was also subjected to some particular policies, all of which were intended to highlight the republic's separate existence from Romania. Like all other Soviet republics, local culture and customs were relegated to a secondary importance, frozen in a showcase of 'folklore' which had little to do with genuine Moldavian traditions. Few dance groups and popular music bands were allowed to operate, and Russian culture was elevated to the role of supreme importance. The republic was portrayed in the official propaganda as the ideal holiday resort, a land of cheap and plentiful wine, merry girls, sun and simple peasants. Chisinau's cultural life was dominated by Russian-language theatres, and Pushkin (who spent a short time in Moldavia) was particularly favoured precisely because he appeared to provide a bridge between Moldavia and Russia's cultural traditions.

However, the authorities in Chisinau had another difficulty: across the frontiers, in independent Romania, indigenous literature continued to be published. Should this be available to the Moldavians, the entire Soviet policy of creating a separate Moldavian nation could have collapsed. For this reason, the importation of Romanian books was strictly controlled. During the period of de-Stalinisation and even during Brezhnev's rule the ban on Romanian literature was relaxed to a certain extent. However, there never was any question of just importing Romanian books, for that would have contradicted the authorities' claim that Moldavian was a separate language. Instead, Romanian authors were selectively published in Moldavia, in the Cyrillic script and only after a political decision at the highest level.[11] History was equally heavily controlled and rewritten. Here, again, the Soviet aim was not simply to show that Moldavia belonged to the USSR. Much more importantly, official historiography sought to 'prove' that Moldavians had nothing to do with neighbouring Romania. Thus, paradoxically, while in many other republics Moscow usually sought to play down their previous independent existence, in Moldavia the authorities fought hard to buttress it.

The fact that these attempts were undertaken in one republic which was never truly independent only made them more ironic. According to the official history, Moldavia was never part of Romania: it was occupied by Ukrainians, Poles and Turks and ultimately 'liberated' by Russians in 1812. The tsarist rule may not have been benign, but it was, on the whole, 'beneficial' by raising local standards of literacy and by laying the foundations of local industry. These industrial enterprises led to the formation of a 'working class' who seized power in 1917, only to be crushed by Romanian 'occupiers'. After twenty years of this occupation and at the first possible moment, the first workers' state came to the 'liberation' of the province and since then, the 'Moldavian' nation has lived happily ever after.[12]

To any experienced observer, it should have been clear that the laughable attempts to create a nation with its own language, history and identity could not succeed under the best of circumstances. However, the clumsy application of the Soviet policies in Moldavia made their failure clearly inevitable. In reality, Moscow was pursuing not one, but two inherently contradictory aims. On the one hand, it sought to buttress the Moldavians' sense of identity, as the only means for severing their connection with Romania. Yet at the same time, the authorities could not forget that the creation of a strong local identity might not, after all, be to their advantage either. In this sense, therefore, Moldavia was squeezed between two Soviet policies: the traditional one of suppressing any national consciousness as much as possible, and the particular one of encouraging Moldavian peculiarities at the expense of the Romanian connection. As a result, none of the Soviet policies in Moldavia were implemented to their logical conclusion.

In language questions, for instance, the imposition of the Cyrillic was coupled with a steady reduction in the teaching of Romanian in all the republic's schools and the elimination of the language from the republican administration. As a result, more than 40 per cent of those who claimed to speak 'Moldavian' also admitted that they did not have complete command of the language, according to the preliminary figures of the 1989 census. Moldavia's cultural policies also displayed the same 'stop – go' mentality. On the one hand, the availability of Romanian literature was heavily restricted while, at the same time, local Moldavians were also discouraged from publishing their works. The result was a domination of everything Russian: not even one Moldavian dramatist could be found to grace with his name one of the local theatres; in the republican Central Library (inelegantly named Krupskaya) not more than one-third of all holdings had anything remotely to do with local culture and literature,[13] while regional libraries often had not even one Moldavian book.[14]

Finally, the rewriting of history was equally stunted: while the authorities remained eager to emphasise that Moldavia was not part of the territories which ultimately formed independent Romania, they were also keen to show that the 'Moldavians', on whose behalf the republic was ostensibly created, were themselves not the first inhabitants of the land. Strikingly, the entire history of the area was written not by local Moldavians, but by Russians or Ukrainians, whose personal, sterotyped perceptions served as the icing on layers of mystifications. Thus, Moldavian children learned at school that their republic was a land of migrants, of boorish peasants and superstitious priests, a *tabula rasa* of civilisation only saved with the arrival of Slav settlers. Russians and Ukrainians dominated the Moldavian Academy of

Sciences and its History Institute and the best professional position for a young Moldavian historian was a country primary school. Only in Moldavia was it still possible as late as 1988 to write a historical thesis based on no primary sources and without the slightest knowledge of the local language; only in Moldavia was it still normal to encounter during the 1980s official historians who fervently argued that their republic was 'multi-national' even before the political concept of the nation became a consideration in international relations.

The disastrous results of this haphazard policy of encouraging and at the same time discouraging the creation of the Moldavian nation were not immediately apparent for three reasons. First, as long as neighbouring Romania was ruled by a Communist regime which was equally subservient to Moscow's interest, Moldavians were kept in check by the Russian rulers and their ostensible nation-state at the same time. Second, as long as local cadres continued to be imported from Russia and the Ukraine and the majority of Moldavians remained confined to their villages, the possibility of an organised opposition remained remote. Finally, as long as Moscow's rule in the republic was conducted with an iron fist, any opposition could be crushed immediately.[15] Yet the greatest failure of the authorities was not to realise that none of these three facts is immutable or permanent, and that, in the absence of any alternative policy, all that would happen the moment Moldavians were allowed their say would be a veritable social explosion.

Soviet control over Romania was the first to go: in the 1960s, Romania's Communists (for reasons quite independent of the Moldavian question) initiated a policy of differentiation from the Soviet Union and an opening to the West. President Nicolae Ceauşescu's rule remained that of a particularly vicious and nepotistic Balkan family, but it was remarkably effective in manipulating Romanian nationalism in general and traditional hatred of the Russians in particular. Romania's challenge was never considered serious enough to merit a Soviet invasion, precisely because Ceauşescu's policies never seriously challenged the rule of the Party in that country or Moscow's interests in Eastern Europe. Nevertheless, the estrangement between the two states meant that Romanian nationalism became a force to be reckoned with in Soviet Moldavia, where it found a more receptive audience. Throughout Brezhnev's rule more and more Moldavians migrated to the towns, and, especially in the 1970s, the local press and literary life were slowly 'nationalised'. However – and unlike other republics – this process continued by default in spite of, rather than because of, a conscious official policy. Moldavian intellectuals started to emerge; Moldavian economists and skilled labourers left the land and found opportunities in towns. Yet they could not be accommodated in the republic's administration which remained firmly under Russian and Ukrainian control. By the early 1980s, it was clear that nationalist grievances, combined with economic difficulties, created a potentially explosive situation, but the local Party leadership did nothing until Mikhail Gorbachev removed the third and last instrument in their traditional policy: that of the persistent use of coercion.

Unlike any other republic in the Soviet Union, the Moldavian leadership was bereft of any vehicle for conducting a dialogue with its population: it could not encourage Moldavian nationalism, for it feared that this would spill into demands for unification with Romania; it could not encourage purely regional pride, for Moldavia was never an independent state and therefore had none. The Moldavians were left in a state of limbo, a dead end which precluded any compromise but also offered no alternative. Moldavia has the dubious distinction of having been governed by two men who subsequently became the USSR's leaders,[16] and the local Party, commonly entitled the 'Moldavian Mafia', was assumed to have good contacts in Moscow. It was not only the collapse of Brezhnev's cabal in 1985 which stunned the Moldavian leaders; much more important for them was the fact that Gorbachev's policies were demanding a dialogue with the local population. Chisinau deemed this impossible and actually dangerous, and it is clear that Simeon Grossu, the republican party leader, remained in power until 1989 precisely because Moscow was persuaded that Moldavia might be a special case which was best treated by old, Brezhnevite hands.

MOLDAVIA UNDER GORBACHEV

The Rise of Organised Opposition

It is undoubtedly true that Moldavia was one of the last republics to stir under Gorbachev's policies. This is due to many reasons, among which the republic's continued agricultural character, the comparatively low number of Moldavian intellectuals and the ethnically mixed nature of the republic's urban areas are clearly important. Nevertheless, by the end of 1987, some members of the local Writers' Union put forward vague demands for political liberalisation which, although quickly brushed aside, ultimately created the mass opposition movement during the summer of 1988.[17] One of its most striking features is not that it started by advancing cultural and political demands (for this was the case in most other republics) but, rather, that demands for changes in the economic mechanism were entirely absent from the opposition's platform.

The reasons for this are clear enough: while the opposition movements in the Baltic republics knew very well from the start that only by controlling their economy, environment and political administration would they stand a chance of prising power from Moscow, their Moldavian counterparts had a much simpler aim. The aim was nothing less than the destruction of Moscow's artificial creation of a Moldavian nation, and this was achieved in a very simple and effective way. Essentially, all the opposition movements did was to turn their rulers' justifications against them: if the Moldavians had their own language, why should this not be the state language in the republic and why should it not be taught at all levels? And, if Moldavians were indeed a nation, why should their right to their land be doubted and their culture circumscribed? There is no doubt that the Moldavian intellectuals understood very well the difficulties hiding behind their seemingly naïve questions. In essence they were challenging the entire official policy of forty years, which was based on a delicate balance between the appearance of a nation and the reality of Russian domination. And in reality, Moldavians were convinced that whichever tactic Chisinau ultimately adopted, the result would be the same: a reassertion of their true ethnic identity.

It cannot be assumed that, at least at the beginning of their struggle, the Moldavian activists had any clear idea of what that ethnic identity would entail. Rather, their demands were much more basic and entailed the affirmation of their attributes as a nation. However, once these were obtained, it quickly became clear to most opposition groups that their nation and their republic could not be defined without a reference to the Romanians and their independent state. The same process operated in East Germany as well and essentially for the same basic reason: in the search for obvious attributes of their separate nations, both the East Germans and the Moldavians discovered – sometimes to their own dismay – that these simply did not exist.

Thus, although the Moldavian popular movement of opposition started by borrowing freely from the political platforms of their counterparts in other Soviet republics, it ended up with a policy which was entirely its own and which can only lead (if continued on the present scale) to demands for union with Romania. From the viewpoint of the authorities, therefore, the worse has already happened: far from acquiring a new pride in their republic, the Moldavians are drawn to everything Romanian. Yet the responsibility for this phenomenon is squarely that of the Soviet authorities, who never considered it necessary to fill their fiction of a 'Moldavian' nation with any real content.

The Battle for a Language and Culture

It was to be expected that the issue of the language should provide the first conflict with the authorities. Language policies were at the heart of Soviet attempts to create a separate nation, and the language has always provided the most potent rallying symbol for all Romanians. By 1988, the Moldavian opposition groups advanced three demands:

that Romanian should be recognised as the state's language; that it should again be written in the Latin alphabet; and that the government should acknowledge that 'Moldavian' and Romanian are one and the same tongue.

The first skirmish was conducted along predictable lines: the government asserted that a return to the Latin alphabet was unnecessary and unworkable; the opposition replied that only the Latin alphabet could render the language's sounds accurately. Yet both protagonists knew only too well that their clash was hardly a linguistic one: its essence was the definition of the nation, a definition on which everything else would ultimately depend. At the beginning, Simeon Grossu reacted to these demands in a predictable manner, by accusing the opposition groups of 'nationalism', 'separatism' and other heinous crimes and by refusing to contemplate any change.[18] However, his position quickly changed when it became clear that some concessions would have to be made. As a consequence, the reintroduction of the Latin alphabet was accepted, but the adoption of Romanian as state language continued to be rejected, with an explanation which revealed the true extent of the leadership's fears. According to Grossu, Romanian could not be considered a state language, for the Moldavian republic was 'multi-national', and any move according preference to any tongue would automatically discriminate against others.[19] To the Moldavian opposition movement Grossu's stance was clear enough: just when the population started taking the government's concept of the Moldavian nation seriously, the government tried to discard it.

The bitter conflict which developed was not without its irony for, out of the opposition's three linguistic demands, the adoption of Romanian as a state language was certainly not the most provocative from the government's viewpoint. Much more serious was the demand for an official acknowledgement that 'Moldavian' and Romanian are one and the same language. Yet it was precisely on this issue that government and popular opposition managed to reach a swift compromise. The reasons why this compromise could be reached are clear enough: once the use of the Cyrillic alphabet was discarded, it was obvious that the fiction about the existence of a 'Moldavian' language could simply not be maintained. At the same time, leading members of the opposition were also aware of the fact that to extract an official admission from the government on this point was of little practical value and amounted to a dissipation of their energies. The 'linguistic identity' question (as it came to be known) was essentially won by the opposition, and all that remained was to create a suitable mechanism through which the government could accept defeat without undue loss of face.

The 'identity issue' was therefore assigned to a special committee of the Moldavian Academy of Sciences, who reported, to no one's surprise, that 'Moldavian' and Romanian were, indeed, identical.[20]

However, since this report was not presented to the Supreme Soviet, and did not form part of the language legislation, it allowed the government to continue referring to the 'Moldavian' language rather than to Romanian. The final version of the Languages Law mentions 'the Moldavian-Romanian linguistic identity which really exists'. As part of the compromise, this statement is contained in the preamble to the Act. The government has since tried to dismiss the importance of the clause by suggesting that it only applies to 'the Moldavians in the republic and the Romanians resident elsewhere in the USSR';[21] Moldavian intellectuals, well aware that their authorities are merely shielding behind an even bigger nonsense that before, are happy to ridicule this stance and refer to their language as Romanian.[22]

Yet, on the subject of the state language, the battle continued throughout 1989 and led to a progressive radicalisation of all ethnic groups in the republic. For an increasingly desperate leadership, this question was its last stand. Once it became clear that the notion of a Moldavian nation would actually mean something, the authorities in Chisinau therefore rushed to limit its consequences, and the official assertions about the need to protect the rights of other 'nations' in the republic grew in direct proportion to the opposition's linguistic demands. By the summer of 1989, Chisinau was confronted with a veritable surge of dissent and a united Moldavian Popular Front which included not just urban intellectuals but also workers. On the 28 August 1989 they filled the streets of the capital. The presence of half a million demonstrators surprised even the opposition.

No compromise – even one offered by Gorbachev on the telephone to members of the republic's Supreme Soviet which by then was in an almost permanent session – seemed to work. The debates in the Supreme Soviet encapsulated the entire problem: while Eugen Sobor, Moldavia's Culture Minister, spoke of the imperative to respect the language of the nation which 'gave its name to this republic',[23] Russian deputies complained against discrimination of 'other nations, living in compact formations throughout Moldavia'.[24] After a few weeks when the republic seemed to be slipping out of anyone's control, the Supreme Soviet ultimately voted a law which enshrined Romanian as the state language, while according other ethnic groups the right to use their own language in regions in which they live. Nevertheless, all members of the administration and of local authorities would be obliged to learn Romanian and speak it at all times. There is little doubt that the Moldavians had won their most important victory. This had little to do with the language issue *per se;* rather, it amounted to extracting an open admission from their government that the republic was theirs and theirs alone, and that all other ethnic groups in Moldavia were not 'nations', but rather ethnic minorities whose rights should be respected but whose claims could not be considered as equal to the interests of the majority. The concept of a 'Moldavian' at last had a meaning.

The Disintegration of Party Control

The prolonged dispute over language questions affected all political bodies in the country. Simeon Grossu, the Party leader who swore not to consider Romanian as a state language and who claimed that to return to the Latin alphabet would mean rendering the entire population illiterate, was thoroughly discredited in the eyes of everyone. The Moldavians considered him beyond the pale; the Russians regarded his climb-down as little short of treason. In the cities of Tiraspol and Bender – major centres for ethnic Russians in the republic – general strikes were declared and the entire railway network was paralysed for almost a month. The Russians openly declared their strikes to be political and the local soviets in the two cities vowed not to apply the language law, with the unreserved support of the regional Party leader. Chisinau, however, did nothing, and the pace of protests accelerated, with the Moldavians concentrating on the rehabilitation of their literature and history. The Popular Front began demanding that restrictions on the importation of Romanian literature be rescinded and that their republic's history should not be falsified. The government responded with a pledge to enact a 'complex plan of cultural development' which, by the year 2005, would supposedly answer all the population's needs.[25] Yet Moldavia's intellectuals quickly perceived that, irrespective of their government, they did have an alternative route to speed up their cultural revival.

Unlike the citizens of any other Soviet republic, the Moldavians did not have to revive an indigenous culture, nor wait for years until local writers saw their works in print; they could simply publish Romanian literature, easily accessible across the border. And, since the authorities continued to refuse any direct importation of Romanian books, either by pleading poverty[26] or by citing 'technical difficulties',[27] Moldavians simply started publishing them in their literary periodicals. A poem by Mihai Eminescu, Romania's foremost poet, was published in all its versions not merely once, but many times[28] and in most periodicals as well.[29] The poem, imbued with hatred of anything foreign and particularly anything Russian, needed no explanation and remained one of the most evocative symbols of Romanian unity. In effect, the Party lost control over the entire press: the Russian and Romanian-language versions of the Party daily are constantly at loggerheads with each other and represent diametrically opposed views on almost any subject; the majority of the other papers devote the majority of their issues to nationalist and religious symbols. No amount of warnings against 'undue interest in foreign countries' – a jibe clearly aimed at Romania – has worked and, most spectacularly, Grossu even failed to dismiss the adventurous editor of the Party daily when the latter published the text of an opposition letter without explicit permission.[30]

Yet even the restoration of Romanian literature was insignificant

compared to the attacks of the opposition against the official interpretations of Moldavia's history. The quest for establishing the 'truth'
about Moldavia's past could only lead – as everyone was perfectly
aware from the start – to questioning the incorporation of the republic
into the USSR. Similar movements took place throughout the union,
but in Moldavia's case the demands for the rewriting of history
were particularly virulent because they were led by a large number
of young and competent historians who were constantly deprived of
useful employment and scholarly pursuits. They rebelled not only
against the falsehoods advanced by the authorities as historical facts,
but also against the entire historical establishment in the republic which,
as already noted, was dominated by members of other ethnic groups.
Disorientated and unable to offer any clear response, the Moldavian
authorities sought to deflect this movement by rehabilitating former
Communists exterminated by Stalin during various purges and re-
working arcane explanations about the 'development of social classes in
Moldavia'.[31] Yet this failed to project an image of change, for the simple
reason that the overwhelming majority of the Moldavian Communists
before the Second World War were members of other ethnic groups
and usually had little connection with the republic. The rehabilitation
of people unknown to anyone born in the last forty years was therefore
no substitute for what the Moldavian historians really wanted discussed:
how was their territory incorporated in the USSR and how was the local
population treated under Soviet rule?

The crucial conflict revolved around the interpretation of the
Molotov–Ribbentrop Pact. On this issue, Chisinau's predicament
was ostensibly eased by the Kremlin's decision in the summer of
1989 to admit that a secret protocol dividing European territories
had actually been signed between Nazi Germany and the Soviet Union
fifty years earlier. However, this official admission, far from allowing
the Moldavian leadership room for manoeuvre, actually compounded
its difficulties. Moscow could admit to the existence of this protocol
and still claim that the Baltic states freely joined the USSR; the same
argument could not be applied to Moldavia, which was never an
independent state and which therefore could never be considered as
having 'opted' for incorporation into the USSR. But there was worse
to come. Essentially, the Soviet ultimatum delivered to Romania in
1940 did not speak of 'Moldavians' at all. Instead, it referred to the
inhabitants as 'basically Ukrainians' whose 'wish' to be united with
their brethren in the Ukraine would be satisfied through the cession of
the Bessarabian territory. Furthermore, the ultimatum also demanded
half of the Romanian province of Bukovina – which was never part of
the Russian empire – not for ethnic or historical reasons, but simply
as a compensation which Romania had to pay for its twenty year
'occupation' of 'Soviet territory in Moldavia'. Finally, the territory
seized from Romania in 1940 did not coincide with the final frontiers

of the Moldavian republic: northern and southern parts were annexed to neighbouring Ukraine and the latter ceded some territory to Moldavia. In sum, therefore, the 1940 Soviet ultimatum demanded Romania's territory on behalf of a nation which at the time the Kremlin did not believe existed, and led to the creation of a republic which should have never been there and which did not correspond to Moldavia's current frontiers. No wonder Chisinau resolved to say nothing on this matter, for no reasoning could have explained these uncomfortable truths.

The government's inability to even begin confronting its historical legacy led to the creation of a unique Moldavian dissident organisation: the Association of Historians, which seeks to open the state archives and publish the 'historical truth'.[32] As a result, Moldavia has two histories: the official one which remains unchanged and the unofficial one, published in instalments in the literary press. Chisinau continues to attack 'falsifiers of history' and threatens dissidents with KGB action,[33] while the independent historians continue to publish hereto forbidden documents, all of which challenge the presence of Soviet power on their land.[34] And, whereas in most other Soviet republics access to archival material has improved, in Moldavia restrictions have intensified. Items recently locked away include all the Romanian-language newspapers published between the wars and even the most ephemeral papers of Moldavia's short-lived parliament, the Sfatul Tarii.[35] Knowing that there could be no going back to the old historical justifications but unable to contemplate any change, the government has essentially retreated into its own shell: it does not refute the historical studies put forward by Moldavians, but nor does it accept them.

The same attitude was adopted towards the problem of the republic's flag and national symbols. One of the first demands of the Popular Front was for a change in Moldavia's flag, from the stereotyped Soviet version bequeathed by Stalin to all republics to a flag which would represent the Moldavians' true 'heritage'. The Popular Front had no doubt which flag could achieve this aim: no other than the Romanian vertical tricolour of red, yellow and blue. Romanian tricolours started appearing in the late spring of 1989 and, very quickly, spread throughout the republic. Displayed on lapels, cars, buildings and present at all demonstrations, the tricolour became the most visible symbol of dissent and at the same time the most potent example of Moldavia's historic connection with Romania.

At least on this issue, the authorities moved quickly and established a special committee in order to discover Moldavia's 'real' flag. The committee searched through historical documents at home and as far afield as Greece and Austria, yet in vain: according to all available evidence, Moldavia never had a flag of its own; it either employed the Romanian flag or the Soviet one. Yet this did not prevent the government from offering various compromises. One such compromise promised the adoption of the red and blue colours only;[36] another suggested retaining the current flag with the addition of yellow (in order to answer the opposition's demands for the inclusion of all the three colours).[37] Needless to say, this 'multi-chrome policy' was nothing but a belated attempt to sustain the former policy of differentiation. Indeed, Moldavian officials were even terrified of mentioning the name of Romania in public. During a televised discussion on the subject, officials merely argued that they could not accept the tricolour as Moldavia's flag, for 'it already represented another sovereign state'. Asked by the television presenter – with some mischief in mind – which state that might be, the official quickly obliged: it was 'the African republic of Chad'.[38]

Most Moldavians understood that they had reached yet another stalemate. And so, after having two interpretations of the Moldavian nation and two versions of its history, Moldavia also acquired two flags: the one flown by the government from public buildings and the one flown by most people during their activities. The dysfunction between the official and the real was complete, and it had catastrophic results on the life of the republic. In one year, Moldavia's crime rate climbed to the highest in the USSR; its economic performance plummeted to the tenth place in the union and barely above that of the Asian Soviet republics.[39] After length strikes and factory lockouts, all production plans were in tatters and all Moldavia's ethnic groups decided to take matters into their own hands. The small Gagauz minority, emboldened by the government's assertions that it was a separate 'nation', promptly declared the Gagauz an 'autonomous republic'[40] and the Russians followed suit by establishing their claim to a 'Dniester republic'.

The government, meanwhile, continued to behave as though nothing was happening: it ordered a military parade for the October Revolution day, and it was genuinely shocked to find out that this resulted in widespread riots for days thereafter.[41] Having survived longer than any other Brezhnevite republican leader but failing to quell the nationalist unrest, Simeon Grossu was clearly a spent force. Yet Moscow's choice for his replacement was not another man from the republic: aware that the Moldavian leadership was hopelessly split and discredited and remembering the sensitivity of the Moldavian question, the Kremlin imposed Petru Luchniskyi, an ethnic Moldavian who spent most of his political career in other parts of the USSR. There can be little doubt that Luchniskyi's task is very heavy indeed: he inherited a republic which has yet to find a purpose and rules over a nation which does not consider itself as such.

Soviet Moldavia as a Case of Irredentism

Nothing prepared Party leader Luchniskyi or his masters in Moscow for what followed in December 1989. The Romanian Revolution started with the removal of Nicolae Ceauşescu's dictatorship in that country; its long-term effect would be the elimination of Communism in Romania and the re-emergence of the 'Moldavian question' as an important dispute between the two neighbouring states.

There is little doubt that Moldavia represents a classic irredentist situation: its population is manifestly identical in language, traditions, religion and culture with that of Romania. Furthermore, there is a territorial continuity between the borders of the nation-state and its 'unredeemed' territory, in this case, Moldavia. Finally, a long-standing historical connection is complemented by a clear, if unstated, desire for unification between the nation-state and its 'unredeemed' people. In fact, the Moldavian situation could only have been contained in the last forty years with one instrument: the threat or use of force. It was force which prevented Moldavian nationalism from manifesting itself, and it was Ceauşescu's dictatorship which prevented Romanians from expressing their desire to help the Moldavians. At least for the moment, the direct threat of the use of force has been removed from both Romania and the USSR.

In every irredentist situation, there are three actors: the nation-state, the unredeemed ethnic group, and the state which possesses the unredeemed territory. The latter is usually reactive: it is interested in limiting as far as possible the contacts between its unredeemed people and their nation state, and it therefore pursues an essentially defensive policy intended to preserve a territorial status quo. This is precisely the policy which the Soviet Union has undertaken under Gorbachev. And, as long as Nicolae Ceauşescu ruled in neighbouring Romania, it was also the policy which the Romanians adhered to. Despite his increasingly shrill attacks against Gorbachev's economic and political reforms, the former Romanian ruler was careful to distance himself from any claims on Moldavia, for obvious reasons. First, it was clear that if Romania advanced any such claims, Moscow could encourage the Hungarians to advance similar claims to Romanian territory in Transylvania. More importantly, the nationalism which Ceauşescu practised was one guided from above and manipulated by his regime. Yet the nationalism which the Moldavians promoted was one that grew from below, with strong religious and popular overtones, precisely the kind which Ceauşescu always repressed. Finally, the Romanian ruler understood perfectly well that the Moldavians were not only challenging Russian rule; they were also attacking dictatorial methods of government and Communist power. For all these reasons, Ceauşescu's Romania simply ignored the rebirth of Moldavian nationalism and actually rebuffed Soviet offers to open the borders between the two states.[42] Romania also reduced its imports of Moldavian literature and a veritable 'Great Wall of China' went up on the Romanian border, frustrating any Moldavian attempt to establish better contacts with their kith and kin.[43] Ceauşescu's stance changed only when the Romanian leader became isolated both at home and abroad. Thus, at his Party Congress in November 1989, Ceauşescu openly called for the elimination of the 'consequences' of the Molotov – Ribbentrop Pact, a clear reference to the redrawing of frontiers between his state and the USSR.[44] Yet, even this reference hardly amounted to a change of heart, for Ceauşescu still viewed Moldavia as essentially an instrument – rather than an object – in his wider battle with the Soviet Union.

These considerations were wiped out with the Romanian Revolution in December 1989. From the start, the overthrow of Ceauşescu evoked an instant response in Moldavia, whose citizens sent vast quantities of food and medical aid to the Romanian revolutionaries. Furthermore, in the heat of the revolution, many Moldavian nationalists crossed the river separating the two states, and immediately voiced demands for unification with Romania.[45] The provisional authorities in Bucharest – realising how sensitive the issue was – remained noticeably coy about mentioning such developments, preferring instead to refer to broad Soviet support for their struggle against the dictator. Nevertheless, the newly freed Romanian press had no such compunction and news items from neighbouring Moldavia became a regular feature.[46] And, despite the fact that from Bucharest's viewpoint the issue of Moldavia can only complicate Soviet–Romanian relations at a time when Soviet economic support is needed most, it is obvious that no Romanian government would be able to prevent the conflict from being raised. Political activists in the Romanian city of Iasi consider this issue most important, and intellectuals in most other Romanian cities have already drafted proposals for union with their brethren in the Soviet Union.[47]

The Soviet authorities, realising that the problem of Moldavia can no longer be avoided, have resolved instead to meet it head on. Thus, while promising the Romanian revolutionary government additional financial and technical support (and thereby reminding Bucharest of its economic dependence on its mighty northern neighbour), Moscow has also lessened travel restrictions at its frontiers and has promised to allow Moldavians greater cultural rights. These measures are essentially only palliatives, intended to stabilise rather than solve an explosive situation, for the truth still is that neither Moscow, nor Bucharest, can control the Moldavian problems any longer. Short of the use of force, it is clear that the initiative is in the hands of the Moldavians themselves. Regardless of the arrangements which may be reached between the Soviet Union and Romania, regardless of the understanding that territorial changes cannot be contemplated, the Moldavians would probably not cease to express their own aspirations. They are unlikely to be satisfied with 'greater' freedoms and are unlikely to be grateful to Gorbachev for contributing to their national emancipation. Nationalism was always an irrational concept, more a matter of feeling rather than a question of cool-headed judgement. The chances are that once

Romanian nationalism has been rekindled, it would not be easily contained.

NOTES

1. G. F. Jewsbury 'An overview of the history of Bessarabia' in M. Manoliu-Manea (ed.) *The Tragic Plight of a Border Area: Bessarabia and Bucovina* (Humboldt State University Press, CA 1983), pp. 1–18.
2. In this chapter, the terms 'Moldavian' or 'Moldavia' are used purely for reasons of brevity.
3. I. G. Pelivan *The Union of Bessarabia with the Mother Country* (Paris 1920). This work was prepared for the Paris Peace Conference which met at the time.
4. See, for example, V. V. Tilea *Actiunea Diplomatica a Romaniei* (Sibiu, 1925), pp. 221 ff.; for a not too objective discussion of the legal ramifications of the problems, see A. Popovici *The Political Status of Bessarabia* (Washington, Randsdell, 1931).
5. The most promising attempts at mediation between the Soviet Union and Romania are documented in W. M. Bacon *Behind Closed Doors: Secret Papers on the Failure of Romanian–Soviet Negotiations, 1931–1932* (Stanford, CA, 1979).
6. Despite the recent revelations in the Soviet press, the fullest documentation is still US Department of State *Nazi–Soviet Relations, 1939–1941: Documents from the Archives of the German Foreign Office* (Washington, DC 1948).
7. The union of all strands of the Ukrainian nation under Soviet control was one of the principal reasons for Stalin's annexation of Czechoslovak, Hungarian and additional Romanian territory in 1945.
8. See *Nistru* Nov. 1988.
9. *Moldova Socialista,* 17 June 1989.
10. A. Lazarev, *Moldovanskaya Sovetskaya gosudarstvenost i Bessarabskiy vopros* (Chisinau, Cartea Moldoveneasca 1974), pp. 739–42.
11. For an example of the selection, see G. Cozonac and A. Borodin (eds) *Literatura artistica editata in RSS Moldoveneasca, 1924–1964* (Chisinau, Cartea Moldoveneasca 1967).
12. *Kommunisticheskoye Podpolyie Bessarabyii (1914–1944 gg). Sbornik dokumentov ii materialov* (Chisinau, vol. I, 1987; vol. 2, 1988); and *Sovyetskaya Moldavyia* 21 June 1988.
13. *Invatamintul Public* 29 Sept. 1989.
14. *Moldova Socialista* 2 Sept. 1988.
15. N. Lupan *Basarabia: Colonizari si Asimilare* (Madrid, Editura Carpati 1979), pp. 17–20; M. Bruchis *Nations-Nationalities-People: A Study of the Nationalities Policy of the Communist Party in Soviet Moldavia* (New York, Columbia University Press, 1984), p. 91.
16. Leonid Brezhnev ruled the republic as First Secretary in the early 1950s; Konstantin Chernenko was Moldavia's chief ideological secretary for a long period.

17. B. Nahaylo 'National ferment in Moldavia' Radio Liberty Research, RL 32/88, 24 Jan. 1988.
18. *Moldova Socialista* 11 Nov. 1988.
19. J. Eyal 'Soviet Moldavia: history catches up and a "separate language disappears" Radio Liberty, Report on the USSR, vol. 1 (8), 24 Feb. 1989, pp. 25–9.
20. *Limba si Literatura Moldoveneasca* no. 2 (April–June 1989), p. 15.
21. *Moldova Socialista* 3 Sept. 1989.
22. *Literatura si Arta* 13 July 1989, p. 8.
23. *Moldova Socialista* 5 Sept. 1989.
24. *Moldova Socialista* 29 Aug. 1989.
25. *Moldova Socialista* 9 Oct. 1988.
26. A paltry additional sum of only 32,000 roubles was allocated for the purchase of Romanian literature for the whole of 1989: *Literatura si Arta* 29 June 1989.
27. *Nistru* April 1989, pp. 85–7.
28. *Nistru* June 1989, pp. 33–43.
29. See, for instance, *Tinerimea Moldovei* 10 Sept. 1989.
30. *Literatura si Arta* 25 May 1989.
31. *Comunistul Moldovei* April 1989, pp. 92–4.
32. *Invatamintul Public* 21 June 1989.
33. *Orizontul* Aug. 1989, p. 69.
34. On the events of 1812, see *Literatura si Arta* 10 Aug. 1989; on 1918, see *Moldova Socialista* 16 Aug. 1989; on the interwar period, the most notable articles were published in *Moldova Socialista* 18 and 27 Aug. 1989; on the events of 1940, see ibid., 23 Aug. 1989 as well as every issue of *Literatura si Arta* since August 1989.
35. *Tinerimea Moldovei* 8 Sept. 1989.
36. *Moldova Socialista* 16 April 1989.
37. *Moldova Socialista* 28 July 1989.
38. *Literatura si Arta* 13 July 1989. Chad does, indeed, have an identical tricolour flag.
39. *The Economist* 23 Sept. 1989, p. 70.
40. *Moldova Socialista* 6 Dec. 1989.
41. *Moldova Socialista* 9 and 11 Nov. 1989.
42. *Moldova Socialista* 11, 24 and 27 May 1989; *Nistru*, April 1989, pp. 79–80.
43. *Literatura si Arta*, 17 Aug. 1989.
44. *Scinteia*, 21 Nov. 1989.
45. *Le Monde*, 3 Jan. 1990.
46. *Scinteia Poporului*, 23 Dec. 1989; *Romania Libera*, 27 Dec. 1989.
47. *The Times*, 5 Jan. 1990; *Independent*, 8 Jan. 1990.

PART III

Transcaucasia

Transcaucasia is a small but relatively densely populated area separated from Russia by the Caucasian Mountains and bordered on each side by the Black and Caspian seas. It is divided into three republics: Armenia, Azerbaijan and Georgia. Although formed as individual republics in 1920, in March 1922 all three were incorporated into the newly established Transcaucasian Socialist Federative Soviet Republic, which lasted until 1936. Since then each has constituted a separate union republic. In 1989, the population of the region stood at 15.8 million.

Culturally the region can legitimately claim to contain the most ancient cultures in the Soviet Union. Each of the three major nationalities, the Armenians, Azerbaijanis and Georgians, have their own distinctive language; whereas Armenians and Georgians have been Christian since the third century, the Turkic-speaking Azerbaijanis are Shiite Muslim. Transcaucasia's geo-strategic location at the crossroads of Asia and Europe has also resulted in subjugation to Persian, Turkish and Russian rule. As part of the Soviet federation, the region's economic development has been achieved without the runaway industrialisation experienced by many other national republics, which has also limited Russian immigration, making Transcaucasia the least ethnically Russian of the non-Russian periphery. Both the Georgians and Armenians enjoy a standard of living well above average.

Transcaucasia is also the homeland of a number of other nationalities, with the Abkhazians and South Ossetians, as well as the Adzharians (Muslim Georgians) having their own territorial-administrative status. Present territorial arrangements also reflect the past difficulties of drawing boundaries according to strict national criteria (Figure 2). Consequently, the predominantly Azerbaijani community of the Nakhichevan ASSR, although administered by Azerbaijan, is found within the Armenian republic, while the Armenian majority of Mountainous Karabakh (or Nagorno-Karabakh ASSR) is also administered as part of Azerbaijan. National rivalries and tensions, fuelled by religious, territorial and ethnic divisions, are longstanding, most notably between Muslim Azerbaijanis and Christian Armenians, Georgians and Abkhazians, and between Azerbaijanis and Georgians.

It has been Transcaucasia which provided the first major test for the Gorbachev administration of how to handle the national question, with the region experiencing a series of general strikes, demonstrations and level of ethnic violence hitherto unknown in the Soviet Union. At the forefront has been the issue of territorial ownership of Nagorno-Karabakh, triggered off in February 1988 by the Nagorno Soviet calling for their enclave's accession to Armenia. In April 1989, the focus of attention switched to Tbilisi, the capital of Georgia, when, following an escalation of tensions between Abkhazians and Georgians, Russian troops were sent to disperse demonstrators calling for greater autonomy for the Georgian republic.

FIGURE 2: TRANSCAUCASIA

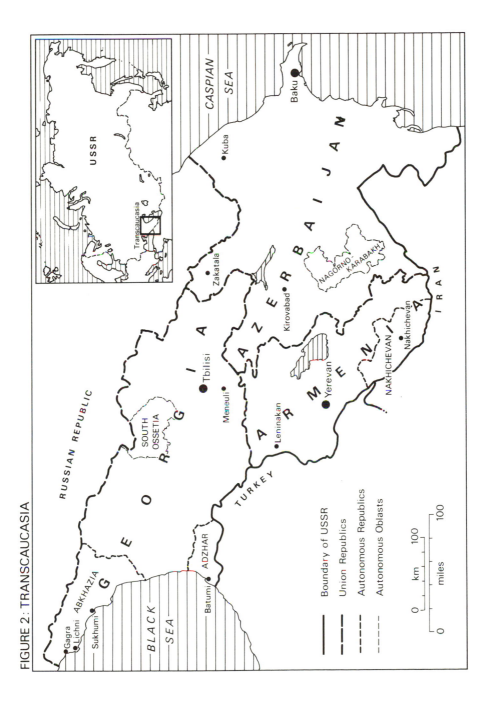

Boundary of USSR

Union Republics

Autonomous Republics

Autonomous Oblasts

CHAPTER NINE

Armenians

Edmund M. Herzig

BACKGROUND

The first historical records of a people, 'the Armenians', and their country, 'Armenia', date back to the middle of the first millennium BC, but the survival of the Armenian people to the present day, when so many of the other ancient nations of the region have disappeared, was a result of later developments: the conversion to Christianity around AD 300, and about a century later the creation of the Armenian alphabet, and with it a distinct Armenian literary language and culture. The Christian faith and the Armenian language have been the cornerstones of national identity ever since, and the experience of history has shown that whenever Armenians have abandoned their church, assimilation in the larger and more powerful communities around them has been quick to follow.

Armenia's history has been a succession of wars, conquests and partitions. The country's geographical position has made it both a natural bridge for conquering armies, and borderland between powerful states centred on the Iranian and Anatolian plateaux. Occasionally parts of Armenia have achieved a temporary partial independence between powerful neighbours, but such interludes have been rare as well as brief. The Roman empire and Sassanian Iran fought over Armenia, then Byzantium and the Arab Caliphate, before the Seljuq Turks conquered the whole country in the eleventh century. Thereafter, there was no independent Armenian state in historic Greater Armenia until 1918. The Seljuq armies were followed by those of Ghengis Khan and Timur, each bringing new massacres, the flight of more of the Armenian population, and the loss of land to growing numbers of Turkish nomads.

Between the fifteenth and seventeenth centuries, Turkey and Iran fought over Armenia and partitioned it into western and eastern halves, a division given permanence by the development of distinct western and eastern Armenian languages. In the nineteenth century tsarist Russian won eastern Armenia from Iran, and then part of western

Armenia from the Ottomans. As the century progressed, the already fragile and complex ethnic jigsaw of the Ottoman empire and Russian Transcaucasia began to break up with the emergence of Western-style, secular nationalism among Turks, Armenians and the other peoples of the region, nationalism that brought with it a new element of overt racism, and new territorial ambitions to secure national homelands. Nineteenth-century Armenian nationalism was mainly restricted to the educated and progressive elites of the big cities, particularly Istanbul and Tiflis (Tbilisi). It was characterized by a fierce attachment to the religion, language, literature and ancient history of the Armenian people, and by an ambition to achieve independence from the Ottoman empire that was strongly influenced by the example of the Balkan independence movements, by the comparative freedom of Armenians under Russian rule, and by contemporary European political thought and literature. Together with Armenia's sensitive position on the border between an expansionist Russia and a weak and defensive Ottoman empire, the new nationalisms of Turks and Armenians paved the way for the national tragedy of 1915, invariably referred to by Armenians as 'The Genocide'. That year a desperate Turkish government facing Russian attack determined to prevent the Armenians on its eastern borders assisting the advancing enemy by eliminating them once and for all. As many as 1.5 million died as a result of execution, massacre and forced marches across Turkey to concentration camps in northern Syria. Tens of thousands more fled to Russian-controlled eastern Armenia, the Middle East and the Western world. The Armenian population of the western part of historic Greater Armenia was wiped out and has never returned.

The most recent figures for Armenian population world-wide show that in 1979 there were more than 4 million Armenians living in the Soviet Union (3 million of them in the Armenian republic), while in 1966 there were estimated to be about 2 million Armenians in the diaspora communities, chiefly in the USA, France, Iran, Syria and Lebanon, with about a quarter of a million more in Turkey.

THE INCORPORATION OF ARMENIA INTO THE SOVIET UNION

In the aftermath of the 1917 February Revolution Transcaucasia was cut adrift from Russia and left to fend for itself. The years from then until the final establishment of Soviet power in 1920–21 were a period of continuous acute crisis for Armenia. Initially, Transcaucasia was united in a single republic, but on 26 May 1918 the Assembly of the republic dissolved itself, and the same day the Georgian Mensheviks set up their own independent state. Azerbaijan declared its independence the next day, and on the 28 May Armenia reluctantly followed suit. Armenia was much the weakest of the three new republics, and lacked the powerful protector possessed by Georgia in Germany, and by Azerbaijan in Turkey. The territory of the Armenian republic was based on the old tsarist governorship of Erevan – a small, mountainous, backward and impoverished area, for although Armenians possessed considerable wealth and economic power in Transcaucasia, these were concentrated in Tbilisi and Baku – also the centres of Armenian political and cultural life – not in Armenia itself. Erevan, with a population of 30,000 (a tenth the size of Tbilisi or Baku), was a minor provincial centre with none of the resources or administrative machinery to manage an independent republic.[1]

These basic disadvantages facing the government formed by the nationalist and socialist Dashnak Party were greatly exacerbated by the problems created by the years of war and the current political situation. Before 1914 Armenia had imported much of its food from Russia, but following the 1917 Revolution this source of supply was cut off, and the landlocked new republic had neither the lines of communication nor the resources to open up alternatives. Agricultural production had fallen drastically during the war years, and of a population of 750,000 as many as 300,000 were refugees from western Armenia, who had to be fed but could not initially contribute to the national economy. Perhaps 20 per cent of the population died of famine and associated diseases in the first eighteen months of the republic's existence.[2]

As if internal difficulties were not enough, the republic of Armenia was born into a state of war with Turkey (rapidly brought to an end by the humiliating treaty of 4 June 1918), and soon became involved in territorial disputes and ethnic clashes with neighbouring Georgia and Azerbaijan. These were mostly suspended after the British military intervention in Transcaucasia in autumn 1918, following Turkey's surrender at the end of the First World War, but the British did nothing to provide permanent solutions to the underlying problems. As soon as they departed in summer 1920 the conflicts resurfaced, and Armenia was soon at war with Kemalist Turkey. The campaign went disastrously, and at the end of 1920 the Dashnak government surrendered without resistance to the Bolsheviks, preferring a Soviet takeover to annihilation by the Turks.[3]

THE SOVIET ACHIEVEMENT

Armenia in 1920 was a devastated and desperate land – the post-First World War equivalent of today's Ethiopia or Sudan – and the Soviet achievement must be measured against this background. With starvation claiming thousands of lives, the first need was to provide food. Within six years agricultural land under cultivation had risen from around 30 per cent to 90 per cent, and food production to nearly three-quarters of pre-war levels. Several major irrigation projects were under way, and considerable progress had been made in repairing and extending the road network. Industrial reconstruction was slower, and unemployment remained a serious problem throughout the 1920s, aggravated by the number of refugees and the influx of peasants into the cities.[4] During the first ten years of Soviet rule, economic reconstruction took priority over other considerations, and there was little progress towards the ideal of a new urban social order. The great majority of Armenia's population remained rural, with only 12.69 per cent classed as proletarians.[5]

The real revolution came only after 1929, when Armenia was forced through the colossal upheaval of collectivisation and industrialisation. The human and material costs were immense, but the achievement undeniable: in 1929 just 3.7 per cent of peasant households were in collectives, by 1936 the figure was 80 per cent.[6] All Armenia's main industries developed significantly, and by 1931 unemployment was officially eradicated. The gross product of industry in 1935 was 650 per cent that of 1928, and industry's share in the value of total economic production rose from 21.7 per cent to 62.1 per cent.[7] Social change followed in the wake of the economic revolution, and family and village, the traditional units of rural life and agricultural production, were replaced by the collective. In towns a new sovietised urban proletariat came into existence.[8]

The social and economic progress so violently initiated in the early thirties has continued since, though not at the same break-neck pace. The population is now approaching 3.5 million (65 per cent live in towns, including 1.2 million in Erevan), and is continuing to expand rapidly, with almost half aged twenty-five or under.[9] In 1975 38 per cent of the labour force were industrial workers, 42 per cent worked in the service sector, and only 20 per cent were still in agriculture and forestry.[10] Education, health care and standards of living have all improved markedly in the post-war period. The economy has continued to develop rapidly, although the rate appears less impressive calculated per capita because of the vigorous demographic growth. The impressive growth notwithstanding, by most measurements both economic development and living standards in Armenia still lag behind Soviet national average levels. Such measurements do not, of course, take into account the role of the thriving unofficial economy, which makes a considerable contribution to the living standards of many Armenians.[11]

ARMENIAN NATIONALISM IN THE SOVIET PERIOD

National consciousness was already highly developed among educated Armenians by the time of the 1917 Revolution. Pro-Russian sentiment was strong, since Armenians under Russian rule were generally in a far more enviable position than those in Turkey. The century-long division of the Armenian people between the two empires did much to shape the Armenian self-image. Armenians rejected (by and large still do reject) the Middle Eastern elements in their heritage, choosing to see themselves as an island of civilised Christian 'Europeans' in a hostile sea of barbarous Muslim Asiatics.[12] This preference, already evident in past centuries, was ineradicably scored into the Armenian psyche by the national tragedy of 1915, leaving what perhaps can best be described as a wounded historical consciousness – a continuing sense of outrage at the Genocide, made more bitter still by the betrayal by the Western Allies (who never fulfilled promises of compensation and an independent Armenian homeland after World War I).[13] Nationalist aspirations have since been directed towards avenging 1915 and achieving retrospectively a territorial settlement more in line with Armenian claims and the Allies' promises. Armenian nationalists have often shown less interest in working from existing political realities than in starting the game again with the pieces more fairly distributed across the board.

From a nationalist viewpoint, incorporation into the Soviet Union had both positive and negative aspects. Over-riding all other considerations was the fact that Russia, this time Soviet Russia, had shown itself once again to be Armenia's only source of practical help in the hour of need. The price, however, was the loss of full independence, and of much of the territory to which Armenia laid claim. The Bolsheviks renounced all claims to tsarist gains from Turkey in western Armenia, and were, moreover, broadly sympathetic towards Kemalist Turkey, which they perceived as a natural ally in the struggle of oppressed peoples against Western imperialism. Armenian hopes of Western support for their territorial claims and of a mandate for Armenia were completely out of line with the Bolsheviks' international position.[14] The territorial settlement in 1921 between the Soviet Union and Turkey (Treaties of Moscow and Kars) entailed giving up not only the Armenia proposed by the Treaty of Sevres (1920) and the western Armenian provinces that had been part of Russia since 1878, but also the Surmalu district of Erevan (Russian since its cession by Iran in 1828) in which stands Mount Ararat, a potent symbol of the Armenian homeland. The Treaties stipulated further that Nakhichevan should become an autonomous oblast under Soviet Azerbaijan, not a part of Armenia. Other border disputes with Georgia and Azerbaijan were also settled to Armenia's disadvantage.[15]

Soviet cultural policy has also been ambivalent towards Armenian nationalist expression. In the 1920s pragmatic Communists accepted the fact that 'the international outlook is the future ideal, not the immediate one'. The Soviet government did not perceive any implicit threat to its power from the development of separate national identities among the various peoples of the Union; the policy of *korenizatsiya* or 'nativisation' was pursued simultaneously with the reconstruction programme, and there was toleration of the overtly nationalist aspirations of the intelligentsia.[16] Armenian was made the official language of the republic, employed in government, administration and all schools except those for the very small percentage of ethnic minorities. Armenian art and culture were promoted, and until the later 1920s the Communists showed caution in their relations with the Armenian church.[17]

This period of toleration came to an abrupt end in the mid-1930s. During the Great Purge of 1936–38 in particular, the ranks of the Armenian political leadership, Communist Party and intelligentsia were decimated, most of the victims being charged with nationalism.[18] Control from Moscow tightened, and no deviation from the strict Party line was tolerated. Later, during the war years, those aspects of national culture and consciousness that were felt to be a source of loyalty to the Soviet regime were again encouraged, but from 1947 to 1953 the situation reversed and 'bourgeois nationalism' was again subjected to violent attacks.[19]

In the years between Stalin's death and Gorbachev's election as Party General Secretary, greater tolerance returned, and official encouragement was given to many manifestations of Armenian national consciousness.[20] This leniency did not, however, extend to any increase in the republic's real autonomy, and the borderline between official, approved national expression and unofficial, dissident nationalism was ill-defined.[21] In general, Armenian nationalism has retained its Russophile character. Few dissidents have called for secession from the USSR, and most Armenians would agree that the benefits of belonging to the Union – principally security and socio-economic development – have far outweighed the sacrifice in autonomy.[22] Nevertheless, two important issues have remained controversial.

The first is language. While Armenian is the official language of the republic, there is a widespread anxiety that Russian has been steadily gaining ground. A knowledge of Russian has come to be a prerequisite for career success, and many parents now prefer to send their children to Russian-medium schools. When the new republican Constitution of 1978 was being drawn up, a proposal to remove the clause guaranteeing Armenian as the official language had to be dropped following a demonstration in Erevan.[23] The other issue that has never ceased to stir strong passions is that of the wrongs done the Armenians at the beginning of the century. The first major outbreak of dissident nationalism was a demonstration in Erevan in 1965 to commemorate the fiftieth anniversary of the Genocide. Since then the anniversary has been celebrated officially, and a monument to the victims erected.[24] It is the historical issue that has erupted with such force in the Gorbachev period.

THE GORBACHEV PERIOD

When Gorbachev launched his programme of democratising reforms, there were many voices, critics inside the Soviet Union as well as foreign commentators, predicting difficulties over the nationalities question, but the eruption of nationalism[25] in Armenia took everyone by surprise. The Baltic republics, the Ukraine and 'Muslim' Central Asia are all areas with a tradition of strong, frequently anti-Russian, nationalism, but Armenia has always appeared politically docile. The sudden development of a radical popular nationalist movement there can only be understood in relation to the central motivating issue: the question of Karabakh.

The Autonomous Oblast of Mountainous Karabakh[26] is 4,400 square kilometres in area and had in 1979 a population of 162,200, of which 123,100 (76 per cent) were Armenian, and 37,200 (23 per cent) Azerbaijani.[27] The region was conquered by the Seljuqs in the eleventh century, and since then there has always been a Turkish element among the predominantly Armenian population. Despite occasional periods of partial independence, Karabakh was invariably part of some larger Islamic state until Iran ceded the territory to Russia in 1813. It was later fought over by the independent republics of Armenia and Azerbaijan and finally, in the Soviet period, declared an autonomous oblast within the republic of Azerbaijan.

There are a number of reasons for Karabakh being what a historian writing in 1983 described as 'the single most volatile issue among Armenians'.[28] The first is that Armenian nationalists equate the Azerbaijanis with the Turks of Turkey (they may refuse to use the word 'Azerbaijani' at all, preferring simple 'Turk' or 'Tatar'), and see their possession of Karabakh as a symbol of the Turks' successful evasion of punishment for the Genocide and occupation of Armenian lands.[29] Second, Karabakh's incorporation into Azerbaijan was facilitated by the British occupying forces in Transcaucasia in 1918, and is thus a reminder of Armenia's betrayal by the Western Allies.[30] Third, Karabakh epitomises for the Armenians the unsatisfactory resolution of international and republican boundaries at the outset of the Soviet period. The day before the Dashnak government stepped down, the Soviet government of Azerbaijan sent a telegram to the incoming Soviet government of Armenia ceding Karabakh – a move doubtless intended to sweeten the decision to join the Soviet Union.[31] Subsequently, however, the cession was never given effect, and in 1921 a plenary session of the Caucasian Bureau of the Central Committee of the Communist Party of Soviet Russia decided (Armenians maintain it was on Stalin's insistence) that

'considering the necessity of national harmony between Muslims and the Armenians, the economic linkage between upper ("plains") and lower ("mountainous") Karabakh, and its permanent ties to Azerbaijan', Mountainous Karabakh should be left within the boundaries of the Azerbaijani Soviet Socialist Republic, while declaring it an autonomous oblast.[32]

Karabakh was formally incorporated into Azerbaijan in July 1923 –

a reversal of the 1920 decision which nationalist Armenians view as a serious betrayal. Finally, since medieval times the mountains of Karabakh have been a centre for the survival of Armenian folk traditions and culture. These, and the future of Armenian settlement in Karabakh, have been threatened by the alleged discriminatory policies and deliberate underdevelopment of the oblast by Azerbaijan.[33] Armenian nationalist aspirations have focused on it also as the only territory claimed by Armenia which has a majority Armenian population today and which there is therefore any realistic short-term possibility of recovering.[34]

Agitation for a reconsideration of the Karabakh question increased soon after Gorbachev's election as Party General Secretary. Several well-connected Armenians spoke out in a way that encouraged the belief that the new leadership might view the transfer of Karabakh more favourably than in the past. Campaigners sent memoranda and petitions to Moscow and linked Karabakh to the whole issue of *glasnost'* and *perestroika* by suggesting that the democratic demands of the people of Karabakh were essentially in harmony with the process of democratisation.[35] In October 1987 there were reports of demonstrations in Erevan on environmental pollution and Karabakh involving up to 3,000 people, and clashes took place between Armenian and Azerbaijani villagers in Karabakh. At the beginning of 1988 a petition signed by 75,000–100,000 demanding the transfer of Karabakh was presented to the authorities in Moscow.[36]

This simmering local dispute was transformed into a major national crisis after 20 February 1988, when the Mountainous Karabakh Soviet of People's Deputies passed a resolution demanding to be transferred to Armenian jurisdiction.[37] Armenians expressed support for the resolution by demonstrating in Erevan and other Armenian towns, in Karabakh itself and in Moscow. Erevan's first demonstrations, with about 5,000 participants, took place on 20 February, a Saturday. The next day the numbers doubled and, in response to Moscow's rejection of the petition, grew to 250,000 on the Monday, 400,000 on the Tuesday and Wednesday, and as many as a million on the Thursday and Friday. The demonstrations were peaceful, and demonstrators emphasised their Soviet patriotism by carrying placards of Gorbachev and the flag of Soviet Armenia.[38]

Initial government response was fairly muted. On the day that the Central Committee of the Communist Party of the USSR rejected the Karabakh Soviet's request for transfer (22 February 1988), Karen Demirjian (Armenian Party Secretary) made a televised appeal for calm. The next day he and two party officials from Moscow met with leading Armenian academics and intellectuals, and the meeting asked the All-Union Central Committee to examine the Karabakh question at the planned plenary session on nationalities policy. The Central Committee placed the burden of responsibility for dealing with the situation squarely on the shoulders of the leadership in Armenia and Azerbaijan. At the same time, high-ranking party officials were despatched to the Caucasus to monitor the situation and help provide solutions.

Moscow's one major concession at this time was acquiescence in the installation of Genrikh Poghosian – a leading campaigner for transfer – as Karabakh Party Secretary. On 25 February troops were despatched to Erevan, though not used against demonstrators, and the same day the Catholicos – head of the Armenian church – added his voice to the calls for calm. None of this had any effect, and when Demirjian appeared in person to talk to the demonstrators, his speech (delivered in Russian) was greeted with jeers and whistles. The demonstrations only subsided after 27 February, when two leading intellectuals returned from an unannounced meeting with Gorbachev. They had been given a promise that the question would be fully investigated at the highest level, and on the strength of this called for a month's suspension of demonstrations to allow the leadership to consider the matter. A broadcast message from Gorbachev to the Armenian and Azerbaijani peoples accepted that mistakes had been made but emphasised the danger in giving way to emotion when tackling complex issues, and pointed a way forward through maturity, restraint and overcoming concrete problems.

The proposed breathing-space was shattered only two days later by the outbreak of violence in Azerbaijan, the most serious incident being the massacre of Armenians in the industrial city of Sumgait. In Armenia the news led to an immediate hardening of attitudes. After Sumgait little attempt was made to restrain overtly racist, anti-Azerbaijani rhetoric. The official version of events, thirty-two killed and 100 injured, was widely disbelieved in Armenia, where rumours have circulated ever since of a death toll in the hundreds or even thousands. In an atmosphere of escalating racial hostility, large-scale emigrations from both Azerbaijan and Armenia began. The refugees have since been instrumental in keeping emotions and fears at fever pitch by retelling their stories, as well as rumours, of the injustices and atrocities inflicted on themselves and their compatriots in the neighbouring republic. The treatment of the issue in the Soviet press also hardened attitudes. While acknowledging the complexity of the problem and criticising the past and present republican and Karabakh leaderships, the national press branded the Karabakh campaigners as opportunist nationalist extremists, and stooges of foreign powers and anti-*perestroika* forces, even suggesting that the demonstrations in Erevan were not spontaneous, but carefully orchestrated by external enemies.[39]

Yet there can be no doubt that the movement for the transfer of Karabakh was genuinely popular in Armenia, and was not initially perceived as anti-Soviet or even anti-Moscow. The February demonstrations appear to have lacked any organised leadership, and the people who came to the fore at this time were simply the most effective demagogues. By the summer things had changed. Small support committees sprang up in factories, institutes and offices across Armenia, while a stable eleven-member Karabakh Committee was recognised as the *de facto* leadership of the movement. Most of the members were academics or writers, many of them respected authorities in their fields; several belonged or had belonged to the Communist Party. They certainly did not see themselves as anti-Soviet or dissident (though dissidents also called for the transfer of Karabakh).[40]

The legal and constitutional implications of Karabakh's vote to transfer to Armenian jurisdiction were unprecedented in Soviet history, and could only be resolved at the highest level. Opponents of the transfer based their case on Article 78 of the Soviet Constitution, which stipulates that any border changes between republics must be approved by both parties. Armenian activists, on the other hand, argued that the guarantee of national self-determination enshrined in the Constitution gave Karabakh the right to secede. Failing this, they hoped Moscow would compromise by incorporating Mountainous Karabakh into the Russian republic as an autonomous oblast, or even an autonomous republic. Decision on this vital question took a long time to reach, but in March Moscow put forward a package of reforms for Karabakh which involved an investment of 400 million roubles over eight years. By the end of April Karabakh was receiving Armenian television broadcasts for the first time, but with the central issue of the oblast's territorial status still unresolved, such measures could be no more than temporary palliatives.

In May and June divergent tendencies began to emerge in Armenia, where after a brief lull, regular mass demonstrations had recommenced. The dominant mood still favoured a single-issue campaign directed solely towards the transfer of Karabakh. Others, however, were interested in a broader movement with an agenda that included international recognition of the Genocide, reparations from Turkey, the strengthening of the Armenian language, moves to reduce Armenian emigration, and increasing links with the diaspora. A third group looked on the movement as part of a nation-wide struggle for democracy and other reforms, and took on issues with no specifically Armenian connection. In the atmosphere of continuing uncertainty, the mood of the demonstrations became increasingly impatient and radical. Speakers advocating moderation and patience were jeered by the crowd, and calls for a general strike were heard with increasing frequency. On 28 May, independence day of the short-lived Armenian republic, demonstrators raised the tricolour of independent Armenia.[41]

On 13 June there was a general strike, intended to put pressure on the republican government, whose Supreme Soviet was due to meet two days later. Some 700,000 demonstrators crowded around Opera Square, where Party Secretary Harutiunian (who had replaced the sacked Demirjian in May) read a draft resolution on Karabakh. On 15 June all Armenia stayed at home to watch the session of the Supreme Soviet (televised for the first time). When coverage was suspended at 12.30 p.m., tens of thousands converged on the Supreme Soviet building. In its decision the Erevan government bowed to popular demand, and endorsed the Mountainous Karabakh Soviet's call for transfer to Armenia, asking the Supreme Soviet of the USSR to 'positively resolve' the question and, in separate resolutions, condemned the killings in Sumgait and established a permanent multi-ethnic commission to deal with ethnic problems in Armenia. These resolutions generated public euphoria and a tremendous feeling of optimism and strength in the popular movement. Two days later, the Azerbaijani Supreme Soviet rejected Karabakh's demand. This brought the republican governments of Armenia and Azerbaijan into direct confrontation for the first time, and left no alternative to arbitration by the central government in Moscow.

Meanwhile in Karabakh itself a virtual general strike prevailed, and in Armenia and Azerbaijan strikes, demonstrations, ethnic violence and emigration continued unabated. The republican governments and law-enforcement agencies appeared to have lost both the will and the ability to control a situation that was rapidly becoming explosive. Central government forces had been in the region in readiness since February, but there had been great reluctance to use troops against the protestors. Nevertheless, when demonstrators succeeded in closing Erevan airport to traffic on 4–5 July, troops were brought in, and there were numerous injuries and at least one fatality in the operation to clear the airport.

It was against this background of acute crisis that finally, on 18 July, the long-awaited decision from Moscow came. After an all-day session of the Presidium of the Supreme Soviet (at which Azerbaijani and Armenian delegates were in open confrontation), the transfer of Karabakh to Armenia was rejected. During the session, Gorbachev particularly emphasised that the resolution of the Karabakh issue must set a precedent for nationalities problems throughout the Union. Many delegates stressed that a successful solution could only be reached if it was approached in a spirit of legality, compromise and friendship, a spirit noticeably lacking in the Armenian and Azerbaijani goverments and intelligentsias. At the meeting the possibilities of placing Karabakh under central government jurisdiction, or of raising its status to that of an autonomous republic were discussed, but the resolution adopted, while recognising Karabakh's acute problems and criticising past and present republican and oblast leaderships, put forward only limited concrete proposals: to send representatives to Karabakh to work in close cooperation with the republican governments, and to refer further consideration of the question to a special commission with a remit to submit its proposals to the Supreme Soviet in due course.[42]

The 18 July decision was a severe blow to Armenian hopes, and left many disillusioned with Gorbachev and his reforms. From this point on, demonstrations became increasingly anti-Moscow, though tougher security measures reduced their size and led to a return to work and some semblance of normality. The Karabakh Committee began openly to attack Moscow, Armenian officials and even the Catholicos for accepting Moscow's ruling. Confrontation with the state appeared inevitable, and the Committee began to think of a broader Armenian national movement working through electoral politics backed by the threat of civil disobedience. Calls for full independence became more frequent, and attempts were made to establish links with the Baltic popular movements.

In addition to the transfer of Karabakh, the campaigners now demanded greater Armenian autonomy on a range of issues: the power of veto on all federal projects in Armenia; fuller control of economic, cultural and educational affairs; Armenian consulates in countries with large Armenian communities; the promotion of the Armenian language; the de-Russification of the bureaucracy and the removal of the Russian Deputy Party Chief; and the creation of Armenian military detachments. Historical issues on the agenda included official forums to force international recognition of Turkey's guilt for 1915, a historical reappraisal of the independent republic of Armenia and the right to fly the Armenian tricolour. Ecological issues were also prominent, with calls to close Armenia's nuclear power station and the Erevan rubber factory, and to tackle the depletion and pollution of the waters of Lake Sevan.

In the second half of September and again in November ethnic tension flared up once more in both Armenia and Azerbaijan, leaving close to 100 dead. Emigration escalated, and by early December more than 200,000 refugees had crossed between the two republics. Government response was two-pronged. Security was tightened, and outbreaks of ethnic violence were vigorously investigated and their perpetrators punished. A state of emergency and curfew was imposed in Karabakh itself, in Erevan, Baku and many other districts. There was a determined attack on the instigators of unrest, including the arrest of the entire Karabakh Committee, and on officials and law-enforcement officers whose negligence had allowed the disorders to continue. Some fifty Armenian Party and government officials were sacked and the Prime Minister replaced by an Armenian who, like the new Party Secretary Harutiunian, had a career background in the Russian, not the Armenian, Party.

On the other hand, there were important concessions. The trials of those accused of the Sumgait violence were transferred from Baku to Moscow, and the Armenian republican government also showed some readiness to listen to public demands. It announced the closure of the nuclear power station within three years, and agreed to consider the pollution problem, to expand the use of Armenian in schools and to strengthen links with the diaspora communities.

But the most important initiative came on Karabakh. The special commission on Karabakh, its members high-ranking party officials answerable only to Moscow, showed a determination to tackle seriously the problems in Karabakh and to conciliate popular opinion. In January 1989 the commission was given full powers to implement the development programme for Karabakh, and the powers of the oblast's own legislature and executive were suspended. In effect, though the territorial status of Mountainous Karabakh was officially unchanged, its administration was removed from Azerbaijani hands – a move described by the Soviet Prime Minister Ryzhkov as 'a compromise under which a mutually acceptable balance of interests of the two Republics is observed'.[43]

This significant development received a cautious welcome in both Erevan and Baku, but in May, after four months of comparative quiet, disturbances and strikes broke out again in Karabakh, followed by demonstrations in Armenia and Azerbaijan. The Erevan government made further concessions, including the recognition of 28 May as Armenia's national day, and the release from custody of members of the Karabakh Committee, but the situation has remained tense and volatile, and there is no indication that the special commission has succeeded in solving any of Karabakh's problems, or even in winning the full confidence of the inhabitants, nor have nationalist feeling or the nationalist movement in Armenia lost any of their strength or support.

Before this, however, an event took place which suddenly pushed the whole question of Karabakh and nationalism to one side. On 7 December 1988 Armenia suffered a catastrophic earthquake, which completely destroyed the town of Spitak (population 25,000), as well as 80 per cent of the buildings in Armenia's second city, Leninakan (population over 200,000). One hundred and thirty villages were affected, fifty-five of them utterly destroyed, and half a million left homeless. The official death toll was put at 25,000, but it was acknowledged that more may have died, and that many bodies would never be recovered from the ruins of tower blocks which collapsed like packs of cards. A massive national and international relief operation was set in motion, with Prime Minister Ryzhkov taking an active role in organising relief work. The damage done to the republic's agro-industrial complex has been estimated at 2 billion roubles, and the cost of reconstruction at 6 to 6.5 billion.

The earthquake distracted attention from the issue of nationalism, but its aftermath did not by any means generate full national unity. The leaders of the Karabakh movement accused the republican government of inefficiency in handling the crisis, and even suggested that the popular movement should have been entrusted with the relief operation. Official sources in turn attacked the Karabakh activists for attempting to make political capital out of the disaster.

The Karabakh crisis and the earthquake have inflicted enormous damage on Armenia's economy, and far outweighed any possible economic benefits of Gorbachev's reforms. The strikes and work-stoppages of the Karabakh campaign caused huge losses (Party Secretary Harutiunian put lost production during July 1988 at 93 million roubles); and the closure of the nuclear power station (which produces 30 per cent of Armenia's electricity) will prove expensive over a number of years, as will the promised action against pollution. Reports suggest that the only noticeable effects of greater economic freedom in Armenia have been an increase in speculation and hoarding, the disappearance of products from state shops and an increase in unregulated private retail. Only with the reconstruction of earthquake damage and a full return to normal work throughout the republic will it be possible to start measuring the progress of economic *perestroika* in Armenia.

CONCLUSIONS AND PROSPECTS

The Karabakh crisis of 1988 presented the Gorbachev leadership with the most serious internal political challenge it had faced. It cast doubt on the viability of the movement towards a more open, democratic, responsible society, by showing that greater freedom might lead not to a stronger, fitter USSR, but to national disintegration. It also showed how readily a nationalist movement could grow more radical if it was not handled with sensitivity, but also with decision. Armenia is certainly not unique in having a burgeoning popular movement pressing essentially nationalist demands, but in Armenia the questions about nationalities policy raised by *glasnost'* and *perestroika* became focused around a single issue, and the Karabakh crisis has been universally viewed as a possible precedent for developments and responses elsewhere.

In the broader context of the nationalities question throughout the Soviet Union, it is clear that Gorbachev had very little room for manoeuvre on the Karabakh question. A decision to allow the transfer to Armenia would have established a precedent for national self-determination by minorities that could have the most far-reaching and disruptive consequences for the Union. Such a decision would also have deeply alienated Azerbaijan, and perhaps the other Muslim nationalities too. What Moscow had to avoid at all costs was appearing to take sides, creating winners and losers, so the decision to maintain the official status quo while taking actual control out of Azerbaijani hands and giving it to a centrally appointed special commission was perhaps the best available course. Nevertheless, the current solution is viewed as a temporary one by all parties, and in the long term the Armenians' determination to achieve reunification and the Azerbaijanis' to prevent it remain as firm and as irreconcilable as ever. Moscow's delay in reaching its decision, and its failure to recognise the genuinely popular and, in some respects, progressive nature of the Armenian nationalist movement undoubtedly contributed to the radicalisation of the movement and its growing disenchantment with Gorbachev's leadership.

Armenia faces daunting challenges in the next few years. There is the huge task of reconstruction after the earthquake, but no less urgently needed is a solution to the political situation. Unless the republican government can regain public confidence by taking effective action on such problems as earthquake reconstruction, pollution and corruption, while simultaneously moderating popular demands over Karabakh sufficiently to be able to enter a dialogue with Azerbaijan over the region's future, it appears almost inevitable that the unofficial nationalist movement will retain the political initiative, and that there will be more demonstrations and strikes, and further confrontations with Azerbaijan, and eventually the Soviet state.

NOTES

1. R.G. Hovannisian 'Caucasian Armenia between Imperial and Soviet rule: the interlude of national independence' in R.G. Suny (ed.) *Transcaucasia: Nationalism and Social Change* (Ann Arbor, MI, University of Michigan 1983), p. 260 (hereafter, Suny *Transcaucasia*); S. Afanasyan *L'Arménie, l'Azerbaïdjan et la Géorgie de l'indépendance à l'instauration du pouvoir soviétique (1917–1923)* (Paris, Éditions L'Harmattan, 1981), pp. 56–9.
2. Hovannisian Caucasian Armenia, p. 270; Afanasyan *loc. cit.*, and p. 95; R.G. Suny *Armenia in the Twentieth Century* (Chico, CA, Scholars Press 1983), p. 29 (hereafter, Suny, *Armenia*); M.K. Matossian *The Impact of Soviet Policies in Armenia* (Leiden, E.J. Brill 1962), p. 26.
3. Hovannisian, *Caucasian Armenia*, pp. 261, 268–69; Afanasyan, *L'Arménie*, pp. 72–3, 88, 136–51; Suny *Armenia*, pp. 26–7; A.H. Arslanian 'Britain and the Transcaucasian nationalities during the Russian Civil War' in Suny *Transcaucasia*, pp. 293–304.
4. Matossian *Impact of Soviet Policies*, pp. 53, 57–8.
5. Ibid., pp. 59–60, 62.
6. Ibid., pp. 102–12, 116.
7. Ibid., pp. 112–16.
8. Ibid., p. 116.
9. Based on the preliminary results of the 1989 census, *Current Digest of the Soviet Press* (hereafter *CDSP*) 42 (17); Suny, *Armenia*, pp. 76–7; *The Armenian Reporter* (New York, Fresh Meadows, 10 March 1988), citing Armenian republic state planning committee statistics.
10. Suny *Armenia*, p. 75.
11. G.E. Schroeder 'Transcaucasia since Stalin: the economic dimension' in Suny *Transcaucasia*, pp. 397–416.
12. Suny *Armenia*, pp. 10–11.
13. C.J. Walker *Armenia: The Survival of a Nation* (London, Croom Helm 1980), pp. 265–67, 276–77, 280–81, 291–92.
14. Suny, *Armenia*, pp. 23–4, 31; Afanasyan *L'Arménie*, pp. 88–97.

15. Hovannisian *Caucasian Armenia*, p. 291; Afanasyan *L'Arménie*, pp. 181, 199.
16. Matossian *Impact of Soviet Policies*, pp. 78–9.
17. Ibid., pp. 80–1, 90–5.
18. Ibid., pp. 127, 141–47, 155–62.
19. Ibid., pp. 162–69, 194.
20. Suny *Armenia*, pp. 78–9.
21. Ibid., p. 78.
22. Schroeder, 'Transcauasia since Stalin', p. 416; D.M. Lang *The Armenians: A People in Exile* (new edn, London, Unwin Hyman Ltd 1988), pp. 118–19.
23. Matossian, *Impact of Soviet Policies*, p. 190; Suny *Armenia*, p. 80.
24. Ibid., pp. 78–9.
25. The terms 'nationalism' and 'nationalist' are used in the neutral Western sense. In the Soviet context, negative connotations are still attached to them, so that 'nationalists' often prefer to describe themselves as 'patriots'; G.J. Libaridian (ed.) *The Karabagh File: Documents and Facts on the Region of Mountainous Karabagh 1918–1988* (Cambridge, MA, and Toronto, The Zoryan Institute 1988), pp. 66, 72, 98.
26. In Russian, *Nagorno-Karabakhskaya Avtonomnaya Oblast'*. The name is of mixed Turkish-Persian origin: Turkish *kara* 'black', Persian *bāgh* 'garden'. 'Mountainous' or 'Upland' distinguishes this from 'Plains' or 'Lowland' Karabakh to the north, whose centre is Kirovabad (tsarist Elizavetpol, medieval Ganjah/Gandzak). Karabakh corresponds to the medieval Islamic province Arrān and the Armenian Artsakh. The latter name is often used by nationalists calling for reunification. *Encyclopedia of Islam* (Leiden, E.J. Brill, new edn., vol. IV, 1978), entry 'Karābāgh'.
27. B.S. Mirzoyan 'Nagornyi Karabakh' *Lraber Hasarakakan Gitutyunneri*, no. 7 (July 1988), p. 43. Preliminary results for the 1989 census put the population at 188,000; *CDSP*, 41 (17).
28. Suny *Armenia*, p. 80.
29. For an example of such Armenian rhetoric, see Libaridian (ed.) *The Karabagh File*, pp. 76–7.
30. A.H. Arslanian 'Britain and the Armeno-Azerbaijani struggle for Mountainous Karabagh, 1918–1919' *Middle Eastern Studies* No. 1 (1980), pp. 92–104.
31. Libaridian (ed.) *The Karabagh File*, p. 34.
32. Ibid., pp. 36–7. These historical issues were raised by an Armenian delegate at the 18 July 1988 meeting of the Presidium of the Supreme Soviet to decide the question of Karabakh; *CDSP* 40 (29).
33. Mirzoyan 'Nagornyi Karabakh', pp. 43–56; A.E. Ter-Sarkisyants 'Nekotorye tendentsii etnokul'turnogo razvitiya armyan Nagornogo Karabakha', *Lraber Hasarakakan Gitutyunneri* 8 (Aug. 1988), pp. 14–23. The report of the Supreme Soviet special commission to Karabakh confirms these allegations; *CDSP*, 40 (51).
34. Libaridian (ed.) *The Karabagh File*, pp. 69, 73–4.
35. Ibid., pp. 69, 71–7, 81–8.
36. Ibid., pp. 88–9.
37. Ibid., p. 90.
38. Estimates of the numbers of demonstrators cannot be relied on. Those

given here are taken from the eyewitness account of a Western student, *Armenian Reporter* 21 July 1988. Soviet official sources have refrained from giving figures for the numbers attending demonstrations. The course of events from February 1988 can be followed in newspaper reports, the weekly *Armenian Reporter* being particularly useful since, in addition to exerpts from the Western and Soviet press, it contains unofficial eyewitness accounts from Armenia. The *Current Digest of the Soviet Press* provides a cross-section of reports from the Soviet national and local press in English translation. A summary of the principal events to September 1988 is given in T. Dragadze 'The Armenian-Azerbaijani conflict: structure and sentiment' *Third World Quarterly* 11 (1) (Jan. 1989), pp. 55–71; see also Libaridian (ed.) *The Karabagh File*, pp. 90–103.

39. See, e.g., the articles in *Pravda* 21 March 1988 and 4 April 1988. Other reporting showed greater sensitivity, e.g. *Izvestiya* 24 March 1988.
40. *CDSP* 40 (30); *Armenian Reporter* 8, 15 and 29 Sept. 1988.
41. *Armenian Reporter* 4 Aug. 1988.
42. *In Common Interests: On the Solution of the Nationalities Problems in Nagorny Karabakh* (Moscow, Novosti Press Agency Publishing House 1988). For selections from the discussion at the meeting, see *CDSP* 40 (29).
43. *CDSP* 41 (2).

CHAPTER TEN

Azerbaijanis

Tamara Dragadze

At the beginning of 1988, Soviet Azerbaijan was propelled into world focus as a result of the dispute over Nagorno-Karabakh, the ensuing communal conflict having become one of the hallmarks of Gorbachev's term of office. The determination of the Azerbaijanis to retain their territorial integrity, as established when they were incorporated into the Soviet Union, has provided Gorbachev with one of the most intractable problems he has had to face so far.

BACKGROUND

The Azerbaijanis inhabit a land along the eastern edge of the Caspian Sea, sharing borders with Iran, Armenia, Georgia and Daghestan. Southern Azerbaijan, with its capital Tabriz, is in Iran, and for the whole of the Soviet period it has been more or less constantly cut off from Northern Azerbaijan, which now forms Soviet Azerbaijan, despite linguistic, cultural and kinship links between the two halves.

Today Soviet Azerbaijan covers a territory of 86,000 square kilometres and boasts a rich and varied countryside with high mountains along the Great Caucasian Range and a tropical micro-climate to the south of the republic.

The Azerbaijanis view themselves as the direct inheritors of the many cultures and civilisations which thrived on their land over the centuries. Undoubtedly, as in other parts of the Caucasus, the territory witnessed very early human habitation, with rock carvings in Gobustan and evidence of Zarathustrian worship being a source of national pride. Its location provided a crossroads between East and West which was enjoyed by scholars and merchants in antiquity and in the Middle Ages, but coveted by powerful conquerers from the neighbouring areas. Thus the Medians were succeeded by the Aechemenid state in what is now Southern Azerbaijan but by the second century AD the

163

Caucasian Albanian kingdom began to establish itself in the northern areas, in whose name outstanding Christian churches were later to be built, and whose origins are now fiercely disputed by the Armenians. Turkic-language tribes began to settle in the area from around the second century but Azerbaijanis today insist that they assimilated with the native peoples and only the settlers' language type came to dominate and not their population or culture.[1]

By the end of the seventh century AD much of the territory came under the rule of the Arab caliphates. Islam became the predominant religion, although Christianity and other religions persisted among some sections of the population. There subsequently flourished a series of Islamic cultural centres where poets such as Nizami of Ganja, Fizuli and others made their names and whose poetry is now recited at public meetings. The more independent state of Shirvan was established and is said to have fiercely resisted the invasions first of the Seljuk Turks and then of the Mongols. Later the Safavids were to unite Azerbaijan before a series of small feudal states was established, under the Persian sphere of influence.

The turning point in Azerbaijani modern history came with the entry of Russia into the Caucasian arena, Russia's Caucasian frontier with Iran being 'in many ways as important an arena of nineteenth century Great Game as British India's frontier with Afghanistan'.[2] The first accord with Persia, the Treaty of Gulistan in 1813, and the Treaty of Turkmanchay in 1828 resulted in Azerbaijan being divided in two, with Northern Azerbaijan being ceded to Russia, establishing the political pattern which has continued to this day. The economic and cultural consequences of Russian colonisation have bred in today's Soviet Azerbaijanis an ambivalence towards Russia. On the one hand, Russia opened the door to Europe in the nineteenth century, bringing industrialisation and new ideas to the region. On the other hand, the Azerbaijanis lost control of their own destiny and over their resources, a theme to which we shall return later.

By the end of the nineteenth century, Azerbaijani intellectuals had turned Baku into an important centre of modern Muslim culture. Thus Azerbaijanis can boast that the first modern theatre in the Muslim world and the first Muslim opera were opened in Baku. In the nineteenth century there were already several newspapers and a growing native literature.[3] A few Azerbaijanis had grown oil-rich, along with a majority of West Europeans, Armenians and Russians. The Azerbaijani magnate Taghiyev subsidised every kind of cultural activity, including a grammar school for Azerbaijani girls. The cultural universe in Baku at the time extended out to Istambul and Tabriz, to Kazan, where Tatar intellectuals had devised their own form of Jadidism and called for cooperation and a union of Russian Muslims to Moscow and St Petersburg, Paris and Berlin. A literary language had to be devised which would cater for some of the political ideas afloat at the time which focused on integrating the majority of the rural population into mainstream Azerbaijani progress. This inevitably led to reflection on their own ethnic identity[4] as did the development of yearnings for independence from Russian colonial rule. The tactics through which this was to be achieved centred on the choice of three options: Pan-Turkism, Pan-Islamism or Azerbaijani nationalism.

By the early twentieth century colonisation of Azerbaijan also resulted in a shift in the ethnic composition of the population, especially in the urban centres, although Russia had already used rural areas as a dumping ground for Russian dissident sectarian communities. Inevitably, with subtle intervention from various political groups as well as even subtler encouragement, occasionally, from the Russian government, ethnic conflict erupted between Azerbaijanis and Armenians whose numbers in the area had increased since Russian colonisation. Political allegiances were also to develop along ethnic lines, where Bolshevism in particular was to be dominated by non-Azerbaijanis.

With the collapse of the tsarist government in late 1917 the question became even more urgent as to whether the Azerbaijanis were to express their nationhood culturally or territorially.[5] This was no parochial question, since Baku was a leading world oil supplier whose fate could affect Russian and Western interests. The complexities of Turkey's involvement in the peace talks at the end of the First World War only added to the conflicting loyalties of those powers involved in deciding the Azerbaijanis' fate. A multi-national working-class population in Baku provided fertile ground for Bolshevik recruitment; not so in the countryside, however. The heightened tensions and further misguided intervention from external interested parties undoubtedly contributed to a massacre by Armenians of Azerbaijanis in March 1918 followed by a revenge massacre of Armenians in September of the same year. Amidst the affray the Baku Commune was established in the capital,[6] whose business was carried out in Russian and whose aims were 'internationalist'. A section of the indigenous population and many leading native intellectuals doubted the system's capacity to serve their interests as effectively as would a sovereign Azerbaijani nation. With the collapse of the Commune and the flight of the Baku commissars, of whom few were Azerbaijani, an independent republic of Azerbaijan was declared in 1918, as it was in the other two Transcaucasian republics. Largely tolerant of political diversity and dominated by a benevolent bourgeoisie, a government led by the Azerbaijani Moussavat (literally, 'equality') Party was established. Immediately, the attributes of a national culture befitting an independent country were also created, such as the University of Baku, in 1919. This brief period of independence has fired the imagination of Azerbaijanis in Gorbachev's time.[7] The national flag has resurfaced as an emblem and the 11th Division of the Red Army whose entrance in April 1920 brought about the end of Azerbaijani independence and established Soviet rule has sometimes been referred to in recent *samizdat* as an army of occupation.[8]

In the process of carving out the three Caucasian republics by the Bolsheviks, Azerbaijan was seen by Georgia and Armenia to have gained territorially relative to themselves, notably, for the Armenians, by the allocation of Nagorno-Karabakh to the Soviet Azerbaijan republic.[9] Yet the Azerbaijanis are resentful of the divisive 'autonomous region' status accorded to Nagorno-Karabakh and that their province of Nakhichevan is isolated by Armenian territory since Zangezur was allocated to Armenia, again by the Caucasian Bureau in which there was only one Azerbaijani.[10] Other members of the KavBureau, as it was called, were denounced as enemies of the Azerbaijani people at the November 1988 demonstrations; in particular, Armenian Bolsheviks such as Shaumian. The leading Azerbaijani Bolshevik convert, Nariman Narimanov, died in 1925 in what Azerbaijanis see today as sinister circumstances. The events of 1920 and 1921 which accompanied the establishment of Soviet power in Caucasia are at the centre of most national debates today.

AZERBAIJAN UNDER SOVIET RULE

The Sovietisation of Azerbaijan had a two-pronged thrust: first, to harness its economic resources so as to serve the interests of the Soviet Union as a whole, and, concurrently, to create as elsewhere in the USSR, both through terror and reward, an acquiescent, loyal population.

As for all Soviet nationalities who were Muslim and used the Arabic script, the alphabet for writing Azerbaijani was changed from Arabic script to Latin and then to Cyrillic. The influence of the Azerbaijani language beyond the borders of the republic – into neighbouring Daghestan, for example – was abandoned.[11] Under Stalin, the border with Iran was closed and Azerbaijanis with Iranian passports were expelled in 1938, thus completing the process of isolating Soviet Azerbaijan. Likewise, in 1937 many surviving intellectuals were imprisoned or executed. The countryside was collectivised, nomads forcibly sedentarised and an anti-religious campaign was unleashed. Thus, historical sites with religious significance were destroyed – for example, the shrine of Bibi Eybat outside Baku, whose natural spring had been legendary for more than a millenium, was dynamited and covered over, ostensibly to make way for the building of a road. Under Stalin, too, deportations of whole populations took place. Thus, in 1948, around 100,000 Azerbaijanis were deported from Armenia.[12] In a recent polemic, Gorbachev reminded the Armenians that before the

Revolution Azerbaijanis had formed 43 per cent of the population of Erevan.[13]

The population of Azerbaijan has in-built complexities because of the large national communities living within its borders. In 1979, the population of Azerbaijan stood at 6,025,500. The ethnic composition was said roughly to be: Azerbaijanis 4,708,000; Armenians 475,500; Russians 475,300; Daghestanis 205,100; Jews 35,500; Tatars 31,400; Ukrainians 26,400; Georgians 11,400; others 57,100.[14] It should be pointed out, however, that successive local governments in Azerbaijan have been nervous of potential claims by ethnic minorities for 'autonomous region' status. As a result, scant attention was paid to the separate identity of the Talysh, the Tats, Muslim Georgians (but not Christian Georgians) and other minorities who until recently had to declare themselves as 'Azerbaijani'.

It is only under Gorbachev that these issues have come to be discussed publicly, and not without acrimony. The most recent conflicts have resulted in further adjustments to population figures because of the influx of new Azerbaijani refugees from Armenia and the departure of Armenians from Azerbaijan. The rights of ethnic groups to schools and culture in their own language have been contested in the wake of the growing assertiveness among Azerbaijanis of the legitimacy of declaring their own language and culture to be recognised as dominant in the Azerbaijani republic as they would be in any other nation-state.

As elsewhere in the Soviet Union, the population is declared to be 100 per cent literate, which is hailed as a great Soviet achievement. Today there are several establishments of higher education, including a national university, a polytechnic institute and an Academy of Sciences of Azerbaijan. There are, however, other establishments which one would be less likely to find in the other two Caucasian republics, such as a branch of a technical institute of Odessa. There is relatively more teaching in the Russian language in Azerbaijan which cannot only be explained by the large non-Azerbaijani population in Baku. Azerbaijani intellectuals who have greater facility in thinking aloud in Russian than in Azerbaijani are more numerous, perhaps, than in the other two republics. In the country at large there has been a greater, or at least more successful, effort to obtain acceptance of Azerbaijan's union with Soviet Russia through the use of particular symbols. Thus one sees in the countryside a proliferation of Russian names for state farms, such as 'Kallinin' or 'Sverdlov' or 'Kirov', which the other two republics have largely avoided.

Industrialisation increased by expanding the already established enterprises and workforce in Baku. In the post-Second World War period large new industrial towns such as Sumgait and Ali Baramly were built, which not only absorbed part of the growing Azerbaijani rural population but also immigrants from elsewhere, as well as, in the case of Sumgait, large numbers of prisoners serving their sentences through active labour.

At the same time, although non-Azerbaijanis were less likely to benefit from patronage, the diverse ethnic groups lived relatively peacefully, racially motivated murder was rare, and the Houses of Friendship and the lip-service devoted to inter-ethnic harmony were loud and clear, albeit largely superficial. Certain sections of the population today look back at this aspect of the period with nostalgia and regret.

The political history of the local leadership has been chequered, and some writers have judged discriminatory many policies carried out in Azerbaijan by the Moscow authorities.[15] Undoubtedly, however, under the Brezhnev regime a successful *pax sovietica* was established in which dissident nationalist elements were ruthlessly suppressed, largely by a local leadership eager to retain the status quo through which relatively lavish lifestyles could be maintained through local networks of corruption.[16] One Brezhnevite whose influence is still remembered is G. Aliev, whom the Moscow authorities installed as First Party Secretary in Azerbaijan in 1969. He pleased his masters by expanding those sectors of the economy which were deemed to be of 'All-Union significance'. In the countryside vast territories which had previously served the local population in fruit and vegetables were turned over to mono-culture, such as to vineyards whose produce was almost entirely exported outside Azerbaijan. The number of enterprises which were run entirely as subsidiaries of Russian factories or by ministries in Moscow increased under Aliev. On the other hand, he was seen to be a 'strong leader', and through an elaborate patron–client system was able to bring, through informal channels, stability despite a population increasingly divided between the privileged and those who were not.

AZERBAIJAN UNDER GORBACHEV

If for centuries the Azerbaijanis have pondered over which way to express their ethnic identity and sense of nationhood, under Gorbachev this aspect has found its expression unequivocally for a majority of the population in the strongest sense of territoriality yet documented.

Apart from difficulties of a more political nature linked to local party inertia and with national conflicts over territory, Gorbachev has been faced with particular problems in Azerbaijan because of the effects of a growing population faced with increasing awareness of their economic deprivations.

The population of Azerbaijan in 1987 had reached 6,811,000, and the excess of births over deaths had been 2.9 per cent in the previous two years. Since 1970 the rural and urban populations had been equal, but the past two years had witnessed an increase in favour of urban dwellers (54 per cent urban, 46 per cent rural).[17] This growing youthful population has demanded education (further education is usually seen as the way to better jobs) and employment. Increasingly, more rural people look for both in the cities. There has been a sharp increase in unemployment, although reliable statistics are hard to come by (unofficially 14 per cent). They believe that the racist attitudes of other peoples of the USSR towards them have increased, and this has promoted a greater reluctance in the population to seek work outside Azerbaijan. Urban housing problems have also grown in consequence, the number of factory workers living in hostels and families living in virtual shacks at the edge of the cities is larger than ever.

In rural areas the land available varies sharply, but gainful employment is hard to acquire for school leavers in a system that remains inflexible and which still gives little scope for improvement. The leasing system in farming promoted by Gorbachev has hardly begun and is rigidly controlled. The state still forbids moving away from mono-cultures such as cotton or grapes. Choices in the use of pesticides are also not allowed, and such decisions are having an increasingly disastrous effect on animal husbandry and soil quality.

The economy, according to official statistics, would be seen to have grown impressively, although in having to demonstrate this the authorities had to resort to devices such as using base dates like 1913 or 1940, to show recent growth in relation to those earlier times and to conceal more recent trends.[18] The 1980–85 Five-Year Plan nevertheless showed an increase of 116.4 million roubles in overall production compared to the 1976–80 period, which yielded 85.9 million roubles.[19] In the very new climate of media openness which only began in Azerbaijan in September 1989, a new picture is emerging. Between 1980 and 1988, it is claimed, one-fifth of annual production was wasted each year.[20] More damning, however, is the alleged fact that no other single republic was afflicted by such disproportions. The lagging behind the rest of the USSR in all indices of economic welfare of the Azerbaijani population has grown from between 1.7 to 2 times in the same period (1980–88). It is revealed that the republic holds one of the last places in the Soviet Union for levels of social and cultural benefits. Per capita use of national income is only 62 per cent of the average level for the rest of the Soviet Union, only 65 per cent of average Soviet social funds and only 59 per cent of consumer goods. The same article, published in the Communist Party's official papers (*Kommunist Azerbaijan* in Azerbaijani, *Bakinskiy Rabochiy* in Russian) declares that the average per capita income in Azerbaijan is 75 roubles per month whereas such a low wage is received by only 12.6 per cent in the rest of the country. Whereas those in the Soviet Union receiving more than 200 roubles per month form 17.2 per cent of the whole, in Azerbaijan only 6.3 per cent of the population benefit in this way. Thus, the Azerbaijanis have asked why they should occupy this humiliating position, having supplied the world and the Soviet Union, in particular, with oil for a century. Even though Siberian oil resources and petroleum products have gained in importance and their own have diminished in recent times, they point to other mineral resources and even to their export of agricultural produce as having no mean significance. Why, too, would so many Moscow ministries control such large sectors of industrial production if Azerbaijani wealth were so inconsiderable? This last question, however, leads one to the riposte of the newly formed Azerbaijani Popular Front, now also adopted by the local Party: most of the gross national product of Azerbaijan is deemed to leave the republic. The Popular Front say 93 per cent of GNP is expropriated, and only portions of this are returned annually in unpredictable handouts from the centre.

In consequence, Gorbachev has to face in Azerbaijan one of the fastest growing and most forceful demands for economic independence in the Soviet Union. The transition to self-financing and accounting encouraged by the centre has been transformed locally into serious demands for control over all production on the territory of the Azerbaijani republic. Insistence from the centre that 'production of All-Union significance' should be excluded from local control has met with fierce resistance. Whereas the Baltic republics have made the same demand firmly but quietly, the Azerbaijani population is viewed by the centre as volatile. The Azerbaijanis appear so dissatisfied that they claim they are willing to take untold risks to achieve this aim. It must also, and importantly, be said that the majority of the working class is Azerbaijani and that it participates more than in any other Union republic in the organisation and expression of national dissent (see Appendix 2, Table 6).

Economic grievances, however, had sharpened the division between the local Azerbaijani Communist Party and the majority of the population who have regarded it as a bastion of privilege paid for by subserviance to the centre. The Popular Front was only recognised officially in September 1989 and it is only force of circumstances, in particular the growth of industrial unrest, that finally forced the local Party to agree to consult the Popular Front and to join it in the struggle for republican sovereignty, particularly in the economic sphere.

The Popular Front of Azerbaijan has achieved unprecedented local prestige and influence in a rapid reversal of fortune which took place in September and October 1989. As will be described below, the way in which it happened reflects some of the new, democratic elements in the Gorbachev era: the direct use of television, mass demonstrations and strikes.

As elsewhere in the Soviet Union, groups of intellectuals have gathered informally, particularly since the mid-1960s, to discuss ways of gaining concessions from the government for personal liberty and, in the case of the minority republics, for national self-determination. The restoration of national monuments, the concern for the ecological devastation caused by mindless policies and other similar issues have always been at the forefront of these mostly clandestine discussions, and it is only under Gorbachev that they have gathered momentum and have been expressed more openly. On the fringes of open dissent in Azerbaijan there have been members of the intelligentsia who have maintained their distance overtly, but have done this as a tactic in order to act as mediators with the local Party which, until recently, was totally hostile.

Exceptionally in Azerbaijan, however, the initiative for the organisation of dissent through mass demonstrations was taken by the working class, notably in November 1988, which at first distanced itself from the intelligentsia whose members it deemed to be mainly corrupt in their pursuit of personal wealth.[21] On that occasion, nearly a million people gathered in the main square in Baku, with workers being joined by students and other citizens. The initial impetus was to protest about Moscow's handling of the Nagorno-Karabakh affair and Armenian hostility, but very soon protests were to centre on economic mismanagement and workers' rights. Workers from the podium tightly controlled the meetings, suppressing what they deemed to be provocative actions such as a group of people who began shouting anti-Armenian slogans. They organised camp fires for warmth in the November chill and distributed food to the demonstrators after insisting that the Russian soldiers who stood surrounding them be fed first.[22] The central authorities, however, became nervous after the tenth day and finally, after repeated and clear warnings about their plans, moved in troops and tanks and cleared the relatively small number of people who had remained in the square, arresting the leaders, among whom was Neimat Panakhov, dubbed the 'Lech Walesa of Azerbaijan'.[23] In an interview with the author afterhe was released from nearly six months in prison, Panakhov affirmed his belief that it was the authorities' fear of an Azerbaijani democratic workers' movement that had motivated their inertia in contending firmly with initial Armenian protest which they knew full well would be highly provocative for the Azerbaijanis. In his view, the November meeting had started spontaneously but could have been disbanded easily, had the government agreed to a genuine dialogue on worker grievances (the local and Moscow officials refused to appear in public at the time).

Since his release, however, and while still awaiting sentence, Panakhov became a member of the fifteen-strong Popular Front Executive Committee whose intellectual members show deference to their more powerful worker colleagues. In a recent document dated 30 October 1989, a member of the Popular Front voices concern at the possibility of a rift between the moderate intellectuals (and a minority of moderate workers) among the few Popular Front leaders and the militant workers on whose support the Popular Front movement depends.[24] Much of their activity has been devoted to finding ways of solving the Nagorno-Karabakh dispute, yet, interestingly, the programme of the

Popular Front of Azerbaijan does not mention Nagorno-Karabakh at all.[25]

First, the programme declares that the aim of the 'Popular Front of Azerbaijan (PFA) is to support *perestroika* as a general social movement aiming to improve and democratise all spheres of our lives'.[26] It supports the aim that the 'social, economic and political norms and practices correspond in spirit and in letter to the basic law of the Constitution of the Soviet Socialist Republic of Azerbaijan'.[27] The PFA 'absolutely condemns the use of force in political struggle', its founding values are 'Humanism, democracy, pluralism, internationalism and human rights'.[28] It does not differentiate 'according to social group, Party membership, nationality or religion'. However, more difficult for Gorbachev is its declaration that 'The main task of the PFA is to achieve political, economic and cultural sovereignty for the republic of Azerbaijan', including independent representation abroad in the UN and Unesco. It also supports the abolition of political barriers which impede the development of economic and cultural ties with Southern Azerbaijan, 'while recognising the indisputable borders between the USSR and Iran'. The programme also advocates that peasants, 'the true owners of the land', should have the land handed back to them for unlimited use, to have complete freedom to cultivate it as individual farmers or in a collective. The PFA also notes that the slogan 'Factories and plants to the workers' can be put into action only by endowing the council of workers' collectives with rights in the management of enterprises and by ensuring that competent managers are in charge of enterprises through free and democratic elections.

The PFA programme has a strong component on human rights: 'Freedom and not just well-being' is stated to be the highest universal good. It also opposes the participation in any military action not declared justified in international law. On ethnic relations it declares that 'The Azerbaijanis as the dominant ethnic group in the republic are responsible for ethnic relations', and the PFA aims for the creation of the best conditions for the preservation and the encouragement of the language, culture and national traditions of the ethnic minorities living in the Azerbaijan SSR. It also would like to encourage broad cultural links with the peoples of the world but in particular with the peoples 'who historically formed the cultural region of the Near and Middle East'. It also hopes to spread a new attitude towards Islamic religion and culture 'so that it should no longer be subjected to the ignorant attacks of philistines'.

There are two reasons why these demands of the Popular Front will eventually have to receive Gorbachev's attention. First, the local Party is weakened and so discredited that it commands authority and respect only in so far as it voices the opinions of the PFA, a trend which has increased since October 1989. Second, a significant number of Azerbaijanis listen to foreign broadcasts, in particular the Azerbaijani-language programmes of Radio Liberty and Voice of America, who themselves are in direct contact with the dissident community in Azerbaijan. Thus, in remote rural areas as elsewhere, the masses appear to be well informed and, until very recently when the press became more open, relied more on these sources of information than other forms of the media. The television has dramatically gained in importance but it is more vulnerable to changes in policies, whereas foreign broadcasts are seen as a stable and long-standing source of communication. Yet it is typically a trait of the Gorbachev era that television has acquired exceptional influence, especially for the urban population. Some incidents in the saga of the struggle for official recognition by the PFA epitomise this trend.

Following mass meetings and occasional work stoppages in August 1989, which elicited no response from the local government, the Popular Front called a national meeting for 2 September 1989, to be followed by a national strike two days later – the first in seventy years (according to Leila Iunusova)[29] – if the local government refused to meet their main demands. These included having an unscheduled meeting of the Supreme Soviet of the Azerbaijan SSR to discuss matters of sovereignty, of normalisation in Nagorno-Karabakh, the release of political prisoners, the recognition of the Popular Front of Azerbaijan and other issues. They demanded that there be direct transmission by television of the Supreme Soviet session, open voting and that all support should be offered to the PFA to facilitate their participation in the work of the session. The government was apparently frightened,[30] and even resorted to leafleting the population on the dangers of the meeting and the strike. On 8 September, following a picket by women of the official press headquarters of Azerinform, the press officers had to deny the wisdom of the leaflets. As tension mounted, new words entered the political vocabulary of Azerbaijan, according to PFA member Leila Yunusova:[31] 'Tatil' (strike) and 'iste'fa' (resign). These words were chanted during speeches at the meetings organised continuously in the open air in Baku from 6 to 10 p.m., at which the national flag of the 1918–20 government was displayed.

Dialogue began between the Azerbaijani government and the PFA. To demonstrate this, the Second Secretary of the Communist Party in Azerbaijan, V. Polyanichko (Moscow usually appoints non-native, invariably Russian, or 'Russianised' Ukrainian, second Party secretaries in the Union republics) appeared at the mass meeting and announced that the special session of the Azerbaijani Supreme Soviet would take place on 15 September, to which the PFA would be invited. However, the PFA leaders announced at the same meeting that if at precisely 8.30 p.m. on 10 September someone from the PFA leadership did not appear on television to call an end to the strike, people were to resume it on 12 September. Indeed, three PFA members and three officials did appear on the television screen together and the strike was halted. The next day, however, A. Vezirov, the First Secretary of the Communist Party in Azerbaijan, flew back from Moscow and was displeased, apparently, with what was taking place in his absence.

The PFA called a meeting on 13 September at which allegedly half a million people were present and announced that Vezirov had till 9 p.m. that evening to sign the prepared protocol to avoid a renewal of the strike, which he did. Two days later, the extraordinary session of the Supreme Soviet of Azerbaijan was covered by direct television broadcast. Crowds nevertheless stood outside the building as heated discussions took place inside, culminating in high tension when the exasperated PFA turned to the television cameras and announced their wish that the strikes resume. It was one o'clock at night and masses of people still stood together outside. Sensing the gravity of the crisis, Vezirov asked for a fifteen-minute break that turned into two hours, after which concessions were made to the PFA demands.

Shortly afterwards, the press agreed to publish the discussion papers for drafting laws on economic and political sovereignty.[32] From now on, the PFA instead of being subject to sporadic arrest and harassment, was officially recognised. The local government leaders appeared on television from time to time to state that the yearnings of the PFA for sovereignty as well as an end to the conflictual situation in Nagorno-Karabakh were identical with their own wishes.

In January 1990, Vezirov was dismissed for inaction, the PFA was attacked in the press and several of its members were arrested or went into hiding. According to General Yazov, the deployment of troops in Baku that month, resulting in several hundred fatalities, had the purpose of dismantling the power of the PFA and restoring it to the local Communist Party. Since the events of September 1989 which were described above, however, the PFA still retains more credibility among the population than the local government.

Nagorno-Karabakh

The majority of the demands of the PFA can be dealt with by the ruling government over a considerable period of time, but a solution to the impasse reached over Nagorno-Karabakh, the cause of such violence and a threat to the stability essential to Gorbachev's credibility, must be sought by him with greater urgency.

That the Armenians' demands to administer the region from Erevan should have been met with such fierce reaction from the Azerbaijanis can be explained in several ways. First, the Azerbaijanis have learned to think of their nationhood in territorial terms. It would have been seen by the Azerbaijanis as the ultimate insult if the Soviet authorities had ordered them to hand over territory which they had thought was their only inalienable resource at a time when they had become increasingly aware of the way they had been economically exploited by the centre. Second, they could not accept the legitimacy of Armenian demands on historical, statistical or political grounds. Third, they felt that the outside world perceived their refusal to cede the territory of Nagorno-Karabakh as provocative. In other words, they feared general acceptance of a minority Armenian view of themselves as aggressive barbarians.

The original decision taken in 1921 on the republican borders had been ceaselessly disputed, however discreetly at times.[33] When Gorbachev came to power, many Armenians in the enclave of Nagorno-Karabakh had become exasperated by what they believed was the deliberate mismanagement of their region by Baku. Some Azerbaijanis today say that those Armenians were not alone in suffering the consequences of bad administration and that corrupt government should have been eliminated rather than allowing nationalist diversions to develop.[34] Instead, indecision in Moscow was the result, it is thought, of a policy seeking piecemeal measures to pamper Armenian nationalist interpretations of events and to create instability in order to gain greater control over the republics at a later stage. Conspiracy theories abound in Azerbaijan as a result of each concession Moscow is perceived to have made to Armenian sentiment, which makes it more difficult for Gorbachev to reach an understanding with the Azerbaijanis.

The Nagorno-Karabakh affair can be divided so far into two phases, the first beginning in November 1987 and the second phase beginning in September 1989. Most articulate Azerbaijanis[35] claim that the issue of Nagorno-Karabakh started in November 1987 when Aganbegyan, one of Gorbachev's economic advisers who is of Armenian ethnic origin, declared that he believed that Nagorno-Karabakh should be handed over to the administration of the Armenian Soviet republic.[36] Systems of personal patronage are customary, and there was nervousness at the thought that someone so close to the General Secretary of the Soviet Communist Party should be of that opinion.

The Azerbaijani version of events obviously differs from the Armenian version, more familiar to the West. Azerbaijanis nearly all believe that the mass protests in Nagorno-Karabakh by the Armenian population were organised not by local inhabitants but by leaders from the Armenian republic. They furthermore point to the resentment felt by the majority of Armenians who lived in Baku at the risks to which they were being exposed by the protests in Stepanakert, capital of the Nagorno-Karabakh enclave. When feelings were heated in both Erevan and the enclave, two Azerbaijani youths were killed and others fled from the area. Up to 2,000 Azerbaijanis were said to have arrived in Sumgait. Baku radio, allegedly believing they could calm the fervent spirit of the Armenians by telling them of the risks involved in their movement, announced the deaths of the two Azerbaijani youths thinking this would make the Armenians regret their actions. Instead, the announcement allegedly backfired:

the Azerbaijani population, hearing the news, was outraged, and the massacre of Sumgait took place in which a disputed number of Armenians lost their lives in the most macabre of circumstances.

The events in Sumgait form a landmark in Gorbachev's rule; ethnic violence had taken place on a scale unknown by his immediate predecessors. The massacre in Sumgait is also a turning point in the history of the modern Azerbaijanis, for it is the one event which has brought this previously little-known nation to world attention, and which attributes to it a reputation the Azerbaijanis resent. The social and ecological conditions in Sumgait are regrettable, it was explained to the author, with 20 per cent of its population being prisoners in forced labour and with one of the highest infant mortality rates because of pollution. Many Azerbaijanis feel obliged to ask the world not to condemn a whole nation because of the atrocities, however horrific, committed by a small number of mostly very young men. They also have to refute the stereotypical image of themselves as 'wild Turks' whom the Armenians have likened to the western Turks responsible for the massacre of Armenians in 1915. Moreover, Moscow, although perhaps not Gorbachev alone, is perceived to have handled the situation in a way that would alienate them further. As public sympathy rose for the Armenian cause, it is argued that Azerbaijanis were not given a chance to obtain equal media coverage for their version of events or for the violence to which they too fell victim.

There was a rapid escalation of violence immediately after the events in Sumgait. The Azerbaijanis insist that numerically they suffered more deaths than the Armenians. There was, however, a dramatic exchange of population between the Soviet republics of Armenia and Azerbaijan. Apparently every single Azerbaijani who had lived in Armenia arrived as a refugee in Azerbaijan, sometimes not even fully dressed. This aroused a public outcry which the authorities and eventually martial law attempted to defuse. When direct rule was imposed in Nagorno-Karabakh by a special committee set up by decree on 12 January 1989, the Russian commander-in-chief A. Volsky in the interests of security asked all 16,000 Azerbaijanis to leave the regional capital Stepanakert, an act interpreted by a majority of Azerbaijanis as showing blatant anti-Azerbaijani bias. More worrying, however, was the portrayal of the special administrative arrangement as a first step towards the rulers in Moscow conceding Nagorno-Karabakh to Armenia. At the Party level there were also resolutions and counter-resolutions between the two Soviet republics of Armenia and Azerbaijan (see Chapter 9).

The second phase in the Nagorno-Karabakh débâcle began in September when reports starting from events in June reached the rest of Azerbaijan that not only were Azerbaijani villages near Shusha in the southern part of Nagorno-Karabakh still cut off, and had been for over a year, from water and electricity supplies, but the remaining

Azerbaijanis were being terrorised by armed bands of Armenians whom the forces under Volsky had ignored. The Popular Front was seen to be more vociferous than the local Party and was gaining momentum. Eventually the strikes began and, more significantly, a railway blockade of goods destined for Armenia.

The blockade (named an 'embargo' by the Popular Front) was thought to be demonstrating two factors: first, that Azerbaijani railway workers and even Azerbaijani passengers were not receiving sufficient protection from any Soviet forces directed from Moscow or the forces of either republic against alleged attacks when travelling through Armenian territory. Second, the blockade was supposed to serve as a demonstration to the world that Armenia was dependent on Azerbaijani goodwill to receive the goods it so badly needed, and, by implication, that having refrained from such action in the past had demonstrated Azerbaijani restraint and good manners. The outcry following the news that badly needed materials for the reconstruction of the parts of Armenia so adversely affected by the earthquake in December 1988 were being withheld or deliberately ruined was met with a certain amount of indifference among the Azerbaijani popular leadership. The facts had never been released that the first Soviet plane to crash, losing around seventy lives bringing relief to earthquake-stricken Armenia had actually come from Azerbaijan. They had instead been accused of being jubilant when the earthquake took place in Armenia, which Azerbaijanis constantly deny.

A decree from Moscow on 28 November 1989 dissolved the special commission ruling Nagorno-Karabakh and returned its administration to Azerbaijan. Rumours spread through the rest of the country that armed Armenian guerrillas were going to seize the enclave by force as well as the two regions separating it from the borders of the Armenian republic. An Azerbaijani 'voluntary militia' was established, and skirmishes took place between protagonists from both republics. Fighting also started north of the enclave and along the border between Nakhichevan and the Armenian republic. In protest, Azerbaijani crowds claimed land along the border with Iran usually kept as a no-man's-land for military use. They also demanded the right to visit relatives in Iran and an opening in the border in the way that the Berlin Wall had been breached in Germany. Finally, in January 1990, with the numbers of refugees arriving in Baku growing constantly, a group of Azerbaijani terrorists vented their wrath on Armenians who had remained in Baku, and another massacre took place as violent as that in Sumgait. It was finally brought under control after several days and a further exodus of Armenian refugees was organised. Throughout the disturbances, local government had been ineffectual, with the restoration of order being carried out by representatives of various organisations affiliated to the Popular Front. On 19 January 1990, Soviet troops were sent into Baku whose actions resulted in between 83 (official) and several hundred (unofficial) deaths. Since then, Azerbaijanis have become hardened in their resolve to achieve independence from Moscow.

PROSPECTS

Under Gorbachev the Azerbaijanis have become aware of themselves as a nation and under his guidance they may either channel their energies to achieving political and economic sovereignty through constitutional procedure or else achieve it through armed struggle. Although economic cooperation would have to be negotiated with the RSFSR through a mutually acceptable pricing system, economic self-management for Azerbaijan would release Gorbachev's leadership from some of the responsibilities of the backwardness in the Azerbaijani economy. With more democratic structures within the Soviet government apparatus the divisions between the state and the popular fronts would probably be resolved. This might finally lead to more genuine dialogue between Armenia and Azerbaijan rather than further belligerence shown in territorial claims. It is interesting, therefore, to see how the destiny of a southern republic such as Azerbaijan has under Gorbachev become a key element in resolving the difficulties which have beset his government.

NOTES

1. Dj. B. Guliev (ed.) *Istoria Azerbaijana* (Baku 1979, Elm Publishers).
2. R. Tapper (ed.) *The Conflict of Tribe and State in Iran and Afghanistan* (London, Croom Helm; New York, St Martin's Press, 1983).
3. T. Swietochowski *Russian Azerbaijan 1905–1920: the Shaping of National Identity in a Muslim Community* (Cambridge, Cambridge University Press, 1985).
4. Swietochowski, *Russian Azerbaijan*.
5. T. Swietochowski 'National Consciousness and Political Orientations in Azerbaijan, 1905–1920', in R. Suny (ed.), *Transcaucasia: Nationalism and Social Change* (Michigan, Michigan Slavic Publications, 1983).
6. F. Kazemzadeh *The Struggle for Transcaucasia 1917–1921* (New York/-Oxford; The Philosophical Library, 1951); Swietochowski *Russian Azerbaijan*; R. G. Suny *The Baku Commune 1917–1918, Class and Nationality in the Russian Revolution* (Princeton, NJ: Princeton University Press, 1972).
7. L. Iunusova 'The End of the Ice Age; Azerbaijan August–September 1989', *Central Asia and Caucasus Chronicle* vol. 8, no. 6 (Dec. 1989–Jan. 1990).
8. Z. Bunyatov 'Istoricheskaya nauka v Azerbaijane na rubezhe dvukh

stoletii; sostayanie i perspektivi' Elm, 24 Sept. 1988. Baku; *'Dirchalish'* (Revival) (May 1989), 1.

9. T. Dragadze 'The Armenian–Azerbaijani Conflict: Structure and Sentiment', *Third World Quarterly* vol. 11, no. 1 (Jan. 1989).

10. Swietochowksi, *Russian Azerbaijan*.

11. S. Crisp 'Language Policy in Daghestan', Paper read at a conference in London on 'The Russian Advance Towards the Muslim World and the Barrier of the North Caucasus' (London: Society for Central Asian Studies, 1988).

12. A. Tabrizli *Histoire du Daglig(Haut)-Garabagh à la lumière de documents historiques* (Strasbourg; Dagyeli Publishers of the Association Culturelle Azerbaidjanaise à Strasbourg, 1989).

13. *Pravda* 11 July 1988; Suny (ed.) *Transcaucasia*, p. 77.

14. *Narodnoe Khozaistvo Azerbaijanskoi SSR k 70 letiyu velikogo oktyabrya 1987*, (Baku; Azerbaijanskoe gosudarstvennoe izdatelstvo).

15. A. L. Alstadt 'Nagorno-Karabakh, Apple of Discord in the Azerbaijan SSR', *Central Asian Survey* vol. 7, no. 4 (1988).

16. G. Smith 'Gorbachev's Greatest Challenge: Perestroika and the National Question', *Political Geography Quarterly* vol. 8, no. 1 (Jan. 1989), pp. 7–20.

17. Derived by author from *Narodnoe Khozaistvo 1987*.

18. *Narodnoe Khozaistvo 1987*.

19. *Narodnoe Khozaistvo 1987*.

20. *Bakinskiy Rabochiy* 21 Sept. 1989.

21. T. Dragadze, Interview with Neimat Panakhov, *Central Asia and Caucasus Chronicle* vol. 8, no. 5 (1989).

22. Ibid.

23. Ibid.

24. Iunosova 'End of the Ice Age'.

25. Programme of the Azerbaijan Popular Front, *Central Asia and Caucasus Chronicle* vol. 8, no. 4 (Aug. 1989).

26. *Ibid*.

27. *Ibid*.

28. *Ibid*.

29. Iunosova 'End of the Ice Age'.

30. Ibid.

31. Ibid.

32. Ibid.

33. T. Kocharli 'Neobkhodimoe utochnenie', *Bakinskiy Rabochiy* 8 June 1989.

34. Dragadze, Interview with Neimat Panakhov, op.cit.

35. Author's interviews in 1989 and Jan. 1990.

36. *L'Humanité*, Nov. 1987 (Paris).

CHAPTER ELEVEN

Georgians

Robert Parsons

BACKGROUND

Sakartvelo, the land of the Kartvelians (as the Georgians call themselves), lies between the Black and Caspian seas and on the southern flanks of the main Caucasian range. A naturally abundant land, it has always attracted the attentions of its more powerful southern and northern neighbours. As a consequence, its history, apart from brief interludes of peace, has been a long struggle for survival.

Georgia has been exposed to a wide range of cultural influences: classical, Byzantine, Persian, Turkish and, more recently, Russian, but the single most important moment in the early coalescence of the nation was Georgia's conversion to Christianity in the fourth century AD.

As Islam spread rapidly through Asia Minor, Georgia, like Armenia, began to forge an identity that marked it off from the surrounding Persian and Arab worlds. With the collapse of the Armenian state in the tenth century, Georgia was left as a solitary outpost of Christianity. Yet it was just at this moment that the Georgian state reached the peak of its powers. From the eleventh century, the term 'Sakartvelo', describing all the land occupied by the Georgians, entered into common usage and, for the first time, all the Georgian lands, stretching from the Black Sea to the Caspian and south into present-day Turkey and Iran, were united under one ruler.

Against a background of political unity, economic prosperity and military success, Georgian culture flourished until the Mongol invasions of the mid-thirteenth century shattered the power of the central state. Fractured by the rivalries of its feudal princes and constantly invaded by the Mongols, Persians and Turks, Georgia entered into a long period of decline that lasted well into the eighteenth century.

In 1783, however, King Irakli II, who had successfully reunited the eastern half of the Georgian state, concluded the Treaty of Giorgievsk with Russia. By its terms, Georgia ceded control of foreign and defence policy to the Russian crown, but retained sovereignty over its internal affairs. It was to prove to be the first step on the road to incorporation into the Russian empire. In 1801, Tsar Paul abrogated the terms of the treaty by forcibly annexing the Kingdom of Kartl-Kakheti (East Georgia).

Over the ensuing sixty years, Russia took over piecemeal most of the remaining Georgian territories, until by the conclusion of the Russo-Turkish war in 1878 much of the medieval Georgian state had been reunited under its control. But, although Georgians were grateful to the Russians for protecting them from their Muslim neighbours and regaining their lost territories, they bitterly resented the division of Georgia into separate administrative provinces and the persistent denigration of their culture and language. It is an ambivalence towards the Russian presence that persists to this day.

By the late nineteenth century, opposition to the Russians had led to the formation of a national liberation movement among the Georgian intelligentsia. But what began as a student movement had by the turn of the century spread to the peasantry and working class. The main beneficiaries were the socialists, who were quick to exploit a coincidence of class and nationality: whereas the bourgeoisie was predominantly Armenian and Russian, the Georgians comprised the peasantry, working class and increasingly destitute aristocracy. Within years, the Georgian socialists, as members of the Menshevik wing of the Russian Social Democratic Party, had created a mass organisation with branches all over the country.

In 1917 the openness and minimalist aims of the Georgian Mensheviks brought them into conflict with the Bolsheviks. Noe Zhordania, the leader of the Georgian party organisation, refused to recognise the legality of the October Revolution, preferring instead to lead Georgia to independence.

GEORGIAN INDEPENDENCE 1918–21

The initial reluctance of the Georgian Social Democrats to separate from Russian proved short-lived. In his declaration of Georgia's independence on 26 May 1918, Zhordania abandoned the ideas of class struggle in favour of national unity and relegated socialism to the status of a distant goal.

But the new government faced enormous problems. Years of exploitation under the tsarist administration had left the Georgian economy unbalanced and unprepared for self-rule. Regarded primarily as a supplier of raw materials, its industrial development had been even slower than that of central Russia, producing in 1915 to the value of 10 roubles of factory-made goods per caput a year.[1] By 1918 war and revolution had undermined even that modest achievement.

Independence, while enthusiastically welcomed, was achieved against a background of economic collapse, sudden loss of the crucial Russian market and Turkish invasion. Communications between the capital, Tbilisi, and the outlying districts were almost non-existent, food was scarce and the administrative infrastructure had collapsed, leaving few with the experience to fill the role of the Russian bureaucracy.

Nor did the end of the war bring relief. Despite its neutrality, both sides in the Russian Civil War were hostile to Georgia. The Whites sought on several occasions to seize parts of its territory, while the Bolsheviks helped organise uprisings in the national minority areas of Abkhazia and South Ossetia. But the Russians and Turks were not the only threat: in December 1918 the Armenians invaded following a futile dispute over the border district of Lore. Only British intervention brought the conflict to an end.[2]

Against this background, the Georgian Social Democratic Party (GSDP) began increasingly to stress the urgency of active popular support for the state, a difficult task in a country where there was no recent history of a united, independent state structure and where the peasantry had grown used to regarding the state as alien and hostile. They saw mass participation in the electoral process and a programme of Georgianisation as the keys to overcoming popular indifference.

Local government elections in 1918 were followed in 1919 by national elections. Under a system of proportional representation, the GSDP won convincingly, securing 109 of the 130 seats in the Georgian Constituent Assembly. Remarkably, 70 per cent of the rural electorate turned out to vote.[3]

Electoral reform was accompanied by a national education programme. Georgian became the official medium of instruction and a crash programme was undertaken to build schools and libraries in the villages. The first Georgian university opened in January 1918. Yet, like so many of the reforms in 1918–21, they were never fully realised. Because of the economic crisis, teachers were badly paid, often close to destitution, and schools had few textbooks. Moreover, the reorganisation of education and the new status of Georgian demanded the creation of an entirely new syllabus and set of textbooks. Neither of these existed by the time of the Russian invasion in 1921.[4]

For all the problems, however, many had believed in 1920 that the worst was over. The Social Democrats still commanded enormous support, particularly among the working class and peasantry, and Soviet Russia had signalled its readiness to recognise Georgia's independence.[5] On 7 May 1920 Lenin signed a treaty renouncing Soviet Russia's claim to Georgian territory and any right to interfere in Georgia's internal affairs. But less than a year later, on 11 February 1921, on the pretext of an uprising in the neutral zone of Lore between Georgia and Armenia, the Red Army invaded. Six weeks later Georgia's short-lived independence was at an end.[6]

THE GEORGIANS AS PART OF SOVIET LIFE

As Soviet historians are now admitting, the invasion was no more than a localised protest among Armenian peasants, engineered by the leader of the Caucasian Bolsheviks, Sergo Ordzhonikidze, a close associate of Stalin.[7] The poor standing of the Bolsheviks in Georgia fell even lower as a consequence of the invasion and, despite a vigorous recruitment drive, its membership in the countryside still numbered fewer than 6,000 by 1924. Most of the new recruits, moreover, were poor, uneducated peasants.[8] But the government faced more than just an ideological struggle. The economy was in ruins, with industrial output in 1921 a mere 13.8 per cent of its 1913 level and inflation spiralling out of control.[9]

Industrial reconstruction in the 1920s moved slowly. Despite investment in several major hydroelectric projects and the creation of a number of large-scale industrial associations, output in 1925 had still only reached 86.4 per cent of its pre-war level, while unemployment remained high.[10]

Georgia was a predominantly rural society. Some 70 per cent of its national income was derived from agriculture and 85.5 per cent of the population lived in the countryside.[11] The Bolshevik land reform of April 1921, which brought Georgia into line with Soviet Russia, did little to improve life, partly because the independent Georgian government's own land reforms had already redistributed most of the available land and partly because of the overall shortage of land. At 40.1 persons per square kilometre, Georgia had one of the highest population densities in the USSR in the 1920s. The all-union average was 7.3.[12]

The Party authorities continued to regard the peasantry as a threat to their authority throughout the 1920s, always fearful that national and economic grievances could fuse into armed resistance. Despite the Party's failure to win active support, however, the stability brought by the first years of Soviet power proved enough to win the peasantry's acquiescence. By 1926, agricultural output was back to 85.5 per cent of its 1913 level.[13]

The change in regime did little to alter established demographic patterns. As a result of the pro-Georgian policies of the GSDP government, independence had witnessed a rise in the Georgian share of the population from 67.7 per cent in 1917 to 71.5 per cent in 1922–23, a development that was partially corrected as Armenians and Russians returned to Georgia after the invasion. By 1989 Georgians comprised 70.1 per cent of the population of 5,448,600.[14]

Political opposition to Moscow continued at least until 1925 from the defeated Georgian intelligentsia, supported to some extent by the working class and peasantry, and, more surprisingly, from the Georgian Communist Party leadership, which resented the attempts of the centre to limit its autonomy. This inner party issue focused on a bitter dispute between the 'national deviationists', led by Budu Mdivani, and the Caucasian Buro, led by Ordzhonikidze, about the pace of the socialist revolution in Georgia and the question of whether Georgia should be incorporated into the USSR as a separate republic or as part of a Transcaucasian federation. In December 1922, the Georgian Bolsheviks were forced to concede defeat. Georgia entered the USSR as a part of the Transcaucasian Socialist Federal Soviet Republic (ZSFSR). The arrangement not only granted the ZSFSR powers to establish overall economic plans for the area and the right to overrule any republican decision, but also deprived the republics of their separate right to secede. That was now invested in the ZSFSR as a whole. The defeat of the 'national deviationists' brought a new centralist Party leadership into power and heralded the beginning of tougher policies in the republic.

The resistance of the nationalist opposition to Soviet power crumbled with the defeat of a popular uprising in August 1924. As many as 4,000 people were subsequently executed.[15] It was a forewarning of the fate that awaited Georgia in the 1930s. The collectivisation and industrialisation of 1928–32 were followed in 1936–38 by political purges that cut a deep swathe through the intelligentsia and wiped out almost the entire Georgian Party leadership.

The full force of collectivisation hit the republic between October 1929 and March 1930. In just four months the number of collectivised families rose from 3.4 per cent to 65.2 per cent.[16] In March, however, the campaign suddenly slackened in response to Stalin's 'Dizzy with success' article in *Pravda*. By the beginning of 1932 the number of collectivised farms had fallen to 36.1 per cent of the total.[17] But the financial penalties of remaining outside the collectives began to have the same effect as the violence of the initial campaign. By the end of the decade 92.3 per cent of agriculture had been collectivised.[18]

The transformation of agriculture was accompanied by an equally dramatic transformation of industry. The total value of production reached 503 million roubles in 1932, almost thirteen times its pre-war level, and then more than doubled in the second five year plan to reach 1,047 million roubles in 1937, 75.2 per cent of the national product.[19] By 1940 industrial output had increased 670 per cent over 1928. Between 1930 and 1934 the size of the industrial workforce grew by 40.5 per cent, while by 1939 the population of Tbilisi had swollen to 519,000, some 225,000 more than in 1926.[20]

The violent economic revolution was matched by brutal purges of the intelligentsia and Party and government apparatuses, orchestrated by Lavrenti Beria, who became First Secretary of the Georgian Party in 1931 and simultaneously head of the Transcaucasian Party in 1932. A cleansing of Party ranks in 1933 was followed in 1934 with a series of attacks on the cultural intelligentisa. In 1936–37 countless Georgian writers, poets, artists, scientists and others were executed or perished in exile. Far from benefiting from Stalin's patronage, it is probable that proportionately Georgia suffered more than any other republic during the purges.[21]

The new constitution in 1936 restored republican status to Georgia but did nothing to restore its former autonomy. As if to underline the point, Budu Mdivani, who had been leader of the Georgian Party during its feud with Ordzhonikidze and Stalin, was arrested and shot in 1937.

By the end of the decade Georgia's social and economic life had been violently transformed. Thousands of peasants had been forced to take up collectivised farming. Thousands had been executed, sent into exile or simply disappeared. Thousands more had abandoned their villages to seek work in the urban factories. In the towns, the old intelligentsia, the product of the greatest flourishing of Georgian artistic talent since the Middle Ages, had either been exterminated or cowed into silent obedience. The new intelligentsia was the product of the Soviet education system, owed nothing to the past and everything to Stalin and Beria, while the old working class, which had jeered Stalin when he came to Georgia after the invasion of 1921, was now either dead or submerged by the new tide that had flooded into the towns with industrialisation. Increasingly few Party members had taken part in the revolution and most of the 18,555 who had joined since 1936 were fully conscious that they owed their careers to the purges.

The upheavals of the 1930s marked another turning point in Georgia's history and the starting point for the pattern of socio-economic development of the next fifty years. By January 1989, the population had grown to 5,448,600, 55.6 per cent of whom lived in towns. Over a million people are concentrated in the overcrowded capital, Tbilisi.[22] Despite this, however, and the destruction of rural life in the 1930s, traditional values and customs continue to influence Georgian cultural preferences.

Somewhat paradoxically too, Soviet policies appear to have strengthened Georgian national identity. *Korenizatsiya* and the importance attached to spreading literacy in the native languages has created a generation that is better educated and read in the Georgian language than any of its predecessors and more conscious of its history and culture. Georgian theatre, film and literature are all flourishing once more and, in many instances, receiving international acclaim.

Economic expansion has continued, though not at the break-neck speed of the 1930s. In addition to manganese and coal mining and its traditional industries of wine, tea, tobacco and citrus fruit, Georgia now produces a wide range of industrial and consumer goods. Industrial output rose by 240 per cent between 1940 and 1958 and by 1979 53.3 per cent of the workforce was employed in industry and only 16 per cent as collective farmers.[23] Georgia has more doctors per head of the population than anywhere else in the Soviet Union, and by 1979 had proportionately more people with a higher education than any other republic (150 in every 1,000).[24] Yet it has become evident that the Georgian economy has not been performing well in recent years. Industrial output in 1960–71 was the third lowest of any union republic and, despite some recovery while Eduard Shevardnadze was Georgian Party First Secretary (1972–85), was struggling to achieve any growth by the end of the 1980s.[25]

GEORGIAN NATIONALISM

By the time of the Russian invasion, Georgia was already a well-integrated national, political, territorial and economic entity. After three years of independence, moreover, national consciousness was high and cultural activity well developed. Initially at least, invasion strengthened national sentiment, although subsequently a combination of physical elimination of opponents and a conciliatory cultural policy won the acquiescence of the Georgian people without ever undermining their underlying attachment to the nation.

In the pre-Gorbachev period, Georgian nationalism manifested itself on several occasions, most notably in 1924, 1956 and 1978, usually with bloody consequences. The attempt in 1924 to restore independence was crushed and led to severe repression; in 1956 Georgian protests against Khrushchev's 20th Congress speech on Stalin quickly assumed a nationalist character, and in 1978 thousands defied armed troops in Tbilisi to demand that Georgian be reinstated as the state language of the republic.

The motives behind the 1956 demonstration are far from clear. Some were simply responding to a sense of injured national pride – they saw Khrushchev's attack on Stalin as an attack on the Georgian people as a whole; others, reflecting a view widely held throughout the USSR, were protesting against the denigration of a man they had grown up to believe was beyond criticism; while others simply took the opportunity to express themselves freely for the first time in their lives. For them it was the first chink of light. The consequences were tragic: hundreds were killed when troops fired without warning. The incident left a deep mark on the consciousness of the post-war generation of Georgians and reinforced national distrust of the state.

Unlike 1956, the demonstration in Tbilisi in 1978 passed without violence and for that reason alone marked an important stage in the recovery of national confidence and the development of the current national movement. Even more importantly, the party authorities gave way to the demonstrators' demands.[26] The status of the Georgian language, resistance to Russification and the defence of human rights became the rallying points of the Georgian intelligentsia's opposition to Moscow through the 1970s and early 1980s.

THE GORBACHEV PERIOD

The effects of *perestroika* were at first slow to reach Georgia, dripping through the filter of conservative Party opposition until popular opinion, encouraged by awareness of what was happening elsewhere in the Soviet Union, began to put pressure on the leadership for faster change. Resistance was strengthened by the insecurity of Dzhumber Patiashvili, the man suddenly called upon to replace Shevardnadze as First Secretary of the Georgian Party when the latter moved to Moscow as Foreign Minister in July 1985.

Patiashvili appeared uneasy in his new post, unsure of both how to respond to the demands of the time and of the people around him. Characteristically, while *perestroika* deepened in parts of Russia and the Baltic republics, he signalled his intentions by delivering a diatribe to the Georgian Party Central Committee more reminiscent of the 1930s. He railed against economic sabotage, moral degeneration and a growing private property mentality.[27]

Despite occasional public statements in favour of *perestroika* and *glasnost'*, Patiashvili did little to put words into practice. For his first two years in office, 1985–87, he was too preoccupied weeding out Shevardnadze's protégés and building up his own power base. By 1987, at least eight former close associates of the Foreign Minister had been dismissed, and some of them imprisoned on corruption charges.[28]

Once he was surrounded by his own men, Patiashvili began to act more confidently. In April 1987, he suggested that disputes within the Party were hindering *perestroika*, a move which left the way open for more personnel changes if need be and absolved him of any blame for the slow pace of reform.[29] Signs had also begun to appear that Georgia was not immune to the changes taking place elsewhere in the Soviet Union. The party's daily Georgian-language paper, *Komunisti*, began to run a series of investigations into the corrupt practices of the Ministry of the Interior,[30] and, at the end of 1986, Tengiz Abuladze's film *Monanieba* (Repentance), an attempt to face up to the legacy of Stalinism, was screened, first in Georgia and then in Moscow. *Monanieba* and the subsequent public discussion broke one of the taboos of Georgian life and so removed one of the psychological barriers to the re-examination of Georgian history that was soon to follow.

Through 1985–86 there was little organised opposition to the authorities, partly because many of the most active figures in the dissident movement were still in prison. In early 1987, however, frustration at the slow pace of *perestroika* began to form around a number of key issues.

The first of these was ecology, a response not just to the wanton damage to the countryside, but also to people's lives. In March 1987 many blamed the heavy avalanches and consequent loss of life in the mountainous area of Svaneti on the construction of too many hydroelectric stations. Whether they were right or not mattered little. The common perception was that the authorities paid no attention to people's needs, were contemptuous of public opinion and more concerned with private gain than the welfare of the nation.

This indeed was what lay at the heart of the opposition in 1987–88 to a plan to build a railway across the Caucasus linking Georgia directly with Russia. The scheme would have been the most expensive in Georgia's history. Not unusually, it went ahead without public consultation or regard for potential pitfalls.

The first dissenting voice was raised in the Georgian Writers' Union paper, *Literaturuli Sakartvelo*, in April 1987.[31] The project brought into focus a number of the issues which Georgian dissidents had been protesting about over the previous decade: damage to the environment, pollution and the destruction of historical monuments, many of which lay in the line's path. It was to prove the catalyst for the formation of the national movement.

By the summer the dispute over the railway had given rise to a vituperative debate in the republican press – the first real evidence of *glasnost'*. The temperature rose still higher as the public became aware that Soviet troops were using one of Georgia's most ancient monasteries for artillery practice.

Zviad Gamsakhurdia, one of the most prominent Georgian dissidents, had been complaining for years that the army firing range adjacent to the Davitgaredzha monastery had been doing incalculable damage to its frescoes and walls, but to no avail. In 1987, however, as public concern mounted over the railway, the threat to Davitgaredzha suddenly assumed new importance. For many it became a symbol of both the physical and spiritual threat posed by Moscow to the survival of the nation. Christianity, which had always formed a central plank in Georgian national consciousness, began to assert itself once more as young Georgians searched for an alternative to the materialist ideology of the state.

The disputes over the environment and the destruction of historical monuments and spiritual values gradually brought *glasnost'* to the Georgian media. By the end of 1987, the press had caught up and was calling for a re-examination of the blank spots of Georgian history. Some areas, like the invasion of 1921, remained temporarily out of bounds, but a lively debate opened over the role of the 'national deviationists', the purges and the 1956 demonstration.[32]

In the face of official procrastination over the demands for an end to work on the Caucasian railway and removal of the firing range, opposition to the authorities expanded to encompass wider issues. At the end of 1987, several prominent dissidents formed the Ilia Tchavtchavadze Society, named after the founder of the nineteenth-century national liberation movement. It demanded, among other things, that all matters concerning the future of Georgia be settled in accordance with the wishes of the Georgian people, that major projects be submitted to the public for approval, that Georgian become the state language of the republic, that fundamental importance be attached to improving the study of Georgian language, history and geography at school and that Georgians be allowed to perform their military service in Georgia.[33]

But while the society declared its ultimate aim to be Georgian independence, it felt that Georgians would have first to travel through an interim period of political and economic education before they were ready for such a step. However, hopes that the society would act as an umbrella organisation for the opposition proved premature.[34]

An influential and more radical wing broke away in early 1988 to set up a loose alliance of groups united in their rejection of compromise with the authorities. Initially at least, this included the Georgian Helsinki Group, the National Democratic Party, the Georgian National Justice Union and the Georgian National Independence Party, all of whom regard any form of cooperation with the state, even when there is potential advantage to be gained, as a form of moral compromise. They see the key task as the moral regeneration of the nation after seventy years of Soviet power. All, to one degree or another, stress the importance of the close association of the future independent state with the Georgian Orthodox church.[35]

This overtly religious strand in the outlook of the opposition groups has undoubtedly struck a chord with young Georgians, who are in the throes of a religious revival. Thousands have recently been christened in mass baptisms in different parts of the country.

Despite making a number of gestures in 1988 to win popular support – greater openness in the media and the reopening of churches – the Party failed to curb the growing influence of the unofficial organisations and in the summer was forced to bow to public pressure on the Caucasian railway. With the Party on the defensive, a series of demonstrations in September called for the closure of the firing range and the rapid extension of democratisation. Startled by the size of the demonstrations, the authorities initially responded with violence but backed down in confusion when this proved counter-productive. Patiashvili then took the extraordinary step of calling an open meeting at Tbilisi University, screened in its entirety on Georgian television, to discuss the demonstrators' demands. He had evidently hoped to drive a wedge between the students and the unofficial organisations by mixing praise and concessions for the moderate majority with criticism of the demagoguery of the leaders of the national movement. But it proved a serious miscalculation, for the spectacle of the First Secretary being publicly subjected to a stream of criticism from students had a cathartic effect on many Georgians, ridding them of their fear of the Party and state apparatus.

The September demonstrations and the university meeting marked a watershed in the development both of the national movement and the attitude of the Party towards it. By its repeated attempts to marginalise the opposition groups and its failure to follow the example of the Baltic Party organisations in co-opting the reform movements, the Party missed an opportunity to bridge the gulf between itself and society. Devoid of any coherent policy and bereft of moral authority, the Georgian Party became increasingly confused in the face of the growing challenge to its authority. Patiashvili once more retreated into indecision, oscillating between tolerance and repression. But in the absence of dialogue with the leaders of the national movement neither could help him. Repression merely widened the gap between the state and society, while reforms were interpreted as concessions to popular pressure.

In November, the Party watched impotently as the size and frequency of the demonstrations increased. Significantly, the demonstrations were now involving large numbers of peasants and workers and their demands were becoming more far-reaching. Complaints began to be voiced about discrimination against Georgians in the Abkhaz Autonomous Republic in north-west Georgia and the republic's demographic situation. In contrast to the Baltic republics, Georgians were not complaining about Russians, who make up less than 8 per cent of the population, but about the rapidly expanding Azeri population in south-west Georgia. What made matters worse was that corrupt Georgian Party officials had been illegally selling state land to Azeris, many of them settlers from neighbouring Azerbaijan. With land at a premium because of the population density, Georgians began to call for the expulsion of Azeri settlers and the establishment of a pro-Georgian demographic policy.[36]

But the catalyst to the November demonstrations was Moscow's attempt to remove the constitutional right of the republics to secede from the USSR. When the Georgian Supreme Soviet went into session at the end of the month to vote on the issue, hundreds of thousands of people gathered outside and a group of students declared a hunger strike.[37]

While the Supreme Soviet was giving in to their demands, the Party leadership again wavered between repression and concessions. Patiashvili, who was out of his depth, seems to have come increasingly under the influence of Aleksi Inauri, the *éminence grise* of Georgian politics since his appointment to head the Georgian KGB in 1954. It is likely that the latter was behind Patiashvili's request to the CPSU Central Committee at the end of November for permission to use the army to restore order in Tbilisi. The request was turned down and Inauri was sacked a week later.[38]

But if Gorbachev had hoped that Inauri's removal would lead to more enlightened policies in Georgia, he was to be disappointed. Not only had the national movement emerged from the November events more confident in the power of collective action, but Patiashvili had again been publicly humiliated. When, in February 1989, he attempted to reassert his authority by warning on television that a protest planned to mark the anniversary of the Soviet invasion of Georgia on 25 February would be forcibly dispersed, his bluff was called. Thousands marched through the centre of Tbilisi.

By denying legal outlets to dissident opinion and by doing nothing to increase the involvement of the people in the political process, Patiashvili widened the gulf between state and society at a time when *perestroika* was supposed to be overcoming it. Nothing better illustrated this than the Georgian leadership's conduct of the March elections to the USSR Congress of People's Deputies. What was intended as an example of the democratisation of Soviet society in Georgia merely confirmed how little had changed: 57 per cent of the constituencies had only one candidate, far above the Soviet average, and the turnout was claimed to be an absurdly high 97 per cent.[39]

Against this background, the political situation deteriorated in March, when ethnic tension between the Abkhaz and Georgians spilled over into violence. Calls by Abkhaz nationalists, among them senior Party members, for separation from Georgia, brought a furious response throughout the republic and were the direct cause of the demonstrations the following month in Tbilisi. But what began as an anti-Abkhaz protest quickly evolved into a massive demonstration for independence.[40]

With factories coming out on strike, the transport system paralysed, peasants pouring in from the countryside, vast crowds choking the centre of Tbilisi and over 100 people on hunger strike on the steps of the government building, Patiashvili called on Moscow to grant him the use of special troops to disperse the crowd. Permission was granted. Gorbachev and Shevardnadze were absent on a state visit to Britain.[41]

Early in the morning of 9 April, airborne troops joined special and regular Interior Ministry units in what the commissions investigating the tragedy have described as a 'punitive operation' against a peaceful demonstration. Nineteen people were killed, sixteen of them women. More than 4,000 people were treated for injuries and over 500 were hospitalised. Two more people were killed by troops later the same day.[42]

Although ultimate responsibility for the use of the troops rested with senior Politburo members and ministers in Moscow – most notably Ligachev, Chebrikov, the former head of the KGB, and Yazov, the Minister of Defence – and although the planning of the military operation and the tactics used were those of the man entrusted with the operation, Colonel-General Rodionov, the Commander-in-Chief of the Transcaucasian Military District, Patiashvili clearly bore responsibility for the chain of events that led up to the April tragedy during the previous year.[43]

But if the attack was intended to intimidate the Georgians, it clearly backfired. Instead, it radicalised popular opinion and greatly boosted the standing of the leaders of the national movement. According to a poll carried out by the Georgian Supreme Soviet Commission investigating the events of 9 April, 79 per cent of the Georgian population felt the unofficial groups represented the national interest, while 71 per cent had a 'negative attitude' towards the former leadership. The commission evidently didn't ask how people felt about the present leadership.[44]

PROSPECTS

While Georgia presses for greater freedom from Moscow, it must also find a way to resolve its own nationalities crisis. In 1989, inter-ethnic violence broke out in Abkhazia, South Ossetia and Marneuli District, an area heavily populated by Azeris, as the local nationalities attempted to assert themselves against the Georgians. None of the underlying causes of the conflicts have been resolved. Indeed, Georgians would probably question whether they can be resolved while Georgia is ruled from Moscow.

Georgians appear genuinely confused by the demands of the Abkhaz for separation from Georgia. They point out that the Abkhaz comprise only 17 per cent of the population of the autonomous republic (Georgians comprise 45 per cent) and yet dominate the leading party, government and economic posts.[45] The Tbilisi authorities are under enormous popular pressure to take action to satisfy the demands of the Georgians living in Abkhazia for fairer treatment, but almost any action they take is likely to lead to counter accusations from the Abkhaz of Georgian nationalism.

Meanwhile, the opposition groups dismiss the claims of the minority nationalities as Moscow-inspired and designed to deflect the attention of the Georgian people away from their struggle for independence. But although Moscow may well be exploiting national rivalries, there is no doubt that the language of certain of the Georgian opposition groups is becomingly increasingly chauvinist.[46] Despite Georgia's history of harmonious inter-ethnic relations, the possibility exists for bitter conflict.

Despite his personal popularity and readiness to talk to the leaders of the national movement, Patiashvili's successor as first secretary, Givi Gumbaridze, has to bridge an enormous gulf if he is to win the confidence of the Georgian people.[47] Since April 1989 attitudes have been sharply politicised and the demand for independence has spread throughout society. According to the Georgian commission's poll, 89 per cent of the Georgian population want Georgia to become a 'democratic, independent state, founded on the principles of justice'.[48] In the meantime, Georgians are demanding that the USSR admit that

Soviet Russia forcibly annexed Georgia in 1921, thereby violating the terms of its treaty with Georgia, signed in May 1920 and recognising Georgia's independence.[49]

This inevitably limits the room for manoeuvre of the new Party leader, whose credibility depends on his ability to catch up with the popular mood. Gumbaridze must also contend with a national movement strengthened by the unification in October 1989 of the opposition groups in the Committee for National Salvation (*Erovnuli Khsnis Komiteti*),[50] and whose leaders regard the readiness of the Baltic opposition groups to participate in the Soviet electoral system as tantamount to collaboration. The problem for the Georgian Party leadership as it seeks to negotiate with the national movement is how to satisfy popular demands without at the same time presiding over the separation of Georgia from the USSR.

NOTES

1. K. Kandelaki *Sak'art'velos Erovnuli Meurneoba, Dsigni Meore* (Paris, Institute for the Study of the USSR, 1960), p. 87. Output per caput in Russia as a whole was 30 roubles.

2. J.W.R. Parsons *The Emergence and Development of the National Question in Soviet Georgia, 1801–1921*, Unpublished Ph.D. thesis, University of Glasgow, 1987, pp. 522–26; and R.G. Hovannisian *The Republic of Armenia*, vol. 1 (Berkeley, Los Angeles, London 1971), p. 115.

3. Parsons *The National Question*, pp. 529–30.

4. Ibid., pp. 512–13.

5. C. Kandelaki *The Georgian Question Before the Free World (Acts, Documents, Evidence)* (Paris 1953), pp. 182–90.

6. N. Zhordania *Chemi Dsarsuli* (Paris 1953), p. 157.

7. S.F. Jones *Georgian Social Democracy: In Opposition and Power, 1892–1921*, Unpublished Ph.D, thesis, London School of Economics 1984, pp. 542–43.

8. Steven Jones 'The establishment of Soviet power in Transcaucasia: the case of Georgia, 1921–1928' *Soviet Studies* XL, (4) (Oct. 1988), p. 617.

9. I. Katcharava 'Sabtchot'a erovnuli sakhelmdsip'oebriobis shek'mna da sakhalkho meurneobis aghdgena sak-art'veloshi (1921–1925 ds.ds)' in I. Katcharava (ed.) *Sak'art'veloshi Istoriis Narkvevebi T.7* (Tbilisi, Sabtchot'a Sak'art'velo 1976), p. 155.

10. *Ocherki Istorii Komunisticheskoi Partii Gruzii, 1883–1970* (T'bilisi 1971), pp. 460–62.

11. Steven Jones, 'The establishment of Soviet power', p. 618.

12. Katcharava 'Sabtchot'a erovnuli', pp. 130–32.

13. Ibid., p. 137.

14. *Komunisti*: 13 Jan 1990: and Steven Jones, 'The establishment of Soviet power', p. 617.

15. Until very recently the 1924 uprising was one of the many 'blank spots'

in Georgian history. Since 1988, however, it has become the subject of numerous articles in the Georgian press and, already, a novel, *Siskhlis Dsvimebi* by Guram Gegeshidze, serialised in the monthly *Mnat'obi* 3,4,5 (1989).

16. *Komunisti* 25 Feb. 1930.
17. T'. Zhghenti 'Kolmeurneobat'a sameurneo-organizatsiuli ganmtkitseba' in *Sak'art'velos Istoriis Narkvevebi* T.7 (Tbilisi, Sabtchot'a Sak'art'-velo 1976), p. 644.
18. I. Chik'ava 'Sabtchot'a sak'art'velo sotsialisturi sazogadoebis ganvit'arebisa da ganmtkitsebis periodshi, 1937–1941 ds.ds.', in *Sakart'velos Istoriis Narkvevebi* T.7 (Tbilisi, Sabtchot'a Sak'art'velo 1976), p. 780.
19. N. Makharadze 'Meore khut'dsliani gegmis shesrulebis shedegebi. Sotsializmis gamardzhveba. Akhali konstitutsiis migheba' in *Sak'art'velos Istoriis Narkvevebi* (Tbilisi, Sabtchot'a Sak'art'velo 1976), p. 675.
20. R. Klimiashvili *K'alak' T'bilisis Demograp'iuli Protsesebis Sotsialuri P'ak'torebi* (Tbilisi, Metsniereba 1974), p. 38.
21. This is a point strongly made by many Georgian writers, who feel that an attempt is being made in the Russian media to attribute Stalin's excesses to his Georgian birth and, at the same time, to suggest that he protected Georgia from the worst excesses of the 1930s. In an open letter to Gorbachev, published in the literary paper *Literaturuli Sak'art'velo* on 21 April 1989, more than 200 writers argued that the bloody action taken by Soviet troops against Georgian demonstrators earlier that month was the 'logical conclusion and crowning of the general denigration of the Georgian people sparked off in the central press, radio and television'. One writer, Guram P'andzhikidze, pointed out in *Literaturuli Sak'art'velo*, 21 and 28 October, 1988, that aside from the repressions of 1924 and 1937, Georgia also suffered in 1951 when thousands were taken from the Tbilisi intelligentsia overnight and exiled to Central Asia. He noted too that Georgia suffered more than 380,000 losses during the war, over 10 per cent of the population and proportionately higher than any other republic.
22. *Komunisti* 15 June 1989.
23. *Vestnik Statistiki* 1 (1981), p. 67.
24. Ibid. 4 (1981), pp. 69–72.
25. Shevardnadze did for a while achieve notable results in revitalising the Georgian economy, although from a relatively low base. In his first two years, industrial output grew by 9.6 per cent and agricultural output by 18 per cent. Georgia was one of only four republics to fulfil the tenth five year plan targets. But today, the Georgian economy, like that of the rest of the USSR, is struggling to achieve any growth at all.
26. J.W.R. Parsons 'National integration in Georgia' *Soviet Studies* 34 (4) (Oct. 1982), pp. 556–57.
27. *Komunisti* 6 Aug. 1989.
28. Soliko Khabeishvili, the former Central Committee Secretary for Industry, had worked with Shevardnadze since their time together in the Georgian Komsomol in the 1950s. In February 1987 he was sentenced to fifteen years' imprisonment on charges of corruption. See *Komunisti* 22 Feb. 1987.
29. Ibid. 28 April 1987.

30. Major-General Guram Gvetadze was forced out of office after a series of articles critical of him and his ministry in *Komunisti* in late 1985 and early 1986. Among other things, it was revealed that convicted criminals were living in luxury in corrective labour camps and continuing to direct their activities from behind bars. The author of the articles was Nugzar Popkhadze, at that time head of the Central Committee Agitation and Propaganda Department. Popkhadze stood firmly behind Patiashvili's opposition to dialogue with the so-called 'informal organisations' and was one of the first to be dismissed when Patiashvili lost his post in April 1989.

31. *Literaturuli Sak'art'velo* 15 April 1987.

32. Since April 1989 all the papers have become more challenging, but the way has been led in Georgia by *Literaturuli Sak'art'velo, K'art'uli P'ilmi* and *T'bilisi*.

33. *Iveria*, 7 (June 1988), pp. 4–5. *Iveria* is one of the publications of the Ilia Tchavtchavadze Society.

34. *Iveria*, 8 (July–Aug. 1988), pp. 60–74. See also *Gushagi* (Paris) 17 (Oct. 1988).

35. The main part of the programme of the Georgian National Democratic Party (Sak'art'velos Erovnul-Demokratiuli Partia) states, for instance: 'The ideological basis of our party is theo-democracy, which, aside from traditional democratic values, means granting the church the leading role in the moral issues of the nation.' See *Moambe* 10 (1989). *Moambe* is one of the party's regular publications.

36. *Literaturuli Sak'art'velo* 11 Nov. 1988.

37. *Literaturuli Sak'art'velo* 2 Nov. 1988, and *Eastern Europe Newsletter* 2, (23), 23 Nov. 1988 and (24) 7 Dec. 1988.

38. *Komunisti* 28 Sept. 1989.

39. Ibid.

40. Ibid.

41. Ibid.

42. Ibid.

43. Ibid.

44. Ibid.

45. *Sakhalkho Ganat'leba* 4 June 1989.

46. Most Georgians are convinced that Moscow's policy in Georgia is to divide and rule, an approach used with varying degrees of success by the tsarist administration during the nineteenth century. The leaders of the Georgian opposition groups claim to have no argument with the Abkhaz, Ossetian or Azeri peoples, whose security and national interests they promise to guarantee if Georgia gains independence. Certain of them, however – most notably Zviad Gamsakhurdia, the founder of the Georgian Helsinki Group – refuse to recognise the separate existence of the Abkhaz autonomous republic or the Ossetian autonomous region. These, they say, are ancient Georgian territories with no claim to a separate administrative existence.

47. One of the first things Gumbaridze did on his appointment as First Secretary was to stress to the Tbilisi Party organisation the need for the party to engage in a dialogue with the opposition and, where necessary, to be prepared to accept its point of view. See *Komunisti* 26 April 1989.

In November 1989, the Georgian Party leadership entered into direct negotiations with the leaders of the Committee for the National Salvation of Georgia on such issues as the right of Georgians to perform their military service in Georgia and the use of referenda to determine the wishes of the Georgian people.

48. *Komunisti* 28 Sept. 1989.
49. At the beginning of November 1989, the party leadership agreed to allow the opposition groups to carry out a referendum to determine whether or not the Georgian people wanted the UN to set up a commission to investigate the circumstances of the Soviet invasion and the legality of Soviet power in Georgia.
50. The opposition had previously been united in the Committee, but had split in the summer of 1989 because of personality clashes and differences over tactics. The death of Merab Kostava, the guiding moral force of the national movement, in a car accident in October 1989, appears to have brought them together again. It is estimated that as many as 500,000 people followed Kostava's funeral cortège in a vast outpouring of national grief.

PART IV

MUSLIM CENTRAL ASIA

Besides sharing a common religion, the native peoples of the five southern republics of Kazakhstan, Uzbekistan, Turkmenistan, Kirgizia and Tadzhikistan also share a Turkic ethnic background (except for the Tadzhiks, who are Iranian). The region, known in pre-revolutionary times as 'Russian Turkestan', remained relatively isolated from Russian influences until the latter half of the nineteenth century when it was absorbed into the Russian empire. Even up until the 1917 Revolution, however, parts of the region, namely the Emirate of Bukhara and the Khanate of Khiva, although under Russian suzerainty, retained a nominally independent status. In 1920, the Turkestan republic (based on Tashkent) and the People's Republics of Bukhara and Khiva were dissolved, and the region divided up into the union republics of Turkmenistan and Uzbekistan, with Kazakhstan and Kirgizia becoming autonomous republics (ASSRs) within the Russian union republic. In 1929, Tadzhikistan was upgraded from autonomous republic status (in which it had been included within the Uzbek SSR) to a full union republic, as were Kazakhstan and Kirgizia seven years later. Although nationality group criteria was adopted in Central Asia's administrative partitioning, which by and large Moscow succeeded in making coterminous with the new administrative boundaries, there is little doubt, given the strength of pan-Turkic and pan-Islamic identities in the region, that Central Asia's Balkanisation was motivated by geopolitical considerations. Such a divide-and-rule strategy thus circumvented mobilisation along Islamic lines amongst peoples whose sense of national consciousness at that time was in a very rudimentary state.

With the exception of Kazakhstan, whose northern half is industrialised and economically similar to adjacent regions of the Russian republic, the rest of Central Asia remains predominantly rural and largely underdeveloped, with some of the lowest living standards in the Soviet Union. Compared with educational and social welfare levels in neighbouring Muslim countries, however, considerable material benefits have accrued to Muslims from Soviet power. Yet while Soviet Central Asia is held up by Moscow to the Muslim world as an example of the success of Soviet socialism, the region's post-war demographic explosion has the potential to present long-term economic and political problems for Moscow. In the 1959–89 period, more or less exclusively due to rising birth-rates, Soviet Central Asia's population increased from 23 million to 49.4 million, representing a growth of 114.8 per cent, compared with the All-Union average of 36.8 per cent. If current demographic trends continue, it is estimated by Soviet demographers that by the turn of the century the number of Soviet Muslims (including those from other parts of the USSR) will constitute approximately a quarter of the total Soviet population. Besides carrying possible political implications – notably greater power within the arena of federal politics – for the present Moscow has the problem of finding solutions to the region's growing rural unemployment and whether to continue with the unsuccessful policy of encouraging Muslim labour to move to labour-deficient regions of European USSR and the eastlands or to embark upon a major scheme of industrial relocation, with the repercussions this could have for undermining Gorbachev's programme for national economic recovery.

CHAPTER TWELVE

Kazakhs

Ingvar Svanberg

On 7 October 1989, about 200 Kazakhs took part in a rally in Moscow to oppose nuclear tests in Semipalatinsk. Simultaneously, a Kazakh anti-nuclear protest group in Kazakhstan's capital city, Alma Ata, declared that the mine workers would strike if the authorities did not refrain from further nuclear tests in Semipalatinsk.[1] Thus the Kazakhs finally brought their protests against environmental problems and Russian hegemony to the capital of the Soviet Union. The Kazakhs were also the first of the many nationalities in the Soviet Union to react in a nationalistic outburst when one of their own prominent but nevertheless corrupt leaders was ousted as part of Gorbachev's *perestroika* policy in December 1986. The resulting riots in Alma Ata that month were a clear sign of the difficulties facing a multi-ethnic country undergoing political reform, and a reminder to the leadership of the problematic nature of *glasnost'* in facilitating the opening-up of previously containable ethnic problems. Yet the situation in Kazakhstan has not reached the level of tension witnessed in the Baltic republics.

BACKGROUND

Despite its huge area, constituting the second largest of the union republics (2.7 million square kilometres), and despite the mention of the name Semipalatinsk in many mass media reports during the last forty years, Kazakhstan and its people are little known outside the Soviet Union. According to the Soviet census of 1979, of Kazakhstan's 14,684,283 population, Kazakhs constituted 36 per cent. Traditionally, animal husbandry played an important part in the republic's economy, followed by cereal culture. It remains one of the main grain-producing regions of the Soviet Union, at one time producing a third of all Soviet wheat. In the southern parts, fruit growing, cotton, sunflower and other oil plants are also major crops. The leading industrial sector of the republic, concentrated in the north, is largely based on the republic's rich resources of ferrous and non-ferrous metals and coal.

Although the vast majority of the 6.5 million Kazakhs live in their namesake republic, there is also a substantial number (nearly a fifth) living elsewhere in the Soviet Union, and a further million located outside the USSR.[2] The main body of those living outside the USSR is found in China – 907,582 persons according to the 1982 Chinese census. Most of them live in northern Xinjiang, but a couple of small enclaves are found in Gansu and Qinghai.[3] The Kazakhs of the Mongolian People's Republic belong to the same stock and are situated mainly in Bayan Ölgiy aymaq and Hovd aymaq. Their numbers were reported to be 84,300 in the 1979 census.[4] The expatriate Kazakh communities found in northern Afghanistan (24,000 according to a 1978 estimate) comprise mainly descendants of those who escaped from the USSR in the 1930s. Minor enclaves – mostly refugees or emigrants originally from Xinjiang – also live in Turkey (about 5,000 according to late 1980s estimates), as well as in Western Europe and the USA.[5]

The Kazakhs speak a Turkic language belonging to the Kipchak branch. The ethnonym *Qazaq* came into use around 1520. In the beginning of this century, the Kazakhs were still referred to as Kirghiz, or Kirghiz-Kazakhs in Russian and Western literature. In 1926, the ethnonym Kazakh was officially introduced in the Soviet Union in keeping with the policy of naming people according to their own ethnonyms. The transcription from Russian has been kept in most Western literature. A more correct spelling in English should be Kazak rather than Kazakh.[6]

The Kazakhs have a complex ethnic history and trace their origins back to various nomadic tribes that lived on the steppes of Turkestan during the days of Genghis Khan. Towards the end of that period, in the late fifteenth and the early sixteenth centuries, these nomadic tribes were united in a political confederation known as Kazakh Orda. From this tribal confederation the Kazakhs emerged as a consolidated ethnic group. During the sixteenth century the Kazakhs enlarged their territory on the Central Asian steppes. Although they were united under Kasim Khan and partly during the reign of his successor, Tahir Khan, they soon split into smaller nomadic tribal federations. The nomadic groups were politically unified in three large, territorially based tribal federations or Hordes known as the Larger, Middle and Lesser Hordes (*Ulu, Orta* and *Kiši Züz*). This division is still kept and comprises an important dimension in contemporary Kazakh identity. The Kazakh Hordes are subdivided in patrilateral lineages which remain a significant cultural factor in their social life. The exogamous lineages not only provide a chart for identifying individuals according to heritage, but also establish the rules for much social behaviour. A correct understanding of the force of lineages is vital when interpreting contemporary Kazakh society.[7]

As a result of the expansion of the Oirat Mongols in Central Asia in the eighteenth century, Kazakh tribes began to seek the protection of the Russian tsar. The first to do so was the khan of the Lesser Horde in 1731, followed by the khan of the Middle Horde in 1740 and part of the Larger Horde in 1742. When the Oirat Mongols were finally crushed and dispersed by the Qing army in 1756, the most potent enemy of the Kazakhs was destroyed.[8] With Russian control Islam also came to the area, as the tsarist government encouraged the Tatars to proselytise in the steppe region.

The Kazakhs became a buffer between Russia and China, the two expanding empires of Inner Asia. Nominal Russian sovereignty existed without any real Russian interference on the steppes, and the khans continued to control the plain. However, under Tsar Aleksander I, a new policy was introduced. The Middle Horde was ruled by two khans, but after their deaths their power was abolished by the tsarist authorities. In the 1820s a new system of administration was introduced in Kazakh territory. In 1822 the territory of the Middle Horde Kazakhs was divided into Russian administrative units, and Russian military jurisdiction was introduced for criminal offences. The Kazakhs were no longer allowed to acquire serfs. The same process was carried out in 1824 for the Lesser Horde Kazakhs. These changes in tsarist policy led to revolts among the Kazakhs, but the tsarist authorities continued their colonial policy towards the nomads. New taxation methods were introduced, and from the 1830s onwards Kazakhs were no longer allowed to cultivate land. In 1847 the Larger Horde finally lost its independence when forced to pledge allegiance to the tsarist government.

After the abolition of serfdom in Russia in 1861 peasants started to move eastward to settle and cultivate land on the Kazakh plain. The increasing number of Russian and Ukrainian peasants led to the emigration of the Kazakhs eastward to Chinese territory. More than 500 villages were established on the steppe by the end of the nineteenth century. An 1895 tsarist Russian commission reserved land for new settlers in areas that had been used mainly by the Kazakh nomads.

During the so-called Stolypin agrarian reforms between 1906 and 1912, when 19 million hectares of land on the Kazakh plain were set aside for farming, a new mass settlement of Russian peasants took place.[9] The increasing pressure of Russian colonists also paved the way for Kazakh nationalism among the traditional Kazakh elite.

In 1916 the tsarist government decided that Kazakhs, who traditionally had been exempted from military service, should be drafted into labour units. This led to a revolt on the steppe and in the Ferghana Valley. More than 50,000 rebels took part in the uprising. As a punishment, General Koropatkin, the Governor-General of Turkestan, decided to drive the nomads who participated in the revolt away from their lands and to make the territory immediately available for Russian settlers. During the February Revolution of 1917 the Kazakhs under the leadership of Ali Bukeikhanov formed a semi-independent state called Alash Orda, whose autonomy came to an end in 1920 when the Bolsheviks finally integrated the Kazakh steppe under their control. In the Soviet Union the Kazakhs became recognised as one of its nations.[10]

The collectivisation programme in Soviet Central Asia and Kazakhstan in the late 1920s led to conflict and great difficulties for the nomads. The Kazahks were forced to settle, and many nomadic families saw their herds starving on pastures which could no longer sustain them. It is estimated that several hundred thousand, according to some authors even as many as 1.5 million, Kazakhs perished due to starvation during the 1930s.[11]

The Soviet Union continued to encourage settlement of Russian peasants in the post-World War period, especially in the 1950s, when many farmers moved into the republic. Under the Virgin Land Scheme initiated by Khrushchev, vast grazing lands were to be put under the plough and opened up for colonisation. Moscow encouraged thousands upon thousands of Russian and Ukrainian farmers to settle there, which caused protests among the Kazakhs. In 1954 the Kazakh First Secretary of the Kazakh Communist Party, Z. Shaiakhmetov, was replaced by a Russian. Due to difficulties with developing projects in Kazakhstan, Leonid Brezhnev was sent there to act as Party leader in 1954. When Brezhnev's skill was needed elsewhere in 1956, a Kazakh, Dinmukhamed Kunaev, was named First Secretary. Due to economic shortcomings in the republic, Khrushchev criticised Kunaev so heavily that he had to resign. Kunaev was, however, back in power in 1964 and later became the first Kazakh to be a full member of the ruling Politburo of the Soviet Union. Under Brezhnev it became a tradition that the First Secretary of the Republics should be recruited among natives; Kunaev was one of Brezhnev's men. The policy under Kunaev gave a good living standard to Kazakhstan. Reforms in higher education allowed a higher percentage of the indigenous nationalities to attend universities and to take advantage of better job opportunities. While Kunaev remained in power, the Kazakhs were over-represented in many administrative and party positions, as well as in numerous official posts.[12]

Kunaev also brought investments to Kazakhstan. The Kazakhs developed a high degree of ethnic pride and the rate of assimilation seemed low. Kunaev could prove not only his quality, but also that of the Kazakh people by building a prosperous republic. The capital grew to a large city during his years in power and became a monument to Kunaev's strength with many prestigious government and official buildings, some even decorated with gold leaf.

Little is known about ethnic unrest during Kunaev's period in office up to the 1980s. Some disturbances near the Chinese border were noted in the early 1960s, when increasing tensions between China and the Soviet Union led to open dispute. The Soviet propaganda in Xinjiang and the harsh economic situation due to the failure of the Great Leap Forward caused unrest among Kazakhs and other nationalities in China. A major influx of Kazakh and Uighur refugees from Xinjiang took place in 1961 and 1962, a total of about 120,000 people being reported in the world press; these refugees settled in the oblasti of East Kazakhstan.

Sharing its border with China, during the 1960s and 1970s Kazakhstan was a centre for Soviet anti-Chinese propaganda. Border clashes occurred several times, and Kazakh infiltrators were sent to neighbouring Xinjiang to spread propaganda among the Chinese Kazakhs.

DEMOGRAPHIC AND CULTURAL DEVELOPMENTS

Kazakhstan was incorporated into the Soviet Union as the Kirghiz Autonomous Soviet Socialist Republic on 26 August 1920 as part of the Russian republic. It became a union republic with its contemporary borders in December 1936, receiving its official name, the Kazakh Soviet Socialist Republic.

In 1926, Kazakhs numbered 3,968,289, their number falling to 3,098,800 by 1939. In the post-Stalin years, their population has grown rapidly, from 3,621,610 in 1959 to 8,137,878 by 1989. Their demographic decline between 1926 and 1959 was probably due to great losses as a result of hunger during the 1930s, but also to emigration to Afghanistan and, to some extent, to China in connection with forced collectivisation in the late 1920s and early 1930s. Into recent times, the Kazakhs have shared a similar demographic fate to that of the Latvians: until very recently, they were outnumbered by the Russians in their own republic. At the 1979 census, the Kazakhs constituted only 36 per cent of the republic's total population, while the Russians made up 40 per cent. Other ethnic groups include the Germans, Ukrainians, Tatars, Iughurs, Uzbeks, Koreans, Azerbaijanis and Dungans, many of whom are recent arrivals to Kazakhstan. The Dungans and Uighurs are refugees who came from Chinese Central Asia in the 1880s; some Iughurs probably also arrived in the 1960s, while the Tatars stem mostly from the Crimean Tatars deported in 1944. Kazakhstan also became the homeland for other deported nationalities, notably the Volga Germans, Balkars, Chechen, Ingush, Karachais, Ossetians, Mesketian Turks and Kurds,[13] as well as Koreans.

Despite its multi-ethnic character, the number of mixed marriages is low in the republic, at 20.7 per cent (1970 census), with exogamy being higher in the cities (23.8 per cent) compared with the countryside (17.1 per cent). Mixed marriages are most common in northern Kazakhstan with its large Russian and other immigrant communities (this contrasts with the southern part of the republic, where Kazakhs and other Turkic people are concentrated). The Kazakhs prefer endogomous marriages (91.1 per cent), while mixed marriages are most likely to occur with other Turkic peoples rather than with Russians.[14]

Although the Kazakhs were outnumbered by the Russians in 1979, the demographer Maqash Tatimov reported that natural population growth and the large Russian out-migration during the 1980s have led to an equalisation of the Kazakhs and Russians in 1985 at 39.5 per cent each. Furthermore, Tatimov forecast that the Kazakhs would reach 42 per cent of the population of Kazakhstan in 1990 and 50 per cent by the year 2000.[15]

Some figures may be quoted to illustrate the living standard of the Kazakh SSR. In 1961 the urban population was only 45 per cent in Kazakhstan, but in 1987 was estimated to have reached 58 per cent.[16] The life expectancy of the Kazakhs and other Central Asian natives has increased in the last two decades, and by 1979 was 69.5 years for Kazakhs compared with 65.9 years for Russians. In the 1950s the Kazakhs had the highest level of natural fertility in the USSR, with 7.4 children per family; in the early 1980s it was still high, 4.8, while net reproduction was 2.2. The total number of induced abortions per Kazakh woman was 3,033 in the 1970s.[17] The average family size for Kazakhs was 5.5 in 1979 (3.3 for Russians in Kazakh SSR). There is a great need for housing in Kazakh urban areas, as well as quality consumer goods. Access to food has certainly been better than in many other areas outside Central Asia, but complaints have been heard.

LANGUAGE AND RELIGION

The Kazakhs of Inner Asia formerly used Tatar as the written language. The traditional secular elite working in the Russian military service and administration in the nineteenth century was literate in Russian. A Kazakh literature developed during the nineteenth century, and the language was written with an Arabic script. In 1928, the authorities introduced a Latin script for Kazakh. This was replaced in 1940 by a modified Cyrillic alphabet with a total of forty-two letters, a high number for a written language.

The spoken language of contemporary Kazakhs is either Kazakh or Russian. Many younger urban Kazakhs prefer to speak Russian instead of Kazakh due to educational and urban values in their family. The census, however, does not indicate any linguistic Russification of the Kazakh population in the Soviet Union. In 1970 about 57.3 per cent of the Kazakh population in Kazakh SSR claimed not to speak Russian freely; in 1979 the same figure was 48.0 per cent. About 41.6 per cent stated they were bilingual in Kazakh and Russian in 1970, whereas 50.6 per cent did so in 1979. Only 0.4 per cent in 1970 and 0.3 per cent in 1979 had Russian as the native language but were fluent in Kazakh. Those knowing Russian but little Kazakh were 0.7 per cent in 1970 and 1.1 per cent in 1979. For Kazakhs outside Kazakh SSR the figures were somewhat higher; about 4.5 per cent of those living outside Kazakhstan with Russian as their native language claimed not to have any command of Kazakh.[18]

There are magazines and newspapers in both languages published in Kazakh SSR. The Kazakh language press amounted to 32 newspapers and periodicals, 169 magazines, and 716 book titles in 1985.[19] In addition, there are several newspapers, magazines and so on, both in Russian as well as in other languages, including German, published in the Republic. *Kazakhstanskaya Pravda* is published in Russian, while the Kazakh language daily newspaper is *Socialistiq Qazaqstan*. In the last few years with *glasnost'* both *Kazakhstanskaya Pravda* and *Socialistiq Qazaqstan* have developed into interesting and outspoken newspapers with detailed reports on the current situation in the republic. Besides traditional Kazakh literature, including heroic epos and the poems transmitted by traditional bards, of whom Dzhambul Dzhabaev (1846–1945) with his many odes to Stalin probably was the most spectacular, there is a rich collection of modern Kazakh *belles-lettres*.

The Kazakhs were traditionally, at least nominally, Sunni Muslims of the Hanafi juridical school. Today, they probably have a much higher percentage of religiously indifferent people than other native populations of Central Asia. Knowledge of the Quran is very limited, and very few Muslim practices are observed. The food taboo against pork is almost non-existent among urban Kazakhs. The only traditional Muslim practice they follow is to circumcise their boys. It is a widely observed custom, even among urbanites and agnostics. However, most Kazakhs still identify themselves as Muslims, although Islam has a very low profile in the republic. The mosques of Kazakhstan are under the jurisdiction of the Spiritual Directorate of Central Asia and Kazakhstan. During the summer of 1989, the *mufti* of the Directorate was removed and replaced by a new *mufti* who was also elected as a deputy to the Congress of People's Deputies. There are about thirty to forty functioning mosques in the republic.[20]

Although most Kazakhs seem rather indifferent to Islamic practice and values, the contemporary situation has also created a seedbed for religious revivalism among the youth. As part of the developing youth culture of Alma Ata and elsewhere in the republic, students have begun to assemble in religious groups. This religious revival could be a part of anti-Russian or nationalistic feelings. The authorities of Kazakhstan have therefore recently been forced to rethink and strengthen their anti-religious propaganda strategy.

KAZAKHS IN THE GORBACHEV ERA

One of the first outbreaks of nationalist riots under Gorbachev occurred in Alma Ata on 16 December 1986, when Dinmukhamed Kunaev was replaced by a Russian national, Gennadii Kolbin. The latter was sent to clean up the corruption and economic mismanagement that had become a hallmark of Kunaev's regime. At the CPSU Central Committee Plenum the following January, Kunaev was also removed from the Politburo.

There is no question that Dinmukhamed Kunaev was a very corrupt leader in a Western sense. Like many other Central Asian leaders, he was accused of favouring his own lineage and kinsmen. The highly cultural-structural nature of the problem can be seen in that the youths who took part in the riots have been identified as coming from the southern part of Kazakhstan, as did Kunaev. The Alma Ata riots, which according to Western estimates cost the loss of two lives (according to some rumours almost fifty people were killed) and about 200 injuries, certainly came as a surprise for both Moscow and many foreign observers.[21]

In a speech to the Central Committee just after the Alma Ata riots, Gorbachev stressed the importance of protecting the youth from the demoralising impact of nationalism. He also criticised the Party and social scientists for not taking the national question seriously. The crack-down on the nationalist riots in Alma Ata in December 1986 was, however, the beginning of many nationalist insurgent problems.

Kunaev's dismissal was followed by that of a number of his associates, many of whom were related to him. His brother, Asqar Kunaev, was removed from his post as President of the Kazakh Academy of Sciences, as was Diusetai Bezekhanov, assistant to Kunaev; Köpzhasar Naribaev, Minister of Higher and Secondary Education, was fired for permitting nepotism, bribe-taking and other crimes. Other relatives of Kunaev, who held posts in the provinces, were fired and even put on trial; a few were sentenced to death. Many people came under scrutiny. In February 1987, it was reported that thousands were overpaid for their jobs. Many were transferred to other jobs, and those responsible were punished. During that spring numerous party officials were compelled to undergo competence tests.

In January 1987 Kolbin presented a plan for setting up a body to ensure fair ethnic representation in all institutions. To restore the national balance the Kazakh Sagidulla Kubashev was appointed Second Secretary. To put an end to the desperate housing problem, Kolbin promised to provide housing by 1991 for everyone on the waiting list in 1987.

Makhtay Sadgiev was named as President of the Supreme Soviet Presidium in Kazakh SSR on 10 March 1989. He succeeded Zakahs

Kamalidenov who had resigned on health grounds in December 1988 after only ten months in office.

The election to the Congress of People's Deputies in March 1989, however, followed almost classical pre-Gorbachev lines. Gennadii Kolbin received 97 per cent of the votes.[22] In September 1989 steps were taken to reform the administrative system. The Kazakh Supreme Soviet will be a full-time legislature and the number of deputies will be cut. The reform also implied that more than one candidate will be nominated in the future to run for each seat.[23] Kolbin was ordered back to Moscow and replaced by Nazarbaev, a Kazakh.

After the removal of Kunaev and his associates there have been reforms in the political and economic structure of Kazakhstan. One might single out three major fields that signify *glasnost'* (*äygilik*) in Kazakhstan: the language question, the demand for a new historiography and the foundation of informal protest groups against environmental problems.

Perestroika (*qayta qurïlïs*) has focused on the system of *nomenklatura* built up by Kunaev. Much propaganda has stressed nepotism and clan thinking in Kazakh society, which is essentially a cultural problem. The reform policy under Kolbin has also emphasised the importance of putting an end to the social injustices endemic to Kazakhstan. Many exclusive shops for the elites have been closed. According to a list published by *Izvestia*, the elite around Kunaev had gained control over no fewer than 247 hotels, 414 guest flats, 84 cottages, 22 hunting lodges, 350 hospital beds and so on for their personal use. Problems with shortage of consumer goods and other needs are discussed openly in the daily newspapers.

Another problem which came to the surface was signs of a youth culture which could be a hot-bed of nationalistic tensions and protest movements. The risks of drug abuse and the youth have become a common topic in Soviet newspapers. Although drug problems were not unheard of previously and were acknowledged among the people, they were seldom openly discussed. The Soviet Union has long been a transit area for drug trafficking to Northern and Western Europe. With the Soviet experience in Afghanistan, drugs became a more common problem throughout the country. A growing youth culture has also implied an interest in cannabis abuse. With *glasnost'* this kind of problem also came to the fore. In January 1987 the police arrested forty-three persons in Alma Ata for selling narcotics, and almost 50 kilograms of hashish were confiscated. Much hashish was said to have been grown in the valley of Chuiskaia, one of the major areas for drug production in the Soviet Union. Drug problems are now a repeatedly mentioned issue. The magazine *Leninshilias* (18 January 1989) describes far-reaching abuse of drugs and youth criminality among school students in Kazakhstan.

In 1988, however, the newspaper reports not only stressed

delinquency among the youth, but also a more conscious kind of informal protest activity. Reports on informal groups increased in the republican press. At the beginning of September 1988, a deputy prosecutor reported that there were then more than 300 informal groups in Kazakhstan with a total of around 3,000 members. Some of these groups were environmental groups. The increasing ecological problems of Kazakhstan are not only the concern of youth, but teachers, scientists and other intellectuals as well.[24] Especially sensitive is the question about the nuclear weapons tests in the Semipalatinsk area. In July 1989, newspapers reported a Semipalatinsk Oblast Peace Committee, which announced that the residents of the area had been exposed to radiation. The chairwoman of the committee, Maira Zhangelova, was interviewed on television and reported preliminary results from a medical investigation showing cases of abnormalities in their blood and immune systems directly proportional to the time people have lived in the area and their proximity to the test site. The anti-nuclear activists held a conference in Semipalatinsk to discuss the health problem linked to the nuclear weapons tests.[25] Much publicised is the protest group 'Nevada-Palatinsk', which has organised rallies against further tests. The mine workers also continue to protest against the nuclear weapons programme in Semipalatinsk.

Language policy is one of the major topics in contemporary national debate in the Soviet Union. In a resolution from the 19th Party Conference it was stated that nationalities outside their territories would receive better opportunities to develop their own languages. The extent to which any steps have been taken among the Kazakhs in the Russian republic or Uzbekistan is not known. Within Kazakhstan the native language has been the topic of the day in local newspapers for the last few years. Letters to the editors complain about poor spelling of Kazakh words in official signs and the quality of instruction in the schools. A Kazakh Central Committee resolution was passed in March 1987 for improvements in the teaching of not only Kazakh, but also Russian.[26] In September 1989, the Supreme Soviet of Kazakhstan adopted a new language law in which Kazakh was made the republic's official language, but Russian will be retained as the language of inter-ethnic communication and widely used alongside Kazakh.[27] As inter-ethnic communication refers to use within the republic, Russian will probably continue to be used on an equal basis with Kazakh. However, in the future anyone dealing with the general public will have to know both Kazakh and Russian. Officials will be compelled to provide facilities for the public to communicate in either language by 1995, and only by the year 2000 will they be required to know both languages.[28] However, this act may have psychologically raised the status of the Kazakh language.

As with many other Turkic languages, the script reforms of the 1920s and 1940s severed the Kazakh language from its cultural background.

There are movements and persons today working for another change in the alphabet. Most prominent in these demands is the Mother Tongue Society (*Anatili Qogami*). In 1989 interest in teaching Kazakh children the Arabic script was reported. The children's journal *Pioner* began to publish a special section to teach the Arabic script to Kazakh youngsters.[29] More interesting, however, is the demand that the study of the Arabic script should at least be a mandatory part of course work in the advanced study of history.[30]

The Blank Spots in History

The Kazakhs have been under the hegemony of tsarist Russia for a long time but the view of how their dependency on Russian rule developed has varied under the Soviet regime. The official version has dominated until today. The Kazakhs have long demanded the right to their own history. Since 1963, the famous Kazakh author Olzhas Süleimanov, has repeatedly called for a real history of the Kazakhs. In an interview in *Komsomol' skaya Pravda* on 3 June 1988, he stressed the need for a new Kazakh history,[31] a demand shared by most Kazakh intellectuals. This was repeated by Süleimanov in *Qazaq Ädibeyatï* on January 1989.[32] *Qazaq Ädibeyatï*, on 23 September 1988, reported that a group of writers is willing to assist the magazine in filling in the blank spots in Kazakh history. In accordance with these demands, several formerly branded Kazakh intellectuals and nationalists have been rehabilitated, such as Ahmed Bayturshin (Baitursunov) (1873–1937), a leader of the Alash movement. More than 650 Kazakh intellectuals were rehabilitated during the autumn of 1988 and in spring of 1989. During the summer of 1989 Kazakh history was repeatedly discussed in the republican newspapers.[33]

Novi Uzen

While the Alma Ata riots were caused by dissatisfaction with Moscow interference in local affairs, ethnic conflicts surfaced with workers from an oil refinery in a small town in western Kazakhstan. A wave of violence swept over Novi Uzen during the summer of 1989.

On 17 June a gang of Kazakh youths was reported to have attacked cooperatives and set fire to vehicles. A Soviet report gives a detailed account of the riots.[34] What is described is a classic type of ethnic conflict known from many Western countries in times of unemployment. The Kazakhs who took part demanded that the

209

immigrant Lezghins and other Caucasian settlers of the area be expelled in order to free jobs for the locals. They accused the Lezghins of taking their jobs and stores run by Caucasian immigrants of overpricing commodities. The disturbances spread northward to most other towns on the Mangyshlak peninsula. By 26 June five people had been killed and 118 injured during the clashes. About 3,500 people were reported to have fled the area, most to Daghestan. Minor protests and disturbances were heard from other Kazakh cities as well.[35]

CONCLUSION

The nationalism of contemporary Kazakhstan is centred on several themes. First, there are economic problems: high unemployment among youths has caused some tension with immigrants. Second, the more intellectual debate has stressed Russo-centric historiography and the Kazakh right to their own history. Third, language is another question which is often discussed in contemporary Kazakhstan. Finally, there is a growing youth culture willing to protest against the persistent Soviet political culture. This has taken many forms, either informal religious groups or more concerned groups working with ecological and other cultural problems of the Kazakhs. Whatever happens in the contemporary Soviet Union, the authorities must take the Kazakhs seriously.

ACKNOWLEDGEMENTS

I am grateful to Professor Sven Gustavsson, Department of Slavic Languages, Dr Marie Clark Nelson, Department of History, Uppsala University, Ms Caroline Taube, Uppsala and Mr Abdulahap Kara, Munich, for generous help in completing this chapter.

NOTES

1. 'Streikdrohung gegen weitere Atomtests in der UdSSR' *Neue Züricher Zeitung* (8–9 Oct. 1989), p. 4.
2. For a general survey on the history and distribution of the Kazakhs of the USSR, see L. Krader and I. Wayne *The Kazakhs: A Background Study for Psychological Warfare* (Human Resources Research Office, Technical

Report, 23, Washington, DC 1955), and the well-researched book by M.B. Olcott *The Kazakhs*, Studies of Nationalities in the USSR Series (Stanford CA, Hoover Institution Press, Stanford University 1987). Basic statistical information is to be found in S. Akiner *Islamic Peoples of the Soviet Union: An Historical and Statistical Handbook*. 2nd edn, (London, New York, Sydney and Melbourne: Kegan Paul International 1987). An excellent but somewhat dated overview is Z. Katz 'Kazakhstan and the Kazakhs' in Z.Katz *et al.* (eds) *Handbook of Major Soviet Nationalities* (New York, Free Press, 1975), pp. 213–37. A gold-mine for information on all aspects of the Kazakhs and of Kazakhstan is *Qazaq Sovet Enciklopedeyasï* 10 vols (Almatï 1972–78).

3. For details on the distribution of Kazakhs in China, see I. Svanberg *The Altaic-Speakers of China: Numbers and Distribution*. Uppsala Multi-ethnic Papers, 14. (Uppsala: Centre for Multi-ethnic Research, 1988).

4. Little information is available on the Kazakhs of Mongolia. Their history is dealt with in Qabïsulï Islam, *Kereyler kerweni (Tarïxïy monografiyalïq qïšqasa solïw)* (Ögiy 1978).

5. For the *émigré* populations of Kazakhs in Turkey, Europe and elsewhere, see I. Svanberg *Kazak Refugees in Turkey: A Study of Cultural Persistence and Social Change*, Studia Multiethnica Upsaliensia, 8. (Uppsala, Almqvist & Wiksell International 1989), *passim*.

6. See the discussion in L. Benson and I. Svanberg 'The Kazaks in Xinjiang,' in L. Benson and I. Svanberg (eds) *The Kazaks of China*. Studia Multiethnica Upsaliensia, 5. (Uppsala, Almqvist & Wiksell International, 1988), p. 2. Kazakh words in this chapter are transliterated in accordance with the system in *Philologiæ Turcicæ Fundamenta*, vol. 1. (Wiesbaden, Franz Steiner Verlag Gmbh 1959), while Russian words are transcribed according to the system utilised in *Soviet Studies*.

7. For details on traditional social structure among the Kazakhs, see Khalel Argynbaev Qazaq xalqïnda ï sem'ya men neke (Tarixi-etnografiyalïq solu) (Almatï: Gïlim 1973).

8. The Oirat Mongol sphere of influence in Central Asia is erronously referred to as the Dzungarian Khanate in Soviet literature. For a discussion, see J. Miyawaki, 'Did a Dzungar Khanate really exist?' *Journal of the Anglo-Mongolian Society* 10 (1) (1987), pp. 1–5.

9. C. Demko, *The Russian Colonization of Kazakhstan, 1896–1916* (Bloomington, IND, Mouton 1969).

10. M.B. Olcott 'The emergence of national identity in Kazakhstan' *Canadian Review of Studies in Nationalism* 8 (2) (1981), pp. 285–300.

11. A. Bennigsen and M. Broxup *The Islamic Threat to the Soviet State*. Croom Helm series on the Arab World (London and Canberra, Croom Helm 1983), p. 22.

12. P.A. Goble 'Gorbachev and the Soviet nationality problem' in M. Friedberg and H. Isham (eds) *Soviet Society under Gorbachev: Current Trends and the Prospects for Reform* (New York: M.E. Sharpe, 1987, pp. 70–100.

13. For background, see I. Kreindler, 'The Soviet deported nationalities: a summary and update' *Soviet Studies* 38 (1986), pp. 387–405.

14. R. Karklins, *Ethnic Relations in the USSR: Perspectives from Below*. (Boston, Allen & Unwin 1986), p. 156.

15. A. Sheehy 'Do Kazakhs now outnumber Russians in Kazakhstan?' *Radio Liberty Research Bulletin* 65/87.
16. *Kazakhstan v tsifrakh. Kratkii statisticheshii sbornik.* (Alma Ata, Kazakhstan 1987), p. 4.
17. For details and discussion, see M. Bernstam, 'The demography of Soviet ethnic groups in world perspectives' in R. Conquest (ed.) *The Last Empire: Nationality and the Soviet Future* (Hoover Institution Press, Stanford University, Stanford, CA 1986), pp. 314–68.
18. See discussion in S. Lallukka 'Some demographic and linguistic trends among Soviet nationalities according to census data' *Bidrag till öststatsforskningen* 10 (1) (1982), pp. 86–110. The language question in Kazakhstan is dealt with in H.E. Krag *Sovjetunionenes mange sprog. Mål og midler i sovjetisk sprogpolitik.* Københavns Universitets Slaviske Institut. Rapporter, 5 (Copenhagen 1982); and in M.B. Olcott 'The politics of language reform in Kazakhstan' in I.T. Kreindler (ed.) *Sociolinguistic Perspectives on Soviet National Languages. Their Past, Present and Future.* Contribution to the Sociology of Language, 40, (Berlin, New York, Amsterdam, Mouton de Gruyter 1985), pp. 183–204.
19. *Narodnoe khozyaistvo Kazakhstana v 1985 g. Statisticheskii ezhegodnik* (Alma Ata, Kazakhstan 1986), pp. 277–78.
20. A. Bennigsen and S. Wimbush *Muslims of the Soviet Empire: A Guide* (London, C. Hurst & Co. 1986), p. 70.
21. The riot following the dismissal of Kunaev is discussed in detail by S. Wimbush 'The Alma Ata riots' *Encounter* 69 (1) (June 1987), pp. 62–8. Comments upon Kunaev are also given in H. Krag 'Kunajev førte Kazakernes kulturtradition til Moskva', *Information* 23. Dec. 1986, p. 2.
22. 'Election to new Congress of People's Deputies' *Keesing's Record of World Events* vol. 35 (3) (1989), p. 36,513.
23. B. Brown 'Informal groups in Kazakhstan' *Radio Liberty Research Bulletin* 549/88 (1988).
24. V. Tolz 'The USSR this week' *Radio Liberty Report on the USSR*, vol. 1 (32) (11 Aug. 1989), pp. 29–31.
25. 'Das Erlernen der Sprachen verbessern' *Freundschaft. Zeitung des Zentralkomitees der Kommunistischen Partei Kasachstans* 24 June 1987, p. 1.
26. Tass, 22 Sept. 1989.
27. V. Ardaev and E. Matskevich 'Sessii Berkhovnykh Sovetov soiuznykh respublik, Kazakhskaya SSR' *Izvestiya*, 23 Sept. 1989, p. 2.
28. A. Bohr and T. Kocaoglu 'Press watch on Central Asia' *Radio Liberty*, 17 March 1989, p. 27.
29. See E. Dailey 'Update on alphabet legislation' *Radio Liberty Report on the USSR* vol. 1 (32) (11 Aug 1989), pp. 29–31.
30. S. Newman 'Suleimenov promotes study of Kazakh history' *Radio Liberty Background Report RL 262/88* (1988).
31. A. Bohr and T. Kocaoglu 'Central Asian notebook' *Radio Liberty. Report on the USSR* vol. 1 (6) (10 Feb. 1989), p. 21.
32. B. Brown, 'Investigation of "blank spots" in Kazakh history moves forward' *Radio Liberty, Report on the USSR* vol. 1 (33) (18 Aug. 1989), pp. 16–18.
33. A. Nurmanov and D. Sidorov 'Novy Uzen – the buildup to explosion'

Moscow News Weekly 27 (1989), p. 5. Cf. 'Kazakh violence spreads' *International Herald Tribune* 26 June 1989.

34. For a brief overview on the events in Novi Uzen, see A. Sheehy 'Interethnic disturbances in western Kazakhstan' *Radio Liberty. Report on the USSR*, vol. 1 (26) (7 July 1989), pp. 11–14.

CHAPTER THIRTEEN

Uzbeks

Shirin Akiner

BACKGROUND

The Uzbeks are a people of predominantly Turkic origin, with a significant admixture of Iranian and Turkicised Mongol elements. They speak Uzbek, a language which evolved out of Chagatai, the chief literary medium of the eastern Turkic world (contemporary and counterpart to Ottoman Turkish in the west). The Uzbeks are Sunni Muslims of the Hanafi school, as are the majority of Soviet Muslims, and also of Muslims outside the Soviet Union.

The Uzbeks, by far the largest group of Muslims in the Soviet Union, are also the third largest Soviet nationality, ranking after the Russians and Ukrainians. Today they number some 16,686,000. Over 14 million, approximately 85 per cent of the total, live within the Uzbek SSR; a further 7 per cent, some 1 million, in the Tadzhik SSR; 3.5 per cent, approximately half a million, in the Kirghiz SSR, and close on 2 per cent each, some 300,000, in the Turkmen and Kazakh SSRs.[1] Outside the Soviet Union, there used to be a colony of some 1.5 million Uzbeks across the border to the south, in Afghanistan; many of these fled to Pakistan during the Soviet occupation of 1979–89, and some moved still further afield, to begin new lives in Turkey. None have so far returned to Afghanistan. There are another 20,000 Uzbeks to the west, in the Xinjiang-Uighur Autonomous Region of the People's Republic of China. Cross-border contacts have become easier in recent years, but are still fairly limited and restricted, in the main, to close blood relations.

The Uzbeks are descendants of the nomadic tribes of the Golden Horde who settled in Transoxiana in the fifteenth to sixteenth centuries and there intermingled with the sedentary population. Independent, rival khanates emerged, the most powerful of which came to be centred on Bukhara, Khiva and Kokand. Tsarist troops invaded the region in the second half of the nineteenth century. They met with little resistance from the local rulers who, distracted by internecine struggles, failed to present a coordinated resistance. Bukhara became a Russian protectorate in 1868, Khiva in 1873; Kokand was annexed, and its khanate abolished, in 1876. However, Russian rule proved to be less onerous than that of most other colonial regimes, and, for the most part, the indigenous population continued to live much as before.[2] The social and material changes introduced by the Russians were relatively few, and limited to the main urban centres. Almost despite themselves, though, they provided a channel for new ideas into a society that had previously been isolated and closed for many centuries. Of even greater significance was the fact that, once part of the empire, the Central Asians came into close contact with other 'Russian' Muslims, notably the Tatars of the Volga and Crimea, and the Azerbaijanis. Far more progressive than the Central Asians, it was they who introduced the *jadid* (reformist) movement to Central Asia. They pioneered a more modern type of education. Many of the privately owned vernacular newspapers that appeared in Central Asia from 1905 onwards were *jadid* publications.[3]

Tsarist rule in Tashkent was replaced by Soviet government in late 1917, but not finally consolidated until April 1919. Nevertheless, in April 1918 the Turkestan ASSR was proclaimed (within the RSFSR), comprising most of Soviet Central Asia. Meanwhile, a fierce struggle was waged between Bolshevik and anti-Bolshevik forces, interventionists and native *basmachi* (lit. 'robber') bands (themselves disunited, with disparate aims). The former protectorates of Bukhara and Khiva were transformed into nominally independent People's Soviet Republics in 1920, then incorporated into Turkestan in 1923–24.[4]

UZBEKS UNDER SOVIET RULE

Whereas the tsarist administration consciously restricted its efforts to change Central Asian society, the Soviet administration, by contrast, sought drastically to remould it. Possibly the most fundamental innovation was the creation of national administrative units. These were based on ethno-linguistic divisions. It would be an exaggeration to say that such divisions did not exist (though this is indeed a view held by some), but certainly prior to this they had had no political significance. Traditionally, religion had provided the key element in self-definition: 'Muslim' as opposed to 'non-Muslim'. The ethonym 'Uzbek' was scarcely used. The most common terms were those derived from place-names, for example, *Namanganlyq* 'someone from Namangan'; the colonial administration referred to the native sedentarised population as *Sart*, a word of Sanskrit origin meaning 'trader'. By the early years of the twentieth century a handful of intellectuals had begun to raise the question of ethnic identity, but in a vague, tentative way. There was nothing in their discussions, nor in the subsequent turmoil of civil war, that in any way prepared the ground for the National Delimitation of the Central Asian Republics of 1924–25, as a result of which the Uzbek SSR and other Central Asian republics were created. Far from being a response to a popular, indigenous demand, the Delimitation was an administrative decision imposed on the region from the centre – part, some would say, of a 'divide and rule' policy.[5]

The Uzbek SSR, which came into being on 27 October 1924, encompassed the districts of Amu Darya, Syr Darya, Samarkand and Ferghana, part of the former Bukharan state, and part of the Khorezm (Khivan) state. It included the Tadzhik ASSR until 1929, when this acquired full union republic status; it acquired the Karakalpak ASSR (originally part of the RSFSR) in 1936. Uzbeks represented 66 per cent of the total population (they are approximately 70 per cent today).

Language and Literacy

The creation of separate administrative units was but the first step in the process of nation-building. The development of distinctive national literary languages, literatures, histories, rituals, symbols and art forms were concomitant necessities. It was not an easy task. It was not that the Central Asians lacked traditions, but that their shared heritage was so great that efforts to parcel it up into 'nationalist' packages led to distorted and grossly anachronistic interpretations of history, not to mention awkward rivalries over medieval scholars. However, artificial though they were, in time these devices achieved a measure of success, and a degree of national pride, even of nationalism, was born. The Uzbeks, for example, have come to believe that they have a unique hereditary claim to the brilliant achievements of ancient Transoxiana. This, along with their numerical superiority, has reinforced their view of themselves as the natural leaders of Central Asia today. The neighbouring republics regard this cultural aggrandisement as yet another expression of 'great Uzbek chauvinism'.

Easily comprehensible literary languages, full literacy and a plentiful supply of printed material were required in order to reach out to the masses, to communicate the new ideology to them and involve them in the new political system. The Uzbeks, unlike some other peoples of Central Asia, already had their own literary language, Chagatai (also known as Old Uzbek). However, it was a refined, learned medium, far removed from the spoken dialects of the region. Moreover, and perhaps more importantly, it was firmly associated with the pre-Revolutionary period. In the 1920s there was a struggle between the so-called 'bourgeois nationalists', who mostly supported the continued use of Chagatai, and the pro-Russian group, who were in favour of developing a new literary form based on the dialects of Tashkent and Ferghana.[6] These were the dialects of the economic and political centres of the new republic, and also of the burgeoning print language.

However, they were atypical of the main body of Uzbek dialects (and most other Turkic languages) in that they had little vowel harmony. Nevertheless, they were adopted as the base for the national language. Terms drawn from Russian were introduced to convey new concepts in such fields as ideology, technology and the general Soviet 'way of life'. The change of scripts gave visual emphasis to the new orientation. The Arabic script continued to be used up to 1930, when it was replaced by the Latin. This in turn was superseded by the Cyrillic in 1940.

One of the chief reasons advanced for the abolition of the Arabic script was that it was an impediment to the spread of literacy. That is a debatable point, but it is undeniable that the literacy rate rose with astonishing speed under Soviet rule. According to the 1926 census, literacy among Uzbeks stood at a mere 3.8 per cent; by 1932, 52.5 per cent of the population were said to be literate. The curve continued to rise, until today it is claimed to be over 99 per cent. There may be some over-optimism in this, but even so what has been achieved is remarkable, and far outstrips literacy rates in neighbouring countries such as Pakistan, Afghanistan and Iran. It required an extraordinary level of organisation and coordination, since virtually everything had to be created from scratch, from the construction of school buildings to the training of teachers, from the compilation of basic textbooks to the provision of paper and printing facilities.[7] Yet there were also losses. The changes of script have meant that the Uzbeks have been bereft not only of the whole of their pre-Revolutionary written culture but also of first-hand acquaintance with sources relating to the formative first decades of Soviet rule. Literacy has given them access to only a small and carefully edited segment of their history.

Islam

In November 1917 the Soviet government issued a declaration 'to all the toiling Muslims of Russia and the East' that henceforth their beliefs and customs would be considered 'free and inviolable'.[8] At first this promise was fulfilled reasonably well. By the end of the 1920s, however, the situation had changed. In Uzbekistan, as in other parts of the Soviet Union, a fierce anti-religious campaign was unleashed. Muslim schools and courts were phased out (initially, since there were few acceptable alternatives, they had been allowed to continue functioning); mosques were closed, often to be turned into clubs or cinemas, religious literature confiscated and destroyed, religious functionaries persecuted. The Arabic script, which had been used for the literary languages of Central Asia for close on a thousand years, and is precious to Muslims all round the world because it is the script in which the Qur'ān was originally recorded, was replaced by the Latin. In short, as far as possible all visible signs of the religion were wiped out and it became dangerous to admit to being a Muslim.

However, it was impossible to eradicate overnight something that had for centuries been the very essence of life. Quite apart from the role the religion had played in shaping the culture and history of Central Asia, almost every custom and tradition had its roots in Islam. The claim that the religion survived owing to the activities of secret Sufi (mystic) organisations is surely too extreme. Even if there had been such activity (which has not been proved convincingly) it could not have been effective had there not been a widespread, deeply ingrained belief that to be a Central Asian was synonymous with being a Muslim. To have abandoned such practices as, for example, circumcision and the special burial rites would have been to cut oneself off from one's ancestors, to become an isolated individual rather than a member of a living community of past, present and future generations.[9]

During and after the Second World War the government adopted a slightly more conciliatory attitude towards Islam. Four regional Muslim Spiritual Directorates were created, to regulate such formal aspects of Islam as were allowed to reappear at this time. The largest and most important directorate had its seat in Tashkent, the Uzbek capital. The first two (until 1989 the only) *madrasa* (religious colleges) in the Soviet Union were reopened in Bukhara and Tashkent. A small number of mosques were also gradually reopened and a few religious publications sanctioned, their print runs tiny and circulation tightly controlled. Some twenty to thirty carefully chosen pilgrims (drawn from the whole of the USSR) were allowed to make the annual *hajj* to Mecca, one of the basic precepts of Islam. These changes were mostly cosmetic and did little to bring greater freedom of worship to ordinary believers. Their primary purpose was to impress foreign Muslims, to pave the way to better relations with Muslim states in Africa and Asia.

Social and Economic Change

Soviet rule brought drastic changes to the social and economic life of the Uzbeks. Under the tsarist administration there had been some industrial development of Central Asia (chiefly the extraction of petroleum, coal and copper), also a substantial expansion of the cultivation of cotton. Short-staple native cotton had long been grown locally, but it was the introduction of higher-yielding American seed in 1884 that revolutionised production and transformed the region into the principal supplier of raw material to the Russian textile industry (the simultaneous extension of the railway system solved the transport problem). The 'great leap forward' in economic development, however, was initiated during the first two Soviet five year plans (1928–38). In order to accomplish this, large numbers of professionals and skilled technicians were brought in from other parts of the Soviet Union. By the 1930s, some 85 per cent of the industrial workforce was composed of immigrants from European Russia. During the war years, a number of industrial enterprises from the western parts of the Soviet Union were relocated in Central Asia, over 100 in Uzbekistan alone; this further helped to accelerate the economic development of the region (and brought in yet more immigrants). After the war, the industrial growth rate remained high for a time, but by the mid-1950s had begun to decline sharply. This downward trend has since continued, occasioned to a large extent by the lack of sufficient capital investment in the post-war years. There was, however, a temporary upturn in the 1970s; this was closely related to an increase in cotton production from 1965 onwards.[10] In 1980 Uzbekistan reputedly produced over 6 million tonnes of raw cotton; in 1983 it almost rivalled the output of the whole of the United States of America. Since then, though, there has been a decrease in production. In 1989 it accounted for just over 5 million tonnes.

The workforce in the cotton fields is entirely Uzbek. Despite all the hardships and lack of facilities in the rural areas there has as yet been very little urban drift; the great majority of the population have remained in their ancestral villages. This has been a very important factor in preserving the traditional way of life, at least within the confines of the family. In the late 1920s there was a vigorous campaign to socialise women; known as *hujum* ('attack'), it sought to draw women out of the home, to give them an education (only 1 per cent were literate), and to turn them into wage earners. It was responsible, too, for causing women to stop wearing the veil. The *hujum* had a lasting effect on the lives of urban women, many of whom now work outside the home, some as highly qualified specialists. In the villages, however, there has been little change. The desperate, hopeless conditions cause several hundred women a year to commit suicide through self-immolation.[11]

UZBEKS IN THE GORBACHEV PERIOD

Perestroika and *glasnost'* have been slow to come to Uzbekistan. Even now they can scarcely be said to be much in evidence. Fear and distrust, legacies of the terror of the 1930s, are to some extent responsible for this. There is also confusion and uncertainty about the true intentions of the centre. No one quite knows what is expected of them. The most powerful reason, however, surely lies in the nature of the society itself. The Uzbeks have a tradition of deferring to those who are senior to them in age or status. Criticism of the *aqsaqaly* ('white beards') is considered unseemly and a fault in the person who shows such temerity, no matter how justified the criticism might be. This attitude, when combined with a system that itself provides few checks and controls on those in power, creates an elite who are doubly insured against the need to account for their actions. The word 'mafia' is frequently used of the ruling cliques in Uzbekistan, not least by the Uzbeks themselves, who suffer acutely from this blight on their society and yet are impotent in the face of it. Virtually every organisation and every neighbourhood is plagued by this phenomenon. It is impossible to characterise a typical 'mafia' member; they are found at every level of society, drawn from every nationality. Inevitably, though, the great majority are native Uzbeks, nurtured, supported and tied into the local networks of power. Loyal neither to Moscow nor to their compatriots, but to themselves alone, their stranglehold on society is very nearly as strong as it was in the days of 'stagnation'. Consequently even the modest moves towards democratisation that have taken place elsewhere in the Soviet Union have hardly begun to make an appearance in Uzbekistan.

Nevertheless, since the late 1980s there has been slightly greater freedom of the press and more opportunity to discuss publicly subjects that were formerly forbidden. It is mainly the writers who have led the struggle for greater openness, but academics, painters, film-makers and other creative artists have also made an important contribution. Social and environmental issues have been widely discussed. It has come as a painful shock to many to discover how serious are the problems that now confront the republic. The catalogue of disasters is vast; it includes the abysmal level of health-care and housing in rural areas (where some 80 per cent of the Uzbeks live); widespread disease, malnutrition and poverty; high infant mortality; a colonial-type economy that uses the indigenous population almost as slave labour to produce raw materials which are purchased at prices far below the world market level, then exported to other parts of the Union to be processed; high unemployment, leading to inter-ethnic tensions; ecological calamities that are making large tracts of land uninhabitable. There is a growing indignation over the extent to which their culture and history have been distorted and manipulated. As in other parts of the Soviet Union, there is a demand for the rehabilitation of those liquidated in the purges of the 1930s; also, for the filling-in of the 'blank spots' of history. Yet by no means everything is open for discussion; the *jadid* period – the period of the first stirrings of political awareness in the early years of the twentieth century – remains a sensitive topic. So, too, does the establishment of Soviet power in the region, the incorporation of the Bukharan and Khivan states into Turkestan, and the whole of the civil war period.

Environmental Issues

The largest and most complex environmental problem is that of the Aral Sea. Not only is the region itself fast being reduced to an irredeemable wasteland, but the effects of the devastation are beginning to be felt, it is reported, as far away as in Pakistan to the east and along the Black Sea coast to the west. It is a cycle of disaster comparable in scale to that of the cutting down of the Amazonian rainforests. In recent years climatic changes have been observed, possibly caused by the shrinking of the sea; dust storms, fiercer and more frequent now, scoop up salts from the exposed seabed and scatter them far and wide; some are deposited on the glaciers, again to be carried down to the sea by the snow melt, but in a yet more concentrated form. Highly toxic and non-biodegradable, these salts are the residue from the fertilisers and pesticides used to boost the cotton crop. The effect of long-term exposure to these chemicals is believed to be similar to that caused by exposure to radiation. Scientists speak of a catastrophe of greater proportions than that of Chernobyl. Physical and mental abnormalities abound. Doctors fear that a genetic mutation has taken place and that the local population is, quite simply, beyond the help of medical science. Some political activists are openly calling it genocide.

Evidence of the approaching calamity has long been available to the authorities, yet they chose to ignore it. Once again, it was left to the writers to force the matter out into the open. A Society for the Protection of the Aral Sea was created under the auspices of the Writers' Union in 1989. It has done much to raise public awareness of the disaster. Solutions to the problem, however, are still very far away.[12]

The plight of the Aral Sea, like so many of Uzbekistan's problems, has its roots in the mono-culture of cotton. The drive for higher productivity initiated by Khrushchev in the 1950s developed a mad momentum of its own during the Brezhnev era. It turned into a fantastic charade, with the centre setting ever more outrageous targets and the republican leadership readily concurring. The strain on the republic was unbearable and every aspect of life suffered. Precious water resources were squandered with no thought for sustainable development; intensive irrigation led, on the one hand, to the creation of saline swamps; on the other, to a severe depletion of the rivers that feed the Aral Sea and, eventually, to the drying up of the sea itself.

It is now openly acknowledged that the mono-culture of cotton has been responsible for some of the worst health problems of the republic. As more land was turned over to cotton, so other forms of agriculture were neglected. Crop rotation declined, leading to an impoverishment of the soil. Less space was available for the cultivation of fruit and vegetables; pasture land, too, was reduced. Basic foodstuffs became scarce and expensive, and the diet of the population suffered accordingly. Vitamin, protein and iodine deficiencies are widespread, resistance to infection low, especially among children; the official infant mortality rate in some parts of Uzbekistan is 118 per 1,000 live births, the actual rate probably higher (cf. the Soviet average of 25.4).

Further health hazards are created by the vast quantities of chemical fertilisers and pesticides that are used on the crop (according to Uzbek scientists, some 54 kilograms per hectare). These have seeped into the soil and the water supply, poisoning both; in many parts of the republic there is no clean drinking water. The food cycle has been contaminated to such an extent that, in the worst affected regions, even the breast milk of nursing mothers shows traces of toxic salts. Butyfos, the most dangerous of the defoliants, was banned in 1987, but others, almost as lethal, are still legal, and continue to be used. It is the women and children, who harvest the crop by hand, who are exposed, without any form of protective clothing, to the full force of these chemicals. The harm they do in the short term is all too obvious, but it is feared that the long-term effects will be even more serious. Apart from the damage to their health, it has been estimated that Uzbek children and young people lose 2 to 3 months out of every academic year, from the beginning of their schooling through to the last year of university, by working in the cotton fields. They are thus seriously disadvantaged in their education.[13]

The cotton mania has brought many other troubles to Uzbekistan. The most spectacular was a giant embezzlement conspiracy linked to the falsification of cotton statistics. It has emerged that in the Brezhnev era some of the plantations, and consequently their harvests, existed only on paper. The profit, however, was real enough and went to highly placed pockets in Moscow and Tashkent. Some of the ringleaders were brought to trial and convicted in 1988, but the 'Uzbek affair', as it has come to be known, remains very much alive, with new rackets and swindles still coming to light. Many thousands of people have been arrested. It is a vivid exposition of the workings of the 'mafia', revealing not only colossal greed, but also total indifference to the sufferings inflicted on others. It shows, too, the international aspect of such operations, involving not only those within the republic, but also those outside. Many Uzbeks deeply resent the manner in which the all-Union press has laid such stress on their part in the affair, as if they alone were guilty. Their indignation is understandable, and to an extent justified; nevertheless, it does seem that corruption and lawlessness flourish more easily in Uzbekistan, behind its many still closed doors, than in most other parts of the Soviet Union.

'Popular Front' Movement Birlik

The Uzbeks have no experience of democratic self-rule. In the time of the khanates power was concentrated in the hands of a tiny few; this was followed by a half-century of colonial rule, replaced, in turn, by another, in many ways yet harsher form of external control. It is small wonder that they find it difficult to formulate a coordinated response to the current situation. Having no political culture of their own, they are forced to look elsewhere for models. The central question is one of orientation: are they Uzbeks who, having accepted the nationality thrust upon them in 1924, now seek to carve out a future for a nationally based republic? Or do they belong to a larger grouping; for example, that of Turkestan? Or Turan? And are they Muslims, striving to create a society organised on Islamic precepts, or do they find inspiration in Western systems? As yet there are no clear answers. The questions themselves are too new.

The intelligentsia are pulled in two directions. Many have a profound respect for Islam, but few have any real understanding of it; now, after seventy years of Communist rule, it has become an alien philosophy. For all their instinctive sympathy for it, they find it hard to comprehend how, in practical terms, Islam could provide the basis for contemporary life. Everything in their education predisposes them towards Western models, and within the Soviet experience, to the example of the Baltic republics, of Moscow, of the Ukraine. *Birlik* ('Unity'), the largest of the contemporary political movements in Central Asia, founded in Tashkent in November 1988 by a group of Uzbek intellectuals, was closely modelled on popular front movements in other parts of the Soviet Union, in particular, that of Lithuania's *Sąjūdis*. The movement grew rapidly under the chairmanship of Abdurahim Pulatov, a lecturer and research scientist in cybernetics at Tashkent University. Thanks to his energy and organisational skills, it succeeded in attracting supporters from all walks of life; at its height it numbered some 500,000 members. It put forward a candidate, the poet Muhammad Salih, in the elections of March 1989 for the Congress of People's Deputies. Despite *Birlik*'s popularity, however, and despite Salih's own very considerable following, he was unsuccessful, defeated by the underhand and highly unconstitutional tactics of the local Party and government representatives.

Nevertheless, the movement persevered and continued to campaign on a number of issues. The struggle to obtain legal recognition for Uzbek as the state language of the republic provided them with their chief platform. Legislation enshrining this in the Constitution was passed in October 1989. Almost simultaneously, *Birlik* disintegrated. To some extent this was the result of personality clashes within the leadership, but collapse was undoubtedly hastened by the strain inflicted by the authorities, who pursued a cat-and-mouse policy, sometimes inviting cooperation from *Birlik* members, sometimes clamping down on them, often intimating that official registration of the movement was imminent, but never actually granting it. The members were politically too inexperienced to withstand such pressure. There are those, like Muhammad Salih and his faction who seem inclined to create a new pan-Turkestan party, while Abdurahim Pulatov is tending towards a more nationalist approach. A number of other small organisations have sprung up recently; none have clearly defined aims and at present are scarcely more than discussion groups.

Islam

Official attitudes towards Islam are ambivalent. In the press, especially in organs of the centre, and even in statements from the senior leadership, including those of Gorbachev, there is not infrequently a critical, almost derogatory, approach to Islam. In practice, however, the last years of the 1980s have shown a marked improvement in working relations between the state and the Muslim community.

The clearest intimation of change came in March 1988, when a new mufti was elected. The post is of more than regional importance, since the incumbent is the mouthpiece of official Soviet views on Muslim affairs for those within the USSR, as well as for those abroad. Three generations of the Babakhanov family fulfilled this function loyally, proving themselves dependable allies of the secular authorities; but times changed, and the leadership they had served fell into disgrace. Shamsuddin Babakhanov, elected in 1982, became an embarrassment to all concerned, not least to the policy-makers in Moscow. Yet there was no formal mechanism by which he could be relieved of his duties. Then, suddenly, the Muslim community held an unprecedented public demonstration in Tashkent, accusing him of licentious and un-Islamic behaviour and demanding his resignation. Their voice was heeded; a few weeks later the Rector of Tashkent *madrasa*, thirty-seven-year-old Muhammad Sadyq Mahammed Yusuf Hoja-ogli, was installed in Babakhanov's place. It was a neat solution to an awkward problem.

Shortly after, a number of dramatic concessions were made towards the Muslims. More mosques were opened over the next few weeks than had previously been permitted in several years. A new edition of the Qur'ān was promised, its 50,000 copies to be the first step towards fulfilling Mufti Muhammad Sadyq's publicly expressed hope that there should soon be a copy of the Holy Scripture in every home. An Uzbek translation of the Qur'ān is in preparation and extracts have already appeared in print. Extensions to the two *madrasa*, in Bukhara and in Tashkent, have been sanctioned and construction is under way. There have been several other notable improvements, but perhaps the most potent symbol of the 'new thinking', and the one that touched the believers most deeply, was the return of the Othman Qur'ān to the safekeeping of the Muslims. Believed by Central Asians to be a seventh-century manuscript, copied soon after the death of the Prophet, it is one of the holiest treasures of Islam. It was taken to St Petersburg by the tsarist administration, returned to Central Asia by the Soviet government, but kept for most of the past seventy years in the custody of the civil authorities.

Not every obstacle to a truly Muslim life has yet been removed, but it is a great deal easier to be a Muslim in Uzbekistan today than it has been at any time since the republic was founded. The general mass of believers have welcomed these developments, which have done much to enhance Gorbachev's popularity. However, the new freedoms place new responsibilities on the Muslim leaders. They are now expected to give moral direction to the community, to act as a counterbalance to 'undesirable phenomena' ranging from hooliganism to nascent fundamentalism. The Mufti Muhammad Sadyq was elected (the single, unopposed candidate in his ward) to the Congress of People's Deputies in March 1989. The government has encouraged him to speak out on matters of law and order as, for example, during the violence in Ferghana in June 1989. He and the other *ulama* (religious scholars) have for so long been accustomed to a marginal role in society, however, that it is not easy for them to find a common language with the community at large. Yet as the euphoria over mosques being open for worship, and Qur'āns legally available, gives way to a commonplace acceptance of such things, the Muslim leaders will have to meet the challenge of their new function, or lose the respect of believers.

A rival form of moral Islamic authority is being provided by the so-called Wahhabis (not apparently linked in any way to those in Saudi Arabia). Eschewing politics and indeed, as far as possible, any form of involvement with the secular authorities, they live by the labour of their own hands. They are greatly respected for their upright, ascetic lives. They began as a small group in the Namangan region, but their influence has now spread to the capital.

CONCLUSIONS

The social and economic problems of Uzbekistan are steadily worsening. As in many developing countries, the population is very young and growing rapidly (the birth-rate is almost double the Soviet average). Unemployment is widespread, especially in rural areas, but attachment to the land remains strong and there has been little out-migration. It is difficult to judge the extent of the crisis since information is incomplete and not always reliable. However, there is now a greater degree of public discussion and this has led to a radical change of attitude. Before, most people were prepared to accept their lot; today, there is growing disillusionment, anger and disaffection, which in turn has led to a rise in nationalism and general xenophobia. This is a new phenomenon, but one that is likely to increase as economic inequalities become more pronounced. Resentment is by no means directed against the Slav immigrants alone; as the clashes in Ferghana in June 1989 involving the Meskhetian Turks showed, even fellow Sunni Muslims are not immune.

The problems are so colossal that it is hard to see how they will be solved. Serious analysis of the economic and related ecological ills has scarcely begun, so though there is much indignation, there are as yet no programmes for implementing change; plans for economic independence remain vague, as do those for saving the Aral Sea or re-aligning the agriculture. The future does not look promising. Even if a major conflagration is avoided, sporadic localised outbreaks of violence will probably spread. The population has lost confidence in the old leadership and new leaders have not yet emerged. It cannot be excluded that fundamentalist elements will fill the vacuum. It is a situation ripe for manipulation.

NOTES

1. Complete data from the 1989 census are not yet available. In 1979 the regional distribution of Uzbeks within the USSR was as follows:

		Percentage
Total number of Uzbeks	12,455,978	100.0
In UzSSR	10,569,007	84.9
In KazSSR	263,295	2.1
In KirSSR	426,194	3.4
In TurkSSR	233,730	1.9
In TadzhSSR	873,199	7.0

Source: *Chislennost' i sostav naseleniya SSSR: Po dannym Vsesoyuznoi perepisi naseleniya 1979 g.* (Moscow: Finansy i statistika, 1984).

In the period 1979–89 there has been an increase of 34% in the overall number of Uzbeks in the USSR.

2. There are several accounts of life in Central Asia under the tsarist administration. Of particular interest are those by the American consul in Moscow, E. Schuyler, *Turkistan: Notes of a Journey in Russian Turkistan* ... (London: Sampson Low, Marston, Searle & Rivington, 1876), and by F. H. Skrine (of the Indian Civil Service) and E. D. Ross, *The Heart of Asia: a History of Russian Turkestan and the Central Asian Khanates from the Earliest Times* (London: Methuen, 1899), pp. 238–428.

3. For a review of the pre-Revolutionary press in Central Asia, see A. Bennigsen and Ch. Lemercier-Quelquejay, *La Presse et le mouvement national chez les musulmans de Russie avant 1920* (Paris–The Hague: Mouton, 1964); T. Ernazov, *Rastsvet narodnoi pechati v Uzbekistane* (Tashkent: Uzbekistan, 1968).

4. The best study to date of the khanates in the tsarist and early Soviet period is S. Becker, *Russia's Protectorates in Central Asia: Bukhara and Khiva, 1865–1924* (Cambridge, MA: Harvard University Press, 1968).

5. Cf. A. Bennigsen, 'Islamic, or Local Consciousness among Soviet Nationalities?', in *Soviet Nationality Problems* (New York: Columbia University Press, 1971), pp. 168–82; T. Zhdanko, in I. R. Grigulevich and S. Ya. Kozlov (eds), *Ethnocultural Processes and National Problems in the Modern World* (Moscow: Progress, 1979), pp. 133–56; R. Vaidyanath,

The Formation of the Soviet Central Asian Republics: a Study in Soviet Nationalities Policy, 1917–1936 (New Delhi: People's Publishing House, 1967).

6. A useful discussion of the political currents underlying the changes of script, etc. is given in E. Allworth, *Uzbek Literary Politics* (The Hague: Mouton, 1964), pp. 169–200; see also S. Akiner, 'Uzbekistan: Republic of Many Tongues', in M. Kirkwood (ed.), *Language Planning in the Soviet Union* (London: Macmillan, 1989), pp. 100–22.

7. See W. K. Medlin, W. M. Cave and F. Carpenter, *Education and Development in Central Asia* (Leiden: Brill, 1971); also T. N. Kary-Niyazov, *Ocherki Kul'tury Sovetskogo Uzbekistana* (Moscow: AN SSSR, 1955), pp. 55–68, 334–60.

8. 'Obrashchenie Predsedatelya Soveta Narodnykh Kommissarov V. I. Lenina i Narodnogo Kommissara po Delam Natsional'nostei I. V. Stalina k vsem trudyashchimsya musul'manam Rossii i Vostoka, 20 noya. (3 dek.) 1917 g.', *Dokumenty vneshnoi politiki SSSR*, vol. 1 (Moscow: Gos. izdatel'stvo politicheskoi literatury, 1957), pp. 34–5.

9. The fullest Western study of Islam in the Soviet Union, though now somewhat out of date, is still A. Bennigsen and Ch. Lemercier-Quelquejay, *Islam in the Soviet Union* (London: Pall Mall, 1967); cf. *Islam v SSSR*, E. G. Filimonov (responsible editor) (Moscow: Mysl', 1983).

10. See, further, A. R. Khan and D. Ghai, *Collective Agriculture and Rural Development in Soviet Central Asia* (London: Macmillan, 1979).

11. For two contrasting views of the lot of women in Soviet Central Asia, see G. Massell, *The Surrogate Proletariat* (London: Princeton University Press, 1974); B. P. Pal'vanova, *Emansipatsiya musul'manki* (Moscow: Nauka, 1982). There have been several reports in the press on self-immolation, e.g. 'The Flames of Feudalism' by E. Gafarov, Head of Burns Unit, Civic Hospital, Samarkand, *International Pravda*, vol. 2, no. 7, 1988, p. 24.

12. *Sud'ba Arala*, R. Ternovskaya (ed.) (Tashkent: Mekhnat, 1988), a collection of some 20 essays by journalists, academics and politicians, presents a survey of the current thinking on the problem; see also 'Aral'skaya Katastrofa', *Novyi Mir*, no. 5, 1989, pp. 182–241.

13. See, e.g., the reports in *Ogonek* by A. Minkin, no. 13, March 1988, 'Zaraza ubiistvennaya', p. 26; and no. 33, Aug. 1988, 'Posledstviya zarazy', p. 25.

CHAPTER FOURTEEN

Turkmen

Annette Bohr

BACKGROUND

Turkmenistan appears to be a bastion of calm amid the rising storm of nationalist agitation that has been sweeping the country since the mid-1980s. Despite the absence of mass demonstrations in the republic and informal organisations, Turkmen nationalist activity has grown significantly since 1987, as evidenced by increasing demands to halt environmental damage and reduce the concomitant health risks, to improve the status of the native language, and to re-examine Turkmen history without ideological constraints. Perhaps most important, new information disclosed since the advent of *glasnost'* – together with abject living conditions – are convincing growing numbers of Turkmen that seven decades of Soviet power have transformed their region into little more than a cheap source of raw materials for the industries of the Russian republic.

While there has been a great leap forward in collective national consciousness, the Turkmen have none the less been slow – in comparison with other Soviet nationalities – to press for greater autonomy. Several factors account for this relatively passive response to Gorbachev's reform programme, the first of which is rooted in pre-Soviet Turkmen history. Before the establishment of Soviet rule, the largely nomadic Turkmen tribes never formed a national state, and were often divided among different powers, such as the Iranian empire, the Khivan khanate and the Bukharan emirate. The territory comprising present-day Turkmenistan, which stretches from the Caspian Sea in the west to the Amu Dar'ya river in the east and from Kazakhstan and Uzbekistan in the north to Iran and Afghanistan in the south, was the last Central Asian territory to be brought under the control of tsarist Russia. When tsarist annexation of the Turkmen region was completed in 1884–85, the tribe represented the highest form of political and economic power.[1]

At present, the Turkmen SSR in many respects still constitutes more of a tribal confederation than a modern nation. The largest tribes are the Tekke in central Turkmenistan, the Ersary near the region of the Turkmen–Afghan border, and the Yomud in western Turkmenistan. Although the tribes have been steadily losing their economic power since the early Soviet period, tribal loyalties still exercise a strong influence on the Turkmen, and are reinforced by rules of endogamy and the persistence of dialects. In fact, tribal loyalties are stronger in Turkmenistan than in any other Muslim area of the USSR, impeding the development of a cohesive and homogenous Turkmen nation capable of pushing for greater independence from Moscow. As one Turkmen journalist recently put it: 'Feuds between tribes are a ruinous occurrence in our life that hamper the development of the republic and often lead to tragedy.'[2]

Second, the low level of economic and social development in Turkmenistan, as in the rest of Central Asia, has thwarted the growth of nationalist behaviour such as that seen in the Baltic republics or even in the Ukraine and Belorussia. Turkmenistan is among the very poorest of the Soviet republics in terms of per capita income, and has the USSR's highest rate of infant mortality as well as its lowest rate of life expectancy. Whereas the largest and most influential of the Soviet Union's popular movements are urban-based, Turkmen society is still predominantly rural, with only 45.3 per cent of the population residing in cities in 1989.[3] Wedged in the southernmost corner of the Soviet Union, this republic of some 3.5 million is also geographically severed from the momentous political changes currently shaking the country. Information on the events occurring in other Soviet republics rarely makes its way to Turkmenistan, since telephones and television sets are rare even in urban areas.

Third, the absence in Turkmenistan of a numerous, active intelligentsia (those with higher education working in professional jobs) has hindered the emergence of a full-fledged national movement. In other Soviet republics, it has primarily been the intellectuals who have spearheaded the move for greater national autonomy. The intelligentsia in Turkmenistan is very small in number, and appears to have difficulty articulating the interests of Turkmen society or mobilising the population. According to the chief editor of the main Turkmen literary newspaper, *Edebiyat ve sungat*, there are no 'energetic commentators and writers [in the republic] whose speeches inspire people to react'.[4]

Fourth, Turkmen officials appear almost fearful of Gorbachev's policy of *perestroika*, and tend to quash any popular initiative in order to retain their fragile ability to govern. 'There are more than enough problems in Turkmenistan. Would we make progress in solving them if people took to demonstrating?,' recently stated Turkmen First Secretary Saparmurad Ataevich Niyazov, summing up his view on the role of popular political participation in his republic.[5] Niyazov's reluctance to embrace economic reforms, such as the transfer to *khozraschet* (full-cost accounting) is understandable in view of the republic's desperate dependency on Moscow for subsidies and imports of food and textiles. However, the Turkmen public is becoming ever more aware that this dependency is the result of decades of a centrally directed policy aimed at procuring the region's natural resources while neglecting the development of industry. As this process continues, the Turkmen leadership may find itself increasingly caught between Moscow's over-ambitious plan targets and vocal opposition within the republic to such central dictates.

TURKMENISTAN UNDER SOVIET RULE

The forging of the Turkmen into a modern nation – albeit one with a rather weak sense of unity – has perhaps been the single greatest achievement of Soviet rule in the region. It is therefore ironic that this national identity was created inadvertently, following the delimitation of Central Asian territory along national lines (*razmezhevanie*) in the first years of Soviet rule. At that time, Central Asia was divided up into distinct nations according to Stalin's four criteria: unity of economy and culture, territory and language. Soviet leaders clearly hoped that these new creations would undermine Pan-Islamic and Pan-Turkic sentiments, thereby forestalling any aspirations to Central Asian unity. Consequently, an autonomous Turkmen region was created in 1921, followed by the establishment of the Turkmen Soviet Socialist Republic in October 1924.

The consolidation of Soviet power in the Turkmen region, however, did not occur without a struggle. Turkmen participated in the *basmachi* guerrilla revolt that swept Central Asia following the Bolshevik revolution. Led by Muhammad Qurban Junayd Khan, Turkmen tribes successfully took the Khivan capital in 1918 and established their leader in power. A Red Army detachment drove him into the desert early in 1920, where he and his followers continued to fight on for several years as part of the *basmachi* resistance.[6] The essence of *basmachestvo* was to expel rural and urban settlers and to protect the traditional way of life threatened by Western civilisation. The collectivisation drive begun in Central Asia in 1929 was particularly traumatic, as it forced many Turkmen, Kazakh and Kirgiz nomads to settle and join collective farms. Turkmen resistance fighters waged war in the area of Krasnovodsk and the Kara-Kum desert throughout the early 1930s, with the last battle fought in 1936.[7]

Peaceful resistance to Soviet rule was offered by the nascent Turkmen intelligentsia. A Provisional Turkmen Congress was formed in Ashkhabad following the 1917 October Revolution that later merged with the Whites late in 1918 to form a Transcaspian government. This government, with limited British assistance, managed to hold off the Bolsheviks for a year before succumbing to Soviet rule. It was between 1930 and 1935, however, that the Turkmen intelligentsia was the most vocal, going so far as to demand political autonomy and the abandonment of the Turkmen language in favour of Anatolian Turkish or Chagatai, a Turkic language with deep literary roots in Central Asia. Soviet authorities began purging Turkmen intellectuals on a large scale in 1934, soon widening the purges to include Turkmen government leaders. In 1937–38, the chairman of the Turkmen Supreme Soviet, Nederbai Aitakov, was executed, and with him perished the last of a generation of Turkmen nationalists.[8]

In 1928, Soviet authorities launched an anti-religious campaign with the aim of completely eliminating Islam among the Turkmen. This campaign was perhaps the harshest of all the anti-Islamic offensives simultaneously begun in Central Asia. Of the approximately 500 mosques that were functioning in the Turkmen territory in 1917, only four were still operating in 1979: two in Mary Oblast in the villages of Bairam Ali and Iolatan, and two in Tashauz Oblast in the cities of Tashauz and Ilialy.[9] As with the rest of Central Asia, all Islamic courts of law, *waqf* holdings (Muslim religious endowments that formed the basis of clerical economic power), and Muslim primary and secondary schools had been liquidated in Turkmenistan by the end of the 1920s.

On the other side of the coin, the strongly developed compulsory school system that replaced the religious schools, together with the mass campaigns against adult illiteracy, produced truly impressive results, although not as great as Soviet figures indicate. (Official statistics claim that the literacy rate in Turkmenistan between 1926 and 1970 jumped from 2.3 per cent to 99 per cent, but this apparently includes a large number of people only able to sign their names and spell a few words.) Literacy rates appear especially impressive given that Soviet authorities changed the alphabet used by the peoples of Central Asia and Azerbaijan twice within a period of twelve years, creating overnight illiteracy for millions of Soviet Muslims. In March 1926, the Congress of Turcology meeting in Baku decided to replace the Arabic alphabet by the Latin, thus breaking Central Asian ties with the language of Islam and with the Arabic world. This change, however, provided an undesirable link with Turkey, and in 1938 the Latin alphabet was replaced by the Cyrillic and the teaching of Russian was made compulsory.[10] Although the alphabet changes were to have disastrous consequences for the studying of Central Asian history and literature, there was little opposition to the move as it occurred at the height of the Stalinist purges when much of the Central Asian intelligentsia had already perished.

During the Second World War, Stalin declared a reprieve in the war on Islam in order to secure greater support for the war effort among Soviet Muslims, as among other believers in the USSR. An official Muslim organisation was established in 1942, consisting of four 'spiritual directorates' or Muftats. Of the four, the Muslim Religious Board for Central Asia and Kazakhstan, seated in Tashkent, is the most important and has jurisdiction over approximately 75 per cent of the country's more than 50 million Muslims. A *kazi* serves as the leading representative of official Islam in each Central Asian republic. After the war, persecution of religion was resumed although the official Islamic establishment remained. Particularly under Brezhnev, the Soviet regime found the official Islamic establishment to be a convenient instrument with which to advance its interests in the world Muslim community.

Following the Islamic revolution in Iran and the Soviet invasion of Afghanistan, anti-Islamic propaganda in the USSR took an especially vicious turn. Distrust of official Islam among Soviet Muslims and the paucity of officially recognised mosques and clerics forced Islam to establish itself underground, where it has thrived in the post-war period and in recent decades in particular. In Turkmenistan, as in the rest of Central Asia, the number of mosques operating illegally far outstrip those operating on an official basis.[11] The observance of certain rituals associated with Islam – such as circumcision, religious weddings and burials, and the celebration of the religious festival of Kurban Bairam – is nearly universal among the native population.

Soviet Rule and the Development of the Turkmen Economy

It was not until the first years of Soviet rule that Turkmenistan entered the industrial age for tsarist Russia had made little attempt at its industrialisation. Central authorities earmarked hefty sums of the All-Union budget for the industrialisation of the republic, and also sent a large number of skilled Slavic workers to facilitate the process. By the end of the 1920s, a number of industrial enterprises had been established, including those for the manufacture of textiles, silk and confections.

Beginning in the 1930s, however, Turkmenistan's economy took on an increasingly agricultural orientation. In fact, the growth of industrial production in the republic between 1949 and 1950 and 1960 and 1970 was the slowest of any Union republic except Azerbaijan.[12] At present, those industrial enterprises established in the 1920s account for virtually all of light industry in the republic.[13] Most heavy industry in the republic is geared towards the exploitation of Turkmenistan's large oil and gas deposits, with the exception of the Kara-Bogaz chemical works industry. The latter, however, has been threatened in recent years by the environmental disaster set in motion when the strait between the Kara-Bogaz Gulf and the Caspian Sea was damned in 1980.[14]

The lack of industry in Turkmenistan together with its orientation towards cotton production has meant that the indigenous population has remained overwhelmingly concentrated in the least modernised sectors of the economy: agriculture and service occupations. The problem has grown more acute in recent decades as Turkmenistan's labour force has expanded disproportionately to that of the rest of the country. The total Turkmen population increased by 42.3 per cent between 1959 and 1970, and by 28.1 per cent between 1970 and 1979. These large increases have made themselves felt primarily in the rural regions where the majority of Turkmen reside.

Before the Revolution, the Turkmen region was already beginning to abandon the production of foodstuffs in favour of producing cotton. In 1912, the tsarist Minister of Agriculture had declared cotton a strategic crop, stating that 'it is better to supply this region with imported cereals even if they are more expensive, and make its irrigated land available for cotton cultivation'.[15] Soviet authorities perpetuated this trend by embarking on a policy of cotton mono-culture. Those Central Asian farmers who opposed the sharp reduction in the amount of arable land available for the production of food were branded kulaks and saboteurs. Due to this policy, the USSR became self-sufficient in cotton for the first time in 1931, and a net exporter in 1937.[16] In the post-war years, cotton production in the republic has grown by an astonishing 450 per cent, primarily owing to the construction of elaborate irrigation projects in the region, such as the Kara-Kum Canal, the USSR's single largest irrigation project.

TURKMENISTAN UNDER GORBACHEV

Economic Issues

Encouraged by *perestroika*, some of the more educated, vocal Turkmen have begun to describe their republic's relationship with Moscow as colonialist in essence. As support for their argument, they point to an investment policy geared towards the export of massive amounts of raw cotton and natural gas from Turkmenistan at artificially low prices, while industries in the region have been growing at a snail's pace. The emphasis on primary production in the republic has led to an excessive degree of dependency on Russia proper and other regions for imports of textiles and food, and has also exacerbated burgeoning unemployment.

While Turkmen have been expressing concern over the distorted development of their economy, it has become fashionable among Russian nationalist groups and others to accuse the Central Asians of taking more from the all-Union economy than they contribute (*izhdivenchestvo*). Such accusations have only fuelled Central Asian resentment, prompting angry retorts. According to one official from the Turkmen Writers' Union:

We also earn our money and are also able to count ... The [Turkmen] republican budget receives subsidies from the central budget of 344 million roubles a year. The enterprises under all-Union subordination located on the territory of Turkmenistan contributed 530 million roubles to their respective ministries [in Moscow] last year, but only half a million roubles to the local soviets. So judge for yourselves – are we really 'poor relations' living at the expense of our 'rich brothers'?[17]

To be sure, enterprises under all-Union subordination are among the most visible signs of Moscow's dominion over the republic. At present, these enterprises contribute only 1 per cent of their annual profits to the republican budget, although they control a preponderant percentage of Turkmenistan's economic activity.[18] According to Turkmen Party First Secretary Niyazov, all-Union enterprises and organisations receive nearly 60 per cent of all capital investment in Turkmenistan, only a miniscule amount of which goes towards the development of the republic's social infrastructure.[19] It is little wonder that the all-Union enterprises in Turkmenistan have become a bone of contention between the republic and Moscow.

In addition to having to import most goods due to lack of industrial diversification, Turkmenistan exports virtually all of its raw materials – more than 95 per cent of all the cotton and gas it produces, as well as 70 per cent of all silk.[20] Understandably, many Turkmen have protested against this policy, since it is much more profitable to manufacture finished products than simply to export raw cotton to the mills of the Russian republic and the Ukraine. Furthermore, the low level of manufacturing has also contributed to the problem of growing unemployment in the region. Moreover, and perhaps most importantly, Turkmen are protesting against Moscow's insistence on maintaining a one-crop cotton system in the republic despite the artificially low state procurement prices that make the cultivation of this crop less profitable than some others. Unprofitability aside, the production of cotton has increased in Turkmenistan by 450 per cent during the post-war period, squeezing out other crops and directly affecting the republic's ability to feed itself.[21]

Perhaps more than any single complaint directed towards Moscow, conditions of abject poverty throughout the republic have provided the greatest impetus for many Turkmen to speak out against central economic control. In 1988, no less than 36.6 per cent of the population of Turkmenistan had an average monthly income from all sources of 75 roubles or less; that is, below the official subsistence level, compared with 6.3 per cent of the Russian republic's population (see Appendix 2, Table 8). Furthermore, the number of Turkmen living below the poverty line is continually increasing as the population grows ever larger.

A precise figure for the current number of unemployed is unavailable, but a Central Committee resolution from 1986 stated that 18.8 per cent of the working-age population in Turkmenistan did not hold jobs in 1984.[22] It should be remembered that this figure includes people engaged in housework (usually women with several children), individual labour activity, personal subsidiary farming, and others not actively seeking employment in the public sector. More recent estimates of the percentage of the working-age population in the republic not employed in the public sector have varied widely: from 9 per cent, according to Turkmen Party First Secretary Niyazov,[23] to nearly 40 per cent, according to an official from the Turkmen State Planning Commission (*Gosplan*).[24] Housing shortages are also severe; more than 118,000 residents of Ashkhabad – more than half the city's population – are living in temporary shanties erected more than forty years ago after a major earthquake hit the capital.[25] Finally, a mere 8 per cent of all households in Turkmenistan's rural regions and 58 per cent of those in urban areas are supplied with gas – a paradoxical situation, since the republic produces 12 per cent of the country's entire gas supply.[26]

However much Turkmen officials may welcome the prospect of greater autonomy, they are well aware that the republic's economy is not prepared to cope with major reform. The eventual transfer of the republic or even regions within the republic to a system of full-cost accounting appears especially daunting, given that Turkmenistan has more than its share of insolvent enterprises that Moscow will not be willing to bail out indefinitely. As Turkmen Deputy Finance Minister I. Kireev recently remarked, 'What talk can there be of a transfer to *khozraschet* when, in the local budgets, expenses exceed revenues by three times?'[27] The weak industrial base in Turkmenistan means that the republic will have a more difficult time than most other areas of the USSR using newly found autonomy to spur economic growth. Consequently, economic *perestroika* in Turkmenistan may prove to be very rough going.

Ecological and Health Concerns

From the time construction began in 1954 on the Kara Kum Canal until recent years, the artificial waterway was hailed as a singular blessing for the Turkmen people, a grandiose project which was to transform the region from an arid wasteland into a fertile oasis. Since the inception of *glasnost'*, many Turkmen have criticised Moscow for using the canal to implement and sustain a policy of cotton mono-culture in the republic, bringing lasting harm to Turkmenistan's ecology and the health of its inhabitants in the process.[28]

The Kara Kum Canal is a primary factor behind the rapid dessication of the Aral Sea, which has been termed 'one of the most extraordinary violations of the environment in modern times'.[29] Once the world's fourth largest inland body of water, the Aral has now lost 65 per cent of its original volume owing to increasing diversions of water for irrigation and leaching purposes from its primary sources of replenishment, the

Amu Dar'ya and Syr Dar'ya rivers.[30] In 1984, the Kara Kum Canal was withdrawing 384 cubic metres of water per second from the Amu Dar'ya, or 25 per cent of that river's average annual flow at Kerki, the canal's starting point.[31]

The slow death of the Aral Sea as a result of short-sighted agricultural policies has had the most acute effects on the Karakalpak ASSR and Khorezm Oblast, both of which are in Uzbekistan, Kyzl-Orda Oblast in Kazakhstan, and Tashauz Oblast in Turkmenistan. Each year the wind scatters millions of tons of dust and salty sand from the Aral's dehydrated seabed on to some of the region's most fertile crop land. Furthermore, the Aral has a decisive influence on the climate of the whole of Central Asia, and the loss of the sea's moderating effect on climatic conditions has reduced the length of the growing season.[32]

Owing to the Soviet practice of simply scooping irrigation canals out of the earth and not lining them with concrete, infiltration losses from the Kara Kum Canal amount to as much as 60 per cent of the flow withdrawn from the Amu Dar'ya.[33] Such inefficient irrigation methods have not only adversely affected the Aral Sea, but have also caused soil conditions in Turkmenistan to deteriorate. Water seepage from unlined irrigation canals and the lack of proper drainage systems have caused groundwater levels to rise, which in turn has led to secondary soil salinisation.[34] The result is that the area of heavily salted lands, which do not produce even half their potential harvest, has rapidly expanded. In 1987, heavily salted lands comprised 51 per cent of all land within the Kara Kum Canal zone.[35]

Chemical pollution, which has also exacerbated soil conditions, has had a grave impact on the health of the Turkmen population. To help meet the plan, an exorbitant amount of pesticides, herbicides and defoliants are used in the cotton fields, much of which end up in the soil, atmosphere and water supply. After irrigating and leaching the Uzbek and Turkmen cotton fields, more than 3 billion cubic metres of water saturated with agricultural chemicals are thrown back into the Amu Dar'ya each year. The Turkmen Health Minister has called this river – which supplies the population with its drinking water – 'little more than a sewage ditch'.[36] Since only a scant 13 per cent of the republic's rural population is provided with water mains, many residents of Turkmenistan are forced to drink this chemically polluted water straight from canals and ditches. Considering that contaminated water is the basis for the spread of severe intestinal infections, it is not surprising that some disease indices in Turkmenistan – for example, for typhoid – exceed all-Union indices by more than eight times.

High disease indices in Turkmenistan are attributable to poor overall medical, sanitary and ecological conditions: primitive and crowded medical facilities, a dearth of skilled personnel, contaminated water supplies, the indiscriminate use of agricultural chemicals, and inadequate supplies of milk and meat (land is sown to cotton rather than used for grazing). These factors, combined with harsh labour conditions for cotton workers, have exacted a heavy toll on general health. As a result, Turkmenistan had the lowest average life-expectancy level in 1986–87 of all Soviet republics: 65.2 years compared with an all-Union average of 69.8 years and an average of 70.1 years in the RSFSR.[37] It also has the country's highest rates of infant mortality.[38]

Restoring the Turkmen Cultural Heritage

Since the introduction of *glasnost'*, a panoply of cultural grievances has surfaced in Turkmenistan, including demands to reassess Turkmen history, remove Russian toponyms, rehabilitate disgraced Turkmen writers and introduce the teaching of the Arabic script. The status of the Turkmen language is of paramount importance for many Turkmen, and, perhaps more than any other concern, has strained relations between the indigenous and non-indigenous inhabitants of the republic. As one Russian living in Turkmenistan complained in the local press: 'We were born and raised here. Now we are uncertain about the future because the native population has begun to demand the impossible from us – either learn the language in a very short period of time, or else. . . . It is this "or else" that alarms us.'[39]

Although the use of Russian in the republic as the language of communication at official levels has struck a deep chord of resentment among many Turkmen, Turkmenistan is the only Central Asian republic that has not yet decreed the language of the republic's titular nationality the state language of the republic. In lieu of taking this step, a commission of the Turkmen Supreme Soviet has worked out a draft language programme that First Secretary Niyazov has described as 'international in spirit'.[40] While carefully avoiding any challenge to the preferential status currently enjoyed by Russian, the programme seeks to broaden the use of Turkmen in public life. In addition to calling for the teaching of Turkmen on a wider scale, certain practical measures, such as the issuance of public notices and street signs in both Russian and Turkmen, are outlined in the programme.[41]

Turkmen officials are reluctant to support legislation that would grant state status to the language of the majority for fear of creating a backlash among the republic's sizeable non-indigenous population. According to census data for 1989, Russians, who form the largest non-indigenous nationality group in Turkmenistan, accounted for 9.5 per cent of the republic's population.[42] However, one Turkmen official has pointed out that the population of Ashkhabad is equally split between Russians and Turkmen, with each group comprising 41 per cent.[43] Uzbeks and Kazakhs also comprise sizeable minorities in Turkmenistan, and members of several other nationality groups, such as Tatars, Azerbaijanis, Baluchis and Armenians, are represented in the republic's population.

Whereas protests by the Slavic communities in the Baltic states and Moldavia following the passage of language legislation there have been well publicised, similar legislation adopted in Tadzhikhistan in 1989 was reported to have prompted an exodus of some 10,000 residents from the capital of Dushanbe.[44] Turkmen leaders undoubtedly wish to prevent such an exodus from their own republic, given that many of the Slavic settlers in Turkmenistan supply the economy with badly needed skills. Moreover, the scale of out-migration from Turkmenistan has already sextupled over the past decade in comparison with the 1970–79 period.[45]

Despite the strain posed by the language controversy to inter-ethnic relations in the republic, demands to upgrade the status of Turkmen are likely to become even more persistent in future, given the impoverished state of the language. Few non-Turkmen residents of the republic – especially among the Slavic populations – have a command of the native language, and many Turkmen send their children to Russian-language schools since they regard the Turkmen language as 'having no future'.[46] Moreover, the quality of Turkmen instruction is very low throughout the republic and complicated by a lack of qualified teachers and teaching materials. Since the Turkmen language has been allowed to atrophy over the years and knowledge of Russian amongst the Turkmen population is generally poor (only 27.8 per cent of all Turkmen claimed a good knowledge of Russian as a second language in 1989),[47] many Turkmen now lack a solid knowledge of *any* language.

Inspired by *perestroika*, several Turkmen scholars have also set about questioning official Soviet interpretations of their history. The most heated discussions to date concern the events surrounding the incorporation of what is now Turkmenistan into tsarist Russia.[48] Official dogma holds that the area was 'voluntarily joined' with the Russian empire rather than won by conquest in the latter half of the nineteenth century. The idea of a voluntary incorporation with Russia offends the sensibilities of many Turkmen, since their forefathers fought the annexation of the region in some of the greatest displays of resistance encountered by tsarist occupation forces. At the battle for the fortress of Geok-Tepe in 1881, Russian troops mined and stormed the Turkmen fortress, killing some 14,500 native defenders. Russian forces then killed all Turkmen males who had not succeeded in escaping from the fort.[49] The memory of those who died at Geok-Tepe, which finally broke the stubborn Turkmen resistance and decided the fate of the rest of the Transcaspia, is still sacred for a great number of Turkmen.

While discussions of Geok-Tepe are now commonplace in Turkmen intellectual circles, the subject was strictly taboo as little as five years ago. The well-known Turkmen writer and historian Rahim Esenov recently recounted how, in 1984, Soviet publishers extracted a detailed description of the battle of Geok-Tepe and the role of Russian General Skobelev before sending his book to press.[50] Despite such censorship, as one Turkmen official put it in reference to the historic battle: 'Every Turkmen official and historian knows how Turkmenistan was incorporated into tsarist Russia.'[51]

The year 1989 saw the official rehabilitation of the Turkmen national epic *The Book of Gorkut Ata*, a cycle of semi-legendary chronicles dating from the Middle Ages that retraces the history of the Oguz Turkmen[52] and gives much valuable information concerning their language, ethnography and socio-economic conditions. In 1951, the Turkmen Communist Party Central Committee condemned the epic, but last year this ruling was reversed and preparatory work for its eventual publication was completed.[53] In addition to seeking rehabilitation for *Gorkut Ata*, Turkmen have been actively rehabilitating the victims of the Stalinist purges in their republic. Since the issuance of a decree by the USSR Supreme Soviet in January 1989, the Turkmen KGB and Procurator's Office have rehabilitated more than 3,500 people, including members of the intelligentsia, former Turkmen officials and common citizens.[54]

A New Era for Islam

In the wake of the removal of Mufti Babakhanov as Chairman of the Muslim Board for Central Asia and Kazakhstan and his replacement by Muhammad Sadyq Mahammed Yusuf Hoja-ogli (see Chapter Thirteen, page 222), the new incumbent has made every effort to expand the rights of Soviet Muslims. For years, Ashkhabad was the only Central Asian capital without a functioning mosque. In July 1989, the foundation of a new, large mosque was finally completed in that city, and traditional Friday prayers were performed there for the first time.[55] This was an event that had been a long time in the making; for several years local authorities had refused to authorise the project or to designate a site for the construction of the mosque, which is being built entirely on the initiative and funds of local believers.[56] Two other mosques have recently been opened in the oblast capital of Chardzhou, one of which, the Sahijan mosque, is a traditional place of pilgrimage in Turkmenistan.[57]

In another concession to Soviet Muslims, Muhammad Sadyq has declared that it will henceforth be easier for believers to make the pilgrimage to Mecca, since Soviet practice has been to allow only a handful of official Islamic functionaries to make the *hajj* each year. There are also plans to print 50,00 copies of the Qur'ān (presumably in Arabic), as well as to import 100,000 copies from Saudi Arabia (although only a small number of Soviet citizens are able to read Arabic or even the Arabic script). More importantly for Turkmen, a special group, comprised primarily of poets but working together with religious consultants, has been formed to translate the Qur'ān from a Turkish-language edition into Turkmen. According to the director of the 'Turkmenistan' Publishing House, 'circulation [of the Turkmen-language Qur'ān] will be somewhat dependent on the availability of paper'.[58]

The concessions granted to Muslims under *perestroika* are a tacit admission by Soviet authorities that official attempts to wipe out Islam – particularly vigorous under Nikita Khrushchev – not only failed to reduce the number of believers, but have also encouraged the growing vitality of unofficial Islamic activity that is beyond Moscow's control. In striking a peaceful coexistence with Islam, Gorbachev is hoping to make the best out of the widespread religious feeling among Central Asians that he cannot eliminate, and to gather support for *perestroika* in the process. A good example of this new policy was the much-publicised official restoration of the traditional Muslim feast of Kurban Bairam on 13 July 1989 – a festival that the majority of Turkmen had continued to observe during the many years its celebration was formally banned.[59]

In another manifestation of *glasnost'*, the all-Union and local Soviet media now regularly publish interviews with Muslim religious leaders that accord these figures a degree of respectability. The leading representative of Islam in Turkmenistan, *kazi* Nasrullo Ibadullaev, who is young, well-educated and a modernist in his approach towards Islam, has used such occasions to denounce the more superstitious variant of Islam that has long been a part of worship in Central Asia. For example, in an interview with *Komsomol'skaya Pravda*, he stressed that the Qur'ān condemns the making of pilgrimages to 'holy places' other than Mecca – a particularly widespread practice in Turkmenistan.[60] His remonstrations have most likely fallen on deaf ears, however, since, over a period of centuries, Islam in Turkmenistan has become a curious admixture of orthodox Islam, Sufi mysticism and shamanistic practices. The cult of ancestors is still observed, and reverence for members of the four holy tribes (the *Awlad*) is still strong. Furthermore, holy places, which are generally tombs connected with Sufi saints, mythical personages or tribal ancestors, have become real centres of religious life in the absence of functioning mosques.[61]

The limited powers of the Turkmen *kazi* to control the direction Islam takes in his republic is underscored by the large amount of religious propaganda directed towards Turkmenistan by its foreign neighbours. One scientific worker, who conducted a sociological survey in Turkmenistan's Tashauz Oblast, concluded that one-third of all young people there listen to Turkmen-language radio broadcasts beamed from Iran and Afghanistan.[62] Such broadcasts, he noted, which aim to encourage religious and national sentiment, tend to be of greater interest to Soviet Turkmen than domestic broadcasts (and this although the Iranians are Shiite and the Turkmen, like the majority of Afghans, are Sunni Muslims).

Mufti Muhammad Sadyq has rejected the possibility of a radical Islamic movement being exported to Soviet Muslims from Iran and

Afghanistan. 'We have our own history, and we have deep roots in Islam,' he stated. 'We have our own view and our own foundation. We can influence others, but others cannot influence us.'[63] While the majority of Soviet Turkmen would not necessarily opt for an Islamic fundamentalist regime in place of the current one, Muhhamad Sadyq's assertion that 'others cannot influence us' may prove to be too categorical, given that *glasnost'* is revealing daily the growing interest on the part of Soviet Turkmen in both Islam and in their fellow Turkmen across the border.

CONCLUSION

While the Turkmen have used *perestroika* to make significant cultural and religious gains during the first years of Gorbachev's rule, the more recent calls by many Turkmen for a fundamental restructuring of the republic's economic relationship with Moscow promise to have the most far-reaching consequences. Although Turkmen leaders and members of the intelligentsia alike have expressed a desire for a devolution of economic power from the centre, they are well aware that such a devolution, in many respects, would put them at a disadvantage *vis-à-vis* the other, richer Union republics. Additionally, a weak industrial base would make it difficult for Turkmenistan to use reforms to spur economic growth.

The question of popular reaction to reform is also a crucial one. The republic's population – already suffering from a high level of unemployment and a declining standard of living – is likely to show a low level of tolerance for economic reform and private enterprise. Many Turkmen are not ready to accept price reform, judging by the protest strike staged by carpet-weavers in 1989 over a planned increase in the state price of wool and a concomitant drop in wages. Regarding the highly anticipated introduction of contract brigades, an official from the Turkmenistan State Planning Commission recently disclosed that labour productivity in such brigades is nearly a third lower than in regular brigades.[64]

Concerning the prospects for private enterprise, as of January 1989, there were a mere 447 cooperatives operating in Turkmenistan compared with 3,616 cooperatives in smaller Armenia.[65] The high prices charged by cooperatives were a major cause behind the riots that took place in the Turkmen cities of Ashkhabad and Nebit-Dag in May 1989.[66] In an even more foreboding sign of the prospects for economic reform, the chairman of Turkmenistan's State Committee for Labour and Social Problems warned that the practice of laying off workers in Nebit-Dag in connection with a transfer to new methods of management had contributed to the turmoil.[67]

The violent clashes in May 1989 in Turkmenistan also provided evidence of growing inter-ethnic tensions in the republic, in so far as anti-Armenian slogans were shouted by the rioters. As the population expands, further outpacing an already sluggish level of social and economic development, resentment against the presence of non-indigenous nationality groups in the republic is likely to become more acute – particularly since most such groups are perceived by the native population to be more prosperous. Officials also worry that the steady stream of religious and nationalist propaganda from the republic's foreign neighbours may fuel existing tensions. Although the majority of Soviet Turkmen would be unlikely to opt for a fundamentalist Islamic regime, they have demonstrated a clear interest in strengthening ties with the large Turkmen communities in Iran and Afghanistan. It is conceivable that increased contact with Turkmen abroad could serve to radicalise many Soviet Turkmen – especially the burgeoning underclass – in their stance against Moscow.

Turkmen leaders, distinguished by their conservatism, appear fearful that *glasnost'* and *perestroika* will further disrupt the social equilibrium and, hence, their fragile ability to maintain control over the republic. Their position is all the more precarious in light of the anti-corruption campaign, in force since October 1986, that has resulted in mass arrests and dismissals at all levels of the bureaucratic hierarchy. The ongoing effort to wipe out rampant bribery, embezzlement and report-padding has also been accompanied by a strikingly large number of replacements in the republican Party apparatus. For example, by 1990 not a single regional Party Committee first secretary from the Brezhnev era still remains in office in Turkmenistan.

Afraid of the forces of change unleashed by *perestroika*, republican authorities have systematically sought to quash popular initiative. Turkmen Party First Secretary Niyazov has taken a public stand against the organisation of informal groups and demonstrations in the republic, citing as a reason his concern that Turkmenistan was about to fall prey to the 'copy-cat syndrome' he said was sweeping the republics.[68] In April 1989, members of the republican intelligentsia in the city of Mary attempted to form a popular movement along the line of the popular fronts in the Baltic republics. The group's members were then invited to local Party headquarters for an open discussion with republican officials, according to a report in *Turkmenskaya Iskra*, where they gave up their cause 'without any sort of force'.[69] More recently, several intellectuals in Ashkhabad appear to have formed a popular movement under the name *Agzybirlik* ('Unity'), despite official discouragement and attacks on the group in the local press. The programme of the fledgeling movement devotes particular attention to the language issue, while also addressing other cultural as well as ecological problems.[70]

Judging by the results of the elections on 7 January 1990 to the Turkmen Supreme Soviet and local soviets, the republican leadership is unlikely to undergo liberalisation in the near future: nearly 90 per cent of those elected are CPSU members, and all of the republican Party Central Committee secretaries won their bids for election.[71] Despite a remarkable degree of conservatism among Turkmen leaders, the dizzying pace of reform throughout the Soviet Union makes it seem a virtual certainty that demands for greater economic, cultural and religious autonomy in Turkmenistan will continue to strengthen. By attempting to maintain an iron grip on popular initiative, local authorities are running the risk that change will arrive in the form of an explosion rather than through a series of democratically-implemented reforms. As a string of violent eruptions rocks the USSR's southern rim, the Turkmen leadership would be well advised to keep in mind that change is unavoidable and time is of the essence.

NOTES

1. Mehmet Saray *The Turkmens in the Age of Imperialism: a Study of the Turkmen People and their Incorporation into the Russian Empire* (Ankara, Turkish Historical Society Printing House 1989), pp. 8–13, 23–61. See also Alexandre Bennigsen and S. Enders Wimbush *Muslims of the Soviet Empire* (Bloomington IND, Indiana University Press 1986), p. 95.
2. 'Iz plena ambitsii', *Turkmenskaya Iskra* 5 May 1988.
3. 'O predvaritel'nykh itogakh vsesoyuznoi perepisi naseleniya 1989 goda', *Turkmenskaya Iskra* 12 May 1989.
4. *Turkmenskaya Iskra* 7 July 1988.
5. 'V otkrytuyu dver' lomit'sya ne nado', *Pravda* 14 Nov. 1989.
6. Aman Berdi Murat 'Turkmenistan and the Turkmens', in Zev Katz (ed.) *Handbook of Major Soviet Nationalities* (New York, Macmillan 1975), p. 265.
7. Chantal Lemercier-Quelquejay, 'Muslim National Minorities in Revolution and War', in *Soviet Nationalities in Strategic Perspective*, S. Enders Wimbush (ed.) (New York, St Martin's Press 1985), p. 54.
8. Helen Carrere D'Encausse 'The Russian Revolution and Soviet Policy in Central Asia', in Gavin Hambly (ed.) *Central Asia* (New York, Delacorte Press 1969), p. 238.
9. Bennigsen and Wimbush *Muslims of the Soviet Empire*, p. 101.
10. Edward Allworth *Uzbek Literary Politics* (The Hague, 1964), pp. 169–78.
11. *Literaturnaya Gazeta* 18 May 1988, p. 10.
12. Aman Berdi Murat 'Turkmenistan and the Turkmens', p. 263.
13. *Ashkhabad* no. 5, 1989, p. 61.
14. *Izvestiya* 15 Jan. 1988.
15. Geoffrey Wheeler *The Modern History of Soviet Central Asia* (New York, Praeger 1964), p. 157.
16. Violet Conolly *Beyond the Urals* (London, Oxford University Press 1967), pp. 91–3.
17. *Ashkhabad* no. 5, 1989, p. 56.

18. 'Delit' ili zarabatyvat?' *Turkmenskaya Iskra* 13 July 1989.
19. 'Byudzhet mestnyi, interes obshchii', *Izvestiya* 18 April 1989.
20. 'O garmonizatsii mezhnatsional'nykh otnoshenii', *Turkmenskaya Iskra* 20 Aug. 1989.
21. *Ashkhabad* no. 5, 1989, p. 57.
22. *Izvestiya TsK KPSS*, no. 5, 1989, p. 29.
23. 'Byudzhet mestnyi, interes obshchii', op. cit.
24. 'Delit' ili zarabatyvat?' ', op. cit.
25. Moscow Radio 1, 9 Feb. 1989.
26. *Turkmenskaya Iskra* 27 Jan. 1990.
27. 'Delit' ili zarabatyvat'?', op. cit.
28. See, e.g., 'Dumat', uvazhat', schitat' ', *Turkmenskaya Iskra* 26 Nov. 1988.
29. 'The Aral: a Soviet Sea Lies Dying', *National Geographic* 2 (1990), p. 76.
30. 'Zona ekologicheskogo bedstviya', *Argumenty i fakty* no. 51, 1989.
31. 'Problema Aral'skogo morya i Karakumskyi kanal', *Problemy osvoeniya pustyn'* no. 1, 1989.
32. It should be noted that another ecological catastrophe, similar to the Aral Sea disaster but on a smaller scale, has already occurred in Turkmenistan: the dessication of the Kara-Bogaz Gulf, located on the republic's north-west border. In 1980, the strait between the Kara-Bogaz Gulf and the Caspian Sea was dammed in order to prevent a further decline in the level of the latter. Bureaucratic in-fighting has obstructed the development of a solution to the problem.
33. Philip Micklin 'Irrigation Development in the USSR during the Tenth Five Year Plan (1976–1980)', *Soviet Geography: Review and Translation* (Jan. 1978), p. 8.
34. When the groundwater rises to a level of only 2–3 m. from the surface, capillary action carries saline solutions to the surface where the salts remain after the water has evaporated. See Philip Micklin 'Irrigation Development in the USSR', p. 15.
35. 'My dumali o pol'ze, kogda stroili Karakumskyi kanal', *Turkmenskaya Iskra* 14 Sept. 1989.
36. *Turkmenskaya Iskra* 20 April 1988.
37. *Narodnoe khozyaistvo SSSR v 1987 godu*, Finansy i statistika, (Moscow 1988), p. 358. Statistics for the year 1988 (*Narodnoe khozyaistvo SSSR v 1988 godu*, Finansy i statistika, Moscow 1989) indicated that average life expectancy in Armenia had dropped nearly ten years over a two-year period (from 73.9 years in 1986–87 to 62.3 in 1988), thereby replacing Turkmenistan in the last place position. However, it seems safe to assume that this anomaly is the result of the 1988 earthquake in Armenia that claimed thousands of lives.
38. *Argumenty i fakty* no. 45, 1989.
39. 'Agzybirlik ne sostoyalsya', *Komsomolets Turkmenistana* 7 Oct. 1989.
40. *Turkmenskaya Iskra* 22 Oct. 1989.
41. The full text of the draft language programme was published in *Yash Kommunist* and *Turkmenskaya Iskra* 31 Oct. 1989.
42. Calculated on the basis of data in the Estonian newspaper *Rahva Haal* 19 Sept. 1989, and 1989 census data in *Pravda* 29 April 1989, as cited in

Ann Sheehy 'Russian Share of Soviet Population down to 50.8 per cent', *Report on the USSR*, RFE/RL, Inc., no. 42, 1989.

43. 'Agzybirlik ne sostoyalsya', op. cit.
44. *Izvestiya* 16 Sept. 1989.
45. Calculated on the basis of data in the newspaper of the Lithuanian popular front *Sąjúdis* no. 37/50, 20–27 Oct. 1989, and 1979 census data, as cited in Ann Sheehy '1989 Census Data on Internal Migration in the USSR', *Report on the USSR*, RFE/RL, Inc., no. 45, 1989.
46. 'Iz plena ambitsii', op. cit.
47. *Rahva Haal* 19 Sept. 1989.
48. See, e.g., *Turkmensaya Iskra* from 19 July 1988, 6 Oct. 1989 and 6 July 1988.
49. For a detailed description of the Battle of Geok-Tepe, see Mehmet Saray, *The Turkmen in an Age of Imperialism*, pp. 175–216.
50. 'Iz plena ambitsii', op. cit.
51. *Yash Kommunist* 29 July 1989.
52. The name 'Oguz' first appeared in the early eighth century in Turkish inscriptions, and refers to one of the main elements of the nomadic Turkish empire. The name 'Turkmen' first appeared in the late tenth century and was the name used by the non-Muslim Oguz for the Muslim Oguz. Later, the Oguz came to use only the name 'Turkmen' in reference to themselves. See Mehmet Saray, *The Turkmen in an Age of Imperialism*, p. 15.
53. *Edebiyat ve sungat* 19 Sept. 1989.
54. 'Vozvrashchenie', *Turkmenskaya Iskra* 16 Aug. 1989. An additional 8,000 people were rehabilitated in the republic in the aftermath of the historic Twentieth Party Congress of the CPSU in 1956.
55. *Edebiyat ve Sungat* 14 July 1989.
56. *Turkmenskaya Iskra* 2 Aug. 1989.
57. *TASS* 25 Sept. 1989.
58. *Yash Kommunist* 1 Aug. 1989.
59. *TASS* 13 July 1989. Results of Soviet surveys conducted in the late 1970s indicated that the feast of Kurban Bairam was observed by nearly the entire populations of Turkmenistan's Tashauz and Chardzhou Oblasts, (Bennigsen and Enders Wimbush *Muslims of the Soviet Empire*, p. 102).
60. 'Zachem mecheti khozrashchet?' *Komsomol'skaya Pravda* 2 May 1988.
61. Bennigsen and Enders Wimbush, *Muslims of the Soviet Empire*, pp. 101–4.
62. 'Beg na meste', *Turkmenskaya Iskra* 7 July 1988.
63. *AP* 15 March 1989.
64. 'Delit' ili zarabatyvat'?', op. cit.
65. *Ekonomicheskaya Gazeta* no. 17, 1989, p. 9.
66. Annette Bohr 'New Information on May Riots in Ashkhabad and Nebit-Dag', *Report on the USSR*, RFE/RL, Inc., no. 29, 21 July 1989.
67. *TASS* 22 June 1989.
68. 'V otkrytuyu dver' lomit'sya ne', op. cit.
69. *Turkmenskaya Iskra* 29 April 1989.
70. *Turkmenskaya Iskra* 21 Jan. 1990.
71. *Pravda* 10 Jan. 1990.

CHAPTER FIFTEEN

Kirgiz

Simon Crisp

BACKGROUND

Kirgizia is the seventh in size of the Soviet Union Republics with an area of 198,500 square kilometres, and ranks tenth by population (4,291,000, according to the census of January 1989). Situated at the north-eastern extremity of Soviet Central Asia, it has borders with the Kazakh, Uzbek and Tadzhik Union Republics, and with the Sinkiang-Uighur Autonomous Region of China. Kirgizia is a predominantly mountainous region with significant mineral deposits, and the fast-flowing mountain rivers have enabled hydro-electric power to be well developed. Agriculture is mostly concentrated in the lowland areas, although livestock breeding is a traditional occupation in all areas of the republic. Modern industrial centres are located around the capital city of Frunze in the north of Kirgizia, and Osh in the south-west.[1]

The overwhelming majority of the Kirgiz (88.5 per cent of a total population of 1,906,271 in 1979) live on the territory of their republic, with smaller communities in the neighbouring union republics, also in China and Afghanistan. The figures for out-migration of the Kirgiz are among the lowest in the USSR[2]. There is a sizeable European immigrant population, predominantly Russians, concentrated mainly in the towns of Kirgizia.

The early history of the Kirgiz is complex, and their origin is disputed. Most scholars however believe them to be of mixed Mongolian, Eastern Turkic and Kypchak descent, with an identity formed gradually over the course of many centuries. Indeed, subnational loyalties at the level of tribe and clan persist to the present day, though the formation of the Kirgiz as a distinct people is reckoned to have been completed by the sixteenth century.[3] In the following century their territory came under the control of the Jungarian Oirots, a Mongol people against whom the Kirgiz waged a protracted struggle until the overthrow of the Oirot empire by the Manchus in 1758. The Kirgiz at this time were loosely organised under their local rulers, but in the early nineteenth century parts of their territory were taken over by the Khanate of Kokand. During the same century the Kirgiz came under the influence of the Russian empire: groups of Kirgiz took oaths of allegiance to Russia at various times in the mid-nineteenth century, while southern Kirgizia was incorporated into the empire in 1876 together with the Kokand Khanate, to which it belonged.[4] The latter years of the century were marked by a number of Kirgiz uprisings and the emigration of part of the population to the Pamirs and Afghanistan; in 1916 a serious revolt broke out in connection with the mobilisation by the tsarist authorities of the indigenous Central Asian population for non-combatant duties, and the suppression of this revolt caused large numbers of Kirgiz to leave for China. After the Revolution and a bloody period of civil war, Soviet power was effectively established in Kirgizia in 1919–20.

Partly because they came into contact with Muslim states at a relatively late date, the widespread conversion of the Kirgiz to Islam dates only from the second half of the seventeenth century, and the place of Islam in their ethnic self-consciousness has traditionally been somewhat ambiguous. Nowadays, however, the Kirgiz are wholly Muslim, and there is every indication that their religious feeling is strong[5].

KIRGIZ IN THE SOVIET PERIOD

Kirgizia entered the Soviet period as one of the least agriculturally, industrially and culturally developed regions of the country. Tsarist colonial rule had done little to improve the material standard of living or the general cultural level of the local population. The period of civil war, also, had caused severe damage to the local economy. The first large-scale measure of the new Soviet government, the land reform of 1920–21, was in part an attempt to redress past injustices by returning to the Kirgiz population lands taken from them; it also, however, represented the first stage of a move to restructure the rural economy along lines more acceptable to the central authorities by encouraging a move away from pastoral nomadism towards more permanent agricultural settlements. Subsequent reforms followed the same pattern, notably the further land reform of 1927–28 in southern Kirgizia and the collectivisation drive of the early 1930s which radically altered the traditional structures of agriculture and the way of life of the rural population.[6]

In the modern period approximately 30 per cent of the republic's economy is derived from agriculture; of this, 54.5 per cent comes from stock-breeding (mainly sheep, cattle and horses) and 45.5 per cent from crop-growing (above all, the so-called technical crops like cotton, tobacco and sugar beet).[7] The main industries are engineering and metal-working, construction, mining (Kirgizia has some of the most important deposits of non-ferrous metals in the USSR), production of electricity and food. The growth of industry has coincided with that of the towns:[8] between 1939 and 1959 the urban population of Kirgizia increased from 18 to 34 per cent, though the rate of growth has slowed somewhat since then (37 per cent in 1970, 39 per cent in both 1979 and 1989).[9] As in other parts of Central Asia, the proportion of non-Kirgiz in the republic's towns and among industrial workers is considerably higher than in the population as a whole.[10]

Before the twentieth century Kirgizia was to some extent isolated from the cultural and political movements taking place in the Russian empire, even elsewhere in Central Asia. In the first decades of this century, however, the pan-Turkic Jadidist movement penetrated Kirgizia and generated a certain amount of literature and the formation of local organisations, though most political and cultural activists from northern Kirgizia joined the Kazakh national movement Alash Orda.[11] The first years of Soviet power saw, as in other regions, a number of concessions to national feeling: the appointment of important figures from the national intelligentsia like Kasym Tynystanov to influential positions in the administration, respect for traditional Kirgiz culture and way of life, and the creation of a Kirgiz Autonomous Oblast as a national administrative unit in 1924.[12]

The 1920s also saw the beginnings of a truly national literature, based in the first instance on the rich traditions of Kirgiz epic poetry, and the formation of a vernacular standard language. The reform of the Arabic alphabet in 1923 allowed the representation in writing of the specific sounds of Kirgiz (notably the rich system of vowel harmony), and the number of publications in the language increased dramatically, helped to some extent by the introduction of a Latin-based script in 1928 which, while it marked a forced break with the existing literary tradition in the Arabic script, did allow the wider introduction of typographical processes.[13] The first Soviet schools were opened in the early 1920s (by 1923 there were 327, including 251 Kirgiz schools, with a total of 20,000 pupils). The level of literacy, however, especially among women, remained low until the concerted literacy drive of the early 1930s.[14]

Despite the general atmosphere of tolerance for national traditions and the prevailing policy of the adaptation of Soviet power to local conditions, relations between the Kirgiz intelligentsia and the central authorities in the 1920s did not follow an entirely smooth path. The Basmachi movement of armed opposition to Soviet power in Central Asia was largely put down in the early years of the decade, but surfaced again during the drive for collectivisation and de-nomadisation of the migrant Kirgiz herdsmen. And although the national Communist movement was not as strong in Kirgizia as in some other regions of the country, there were a number of attempts by the local elite to gain a greater role for the native Kirgiz leadership.[15] The leaders of such movements were excluded from the Party and in some cases exiled or imprisoned, a process which gained momentum during Stalin's notorious purges of the native elites during the latter years of the 1930s; their sacrifices in Kirgizia included not only most of the local Party leadership but also the most prominent cultural figures of the time.[16]

Industrial and cultural development continued apace during the 1930s, but the basis for this development had changed from one of local concessions to overt centralism: the building of 'socialism in one country' left little or no room for concessions to local conditions, in Kirgizia as elsewhere. The increased pace of industrialisation meant a continued influx of mainly Slav workers from western parts of the Soviet Union and a fundamental change in the structure of the republic's economy; the gradual introduction of universal compulsory schooling meant that a new generation could increasingly be educated along politically acceptable lines; and the adoption in 1941 of the Cyrillic script for Kirgiz brought the language firmly within the orbit of Russian influence.[17] Even in the post-Stalin 'thaw' the scale of rehabilitations in Kirgizia was notably less than in other Central Asian republics.[18]

Despite a lengthy period of pressure towards uniformity and the creation of a new Soviet Man, it is clear that Kirgiz national aspirations remained largely intact. Kirgiz identity has for centuries been linked – albeit in a complex way – with Islam,[19] and all the evidence is that the influence of religion continues to be strong, to judge at least by the space devoted to anti-religious propaganda in the local press. There is also evidence from before the recent period of Kirgiz nationalist tendencies in literature and in historical scholarship;[20] furthermore the criticism of the Kirgiz national epic *Manas* made during the course of a concerted campaign against the Central Asian epics in the early 1950s met with spirited local opposition.[21] In addition, although the prevailing line in language policy until very recent times has been to stress the importance of a good knowledge of Russian, voices were occasionally raised to point out the negative effects of this policy on the knowledge of Kirgiz,[22] and at the end of the 1950s a number of changes to the school curriculum in the republic gave a more prominent place to the study of Kirgiz language and history.[23]

Changes in the local Party hierarchy may well reflect tensions in Kirgiz relations with the centre[24] and also a degree of in-fighting at the local level – most notably in the mysterious murder of the Chairman of the Kirgiz Council of Ministers, Sultan Ibraimov, in December 1980.[25] And even in the early 1970s a number of Kirgiz legal specialists published articles in the local press demanding more explicit recognition of the constitutional rights of the republic.[26] There is thus a good deal of evidence that the concerns expressed in recent years in the new atmosphere generated by *glasnost'* reflect issues which have always been close to the heart of the local political and cultural leadership, even during the years now known as the time of the cult of personality and the period of stagnation.

KIRGIZIA UNDER GORBACHEV

The rise to power of Mikhail Gorbachev can hardly have given much indication of the dramatic events to come in the field of inter-ethnic relations. In Kirgizia, as elsewhere in Central Asia, local elites had carved out entrenched positions for themselves during the Brezhnev era, and when the new regime's policy was articulated at the 27th Party Congress in 1986, it was in a form basically hostile to the interests of the non-Russian nationalities.[27] However, the new freedom of expression which has characterised the recent period, coupled with the implications of *perestroika* for the economies and political structure of the individual republics, has led to an undoubted upsurge in nationalist behaviour. In some cases this has taken an extreme form – for instance, in the December 1986 riots in Alma Ata, which, as we shall see below, had repercussions in Kirgizia, or more recently in Transcaucasia, Moldavia and the Baltic republics. Less dramatic but equally significant is the effect of *glasnost'*, which has allowed the expression of opinions and concerns which had lain dormant for years because it was simply not wise to make them public.

All this means that in recent years the increasingly free and outspoken press has become a major source of information and lively debate, rather than a mouthpiece for tedious official clichés. Thus in Kirgizia, if even in the early 1980s the local press was presenting an idealised and not very accurate picture of 'the world as it ought to be',[28] by the present day we can read frank reports on the exploitation of child labour in the tobacco harvest[29] or the need to limit immigration into the republic.[30]

The first signs in Kirgizia of a new openness in the political sphere occurred in the spring of 1985 when the First Secretary of the Kirgiz Communist Party, Turdakun Usubaliev, went into print with some rather sharp criticisms of shortcomings in political work in the republic. In an interview published in *Pravda* on 7 June that year Usubaliev criticised a number of officials and called for a higher level of accountability in their work, and also spoke out for greater participation by ordinary working people in the decision-making process. He stated that 174 officials had been expelled from the Party for various offences since the last republican Party Congress, including a Deputy Minister of Internal Affairs, the Minister of Justice, the Chairman of the State Committee for the Supply of Petroleum Products, the head of militia for Osh Oblast and the Chief of the Central Committee's Administrative Organs Department. Usubaliev also named a number of government officials under investigation for their involvement in a large-scale fraud at the meat combine in Tokmak, and – perhaps most notable in view of subsequent events – sharply criticised the work of Apas Dzhumagulov, Secretary of the Central Committee with responsibility for industry. The severity and wide-ranging nature of these criticisms, coupled with their author's rather studied claim about the degree of openness they represented, led at least one observer to conclude that the First Secretary might be concerned about the security of his own position[31] – and so indeed it turned out, for Usubaliev retired from his post on 2 November 1985, a few days before his sixty-sixth birthday.[32]

From the first there were suspicions that Usubaliev's retirement was not simply on the grounds of age, but that he was forced to resign because of the many problems faced by the republic and as part of a wider campaign to replace top officials too closely associated with the Brezhnev era. The new First Secretary, Absamat Masaliev, immediately replaced the Second Secretary, all three Central Committee secretaries and the first secretaries of two of the republic's four Oblasts[33] and at the 18th Congress of the Communist Party of Kirgizia, held on 23–24 January 1986, launched an outspoken attack on his predecessor's record, accusing Usubaliev of nepotism and cronyism, and of creating an atmosphere of servility and sycophancy while monopolising the processes of decision-making.[34] In December 1986 Usubaliev was expelled from the Communist Party together with two of his principal associates, and there was even talk of his being put on trial;[35] at a plenum of the Kirgiz Communist Party on 21 May 1988, however, his Party membership was restored, ostensibly for his many years of service and because he had admitted his errors.[36]

Whatever may be the full implications of these events, it is clear that the new opportunities for criticism had far-reaching consequences. The fate of the former First Secretary is a particularly clear case of a policy decision from above coupled with local in-fighting, but the replacement of personnel in key positions has been a constant feature of the last few years, when those replaced include the Chief Editor of *Sovettik Kyrgyzstan* and Chairman of the Kirgiz Journalists' Union,[37] the head of the Kirgiz Writers' Union,[38] the President of the Kirgiz Academy of Sciences,[39] the Chairman of the Presidium of the Supreme Soviet[40] and the head of the republic's KGB;[41] and in May 1986 Apas Dzhumagulov, who had earlier been so strongly criticised by Usubaliev, was appointed Chairman of the Kirgiz Council of Ministers.[42]

Alongside these numerous personnel changes there has been a noticeable change in the cultural climate. The question of Kirgiz ethnogenesis has come in for re-evaluation (see note 3), as has the 1916 uprising, which had such a devastating effect on the Kirgiz population.[43] Several speakers at a plenum of the Kirgiz Writers' Union held in June 1987 criticised their colleagues for neglecting the Kirgiz cultural heritage – specifically, the language, historical origins, epic poetry and national-religious customs of the Kirgiz.[44] A new and more open attitude to the study of Kirgiz history is displayed by the newly elected director of the Institute of History in the Kirgiz Academy of Sciences, Salmorbek Tabyshaliev, who singles out the questions of ethnic origin, survivals of the tribal past and the role of the Russian language for the Kirgiz as being in need of major revision.[45]

The language question, indeed, has become one of the key issues in the cultural field. Prior to the Gorbachev period the main emphasis had been – as throughout the Soviet Union – on ensuring a prestigious role for Russian and developing a high level of bilingualism,[46] but this policy began to change at the 18th Kirgiz Party Congress when the new First Secretary devoted considerable space in his report to the need to improve the teaching of Kirgiz.[47] Subsequently the cause of the Kirgiz language was taken up by scholars who criticised shortcomings in the existing orthography and the huge number of superfluous loan words from Russian,[48] and by literary figures who engaged in a sharp debate over the need for specific measures to enhance the status of the Kirgiz language,[49] for example, by increasing the number of Kirgiz-language schools.[50] Although the revival of interest in the native language appears not to have gone as far as in other Central Asian republics where projects have been published to enshrine in law the official status of the local languages, nevertheless there is evidence of some of the same developments as are taking place elsewhere in the Soviet Union – for instance, a call for Russian-speaking residents of the republic to learn Kirgiz.[51]

One more striking result of *glasnost'* in Kirgizia has been a marked change in the treatment of Islam. It is not that the hostile attitude of the authorities towards religion has changed – on the contrary, the flow of anti-religious propaganda continues probably as strongly as ever,[52] but evidence of the continued strength of religious observance is much more plentiful. The tone was set, once again, at the 18th Congress of the Kirgiz Communist Party, when the new First Secretary Masaliev painted a much more candid picture of the persistence of religion than had his predecessor,[53] and continues in recent writing. Although Islam came relatively late to the Kirgiz and the official religious establishment is rather small,[54] the connection between Islam and the preservation of traditional national values is clearly felt by a sizeable proportion of the population. There are numerous reports of Muslim observances by Party workers and other dignitaries,[55] and accounts of a flourishing, unregistered 'parallel Islam'.[56] One very clear case is the rise in popularity of Takht-e Suleiman near Osh, one of the most important religious sites in Central Asia, as a place of pilgrimage.[57]

The relationship between Islam, national traditions and culture continues to be a potent one. As early as 1981–83 an ethnographical survey conducted among the rural Kirgiz population showed a marked preference for national literature, films and plays, and above all for the traditional bards.[58] The importance of the epic poetry declaimed by these bards – and specifically the saga *Manas* which had been criticised in the 1950s – was underscored by the Kirgiz Writers' Union in June 1987[59] in the context of a debate recognising the need to pay more attention to the Kirgiz national heritage (see above and note 44). All the evidence, then, is that allegiance to traditional Kirgiz culture, customs and way of life continues to be quite strong, as shown for instance by the persistence of elaborate and expensive wedding celebrations.[60]

In recent times such expressions of nationalism have begun to move from the cultural into the political sphere. The riots of December 1986 in Alma Ata, for example, had certain repercussions in Kirgizia, with a number of inter-ethnic clashes in the capital Frunze and some quite outspoken nationalist demands reported on the one hand, and on the other sharp condemnation by official spokesmen and some signs of a clamp-down.[61] And early in 1989 First Secretary Masaliev reported – albeit in a strongly critical tone – on the existence of several informal political associations in Frunze.[62] Unfortunately no details are given about the programmes of such organisations, and in this respect developments in Kirgizia would appear to be lagging a little behind those in other republics. None the less, there are clear signs of a greater level of assertiveness on the part of the local elites: a plenum of the Kirgiz Party Central Committee in December 1987 dealt quite frankly with the questions of demographic composition of the republic and nationality representation in the local Communist Party and workforce;[63] the question of independent cost-accounting (*khozraschet*) for the republic has recently been raised in the press by a professor at Frunze University;[64] and First Secretary Masaliev has responded sharply to criticisms of the republic made in the central press[65] – the clear implication being that the Kirgiz leadership do not mind criticising themselves, but are less enthusiastic when such criticism emanates from Moscow. Finally, an event of some importance is the rehabilitation after a protracted struggle of the Kirgiz writers Moldo Kylych and Kasym Tynystanov – the latter of whom in particular played a crucial part in the formation of Soviet Kirgiz language and culture.[66] The publication of the decree rehabilitating Tynystanov and a number of other Kirgiz political figures from the early Soviet period is a fitting symbol of the changes which have taken place in Kirgizia in the years since Gorbachev came to power.

CONCLUSION

We have observed in this chapter that the processes of *glasnost'* and *perestroika* in Kirgizia have been working in a way analogous with developments elsewhere in the Soviet Union: a thorough shake-out of the local leadership, renewed interest in the history and cultural heritage of the Kirgiz, the beginnings of a demand for greater economic and linguistic autonomy. At the same time, the need for increased contact between the Kirgiz in the USSR and their compatriots abroad has become an issue of concern[67] – and recently a significant step has been taken in this respect with the opening of a trading post on the border between Kirgizia and Sinkiang.[68]

Recent months have seen further signs of Kirgiz self-assertion in the economic field, with a serious clash over the right to use land and water occurring on 14 July 1989 on the Kirgiz–Tadzhik border,[69] and a strike on 1 August at the Kirgiz mining and metallurgy combine at Ak-Tyuz.[70] The wider issues of economic autonomy, republican citizenship and state status for the Kirgiz language have also been opened up for discussion, notably in a strongly worded and programmatic article by a prominent jurist which appeared in the local press on 1 July 1989.[71] All the indications are that, while Kirgizia may initially have been slower than some other republics to pursue the implications of the new political atmosphere under Gorbachev, the republic is now set to participate fully in future developments toward greater political, economic and cultural sovereignty.

NOTES

1. Basic geographical information on Kirgizia may be found in K. O. Otorbaev and S. N. Ryazantsev (eds) *Sovetskii Soyuz: geograficheskoe opisanie. Kirgiziya* (Moscow, Mysl' 1970); and in *Kirgizskaya SSR. Entsiklopediya* (Frunze, Glavnaya Redaktsiya KSE 1982).
2. Detailed figures for the Kirgiz population residing outside the USSR are given in Guy Imart, *Le chardon déchiqueté: être Kirghiz au XXe siècle* (Aix-en-Provence, Université de Provence 1982), pp. 42–3. Figures for Kirgiz migration are found in *ibid.*, p. 49.
3. On the formation and early history of the Kirgiz, see S. M. Abramzon *Kirgizy i ikh etnogeneticheskie i istoriko-kul'turnye svyazi* (Leningrad, Nauka 1971), pp. 10–70; *Istoriya Kirgizskoi SSR* vol. 1 (Frunze, Kyrgyzstan 1984), pp. 47–50, 408–41; for recent criticism of the standard account, see Joseph Seagram 'Question of Kirgiz ethnogenesis being reassessed' RL 6/87, 30 Dec. 1986. The most likely etymology of the term 'Kirgiz' is Turkic *kyrk* + *yz*, 'the forty (clans making up a tribal confederation)' (Imart *Le chardon déchiqueté*, p. 208, note c). Because of a terminological inexactitude the term 'Kirgiz' was used prior to 1925 to refer either to the Kazakhs or to the Kirgiz and Kazakhs together, and so the two peoples have been confused in a number of sources (see Ronald Wixman *The Peoples of the USSR: An Ethnographic Handbook* (London, Macmillan 1984), pp. 107–8). On the contemporary tribe and clan structure of the Kirgiz, see Alexandre Bennigsen and S. Enders Wimbush *Muslims of the Soviet Empire: A Guide* (London, C. Hurst & Co. 1985), pp. 78–80.

4. The official (and officially celebrated) date for the 'voluntary incorporation' of Kirgizia into Russia is October 1863. See V. M. Ploskikh 'Golos sud'by' *Sovetskaya Kirgiziya* 26 and 28 Oct. 1988.

5. Guy Imart 'The Islamic impact on traditional Kirgiz ethnicity' *Nationalities Papers* 14 (1–2) (1986), pp. 65–88; Bennigsen and Wimbush *Muslims of the Soviet Empire* pp. 80–3.

6. The standard account of the early Soviet land reforms and collectivisation in Kirgizia is given in *Istoriya Kirgizskoi SSR* vol. 3 (Frunze, Kyrgyzstan 1986), pp. 260–89, 397–432.

7. Data from *Kirgizskaya SSR . . .*, pp. 192 and 211–12.

8. On the industrial growth of the capital Frunze, see *Central Asian Review* 2 (3) (1954), p. 244.

9. Figures from *Naselenie SSSR 1973: statisticheskii sbornik* (Moscow, Statistika 1975), pp. 12–13. The more recent figures are given by Ann Sheehy 'Preliminary results of the All-Union census published', *Report on the USSR* 1 (20) (19 May 1989), p. 4.

10. See John Soper 'Nationality issues under review in Kirgizia' RL 49/88, 29 Jan. 1988, pp. 4–5.

11. *Central Asian Review* 5 (3) (1957), pp. 243–44; Allen Hetmanek, 'Kirgizstan and the Kirgiz' in Z. Katz (ed) *Handbook of Major Soviet Nationalities* (New York: Free Press 1975), p. 240.

12. The Kirgiz Autonomous Oblast became an Autonomous Soviet Socialist Republic on 1 Feb. 1926, and was upgraded to Union Republic status on 5 Dec. 1936.

13. On Kirgiz alphabet reform, see S. Kudaibergenov 'Sovershenstovanie i unifikatsiya alfavita kirgizskogo naroda' in N. A. Baskakov (ed.) *Voprosy sovershenstvovaniya alfavitov tyurkskikh yazykov narodov SSSR* (Moscow, Nauka 1972), pp. 93–8.

14. The relevant figures on education and literacy in the early Soviet period are conveniently summarised in *Kirgizskaya SSR*, pp. 266–67.

15. Hetmanek 'Kirgizstan and the Kirgiz' p. 241.

16. The basic Soviet account of Stalin's purges in Kirgizia may be found in *Istoriya Kirgizskoi SSR* vol. 2, part 2 (Frunze, Kyrgyzstan 1968), p. 70; a more extensive treatment published in the West is Azamat Altay 'Kirgiziya during the Great Purge' *Central Asian Review* 12 (2) (1964), pp. 97–107. The names of those purged are conveniently listed in Imart, *Le chardon déchiqueté*, pp. 103 and 214 (note bc).

17. Imart, *Le chardon déchiqueté*, gives an exhaustive account of the creation and maintenance of a standard Kirgiz language, emphasising that from the very beginning the so-called literary standard was somewhat artificial in nature.

18. Jane P. Shapiro 'Political rehabilitations in Soviet Central Asian Party organizations' *Central Asian Review* 14 (3) (1966), pp. 201–3.

19. Guy Imart 'Kirghizia between Islam and nationalism' *Journal Institute of Muslim Minority Affairs* 7 (2) (July 1986), pp. 343–72.

20. See, for example, *Central Asian Review* 1 (2) (1953), pp. 42–7; ibid. 11 (4) (1963), pp. 331–32.

21. Ibid. 4 (1) (1956), pp. 68–9.

22. Ibid. 13 (2) (1965), p. 183; Hetmanek 'Kirgizstan and the Kirgiz', p. 257.

23. Hetmanek 'Kirgizstan and the Kirgiz', p. 256.
24. *Central Asian Review* 9 (3) (1961), pp. 226–27.
25. See Bess Brown 'Chairman of Kirgiz Council of Ministers reported murdered' RL 469/80, 9 Dec. 1980; *idem* 'Deceased Kirgiz Premier receives belated honors' RL 223/86, 6 June 1986; *idem* 'Soviet journal publishes story about murder of Kirgiz Prime Minister' *Report on the USSR* 1 (15) (14 April 1989), pp. 33–5.
26. Hetmanek, 'Kirgizstan and the Kirgiz', pp. 257–58.
27. Yaroslav Bilinsky 'Nationality policy in Gorbachev's first year' *Orbis* 30 (2) (Summer 1986), pp. 331–42.
28. Momun Mirza 'The world according to *Sovettik Kyrgyzstan*' *Central Asian Survey* 2 (4) (Dec. 1983), pp. 109–26.
29. 'Moral' i pravo' *Komsomolets Kirgizii* 26 April 1989.
30. A. Ismailov 'V otvete pered soboi i potomkami' *Sovetskaya Kirgiziya* 12 May 1989.
31. Bess Brown 'Party chief of Kirgizia acknowledges problems in the republic' RL 238/85, 2 July 1985.
32. 'Kirgiz Party chief Usubaliev retires', RL 368/85, 7 Nov. 1985.
33. Bess Brown 'New Kirgiz First Secretary cleans house' RL 15/86, 31 Dec. 1985.
34. *Idem*. 'Eighteenth Congress of the Communist Party of Kirgizia: an attack on the past' RL 88/86, 20 Feb. 1986.
35. John Soper 'Former Kirgiz Party chief to be put on trial?' RL 173/87, 24 April 1987; see also *Central Asian Newsletter* 6 (3) (July 1987), p. 14.
36. *Sovetskaya Kirgiziya* 22 May 1988.
37. Ibid. 24 Jan. 1986.
38. Ann Sheehy 'Chingiz Aitmatov elected First Secretary of Kirgiz Writers' Union' RL 204/86, 27 May 1986.
39. *Idem*. 'Non-Kirgiz elected President of Kirgiz Academy of Sciences' RL 262/87, 7 July 1987.
40. Bess Brown 'Shepherd elected head of state in Kirgizia' RL 333/87, 11 Aug. 1987.
41. Amy Knight 'Personnel changes in KGB as public relations campaign continues' *Report on the USSR* 1 (10) 10 March 1989.
42. Bess Brown 'New head of government in Kirgizia' RL 206/86, 22 May 1986.
43. *Kyrgyzstan Madaniyaty* 23 June 1988.
44. John Soper 'Kirgiz intellectuals chided for neglect of heritage' RL 331/87, 18 Aug. 1987.
45. *Sovetskaya Kirgiziya* 26 June 1988.
46. See, for example, *Sovetskaya Kirgiziya*, 11 Aug. 1982 and 8 Feb. 1985; *Izvestiya* 6 Jan. 1986. A wealth of earlier material is entertainingly surveyed by Isabelle Kreindler 'Teaching Russian esthetics to the Kirgiz' *Russian Review* 40 (3) (July 1981), pp. 333–38.
47. *Sovettik Kyrgyzstan and Sovetskaya Kirgiziya*, 24 Jan. 1986.
48. Joseph Seagram 'Need for changes in Kirgiz language discussed' RL 141/86, 21 March 1986, and 'Further momentum in Kirgiz language reform' RL 8/87, 31 Dec. 1986; John Soper 'Kirgiz intelligentsia seeking to lessen Russian influence on native language' RL 412/87, 24 Sept. 1987. The poor state of the contemporary Kirgiz standard language is convincingly

documented in Imart *Le chardon déchiqueté*. Its virtually total exclusion from prestigious social functions may be seen from recent Soviet survey data; A. Orusbaev *Yazykovaya politika KPSS i razvitie kirgizsko-russkogo dvuyazychiya* (Frunze, Ilim 1987).

49. John Soper 'Kirgiz writers express concern over their national language' RL 142/88, 17 March 1988; see also *Central Asian Newsletter* 7 (5–6) (Dec. 1988 to Jan. 1989), p. 16.

50. The issue of Kirgiz-language schools was discussed in detail during 1986–87 (see John Soper 'Nationality issues', pp. 5–10). A recent fruit of this debate is an announcement by Radio Moscow on 6 July 1989 that the teaching of Kirgiz in the republic's schools is to increase greatly from September 1989 (see *Report on the USSR* 1 (30), 14 July 1989, p. 34).

51. Bess Brown 'Russian journalist calls for Russian-speakers in Kirgizia to learn Kirgiz' RL 183/87, 13 May 1987. A law giving Kirgiz the status of state language in the republic was in fact passed on 23 September 1989.

52. A number of recent examples of the genre are summarised in *Central Asia and Caucascus Chronicle* 8 (1) (March 1989), p. 5.

53. *Sovettik Kyrgyzstan* 24 Jan. 1986; see the commentary by Joseph Seagram 'The status of Islam in the USSR as reflected in speeches at the Republican Party congresses' RL 120/86, 7 March 1986, p. 1.

54. In an interview in *Sovettik Kyrgyzstan* on 11 May 1988 the Qadi of Kirgizia, Sadikdzhan Kamalov, gave the total number of 'working' mosques in the republic as thirty-four.

55. *Leninchil Zhash* 4 July 1987; *Propagandist-Agitator Kirgizstana* 2, 1988, pp. 2–16; see also *Central Asian Newsletter* 7 (1) (April 1988), p. 11 and (2) (May 1988), pp. 11–12.

56. Sh. Bazarbaev 'Kayra kuruu zhana ateisttik ish' *Kyrgyzstan Kommunisti* 10 (1987) pp. 58–62.

57. *Central Asian Newsletter* 6 (5) (Oct. 1987), pp. 5–6, and (6) (Dec. 1987), pp. 10–11.

58. A. Asankanov 'Izmeneniya v kul'turnoi zhizni sel'skogo naseleniya Kirgizskoi SSR' *Sovetskaya Etnografiya* 1, 1984 pp. 90–8.

59. *Kyrgyzstan Madaniyaty* 18 June 1987.

60. Bess Brown 'The high cost of getting married in Central Asia' RL 451/88, 10 Oct. 1988.

61. *Sovetskaya Kirgiziya* 27 Jan. 19, 24 and 27 Feb. 1987; Elizabeth Fuller and Annette Bohr 'Chronology of ethnic disturbances in Transcaucasia and Central Asia' *Report on the USSR* 1 (27) (7 July 1989), p. 17. For analysis of this material see *Central Asian Newsletter* 6 (2) (June 1987), pp. 9–13 and (3) (July 1987), pp. 13–14.

62. *Leninchil Zhash* 28 Jan. 1989.

63. Soper 'Nationality issues', pp. 1–5. For the background to the contemporary demographic situation and its significance, see Paul A. Goble 'Gorbachev and the Soviet nationality problem' in M. Friedberg and H. Isham (eds) *Soviet Society under Gorbachev: Current Trends and Future Prospects* (New York and London, M. E. Sharpe 1987), pp. 82–4.

64. Ismailov 'V otvete pered soboi i potomkami' (see note 30).

65. Bess Brown 'Kirgiz Party Chief continues feud with Moscow' RL 308/88, 11 July 1988.

66. For earlier unsuccessful attempts to rehabilitate Moldo Kylych and

Tynystanov, see Ann Sheehy 'Renewed attempt to rehabilitate the works of two important Kirgiz literary figures fails' RL 98/87, 9 March 1987; and John Soper 'Status of two Kirgiz literary figures being reluctantly restored' RL 405/88, 31 Aug. 1988. The decrees rehabilitating Moldo Kylych, K. Tynystanov, Yu. Abdrakhmanov and D. Mambetaliev were published in *Sovetskaya Kirgiziya* 4 Jan. 1989.

67. *Kyrgyzstan Madaniyaty* 11 June 1987.
68. Erkin Alptekin 'Relations between Eastern and Western Turkestan' RL 548/88, 30 Nov. 1988, p. 1.
69. See *Pravda* 15 and 16 July 1989; also SWB SU/0510 B/1–2, 17 July.
70. Radio Moscow reported in SWB SU/0528 B/5, 7 Aug. 1989.
71. L. Levitin 'Natsional'naya politika i pravo' *Sovetskaya Kirgiziya* 1 July 1989.

CHAPTER SIXTEEN

Tadzhiks

John Payne

BACKGROUND

The Tadzhiks speak a language which belongs to the Iranian family and is very closely related to the modern forms of Persian spoken in Iran and Afghanistan. They are therefore linguistically quite distinct from the other main national groups of Central Asia, whose languages (Uzbek, Kirgiz, Turkmen, Kazakh) belong to the Turkic family.

Iranian peoples have been settled in Central Asia since ancient times, predating the Turks by at least a millennium. During the seventh to sixth centuries BC, the territory to the north of the Oxus River (Amu-Darya), which forms the present Tadzhik and Uzbek republics, was already occupied by East Iranian peoples: the Bactrians, the Sogdians and the nomadic Sakas. In the sixth century BC, the early independent states of Bactria and Sogdiana were incorporated into the Persian empire by Cyrus the Great, the founder of the Achaemenian dynasty. At this time, the town of Marakanda (modern Samarkand) in Sogdiana was already an important trading centre.

From the fall of the Achaemenians in the fourth century BC until the Arab conquest at the beginning of the eighth century AD, Bactria and Sogdiana were subjected to a variety of non-Iranian influences. The first of these was Alexander the Great's invasion in the fourth century BC, followed after Alexander's death by the dismemberment of the Greek empire and the eventual formation of an independent Graeco-Bactrian state in the middle of the third century BC. Greek rule was ended in the middle of the second century BC by the arrival from the north of the nomadic Yüeh-Chi. One Yüeh-Chi dynasty, the Kushans, founded the Kushan state which at the height of its power (first–third centuries AD) included much of the territory of Afghanistan and northern India as well as Bactria and Sogdiana. As the power of the Kushan state declined, the influence of Persia again briefly asserted itself as the Sassanian dynasty seized control over Bactria. However, the attempts of the Sassanians to maintain control over their Central Asian territories were thwarted by yet more nomadic incursions from the north, those of the Hephthalites and other Hunnish tribes in the mid-fifth century AD, followed by those of the first clearly Turkic tribes in the mid-sixth century AD.

By the time of the Arab conquest of Central Asia, the original territory of Bactria and Sogdiana seems to have been divided into a number of small kingdoms. Despite the admixture of non-Iranian populations, Eastern Iranian languages were still predominant: Sogdian indeed served as the lingua franca of the silk route from Samarkand into northern China. However, the uniting of the Iranian world under the Arab Caliphate led to the gradual displacement of the original Eastern Iranian languages by Persian. Persian (Persian name *parsi*, later Arabicised as *farsi*), which by contrast belongs to the Western Iranian language group, was the main language of the Sassanian empire in Iran and northern Afghanistan. The Arab armies which originally subjugated Central Asia were to a significant extent composed of Islamicised Persians from Khorasan (north-west Iran). Persian subsequently served as an important instrument of Arab propaganda, and Arab power was based on largely autonomous Persian-speaking ruling dynasties. By the time of the Samanid dynasty (tenth century AD), the large towns (such as Bukhara, which was the Samanid capital, and Samarkand) were essentially Persian-speaking, and an extensive literature in Persian had been developed. The poets Rudaki and Firdousi belong to this period.

The name 'Tadzhik' which is currently used for the Persian-speaking population of Central Asia, is based on an Arabic tribal name 'Taiy'. This name was widely used by other peoples to describe the Arabs: for example, the Arabs were known by this name to the Chinese as early as the first century AD. In the Sogdian form '*tazik*' it was used as a name for the Arab invaders of Central Asia, and then by extension applied at the end of the tenth or the beginning of the eleventh century to the Islamicised, Persian-speaking population.

The eleventh to the sixteenth centuries in Central Asia were marked by successive invasions of Turks and Mongols, beginning with the establishment of the Karakhanid dynasty in the eleventh century and ending with the arrival of the Uzbeks in the early sixteenth century. During this period, as the originally Iranian-speaking populations to a large extent assumed the languages of their Turkic overlords and neighbours, the present national groupings in Central Asia were essentially formed. Persian, however, retained its status as a literary language – for example, in the works of the poets Omar Khayyam and Hafiz – and was maintained as the main spoken language for the majority of the population in the area which constitutes modern Tadzhikistan. In addition, Persian survived as the language of significant minorities in Bukhara and Samarkand. The old Eastern Iranian languages seem to have been preserved only in a few remote areas by relatively small groups: a dialect of Sogdian, now called Yaghnobi, was spoken in the Yaghnob valley in the high Zeravshan (now central Tadzhikistan), and other Eastern Iranian dialects, now called the Pamir languages, survived in the inaccessible western valleys of the Pamir massif (now the Gorno-Badakhshanskaya Avtonomnaya Oblast).

At the beginning of the nineteenth century, after centuries of conflict between rival khanates, rule over the territory of modern Tadzhikistan was divided between the Emirate of Bukhara and the Khanate of Kokand. Kokand fell militarily to tsarist Russia in 1866, and in 1876 was formally incorporated into the General-Governorship of Turkestan which had been established in 1867 to consolidate Russian military power in Central Asia. A treaty between the Tsar and the Emir of Bukhara in 1868 ceded to Russia many of the Emirate's northern territories, including some areas which are now in northern Tadzhikistan. By the same treaty, the rump of the Emirate of Bukhara (including the territory which is now central and southern Tadzhikistan) became a Russian protectorate. The Eastern Pamir, occupied by nomadic Kirgiz, was incorporated directly into the tsarist empire as part of the Kokand Khanate. However, the Western Pamir, which was divided into semi-independent, feudal khanates, was only incorporated later into the Emirate of Bukhara following discussions in 1895 between England and Russia on the demarcation of the borders of Afghanistan.

Under tsarist rule, some degree of economic development was brought to the essentially feudal Muslim regions which made up the General-Governorship of Turkestan, including the territories which now form part of northern Tadzhikistan. Railways were built, and in order to ensure supplies of cheap raw materials for the Russian textile industry, particular attention was paid to the production of cotton. Small factories were set up by Russian industrialists in and around Khodzhent (now renamed Leninabad), and the mineral resources of the area, including coal, began to be exploited. At the same time, Russian settlements began to develop, often with forced expropriation of land. Economically and politically, the Bukharan Emirate was rather more backward, and many of its artisans turned to Russian Turkestan for employment where the wages could be up to three times higher.

THE TADZHIKS IN THE SOVIET UNION

The Tadzhik towns which belonged to Russian Turkestan were the first to be affected by the events of 1917. Following the February Revolution, Soviets were quickly established in all the major centres, including Khodzhent, Ura-Tyube and Kanibadam. However, these were composed primarily of Russian railway workers, miners and factory employees, rather than native Tadzhiks. During the summer of 1917, as opposition to the provisional government grew in strength, some Tadzhik groups emerged; for example, the 'Union of Muslim

Workers' in Khodzhent. These were persuaded to support the Bolsheviks, who finally took control in Khodzhent in November 1917. Despite resistance from anti-Bolshevik forces in other areas – notably Ura-Tyube, Kokand and the Pamir – the northern and eastern territories of Tadzhikistan were effectively under Bolshevik control and had been administratively incorporated into the newly formed Turkestan ASSR by the end of 1918.

By contrast, the Emir of Bukhara, whose army consisted of nearly 95,000 men, including 13,000 cavalry, was not overthrown until 1920. The first attempt at Soviet intervention in February 1918, in support of a revolutionary group called the 'Young Bukharans', ended in military failure. Only after Soviet power had been consolidated in the rest of Turkestan, and after the fall of the Khanate of Khiva in February 1920, did the Red Army again intervene in Bukhara under the command of M. V. Frunze. After a four-day battle, the Emir was driven out of Bukhara in September 1920 and the Bukharan People's Soviet Republic was declared. However, resistance by the remnants of the Emir's forces continued in Eastern Bukhara (central and southern Tadzhikistan), where a number of armed, anti-Soviet groups known as the Basmachi eventually joined forces under such commanders as the Turkish general Enver Pasha. By the end of 1921, Enver Pasha had 20,000 men under his control, and he remained undefeated until the summer of 1922. Despite this setback, Basmachi resistance to Soviet power continued until 1926, and even in 1929 and 1931 isolated incursions were made into Tadzhikistan by Basmachi bands based in Afghanistan.

Tadzhikistan only became a political entity in the delimitation of Central Asia which took place in 1924. Prior to this, 47.7 per cent of all Tadzhiks in Soviet Central Asia were living in the Turkestan ASSR (403,700 people), and 52.3 per cent were living in the Bukharan People's Soviet Republic (420,100).[1] The new boundaries proposed by the Central Executive Committee of the Turkestan ASSR and the All-Bukharan Soviet of People's Deputies envisaged that Tadzhikistan would be merely an Autonomous Region within the new Uzbek SSR; however the second session of the All-Russian Central Executive Committee overruled this decision, giving Tadzhikistan the status of an Autonomous Soviet Socialist Republic within the Uzbek SSR. The republic was formally proclaimed on 15 March 1925, with its capital in the town of Dushanbe.

At the time of its formation, the Tadzhik ASSR had a population of 739,500 (135,700 from the Turkestan ASSR and 603,800 from the Bukharan People's Soviet Republic).[2] The borders were mostly drawn in such a way as to include all the districts with a majority of Tadzhiks. However, the Tadzhik and Uzbek populations were so interwoven that the new Tadzhik ASSR nevertheless contained a sizeable Uzbek minority. For the proportions, the *Tadzhik Soviet Encyclopaedia* suggests figures of 65.4 per cent Tadzhiks and 32.4 per cent Uzbeks.[3] However, later figures from the 1926 census present a slightly different picture, with a total population of 827,100 (74.6 per cent Tadzhiks, 21.2 per cent Uzbeks, 1.4 per cent Kirgiz, 0.7 per cent Russians, 0.5 per cent Turkmen, 0.2 per cent Kazakhs, 0.1 per cent Ukrainians and 1.1 per cent other nationalities).[4]

At the same time, a sizeable proportion of the total number of Tadzhiks (36.9 per cent, according to the 1926 census) remained outside the Tadzhik ASSR, primarily in the neighbouring regions of the Uzbek SSR, including Samarkand, Bukhara, and Khodzhent. In October 1929 the district of Khodzhent, which despite its Tadzhik majority had remained in the Uzbek SSR, was transferred to the Tadzhik ASSR, raising its population to 1,200,000 (901,400 Tadzhiks (78.4 per cent) and 206,300 Uzbeks (17.9 per cent).[5] More or less simultaneously, on 16 October 1929, the Tadzhik ASSR was raised to the status of a full Soviet Republic, becoming the Tadzhik SSR.

The establishment of Soviet control in Tadzhikistan, as in the other Central Asian republics, led to the gradual elimination of illiteracy. A number of serious problems had to be overcome: the opposition of the mullahs to the development of a secular education system, the reluctance of Muslim women to attend schools, and the shortage of teachers, buildings and textbooks. In addition, a major difficulty was presented by the divergence of the spoken Tadzhik dialects from the classical Persian literary language, both in grammar (the dialects had developed a number of new grammatical forms, with the northern dialects in particular being influenced by the neighbouring Uzbek language), and in vocabulary (the classical language contained a large proportion of Arabic words). Some pre-revolutionary Tadzhik authors, notably Ahmadi Donish, had attempted to bring the spoken forms into the written language, and this movement was continued by the Soviet Tadzhik author Sadriddin Aini, whose early stories and novels, *Odina* (1925) and *Dokhunda* (1927), based on the dialects of Bukhara and Samarkand, served as the model for the new Tadzhik standard language. By the end of 1927, 175 'Likbez' (Likvidatsiya Bezgramotnosti, Liquidation of Illiteracy) schools had been set up in the republic, with the primary aim of training party cadres. This figure had expanded by the 1932–33 school year to 4,069 schools with more than 140,000 pupils, including 25,314 women, and by 1939 the official literacy rate for the whole population had reached 71.7 per cent.[6] In 1927 a decision was taken to replace the Arabic alphabet of the classical language with an adapted version of the Latin alphabet. The Latin alphabet was used until 1940, when in its turn it was replaced by the present Cyrillic-based alphabet.

The drive towards the elimination of adult illiteracy was accompanied by the development of a system of education for school-aged pupils, and eventually a full system of higher and technical education. The number of schools rose from 382 in 1928–29 to 2,628 in 1940–41, with 303,500 pupils.[7] However, universal secondary education was

FIGURE 3 : ETHNIC AND LINGUISTIC MINORITIES IN TADZHIKISTAN

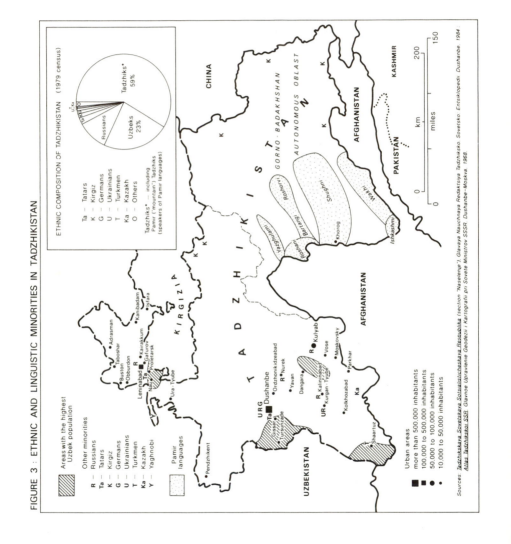

ETHNIC COMPOSITION OF TADZHIKISTAN (1979 census)

Ta – Tatars
K – Kirgiz
G – Germans
U – Ukrainians
T – Turkmen
Ka – Kazakh
O – Others

Tadzhiks* – including
Pamir ('mountain') Tadzhiks
(speakers of Pamir languages)

Tadzhiks*
59%

Russians

Uzbeks
23%

Areas with the highest
Uzbek population

Other minorities

R – Russians
Ta – Tatars
K – Kirgiz
G – Germans
U – Ukrainians
T – Turkmen
Ka – Kazakh
Y – Yaghnobi

Pamir
languages

Urban areas

■ more than 500,000 inhabitants
■ 100,000 to 500,000 inhabitants
● 50,000 to 100,000 inhabitants
• 10,000 to 50,000 inhabitants

Sources: Tadzhikskaya Sovetskaya Sotsialisticheskaya Respublika (section 'Naselenie'). Glavaya Nauchnaya Redaktsiya Tadzhiksko. Sovetsko. Entsiklopedii. Dushanbe. 1984
Atlas Tadzhikskoi SSR. Glavnoe Upravlenie Geodezii i Kartografii pri Sovete Ministrov SSSR. Dushanbe–Moskva. 1968

developed in the post-war years: in 1949–50 Tadzhikistan moved towards a universal seven-year education, this being extended to eight years in 1959–60. Official Soviet figures claim that by 1976 90.3 per cent of the young population were in secondary schools, rising to 99.7 per cent in 1980.[8]

The first pedagogical institution to open was the Pedagogical Tekhnikum in Dushanbe (1926), followed at the beginning of the 1930s by similar technikums in Kurgan-Tyube, Kulyab, Nau, Ura-Tyube, Kanibadam, Pendzhikent, Khorog and Yangi-Bazar (now Ordzhonikidzeabad). In deference to Muslim prejudices, the student population initially consisted only of males: separate female teacher-training institutes or colleges were established in Dushanbe, Leninabad and Kanibadam. Other important centres were founded in the pre-war years, for example, the Medical Institute in Dushanbe in 1939. However, the main expansion of higher education, like that of secondary education, took place in the post-war period. The Tadzhik State University was opened in 1948, and the Tadzhik branch of the USSR Academy of Sciences, originally established in 1932, was formed into the Tadzhik Academy of Sciences in 1951. In 1984 the Academy consisted of sixteen research institutes with a total of 1,389 workers.[9]

Modern figures for the participation of women in education show that, despite the dramatic increases which have taken place since the 1950s (when Asian girls represented only 19 per cent of those enrolled in the final three years of secondary schooling)[10] Tadzhikistan still lags to some extent behind the rest of the USSR. including the other Central Asian republics. This can be seen especially in the proportion of women enrolled in higher and special secondary institutions: at the beginning of the 1986–87 academic year, the proportion of women enrolled in higher education was 42 per cent, compared with 56 per cent for the USSR average, 59 per cent for Kirgizia, 56 per cent for Kazakhstan, 46 per cent for Uzbekistan and 44 per cent for Turkmenistan. The figures for the proportion of women in special secondary education are similar: Tadzhikistan 44 per cent, USSR average 58 per cent, Kirgizia 59 per cent, Kazakhstan 58 per cent, Uzbekistan 51 per cent, and Turkmenistan 49 per cent.[11] At the highest level, 28 women in Tadzhikistan held the degree of doctor of science in 1986, compared with 6,112 for the USSR as a whole. This is a proportion of 0.77 per cent, while the female population of Tadzhikistan represents 1.63 per cent of the total female population of the USSR. The total number of women engaged in academic work was 3,627 in 1986, 0.61 per cent of the USSR total of 598,057.[12]

In the field of economy, the main thrust of the Party's activity in Tadzhikistan was the collectivisation of agriculture and the increasing development of cotton as the republic's main contribution to the total USSR economy. The process of collectivisation was slower than in the central USSR, especially in the remoter mountain regions, and seems to have met with considerable resistance. By 1932, collectivisation had encompassed 41.9 per cent of all peasant households (USSR total 61.5 per cent) and 65.3 per cent of the agricultural land (USSR total 77.7 per cent).[13] These figures, however, conceal a large discrepancy between the collectivisation of cotton-growing areas, which were made into a USSR priority and selectively resourced, and the collectivisation of lands devoted to grain production and livestock rearing. By 1932–33, 84.2 per cent of the cotton-growing land had been collectivised, compared with 26.5 per cent of the land for grain production and livestock rearing.[14] The mass collectivisation of these remaining areas took place in 1937–38. Table 16.1 shows the absolute growth in the area of cultivated land during the early Soviet period, together with the relative increase in the area devoted to cotton production.

Table 16.1   Cultivated land in Tadzhikistan (1913–80)[15]

Area (1000 hectares)	1913	1940	1950	1960	1970	1980
Total cultivated land	494.3	807.1	836.9	724.3	764.9	763.3
Grain	437.8	567.4	551.5	360.6	320.5	195.0
Cotton	26.7	106.1	126.0	172.4	254.0	308.5
Vegetable oil	10.4	51.2	96.3	40.7	7.8	3.7
Animal feed	13.4	55.3	48.9	131.2	150.8	217.0

Although Tadzhikistan with its relatively small area has a smaller acreage under cotton cultivation than the neighbouring republic of Uzbekistan, the cotton yield per acre in Tadzhikistan is the highest in the USSR.

The overall growth rate for Tadzhikistan over the Soviet period has been very high, starting from a relatively low base point. However, industrial development has been concentrated in urban areas, especially around the major cities of Dushanbe and Leninabad, and the relative weight in the republic of the USSR national economy has remained lower for the majority of products than the relative size of its population, which like that of the other Central Asian republics has been growing at a very high rate. The main exceptions reflect the status of Tadzhikistan as a cotton-growing republic, and traditional specialisms such as silk. Almost half the territory of Tadzhikistan lies at a height of over 3,000 metres, and within the Central Asian economic region it has become an important source of hydroelectric energy (see Table 16.2).

The general picture of Tazhikistan in the period 1917–85 is therefore one of considerable development, both in the field of education and in the economy. Given, however, the rapid increase in the size of the population, this development has not been sufficient to raise Tadzhikistan to average USSR levels. The main role of Tadzhikistan in

Table 16.2   Relative weight of Tadzhikistan in the USSR economy and in
the Central Asian economic region (1940–80) percentage[16]

	1940		1970		1980	
	in USSR	in Central Asia	in USSR	in Central Asia	in USSR	in Central Asia
Population	0.78	14.1	1.21	14.6	1.5	15.0
Electrical energy	0.13	0.92	0.48	14.0	1.0	21.5
Cement	–	–	0.92	20.0	0.84	14.4
Coal	0.12	12.1	0.14	10.2	0.11	7.8
Cotton fibre	7.2	8.8	11.0	12.0	10.3	11.7
Raw silk	14.0	21.5	10.6	17.3	9.5	14.3
Cotton textiles	0.0	0.01	1.3	30.0	1.3	25.7
Silk textiles	2.1	25.2	3.3	38.6	3.3	31.0
Leather shoes	0.02	9.3	0.9	17.0	1.05	7.02
Canned goods	0.04	22.5	1.6	29.0	1.75	22.6

the USSR economy is as a supplier of raw cotton, only a relatively small percentage of which is converted into textiles within the republic.

TADZHIKISTAN IN THE GORBACHEV ERA

The most striking feature of Tadzhikistan in the Gorbachev era is undoubtedly the open expression, under the policy of *glasnost'*, of Tadzhik nationalist sentiment. However, this sentiment has not yet resulted in the kind of popular demand for political independence, or even for total secession from the USSR, that we have seen develop in such republics as Lithuania and Moldavia. Unlike the Baltic states, Tadzhikistan does not have any recent history of independence, and indeed owes its existence as a separate republic to the decision of the early Soviet leadership not to treat the Tadzhiks as an ethnic minority within Uzbekistan. Also, unlike Moldavia, Tadzhikistan has not had any recent political ties with states outside the USSR. The link with the Persian-speaking populations of Iran and Afghanistan has for centuries been linguistic and cultural rather than political.

Instead, the main issue that has aroused nationalist passions in Tadzhikistan has been the increasing dominance of the Russian language. In 1926, the Russian and Ukrainian population of Tadzhikistan was still extremely small, at 6,700 (0.8 per cent of the total population).

By 1939, this figure had increased to 153,000 (10.3 per cent), and by 1959 to 289,500 (14.6 per cent). Since then, the absolute numbers of Russians and Ukrainians have continued to grow (to 375,800 in 1970 and 430,900 in 1979). Because of the very high Tadzhik birth-rate, the overall proportion of Russians and Ukrainians in the republic has in fact been slightly decreasing in recent years (to 13.0 per cent in 1970 and 11.3 per cent in 1979).[17] However, the main Tadzhik (and Uzbek) population growth has taken place in rural areas, while the Russian and Ukrainian population is concentrated in the towns and cities. Russians represent 30 per cent of the total urban population, and in the capital, Dushanbe, the proportion of Russians is even higher.[18]

The increasing dominance of the Russian language, and the consequential decline in the status of Tadzhik, is catalogued in an important article in the local press (19 February 1989) by four leading Tadzhik intellectuals: M. Shukurov, R. Amonov, Sh. Rustamov and A. Sayfullaev.[19] The first three are heads of department in the Rudaki Institute of Language and Literature of the Tadzhik Academy of Sciences, and the fourth is a doctor of philological sciences. Shukurov and his co-authors attribute the decline of Tadzhik to the post-war period, blaming the command-administrative system for enforcing a policy under which Russian is the language of administration, the language of the work-place, and the language of instruction in the majority of institutes of higher and secondary education. Only Tadzhiks who are educated in Russian-language primary schools and become bilingual can progress to higher levels. The result is that Tadzhik is not used, even between native Tadzhiks, in the medical, agricultural, polytechnical and other institutes, or as a working language in the research institutes of the Tadzhik Academy of Sciences (with the exception of the Rudaki Institute of Language and Literature, the Oriental Institute and the Philosophy Department). The complaint is made that standards of literacy in Tadzhik are generally low, that Tadzhik is becoming restricted in its sphere of usage to the home and to Tadzhik-language schools, and that there may even eventually be a danger of total language loss if nothing is done.

The measures proposed by Shukurov and his co-authors are analogous to those pioneered in the 'Laws on Language' already under discussion or adopted by the Baltic republics, Georgia and Moldavia. Tadzhik, they suggest, should be named as the 'state language' of Tadzhikistan, while Russian should be given the status of a language for 'communication between nationalities'. The naming of Tadzhik as the state language should not 'lead to discrimination against the other nationalities, peoples and national groups of Tadzhikistan, or to the infringement and restriction of their language rights'. A detailed codex will be necessary to determine exactly where Tadzhik alone should basically be used (in legislation, official records, official correspondence within the republic, national pre-school establishments, secondary professional and higher education, and so on), where Tadzhik and Russian should be equally used (in sessions of the Supreme Soviet, and in local Soviets), and when Russian alone is appropriate (in technical documents, in communications with other republics, in official communications between predominantly Russian-speaking collectives within Tadzhikistan, and so forth). In order to achieve these goals, the higher education system should train highly qualified teachers to run Tadzhik-language courses in the republic's institutions, organisations and enterprises. Financial incentives should be provided to non-Tadzhiks who learn Tadzhik well – for example, 20 per cent or 10 per cent increases in salary for those who achieve an examination mark of 'excellent' or 'good'. Realistically, an equal knowledge of Tadzhik cannot be expected from all social groups within the non-Tadzhik population. However, officials should be able to converse in the language of their subordinates and visitors, shop assistants should speak the language of their customers, doctors should speak the language of their patients, and so on. The time-scale envisaged for the conversion of all official communications into Tadzhik is three to ten years.

Not all Tadzhik intellectuals share these views.[20] R. Khashimov, a member of the 'Language and Society' research unit in the Institute of Language and Literature, points to the polarisation which occurred between Russians and Estonians, when the Estonian Supreme Soviet voted on the Estonian 'Law on Language': the Russian delegates refused to take part in the vote and left the hall. 'Are such extremes necessary?,' Khashimov asks. Declaring Tadzhik to be the state language goes counter to Lenin's view (expressed with respect to the Soviet Union as a whole) that there should be no single state language in a multi-lingual state, and may also conflict with the Universal Declaration of Human Rights, which *inter alia* forbids discrimination on the basis of differences in language. In a counter-proposal, Khashimov suggests that the status of Tadzhik should be improved by making it the 'means of communication between different nationalities within the republic'. However, recognising the relative weight of the different nationalities in the republic, all three major languages (Tadzhik, Russian, Uzbek) should be equally regarded as official 'working' languages of the republic, and in areas where there are compact groups of various minority languages (Kirgiz, Kazakh, Tatar, German, Turkmen, various Pamir languages), these too should be considered as working languages in those areas. Official interpreters should be available to enable all citizens to use their native language when they wish.

The view that Tadzhik should be the single state language has however been officially accepted. A special commission set up by the Presidium of the Tadzhik Supreme Soviet recommended in February 1989 that a corresponding 'Law on Language' should be drafted,[21] and this draft law was ratified during the 10th session of the Supreme Soviet in July 1989.[22] Both meetings seem to have been accompanied by large demonstrations in Dushanbe. For example, on 24 February 1989 hundreds of students are reported to have gathered in Lenin Square in the centre of the city shouting slogans such as: 'Tadzhik should be made the state language!', 'We demand the renaissance of the ancient Tadzhik culture!', and 'We support *perestroika!*'. The local newspaper applauds the decision of senior officials and academics (for example: G. P. Pallaev, the President of the Presidium of the Supreme Soviet; M. Kanoatov, the First Secretary of the Union of Writers; A. Tursunov, director of the Oriental Institute of the Academy of Sciences; and M. Asimov, member of the Praesidium of the Academy of Sciences) to take an active part in the demonstration by reporting the decisions of the special commission to the crowd. Although passions were aroused, this crowd seems to have dispersed without any major disorder.[23] More disturbing, however, are oral reports from the same period that gangs of Tadzhik youths were beating up visitors to cinemas showing Russian-language films.

The effects of the new language law are already becoming visible. Most noticeably, the name of the Tadzhik language has been altered in the official press to the 'Tadzhik (Farsi) language', emphasising its closeness to literary and spoken Persian. School timetables have been changed to give greater emphasis to Tadzhik language and literature, including classical Persian texts. Children in Russian-language schools will study Tadzhik from the first to the eleventh class, beginning at age seven.[24] From 1 January 1990, doctors will be required to write case-histories in Tadzhik rather than Russian.

There is some evidence that the increase in Tadzhik national sentiment is being accompanied by increased tensions between the nationalities. Russian workers are reported to be leaving Tadzhikistan, and in 1989 the opera house in the centre of Dushanbe, which usually carries a banner with the leading political slogan of the day, carried the slogan: 'Russians, do not leave!'. A press report deals with a certain I. S. Makhmudov, a Tadzhik industrial worker from Kanibadam, who was convicted under Article 71 of the Tadzhik legal code ('The Infringement of National and Racial Equality') for hanging anti-Russian posters outside local cinemas. A violent land dispute was reported in the summer of 1989 between Tadzhik and Kirgiz collective farmers on the border between the two republics.[25] Complaints are voiced by Tadzhiks about the treatment of the Tadzhik minority living in Uzbekistan – for example, the reduction during the Brezhnev years of the number of schools and classes in which Tadzhik was the language of instruction, and the unavailability of Tadzhik television in Bukhara and Samarkand. Some segments of the Tadzhik intelligentsia are referring to the 'assimilation' of the Tadzhiks in Bukhara and Samarkand provinces, and trying to question some of the historical aspects of the territorial demarcation of the Central Asian republics in 1924. In an attempt to improve relations, high-level bilateral contacts between Tadzhikistan and Uzbekistan have been taking place.[26]

During the Gorbachev era, certain manifestations of Islamic fundamentalism have been reported in the Tadzhik press. Anonymous
leaflets have been distributed calling on parents to educate their children
according to Islamic law, and demanding that Tadzhik girls abandon
their European clothing. The distributors of the leaflets range from
unemployed workers to schoolboys and students.[27] One consequence
seems to have been an increase in the number of cases of self-immolation
by Tadzhik girls who have been criticised for their European behaviour,
or more seriously, have been prevented by their fathers from attending
school and required to marry against their will.[28] 'Self-appointed mullahs' are reported to be travelling around the villages in Kurgan-Tyube
Province, reading the Qur'ān. Special criticism is directed against a
certain Abdullo Saidov, a driver and geodetic engineer, who as 'mullah
Abdullo' called on collective farm-workers to support the creation of
an Islamic state in Tadzhikistan.[29] The purveyors of Islamic ideas are
accused in the press of 'playing with fire'. There is however no evidence,
as yet, that this fire has taken hold.

The most serious problem facing the Tadzhik economy during the
Gorbachev era seems to be an increasing level of unemployment as the
growth in labour resources outstrips the growth in employment opportunities. Table 16.3 illustrates the growth of the republic's population,
compared with the growth of the city of Dushanbe.[30]

From 1979 to 1989, there was an increase of 34 per cent in the
population of Tadzhikistan, the highest population growth rate in the
USSR (compare Uzbekistan 29 per cent, USSR average 9.3 per cent).
This growth has taken place primarily in rural areas, leading to an
unemployed total of 234,000 in 1986 (219,000 women and 15,000 men;
77.1 per cent in rural areas and 22.9 per cent in urban areas).[31] In his
speech to the Plenum of the Central Committee of the CPSU on 20
September 1989 (the Plenum devoted to the nationalities question), K.
M. Makhkamov, the First Secretary of the Tadzhik Central Committee,
complained that the central authorities have as a rule ignored requests
for the construction in Tadzhikistan of cotton-processing and other
light industrial plant which might mop up this pool of unused labour.

Table 16.3   Population (thousands)

Year	Tadzhikistan	Year	Dushanbe
1940	1525	1939	83
1959	1981	1959	227
1970	2900	1970	374
1979	3801	1979	494
1987	4807	1987	582
1989	5112	1989	n.a.

Instead, 90 per cent of the cotton produced in Tadzhikistan is processed outside the republic, and the price received for the raw product is miserable by modern standards. If Tadzhikistan is to move towards the self-management and self-financing envisaged under *perestroika*, the basic conditions under which its economy operates must be put on a more equal footing.[32]

CONCLUSIONS

The present Tadzhik leadership is clearly opposed to separatism, and defends the idea of inter-republic specialisation within the economy of the USSR. The leadership, however, wishes Tadzhikistan to be given greater autonomy in economic decision-making, and would like a realistic price to be paid for Tadzhik cotton. Only in this way might the per capita income of the Tadzhiks, which is the lowest in the USSR, begin to approach average USSR levels.

Ecologically, Tadzhikistan stands in a better position than some of the other Central Asian republics. Even though the Pamir glaciers are reported to have been affected by wind-borne pesticides from the Aral basin, Tadzhikistan appears to have been relatively untouched by the disaster of over-irrigation and rising water tables which has affected the lower-lying areas of Turkmenistan and Uzbekistan, leading to the disappearance of much of the Aral Sea.

A possible source of instability in Tadzhikistan is that a failure of the economic reforms envisaged by *perestroika*, accompanied by rising unemployment and housing problems, might lead to wide-spread disaffection with the present policies of the leadership and exacerbate the existing tensions between the nationalities. The mob violence which took place in the centre of Dushanbe on 12 February 1990, leading to several deaths and the imposition of a state of emergency, seems likely to have been an organised attempt by a Tadzhik faction opposed to the present leadership to destabilise the political situation in Tadzhikistan prior to the election of people's deputies on 25 February.[33]

NOTES

1. *Tadzhikskaya Sovetskaya Sotsialisticheskaya Respublika* (Dushanbe, Glavnaya Redaktsiya Tadzhikskoi Sovetskoi Entsiklopedii 1984), p. 103 (henceforth TSSR).
2. TSSR p. 104.
3. Ibid.
4. *Vsesoyuznaya perepis' naseleniya 17 dekabrya 1926 goda* (All-Union Census of the Population of 17 December 1926) (Moscow 1929). Cited by S. Akiner, *Islamic Peoples of the Soviet Union* (London, Boston,

Melbourne and Henley, Kegan Paul International 1983), pp. 307–8 (henceforth Akiner).

5. TSSR p. 108; Z. Katz (ed.) *Handbook of Major Soviet Nationalities* (New York, Free Press 1975), p. 325 (henceforth Katz).
6. TSSR p. 113.
7. TSSR p. 260.
8. TSSR p. 261.
9. TSSR p. 271.
10. *Kommunist Tadzhikistana* 26 Aug. 1953. Cited by Katz p. 342.
11. *Zhenshchiny v SSSR 1988. Statisticheskie Materialy* Moscow, Finansy i Statistika, 1988, p. 16 (henceforth Zhenshchiny).
12. Zhenshchiny p. 14.
13. TSSR p. 111.
14. TSSR pp. 111, 115.
15. TSSR p. 205.
16. TSSR p. 201.
17. Katz p. 325; Akiner p. 307–8.
18. TSSR p. 54.
19. *Kommunist Tadzhikistana* 19 Feb. 1989, p. 2.
20. Ibid.
21. A full account of this meeting is given in *Kommunist Tadzhikistana* 25 Feb. 1989.
22. *Izvestiya* 23 July 1989. English résumé in *Current Digest of the Soviet Press* XLI (29) 1989.
23. *Kommunist Tadzhikistana* 26 Feb. 1989.
24. *Kommunist Tadzhikistana* 20 July 1989.
25. *Kommunist Tadzhikistana* 28 June 1989. English résumé in *Current Digest of the Soviet Press*, XLI (28) 1989.
26. *Pravda* 25 June 1988. English résumé in *Current Digest of the Soviet Press* XL (25) 1988.
27. *Kommunist Tadzhikistana* 19 Sept. 1989.
28. *Komsomol'skaya Pravda* 8 Aug. 1987. English résumé in *Current Digest of the Soviet Press* XXXIX (32) 1987.
29. *Kommunist Tadzhikistana* 31 Jan. 1987. English résumé in *Current Digest of the Soviet Press* XXXIX (9) 1987.
30. *Narodnoe Khozyaistvo SSSR v 1987g* (Moscow, Finansy i Statistika 1988). Preliminary report of 1989 census in *Izvestiya* 28 April 1989.
31. *Kommunist Tadzhikistana* 20 Jan. 1987. English résumé in *Current Digest of the Soviet Press* XXXIX (14) 1987.
32. *Izvestiya*, 22 Sept. 1989.
33. *Kommunist Tadzhikistana* 15 February 1990.

PART V

NON-RUSSIANS OF THE RUSSIAN REPUBLIC

The Russian Soviet Federated Socialist Republic (RSFSR) is generally regarded as synonymous with ethnic Russia but in reality it is also the homeland of numerous smaller nationalities. Indeed, the proportion of Russians to the RSFSR's total population has into recent times been slowly declining, from 83.3 per cent in 1959 to 81.5 per cent by 1989. Yet only four of the thirty-one territorially recognised native peoples of the Russian republic number more than 1 million (Tatars, Chuvash, Bashkirs and Mordovians), with the Tatars being by far the largest (5.5 million). In many of the non-Russian administrative homelands, the proportion of Russians has grown under Soviet rule, making them the ethnic majority in the Bashkir, Buryat, Kalmyk, Karelian, Mari, Mordovian, Udmurt and Yakut Autonomous Republics, as in some of the more minor administrative homelands. Less urbanised than the Russian communities and with only rudimentary institutional supports compared with the dominant nationality, the non-Russians have a disproportionately smaller intelligentsia willing and able to champion their nationality interests.

Throughout Siberia there are also numerous aboriginal peoples of whom the Buryats and Yakut are by far the largest (see Appendix 2, Table 1). From the inception of Soviet power, the peoples of Siberia were guaranteed equal and free development, which was partly enacted during the 1920s through the creation of administrative homelands and policies designed to improve the region's education, health care and economic resources, and to secure local native representation. Into modern times, however, the pressures for native assimilation into the republic's culturally and socially dominant language and nationality have been considerable, not least due to Moscow's attempts to replace traditional social and economic practices (such as nomadism, the clan system) with a more modern and culturally uniform way of life. Most of the peoples of Siberia have been unable to effect their cultural protection or to champion nationality interests. Even the Buryats and Yakut, despite being better placed due to formal institutional supports, demography and a larger native intelligentsia than other Siberian peoples, have not embraced the opportunities opened up by *glasnost'* to forward national interests on the scale found elsewhere in the Soviet Union.

CHAPTER SEVENTEEN

Volga Tatars

Marie Bennigsen Broxup

Although possessing an administrative homeland in the Tatar ASSR, according to the 1979 census only 25.9 per cent of the USSR's 6,317,468 Tatars live there, the majority constituting large diaspora communities elsewhere, in the Middle Volga and Urals, in Central Asia and Azerbaijan, the Donetsk region of the Ukraine, and in smaller pockets stretching from the western borders of the USSR to the Pacific Ocean (notably in small rural communities in the original homelands of other historical Tatar groups, such as Astrakhan, Kalmyk, West Siberia and the Baltic republics). Within their namesake republic, they constitute a demographic minority (47.6 per cent according to the 1979 census). The Tatars are Sunni Muslims of the Hanafi school and the most Westernised and Russified of the Soviet Muslims.

BACKGROUND

In August 1989, the Muslim Religious Board for European Russia and Siberia celebrated the anniversary of eleven centuries since the official adoption of Islam by the kingdom of the Bulgars. The celebrations were heralded by the Kazan Tatar intelligentsia and political elite as 'the first true national festival' since the khanate of Kazan, heir to the Bulgar kingdom and the Golden Horde, was conquered and destroyed by the army of Ivan the Terrible, in 1552.

Islam was already widely spread on the shores of the Volga and Kama river when Ibn Fadlan, the envoy of Caliph Jafar Al-Muktadir, reached the kingdom in 922, the year which marks the conversion of the Bulgars to Islam. As the Russian historian S.M. Solov'ev wrote:

For a long time Asia, Muslim Asia built here a home; a home not for nomadic hordes but for its civilisation; for a long time, a commercial industrial people, the Bulgars had been established here. When the Bulgar was already listening to the Quran on the shores of the Volga and the Kama, the Russian Slav had

277

not yet started to build Christian churches . . . and had not yet conquered these places in the name of European civilisation.[1]

The Volga Tatars offer a unique example in the history of Dar ul-Islam, that of a Muslim nation which has survived over four centuries of foreign domination. Since the fall of Kazan the Russians have persistently tried to eradicate Islam, considered as an alien and hostile element. This they tried to achieve through several methods, most notably through colonisation and conversion to Christianity.

Military conquest was followed by a systematic policy of colonisation. The ruling classes were ruined, Muslims were expelled from Kazan, their richest lands were confiscated and distributed among the Russian nobility, the Orthodox monasteries and, later, the peasants. Fortresses were built across the region with merchants and artisans brought from Russian cities. Thus by the end of the sixteenth century the former territory of the khanate of Kazan was already ethnically mixed and by the end of the eighteenth century the present territory of the Tatar ASSR had a majority Russian population.[2]

After an initial period of religious tolerance under Ivan the Terrible, Tsar Feodor launched into an energetic missionary activity. As a result, a relatively large group of natives became Christian Orthodox but maintained the use of Tatar as a spoken and liturgic language. (They have survived until today as a separate community, the Staro-Kryashens.) From the Times of Trouble and the reign of the first Romanovs to that of Catherine II various measures were taken to eradicate Islam: mosques were destroyed, *waqf* property confiscated, special schools were opened for the children of Tatar converts, Muslims were expelled from villages where groups of converts had been formed and deported to remote districts, while Muslim proselytism was punishable by death. Peter the Great gave renewed vigour to the Christian campaign. His reign, and particularly that of Anna (1738–55), can be compared in terms of persecutions to the worst period of Stalin's purges: between 1740 and 1743 alone, 418 out of 536 mosques of the Kazan *guberniya* were destroyed.[3] These policies resulted in a massive exodus of the Tatars throughout the centuries towards Turkestan, the Kazakh Steppes and Siberia, in frequent armed uprisings at first led by the feudal aristocracy, and later in an active participation in the great popular uprisings of Stepan Razin and Pugachev. However, Catherine II did correct the dramatic errors of her predecessors. She halted the anti-Muslim campaign and established a Central Muslim Spiritual Board in Orenburg in 1783 and for a century afterwards the Tatar merchant class cooperated loyally with the Russian government.

The conquest of Central Asia put an end to this rewarding part-nership, and new economic and religious pressures were once again brought to bear by the Russian government. In 1863 Nikolai Il'minsky of the Religious Academy of Kazan devised a policy, not unlike that of the early bishops of Kazan, aimed at creating a new Tatar intelligentsia converted to Orthodoxy but speaking and writing Tatar. This policy achieved some spectacular successes.[4] More than economic harassment (a decree of 1886 forbade the Tatars to own property and companies in Central Asia), the policy of religious assimilation was viewed as a deadly danger by the community and gained the Russians the undying resentment of the Tatar elites. However, the Tatar elites were quick to react. They understood perfectly well that in order to survive they had to regain intellectual, cultural and economic equality with the Russians, preserve Islam as the basis of Tatar society, keep the unity of the Muslim *umma* and reject all social conflicts within the community. This awareness resulted in the first and most widely spread modern reformist movement of the Muslim world – Jadidism. The *jadid* movement began as a religious reform (initiated by Shihabeddin Marjani between 1818 and 1889) seeking to break away from conservative traditionalism in order to allow Islam to survive in a modern world. It encompassed all aspects of social life: religion, education, literature, women's liberation and so on.

The movement flourished thanks to an extraordinary unity of purpose between the Tatar *ulema* and the bourgeoisie. At the end of the nineteenth century the cultural level of the Tatars was extremely high: the percentage of literacy was higher among the Tatars than among the Russians in the Kazan *guberniya*.[5] Kazan, Ufa and Orenburg became prestigious intellectual centres rivalling Istanbul, Cairo and Beirut. Spreading from the Volga, Jadidism, strongly imbued with Pan-Islamic and Pan-Turkic ideals, influenced all the Muslim intellectual elites of the Russian empire.

On the eve of the 1905 Revolution, the Tatars were a 'developed' nation with a sophisticated capitalist and even industrial experience. After the defeat of the Russian army in Manchuria in 1905, the *jadid* movement became politicised. Three Muslim congresses were held in quick succession in 1905 and 1906, and a Muslim Union (*Ittifaq al-Muslimin*) was founded under the aegis of the Tatars Abrurrashid Ibragimov, Yusuf Akchura and Sadri Maksudi. The aims of *Ittifaq* were moderate: equal civic rights for the Muslims, freedom of religion, education and press. Despite this, hopes of achieving liberal reforms and national equality were frustrated when in 1908 the monarchy adopted an intransigent attitude towards nationalist demands. As a result the leadership of the national movement became more radical and revolutionary. Confrontation was inevitable and at the time of the October Revolution the Tatar struggle against Russian centrism was at its height. Two factions could be distinguished: firstly, a Pan-Islamic and Pan-Turkic faction, advocating national and cultural extra-territorial autonomy for all Muslim nations within a unified, but decentralised and democratic, state; and secondly, a more narrowly nationalistic faction represented by the socialist and 'leftist' groups which favoured a federal solution and national territorial autonomy.

Revolution and Civil War were fought in all the Muslim territories. Because of the blunders and tactical errors of the White generals, the Bolsheviks were seen by most of the native leaders as a lesser threat to their aspirations. Lenin and Stalin's clever political manoeuvring (the Appeal to the Muslim Workers of Russia and the Soviet East of the Soviet People's Commissar of 20 November 1917), and the concessions they gave to the Muslims while the outcome of the Civil War was uncertain gained the unstinting support of the Tatar nationalists to the Soviet state until 1921.

On 23 March 1918 a decree of the *NARKOMNATS* (People's Commissariat of Nationalities) proclaimed the creation of the 'Tatar-Bashkir Soviet Republic of the Russian Soviet Federation on the territory of Southern Ural and Middle Volga', but the outbreak of the Civil War in May 1918, with the Tatar-Bashkir territory at the heart of the confrontation, rendered the decree meaningless. The hopes of the nationalists for a large Turkic state on the Volga were crushed with the creation on 23 March 1919 of the Bashkir Autonomous Soviet Socialist Republic, followed by the Tatar Autonomous Soviet Socialist Republic on 27 May 1920. The borders of the republics were drawn arbitrarily – they left 75 per cent of the Tatar population outside the boundaries of their nominal republic while in the Bashkir ASSR Tatars represented the majority ethnic group.

From 1921 Tatar national political life and dissent were channelled through the Party. Muslim National Communism soon became a deviation of the Party line, and from 1923 to 1928 became an active opposition movement. The greatest exponent of Muslim National Communism was the Tatar Mir Said Sultan Galiev. The highest ranking Muslim in the Communist Party, he was the son of a Tatar schoolteacher. He joined the Russian Communist Party in November 1917. His rise through the Party hierarchy was meteoric. He became simultaneously a member of the Central Muslim Commissariat (*MUSKOM*), chairman of the Muslim Military Collegium, a member of the little Collegium of the *NARKOMNATS*, editor of *Zhizn'Natsional'nostei*, and a member of the Central Executive Committee of the Tatar republic. The basis of Sultan Galiev's thinking was the idea of 'proletarian nations'. He argued that all the classes of Muslim colonised peoples had the right to be called 'proletarian' because of the oppression imposed by colonisers. Priority had to be given to national liberation, the class struggle postponed indefinitely, and the cohesion of the Muslim society preserved at all costs. He left no doubts as to the identity of the colonisers: the Russians, including the Bolsheviks, whom he considerered totally incapable of solving the national problem. Sultan Galiev wanted to give Marxism a 'Muslim' national face. He campaigned for the establishment of an independent Muslim Communist Party with its own elected Central Committee and for the creation of a Muslim Red Army with Muslim commanders and officers. He hoped to form a Colonial International independent from the Komintern, and a large Muslim-Turkic state – the 'Republic of Turan', which would have stretched from Kazan to the Pamirs. He dreamed of channelling the energies unleashed by the Revolution in the direction of Asia, rather than the industrial West where 'the fire of revolution no longer burned'. Sultan Galiev was arrested, on the personal initiative of Stalin,[6] in May 1923 'for counter-revolutionary nationalist conspiracy against the power of the Soviets'. Freed in 1924, he was arrested again in 1928, tried as a 'traitor' in 1929, and condemned to ten years' hard labour in the Solovki camp. He was executed in December 1939.[7]

VOLGA TATARS UNDER SOVIET RULE

Between 1924 and 1939 the political battle within the Communist Party of the Volga Tatar ASSR (or Tatarstan) was fought by the 'right' – Tatar partisans of Sultan Galiev – and the 'left' – almost exclusively Russian Communists. The tragic outcome was the liquidation of all the Tatar political and intellectual elite. The conflict between the 'right' and 'left' broke out at the 9th Regional Conference of the Communist Party organisation of Tatarstan in May 1924. For the first time, the Tatar 'right' was directly attacked by the Russian Communists. The Tatars were reminded that 'one should not confuse the objectives of World Revolution with the aspirations of the Tatars. Without denying the importance of the rise of oppressed nationalities, one must not forget that the future of the Revolution depends on the West alone'.[8] Furthermore, it was stated that Russian chauvinism did not exist among Russian Communists and that it was merely an invention of the Tatar nationalists aimed at disguising their own subversive activity. Soviet historians recognise today that the brutal politics of collectivisation, confiscation of *kulaks'* lands and the introduction of the class struggle in the Tatar society between 1923 and 1928 was clumsy and gave rise to a violent outburst of Muslim nationalism within the Tatar Communist Party and the *Komsomol*. Indeed, after April 1926, Tatar Communists, previously divided into 'right' and 'left' factions, united in one national front against their Russian comrades, and for two years attempted to block the policy of the Party and of the Russian Communists whom they accused of leading 'an imperialist policy contrary to the national interests of Tatarstan'.[9]

The condemnation of Sultan Galiev was followed by systematic purges. The first victims were Sultan Galiev's companions and the right wing of the Tatar Communists: Keshaf Muhtarov, president of the executive Central Committee of Tatarstan, Kasym Mansurov, head of the propaganda section, Rauf Sabirov, First Secretary of the *obkom*, Gayaz Maksudov, Mikdad Burundukov and many others. All were accused of having created an illegal 'counter-revolutionary, anti-Soviet, anti-Communist and anti-Russian party' under the leadership of Sultan Galiev, with the aim of installing a bourgeois, capitalist regime. Furthermore, they were accused of having contacts with the Basmachi rebels of Turkestan, Milli Firqa (the Crimean Tatar national party), White *émigrés* and British imperialists.

In quick succession, the Party's offensive was then directed against the university, the literary circles, and in 1931 the Communist Party of Bashkiria, which still sheltered many partisans of Sultan Galiev. By 1933 organised opposition had ceased, but the purges continued until 1939 among the Tatar and Bashkir intelligentsia and affected all those – former partisans or opponents of Sultan Galiev – who defended the political or cultural autonomy of native Muslims. (Even linguists opposing the introduction of the Latin alphabet became a target.)

In 1940 the campaign against nationalism slowed down, which allowed the Tatar Mufti of Ufa, Abdurahman Rasulaev, one of the few *jadid* clerics to have survived the religious and political persecutions, to approach Stalin with the proposal of normalising relations between the Soviet government and Islam. Stalin accepted Rasulaev's proposal. A concordat was signed granting Islam legal status and an official Islamic administration.

In the post-war period, Tatarstan underwent an intensive industrialisation and urbanisation programme together with a heavy Russian immigration. This resulted in a dangerous polarisation of society in Tatarstan where the Tatars represented mainly the rural, peasant communities and the Russians the urban industrial workers and technical cadres. Although urban migration began later among the Tatars than among the Russians, it remained fairly steady between 1930 and 1950, the gap between the two communities beginning to widen in the late 1950s. As an example, the percentage difference between the Tatar and Russian urban population in the republic was 13 per cent in 1926, increasing to 28.4 per cent in 1959 and 30.5 per cent in 1979.[10] Altogether, according to the All-Union census of 1979, the Tatars represented only 38 per cent of the urban population of the republic. It is likely that their proportion of the urban population of Tatarstan is continuing to diminish today as import of Russian and other 'European' labour remains uncontrolled, while Tatars from other areas of the USSR wishing to return to their homeland are discriminated against and find difficulty in settling in the cities. As a result of this imbalance the standard of living of the Tatar population has dropped, the level of qualification of Tatar workers is becoming lower than that of the other national groups of the republic, and the proportion of national cadres in key sectors of the economy is unequal to other nationalities. In recent years, inter-ethnic tension has grown, especially in those areas with a high influx of immigrants.

VOLGA TATARS UNDER GORBACHEV

In the post-Stalin era, Tatar nationalism, more sophisticated and less outspoken than nationalism in Central Asia and the Caucasus, could mainly be discerned in the efforts of the intelligentsia to rehabilitate their literature and political history. New information available since *glasnost'* shows that the Tatar intelligentsia is not sheltering behind arcane academic speculations but is once again playing a leading role in the cultural revival and consolidation of the nation.

Of particular importance in this revival has been the founding of the Tatar Public Centre (Tatarskii Obshchestvenyi Tsentr), or TOTs, which held its founding congress in February 1989.[11] To all intents and purposes the Centre fulfils the role of a national front. The decision to create TOTs was taken in June 1988 during the Party Conference by Tatar intellectuals, mainly the staff of the Kazan Filial of the Academy of Sciences and the Kazan State University who felt that the Communist Party could no longer be relied on to defend national interests. The original founder members numbered no more than 100. By the summer of 1989 TOTs claimed to have over a million followers.[12] In less than a year it had gained the wholehearted support of the overwhelming majority of the Tatar elites in the Tatar ASSR and across the Union, and now serves as a coordinating centre for most Tatar informal groups outside the republic. The Centre has the backing of the majority of the Tatar language press as well as that of the Russian language *Vechernyaya Kazan'*, one of the most outspoken and radical daily newspapers in the USSR.

TOTs' manifesto (*Tezisy k podgotovke platformy tatarskogo obshchestrennogo tsentra*).[13] published first officially in Kazan in an abridged form and later in the Baltic republics in an uncensored version clearly defines the political concerns of the Tatars. Some of the problems it addresses are common to all Soviet nationalities, others are specific to the Tatars. Five issues can be singled out.

The first issue concerns questions of federalism and sovereignty. Dissatisfaction with the 'second-rate' status of the Tatar republic has been endemic since the days of Sultan Galiev. In the last two years an active campaign has been unleashed demanding that the republic be upgraded from 'autonomous' to 'union republic' status. This campaign is endorsed by the majority of the Tatar intellectual and political elites (deputies and soviets). The manifesto states in its introductory lines the need for a genuine federal system which would guarantee the sovereignty of all republics and nations of the USSR. Without this fundamental prerequisite there will be no *perestroika*:

In the course of the establishment of the Soviet state various kinds of national-state structures were formed. Some peoples received the status of 'union', others of 'autonomous' national-state structures. Originally the distinction did not presuppose any limitation in the right of the autonomous republics, and did not hold back the development of their peoples. Later, however, nations in our country turned out to have unequal rights and opportunities.

Union status, it is postulated, would be a first step towards national sovereignty, and would increase Tatar representation in the state organisations of the USSR:

TOTs stands for a single status for union and autonomous republics and for the establishment of legal guarantees of the true independence of the Tatar republic in matters of economics, education, the judiciary, health-care, social provision, culture, science and internal affairs. By agreement with the sovereign organisations of the republic it is appropriate to retain within the competence of the central authorities the function of defence, diplomacy, transport, communications, and a range of questions connected with the financing and control of union-level enterprises.

Further, the manifesto boldly states that 'the national republics do not exist for the sake of the central authorities'. The Tatars were the first to pinpoint the absurdity of a system which divides national territories into 'federal' and 'autonomous' republics, providing autonomous republics with all the regalia of a government while denying such basic cultural requirements as an independent Academy of Sciences. This inherent inequality was recently stressed in a scathing article by the Vice-Rector of the Kazan Institute of Culture, R. Khakimov, in an article in *Komsomolets Tatarii*:[14]

It is essential to equalise the rights of federal and autonomous republics as sovereign governments. If a republic exists it must be sovereign otherwise it amounts to no more than an oblast. The notion of an autonomous republic as a government without sovereignty is a juridical and political nonsense.

Further on he writes:

Why should Tataria and other autonomous republics be part of RSFSR if they can be members directly of another federation – the USSR – and thus avoid unnecessary bureaucratic burdens? The RSFSR and autonomous republics are a political anachronism. National tensions are due, among other reasons, to our classification scale of nations and governmental institutions. The USSR is built on the principle of the *matreshka*: there is a federation within a federation, a republic within a republic, in a *krai* we have an autonomous oblast, in an oblast an autonomous *okrug*. The submission of some nations to others, of some republics to others sharply contradicts the principle of equality among nations and is a breeding ground for conflicts.

Other autonomous republics and oblast are gradually following the Tatar example, demanding that the status of their republics be upgraded – Daghestan, Chechnia-Ingushetia and Abkhazia among others. There is no evidence yet that the Russian population of Tatarstan has taken a position on this question.

The second issue focuses on democracy. The Tatar manifesto echoes the aspirations of the other major nationalities for a democratic society, political pluralism, social justice, equality irrespective of national and ethnic origin, freedom of conscience and human rights. To this end TOTs demands popular participation in the legislative process and wide consensus in resolving key problems of national interest through the use of referenda and free elections, with national deputies and soviets representing minority interests.

Thirdly, like the Central Asians and Caucasians, the Tatars resent the drain of the republic's wealth and the management of most of their national economy (98 per cent of the enterprises in the republic are 'All-Union' controlled). Tatarstan has a developed industrial base, a highly productive agricultural sector and a qualified native personnel. As opposed to Central Asia, which is demanding greater industrial investment, Tatarstan is saturated with heavy industries. A number of industrial and oil-producing complexes are being 'squeezed' by two new atomic power stations, and the ecological situation gives cause for concern. What is more, intensive industrialisation has in the past been an excuse for demographic 'manipulation' through massive Russian immigration to the industrial urban centres in order to reduce the proportion of Tatars in their republic. TOTs demands wide public consultation before any further industrialisation of the region and recommends re-siting light industry in the rural and regional centres. Open discussion of the republic's contribution to the All-Union budget is deemed a vital precondition in the transfer to a self-supporting, self-financing economy (*khozraschet*) in 1991–92. Provisions are included in the TOTs manifesto to take account of inflation in determining wages, to create bodies to defend the interests of consumers, and to introduce labour-saving technology.

Perhaps the most interesting and imaginative aspect of the manifesto concerns the fourth issue, which deals with the extra-territorial national, cultural and political jurisdiction of the Centre. In this, one can see an obvious continuity between the new Tatar intelligentsia and their *jadid* forefathers' demands for extra-territorial national autonomy:

Accordingly TOTs is a movement based on two principles, the territorial and the national (non-territorial). The first principle unites citizens with initiative from all groups of the population of the Tatar republic, while the second brings together initiative groups from the Tatar population living beyond the borders of the Tatar ASSR.

Thus TOTs 'considers it essential to elaborate and put into effect a legal mechanism regulating the relations of the republican cultural, educational and scientific bodies with the Tatar diaspora in order to ensure the cultural consolidation of the nation, and its normal functioning as an integrated formation'. Cultural consolidation can, of course, be viewed as a first step to political consolidation, and to this end TOTs envisages, firstly, the creation of national soviets of people's deputies in rural and urban settlement where the Tatar population lives in compact groups or accounts for 50 per cent of the population; secondly, the creation of cultural autonomy in regions of relatively extensive but non-compact Tatar settlements; and thirdly, local associations in regions of limited settlement. Furthermore, TOTs places special emphasis on developing closer cooperation between the educational institutions and mass media of Tatarstan and Tatar colonies outside the republic, in Siberia, Astrakhan, Lithuania and so on (closer links with Tatar colonies outside the USSR are also recommended). Specifically, Tatarstan should take upon itself the role of a cultural homeland for the diaspora by preparing and publishing textbooks, educational literature, newspapers and journals for the whole Tatar population of the USSR, by providing cultural facilities across the republican borders, training national cadres, organising radio and television programmes and films. A permanent representation of the Tatar republic in the RSFSR Supreme Soviet is also demanded.

And finally, there is the Tatars' concern for the fate of their national language, an issue shared by many other Muslim and non-Muslim nationalities of the USSR. However, their problem is particularly acute. After having been a virtual lingua franca in the Russian empire the threat of Tatar disappearing from public life has now become very real (see Appendix 2, Tables 4 and 5). Linguistic Russification is seen by many as a first step to assimilation by the Russians and the loss of national identity. TOTs demands that Tatar be fully reinstated as the state language of the republic together with Russian – that civil servants should learn Tatar, that opportunity for instruction in Tatar be available from kindergarten to higher educational institutions, and that mass media should be available in Tatar. Knowledge of Arabic script and language is also deemed necessary for a revival of the national heritage.

A related issue, with far-reaching implications for the unity of the Turkic people of the USSR, is that of the alphabet. For some time Soviet writers, such as Oljas Suleymenov, have condemned the artificial division of the Turkic languages created during Stalin's *razmezhevanie*, and have suggested a common standard alphabet for all Turkic languages. The linguists have come to the logical conclusion that the Latin alphabet would be far more suitable for Turkic languages than Cyrillic. The political overtones of this debate are made clear in an article of R. Mukhametdinov, 'Let the People Decide Themselves':

How was the Russian alphabet introduced? It was imposed by force in 1939 in all the Turkic-speaking republics following the genocide and terror of 1937 and 1938. We consider that the forcible change to Cyrillic was a crime of Stalin's clique against the Tatar nation, a mockery of the independence and dignity of our nation and culture. The element of compulsion alone has led people to resent this alphabet. Some opponents of the Latin script claim that a change of alphabet would entail a heavy financial burden. But when whole nations were deported and exterminated thousands of trains and soldiers were available.

Money was not spared when our nation was forced to adopt Cyrillic in 1939, although we were poorer then. Should we assume that money is generously spent for crimes and lawlessness, while denied to correct the consequences of these crimes? This would be an endorsement and perpetuation of Stalin's policy. The future political losses would be considerably higher than the financial.[15]

Following its congress in February 1989 until its official registration in July 1989, TOTs was engaged in an intense lobbying campaign and fencing duel with the obkom of the Tatar ASSR. Despite some harassment and accusations of 'extremism', TOTs has come out so far unscathed and unbowed, also managing to coopt members of the government and the Communist Party. Significantly, the main dispute was over the extra-territorial authority of the organisation – the obkom was willing to allow TOTs to play a parochial cultural role in the republic but not that of a potential figure-head for some 7 million Tatars with influence among all the Turkic nations of the USSR.

The role of Islam

After four centuries of religious persecutions, in the name of Orthodox Christianity or atheism, the Volga Tatars have developed an extraordinary capacity for surviving as Muslims. Today they remain, at least in their original homeland of the Middle Volga and Urals, deeply attached to Islam and provide a relatively high percentage of registered clerics and students attending the two Central Asian *madrasas*.[16] The anniversary celebrations organised by Mufti Talgat Tajuddin on 18–26 August 1989 in Ufa and Kazan were a tribute to the Tatar Muslims' perseverance. The festivities could easily have degenerated into a propaganda exercise for the benefit of foreign Muslims as such occasions have done in the past (the conference hosted by the Mufti of Tashkent in August 1980, for instance). They could also have passed unnoticed in general indifference as an obscure religious occasion. Instead, Tatars from all corners of the USSR – intellectuals, political elites, rural masses and working classes – united in a impressive and moving show of support for their ancestral faith and traditions. A recurrent theme was the role of Islam as saviour of the nation from the time of the Mongol invasions to the anti-Islamic persecutions of Stalin's era. The statement that for the Tatars, Islam and nation are inseparable, was made without ambiguity by the Mufti during a reception of the Presidium on 24 August 1989, when he declared that the celebrations were dedicated to all Tatars, whether believers or not.

Following in the footsteps of the jadid *ulema*, the Tatar clerics have thrown themselves into the political and cultural arena of their community. They have taken position with the informal groups; the summer festivities were planned in collaboration with TOTs, while the young imam of Moscow's mosque, Ravil Gainutdin, is a deputy president of Tugan Tel, a rapidly growing and increasingly influential,

Moscow-based, Tatar informal group. This will undoubtedly ensure their personal prestige and that of Islam among their people.

CONCLUSION

From the nineteenth century until the late 1920s the Tatars have played a leading role in the national and political awakening of the Muslim nations of the Russian empire. Their reformist movement was perhaps the most intelligent attempt of a Muslim society to come to terms with modern times. The Muslim world today is still battling with the ethical and practical problem of how to combine Islam and modernism which the Tatar *jadids* solved a century ago. Later, Sultan Galiev became one of the most serious challengers to Stalin and inspired a generation of Muslim and Third World revolutionaries – from Manabendra Nath Roy, Tan Malaka and Ho Chi Minh to the Algerian FLN. Today his ideas ring a prophetic note and can be recognised in the postulations of the peoples' fronts.

The modern Tatar elites have not broken with the enlightened humanist traditions of their *jadid* forefathers. Their unique position, that of a Muslim nation surrounded by infidels, has helped them keep the ideals of Pan-Islamism and Pan-Turkism alive, yet they have rejected the temptation of Islamic radicalism and fundamentalism. Their nationalism is well reasoned and aimed directly at an oppressive centre, and not at less fortunate, weaker nations. On the contrary, the Tatars' informal groups have actively supported other national movements in the Middle Volga (Jewish, Chuvash, Mari), and in the USSR at large (most notably the Baltic Popular Fronts).[17] The Tatars have faced a challenge similar to that of the Muslims in Spain but, whereas El Andalous was lost forever to the Muslim world, the Tatars have endured in the heartland of Russia. The vigorous reaction which we witnessed today will undoubtedly ensure that the Tatars will survive as a nation. What is more, their sophisticated elites may yet again influence the fate of the Muslim nations of the USSR. A young Tatar intellectual told me in jest: 'The trouble is that when other nations rush to their swords, we Tatars rush into print.' This may prove their strongest asset.

NOTES

1. S.M. Solov'ev *Istoriya Rossii s drevneishikh vremen* vol. 5–6 (Moscow 1959–1965), p. 467, as quoted by Azade Ayse Rorlich in *The Volga Tatars – A Profile in National Resilience* (Stanford, CA, Hoover Institution Press 1986), p. 16.

2. Alexandre Bennigsen and Chantal Quelquejay *Les Mouvements nationaux chez les Musulmans de Russie. Le 'Sultangalievisme' au Tatarstan* (Paris, Mouton 1960), pp. 22–3.
3. Rorlich *The Volga Tatars*, p. 41.
4. It was estimated by Il'minsky that 200,000 Tatars were converted, 130,000 alone in the *guberniya* of Kazan. However, most of these new converts – Novo Kryashens – remained crypto-Muslims and returned to Islam after 1905.
5. Bennigsen and Quelquejay *Les Mouvements nationaux chez les Musulmans de Russie*, p. 40, give the following percentage of literacy for 1897: Tatars 20.4 per cent, Russians 18.3 per cent, and, among the other indigenous Volga peoples: Chuvash 8.9 per cent, Mordvins 9.5 per cent, Udmurts 4.8 per cent and Maris 5.8 per cent.
6. L. Trotsky *Staline* (Paris, Grasset 1948), p. 577.
7. There is a campaign presently in Kazan to rehabilitate Sultan Galiev. Several articles have recently appeared: I. Tagirov 'Kem ul Sultangaliev?', *Kazan Utlary* no. 4, 1989, pp. 163–73 (in Tatar); and B. Sultanbekov 'Sultan-Galiev. Lichnost' i sud'ba' *Sovetskaya Tatariya* 24 May 1989 (in Russian). Sultanbekov's objective article based on new archive material provides information on the later part of Sultan Galiev's life and his death generally unknown so far to scholars in the West.
8. Intervention by Korbut *Stenograficheskii otchet IX-oi oblastnoi konferentsii Tatarskoi organizatsii R.K.P. (b)*, pp. 113–14.
9. Gerhard von Mende *Der Nationale Kampf der Russlands Turken* (Berlin 1936), pp. 158–59.
10. Data provided by D.M. Iskhakov 'Sotsial'no-demograficheskie problemy v Tatarskoi respublike' in *Materialy Uchreditel'nogo s"ezda*, TOTs.
11. Some of the information in the following pages is based on impressions gathered during discussions with the staff of the Kazan Filial of the Academy of Sciences, the Kazan State University, members of the Muslim Religious Board for European Russia and Siberia, and Tatar informal groups such as TOTs, the Marjani Society and Tugan Tel during a visit by the author to Tatarstan in August 1989.
12. Information provided by Farid Mirzovich Sultanov of the Kazan Filial of the Academy of Sciences and a leading member of TOTs.
13. See *Central Asia and Caucasus Chronicle* vol. 8, no. 2 (May 1989), pp. 5–9, for an English translation of the manifesto.
14. R. Khakimov 'Avtonomnaya respublika – politicheskii anakhronizm?' *Komsomolets Tatarii* no. 36 (10 Sept. 1989).
15. R. Mukhametdinov 'Pust' reshit sam nakod' *Nauka* (journal of the Kazan Filial of the Academy of Sciences), no. 31 (25 Sept. 1989).
16. Mir-i Arab in Bukhara and Imam Ismail al-Bukhari in Tashkent.
17. In particular, Rafael Fardievich Mukhametdinov, one of the founders of the Marjani Society and a leading member of TOTs, helped the Jewish community of Kazan establish a cultural association. Also when the Russian population of Estonia went on strike in spring 1989 in protest against the new language and nationality law, TOTs advised the Tatar community to give full support to the Estonian National Front.

CHAPTER EIGHTEEN

Buryats

Caroline Humphrey

The Buryats so far are one of the 'quiet' nationalities of Gorbachev's USSR. Mass demonstrations, and new political parties, are only just beginning to occur. The present First Party Secretary of the Buryatskaya Autonomous Soviet Socialist Republic has been in power since before the Gorbachev era. Recent moves towards democratisation have not yet seriously disturbed the existing leadership.

Explanations for this relative quiescence can be seen in Buryat history, their geographical dispersion, encapsulation by Russians, and perhaps the predominantly religious orientation of their earlier culture. They are similar in this respect to the Tuvinians, Yakut, Altaians and the Kalmyks. But beneath the relatively placid surface there is a revival of national self-awareness and discontent. Of all the peoples mentioned, the Buryats had the most sophisticated pre-revolutionary culture, and their strategic position on the main route between Russian Siberia and the countries of the Far East (Mongolia and China) gave them an early understanding of international relations. New organisations on an ethnic basis have been founded, but they are primarily of a cultural rather than a political nature. The chapter will discuss why this should be so.

It will be argued here that only by building on their literate and many-sided cultural past can the Buryats free themselves from the thraldom of the dogma that 'Buryatness equals backwardness', of a hand-tying gratitude, which appears to pose the only way forward as through Russian-dominated institutions.

BACKGROUND

The Buryats, who give their name to the Buryatskaya ASSR, are a people of Mongolian descent, language group and culture. In the medieval period they were a cluster of tribes living around Lake Baikal in south-east Siberia. The establishing of a frontier between the Russian and the Manchurian empires in the 1680s created the political conditions in which the Buryat could emerge as a separate people. However, they were not administratively unified until the Buryatskaya ASSR was created in 1923. The basis of the traditional Buryat economy was livestock herding, which was nomadic in the regions east of Lake Baikal. Here the round felt yurt was the main type of dwelling. These are the grounds for the Stalin-period view of the Buryats as primitive nomads; but this is not all of the story.

The Buryat tribes are said by Soviet historians 'voluntarily' to have entered the Russian empire in the seventeenth century. In fact, they fought, but not having guns were no match for, the Cossack troops sent by Moscow to conquer eastern Siberia. Gradually, during the eighteenth century, Russian peasant settlement increased. The Buryats were forced off the best land. They sent several delegations to the Moscow tsars to plead for land rights, but to little avail. By the end of the nineteenth century, and especially with the completion of the East Siberian section of the railway, the settlers were taking over ever more land, dividing the Buryats into geographically separate enclaves. The lack of political centralisation of the Buryats and their territorial dispersion must be one of the factors underlying the absence of a cohesive opposition today.

However, the land reforms proposed by the tsarist government at the turn of the century, whereby all households were to be allotted equal shares of land, irrespective of whether they were peasant farmers or nomadic herdsmen, aroused bitter anger among almost all Buryats, and were a first spur to organised Buryat nationalism. This could occur because the Buryats had by now developed an educated elite, conscious of Buryat history, and already engaged in a movement for religious and cultural reform and renewal.[1] The key to this is religion.

The underlying religion of the Buryats was shamanism, based on the idea of spirits in nature which can 'possess' human beings and which are to some extent controllable by tribal shamans. But during the eighteenth century Tibetan and Mongolian Buddhist missionaries were sent to the eastern Buryats. They soon had enormous success. By the end of the nineteenth century there were some thirty-six monasteries in Trans-Baikal, one for each tribal enclave, and the spirits of nature were re-named and classified as Lamaist protector deities. It is estimated that around one-fifth of the male population were Buddhist lamas. Pilgrimages were regularly made to Mongolia and Tibet. The reformers alleged that the great economic power of the monasteries and their close ties with the tribal aristocracy had led to degeneration of the ideals of Buddhism. This 'nationalist' anti-land reform, pro-Buddhist renewal movement was, however, also much influenced by Western liberal ideas.

Right through the tsarist period Buryatiya was a region to which political exiles had been sent. The Decembrists are credited by Soviet scholars with much educational work. Some Buryats were able to benefit from the mixture of Buddhist and Orthodox schooling available, which resulted in the emergence of notable scholars such as the orientalist Dorzhi Banzarov (1822–55). By the beginning of this century Buryat intellectual-religious leaders were in contact – even in vogue – with liberal circles in Russia. A Buddhist temple was built in St Petersburg. The independent-minded, radical Buryat intelligentsia, accustomed to acting as intermediaries between the Russians and Mongolians, was determined to preserve and enhance Buryat language and culture. These people were in close contact with certain enlightened Buddhist lamas who began to instigate a reform of the monasteries. Alongside the traditional theological, philosophical, medical, artistic and other schools which had long flourished in the Buryat lamaseries, there suddenly erupted a complete rethinking of Buddhist culture, and an extraordinary flourishing of debate on ethics, politics, language, the morality of law, and the role of religion in everyday life.

It is not clear to what extent these new ideas penetrated among the Buryat herdsmen. Certainly they were opposed by the *taisha* (prince) of the Khori clan and his allies. Some of the monasteries, which had always had a tendency to compete with one another at the best of times, stirred into open conflict with the reformers.

NATIONALITY AS PART OF SOVIET LIFE

The Buryats played little part in the Civil War which established Bolshevik power in eastern Siberia. They were, however, centrally involved in a series of nationalist movements which aimed to set up a 'pan-Mongolian' state in the east. These movements, a resurgence of the forces which had been so active at the beginning of the century, were ideologically incoherent. Though in several cases they were envisaged as Buddhist theocracies, the main goal was independence from both Russian and Chinese domination. Rapidly swept aside in the military events of the revolutionary period, their place was taken by a grouping of the Buryat intelligentsia with socialist inclinations. The people who formed the Buryat National Committee (Burnatskom) were not Bolsheviks and many of them envisaged a socialist state compatible with Buddhism. It was under their aegis that the Buryat-Mongol ASSR was set up in 1923. Its territory included the region west of Lake Baikal, Trans-Baikal, and the Aga steppes east of Chita. Its capital was the predominantly Russian trading town of Verkheneudinsk, later re-named Ulan-Ude ('Red Ude').

During the 1920s the leaders of the Burnatskom were gradually ousted by Bolsheviks, both Russian and Buryat. As the Communist policies gradually became apparent (expropriation of monastic lands, annihilation of clan leadership, a new territorial basis for administration and so on), there was a series of mass emigrations of Buryats. Some of them fled to northern Mongolia, others to Barga (now part of China). The remaining Buryat leaders were still attempting to accommodate socialism with the national culture – for example, by encouraging the setting-up of agricultural communes of Buddhist lamas. But these were regarded with suspicion both by lay believers and the Bolsheviks. With collectivisation in 1929–37 all such experiments were swept aside. There were further mass emigrations and the monasteries became centres of armed resistance. It would not be correct, however, simply to see the new socialist ideas as implemented by Russians in the teeth of Buryat opposition. Many Russian peasants of the region were Old Believers and highly conservative, and many Buryats of the younger generation had become enthused with the new socialist ideology. Russians and Buryats lived mainly in separate farms.

At this period the population of the Buryat ASSR was largely rural. During the 1930s engineering and railway repair workshops were established, together with some mining, lumbering and manufacturing. These industries and the new towns associated with them were populated largely by Russians, mainly people drafted from outside the republic. Rural Buryats were, however, drawn into the mass education programmes. Young people, often orphans or those without extensive kin networks, were brought to boarding schools in the towns and trained for leadership posts (for instance, as Party officials, local administrators and farm leaders). Some of these were even young ex-lamas. The monasteries were brutally crushed and virtually all of them physically destroyed by 1938.

From around 1931 onwards the cultural policy was one of overt Russification combined with moves to detach the Buryats from their Mongolian connections. Histories began to be published tendentiously portraying the pre-revolutionary Buryats as poverty-stricken, illiterate, tribal people, ground under by extortionate princes, lamas and shamans. Most of the leading figures of the Buryat intelligentsia, branded as 'bourgeois nationalists', disappeared in the purges of the late 1930s. The Mongolian script used to write Buryat was abandoned at the end of the 1920s. A brief experiment with a Latin script orthography was short-lived and Cyrillic was introduced instead. The 'official' Buryat language, which had been based on the Selenga dialect (that is, the dialect closest to spoken Mongolian and most appropriate to the Mongol script), was changed to the Khori dialect. This involved a systemic shift of pronunciation away from Mongol, and was difficult for many groups of Buryats to understand. Vocabulary was changed wherever possible to non-Mongol or introduced Soviet terms, and the use of the old words was criticised as 'archaic'. Schooling and school textbooks were increasingly in Russian. By the 1950s Buryat oral epics were being denounced as 'feudal', and archaeologists were 'revealing' that the Western Buryats were not really Mongolian at all but originally a Turkic people, subsequently Mongolised. This process culminated in the break-up and re-naming of the Buryat-Mongol ASSR. In 1937 the ASSR had been much reduced in size: the territory west of Lake Baikal was ceded to the Irkutsk Oblast, with a small Buryat enclave left as the Ust'-Ordynsk National Okrug, and the eastern steppes were relinquished to the Chita Oblast, the Buryat-settled lands of Aga becoming the Aga National Okrug within it. In 1958 the Buryat-Mongol ASSR was renamed the Buryat ASSR.

It does not seem that this reorganisation was a 'divide-and-rule' response by Moscow to any Buryat nationalist move at the period. The Buryats were too bowed down and encompassed by the Russian population for that. Rather, it seems more likely that the Buryat leaders of the ASSR were attempting to ingratiate themselves with Moscow in the face of demands from the more powerful regions of Irkutsk and Chita. But whatever the reasons, the result was an even greater political fragmentation of the people calling themselves Buryat, a situation which has remained to the present day. According to the 1979 census there was a total population of some 353,000 Buryats in the USSR, 58 per cent in the Buryat ASSR, 20 per cent in the Irkutsk Oblast, 12 per cent in the Ust'-Ordynsk National Okrug and 9 per cent in the Aga National Okrug. A further 30,000 Buryats live in Mongolia and between 10,000 and 20,000 in China.

Nevertheless, the Buryats have of course experienced considerable development during the Soviet period, especially in education. Though they constitute only 23 per cent of the population of the ASSR (with Russians providing over 70 per cent and other nationalities about 5 per cent) the Buryats play a disproportionately large part in governmental and cultural institutions and they dominate the rural intelligentsia. Relatively few Buryats are engaged in mining, manufacturing or lumbering. Many remain in agriculture, especially in livestock farming (precise figures are not available). From the 1950s to the early 1980s collective and state farms in the ASSR were subject to the usual Soviet gigantomania of the period. Amalgamated into even larger units, they remained largely ethnically specific (either Buryat or Russian) but unwieldy, covering areas as large as English counties. The farms of the region have never been very successful in general, but this cannot be attributed to lack of training of the workforce. Rather, it seems to have been caused, as elsewhere, by a combination of inappropriate, over-centralised plans, low prices, neglect of infrastructure, mismanagement and general anomie. Probably the Buryats are at least as well-off in rural districts as the Russians, who tend to concentrate in low-paid labouring jobs in agriculture or else in small-town industry. Buryat birth-rates are much higher than those of the local Russians (though not as high as the rates among the peoples of Central Asia).

Because of the policy of supporting national cadres in the ASSR, which gives Buryats an advantage in obtaining white-collar jobs, Buryats have flooded in from the surrounding regions. Western Buryats from the Irkutsk Oblast in particular have left their homeland and moved to the ASSR, abandoning villages to a few remaining families. In the Russian-dominated Irkutsk and Chita regions, on the other hand, Buryats have been at a disadvantage. People have started to complain that the Ust'-Ordynsk National Okrug was left on the side, bypassed by development, its capital town still in effect a decrepit 1940s village, and its economy no more than a raw-materials base for the industry of Irkutsk city.[2]

By the late 1960s the Buryats already gave the impression of being very Russified.[3] The traditional pastoral economy had been swallowed by the collective and state farms with their mechanisation and bureaucracy. Most education was in Russian, and the vast majority of people spoke Russian fluently. Native housing, the octagonal wooden yurt and the round felt tent, had long since disappeared. People lived in long rows of more or less identical wooden houses of the Siberian type. No one except for a few old women wore Buryat national clothing. Utensils, books, pictures, carpets and furniture were manufactured, the standard Soviet issue. Two monasteries had been resurrected after the Second World War, but on a tiny scale, and the lamas had to study Marxism-Leninism before they graduated to religious texts. Folk ensembles appeared in the most clumsy theatricalised approximations to Buryat clothing, which must have been the product of non-Buryat imagination. Yet they were enthusiastically applauded by the shepherds as they portrayed wicked feudal princes, solidarity with Vietnam, and the helping hand of the 'older brother'. People seemed matter-of-fact and secular, if grim and dependent on alcohol, as they struggled to make collectivised agriculture work in the Siberian cold.

But to some extent the impression of Russification, if not Sovietisation, was misleading. People spoke Russian, but they had not forgotten Buryat, nor the domestic side of Buryat culture. Above all, they remembered long genealogies, whole lineages of ancestors, and they still observed the exogamic marriage rules. Almost everyone knew Buryat legends and myths. Sacred places of the spirits of nature were given surreptitious worship. Ancient burial rites were still practised. With the repression of Buddhism shamanism had re-emerged during the war and never entirely died out. But all of this was hidden. Only the occasional drunken brawl in the towns, where Russians and Buryats lived in separate quarters, gave an indication that there might be tension under the surface.

THE BURYATS IN THE GORBACHEV ERA

Although Buryats are only 23 per cent of the population of the ASSR they comprise 50 per cent of the obkom (ASSR) Party apparat, 45 per cent of the raion and city Party cadres, and 60 per cent of the leading officials in the ministries and ASSR administration.[4] In a situation of general criticism of the Party there seems to be an obfuscation in the official line about the significance of these figures. On the one hand, the First Party Secretary in a recent speech stressed the need to renew Buryat Party officials and for an influx of younger, better-qualified people from the native 'core nationality', and on the other hand he stated that the 'national correspondence' in cadres should be carefully assessed.[5] The impression is that an ageing and old-fashioned Party leadership, numerically dominated by Buryats, is now being challenged by go-ahead, better-qualified people, who may well be mostly Russian. This is being expressed by a subdued conflict between the Party and the Komsomol.[6] This pattern is quite different from that found in Union Republics and, as Smith[7] has pointed out, is to be expected in regions where the nationality had no *political* coherence before the Soviet era.

The Party of the Buryat ASSR is unusual even in Siberia in retaining a First Secretary from the pre-Gorbachev era.[8] The leadership seems firmly wedded to a 'conservative' line: warnings are issued that the slogan 'All power to the Soviets!' must not be taken to moderate the influence of the Party or place its leading role in society in doubt; speeches give evidence that the national movements in the Baltic republics are regarded with fear and suspicion, and sympathy is expressed for the Russians of those regions; and there are constant calls for renewal of the best traditions of Bolshevism and ideological work to promote the idea of socialism as the pre-eminent way of life. All of this suggests, of course, that alternative views are rife in Buryatiya.

The Party in the Buryat ASSR has experienced a severe drop in esteem and authority. During 1986–87, for example, 1,198 members and candidate members were removed from Party rolls, 220 for 'hooliganism, drunkenness and moral degradation', 269 were punished by the Party, and 630 received sobering up. In spite of Party regulations, 18 people convicted of crimes, and 25 oblast and raion leaders banned from office, were found again in leadership roles.[9] Young people (of any nationality) are not joining up, and there has been a haemorrhage of members simply leaving the Party, including *nomenklatura* officials[10] and young members of less than five years' standing. It is difficult in some places to find people willing to stand as party secretaries at the lower levels in the hierarchy ('Only let it not be me!').[11] Members are starting to complain about the Party dues deducted from their pay. This is not surprising when we learn that Party officials earn around 35–40 per cent less than the directors and main specialists in industrial and farm enterprises. What is new is the fact that the ideological privilege of Party membership is now being questioned and directly discussed in relation to such subjects as pay.

The question of national representation has been raised in relation to elections to the Soviets, because again, as in the Party, the Buryats have had 50 per cent of the deputies despite their minority status. Buryats feel under threat because in other regions of the RSFSR native peoples have lost out in the recent elections to the Congress of People's Deputies of the USSR. While stressing that ethnic relations in the ASSR are peaceful, the Union of Writers of Buryatiya nevertheless has proposed a new organisation of the elections to the Soviets to prevent bad feeling, whereby each constituency would have both a Buryat and a Russian delegate. The move, they say, is urgently necessary to counter the mistrust and strained relations aroused by the present system.[12] We are left in no doubt that a great deal of bitterness exists between the Buryat and Russian communities.

Despite this kind of rethinking, on the evidence of the elections in 1989 the deputies to the Soviets seemed to arouse as little enthusiasm as their Party counterparts. On their return to Ulan-Ude from the Congress in Moscow they were subject to a barrage of criticism. Why had the 'Buryat' deputies not made speeches? Why had they not spoken up about the ecological damage to Baikal? Why did they vote against Yeltsin? The replies were weak. One deputy, admitting that she had not even applied to speak, responded, 'On such an important occasion one should have something definite and businesslike to propose.'[13] We are presented with a picture of official representatives of Buryatiya (not necessarily themselves Buryats) unused to taking the initiative, and incapable of articulating the views of their constituents. This compounds the problem experienced by all non-Russian nationalities of the RSFSR in getting their voices heard at all, a subject of bitter complaint by those few speakers from these groups at the Congress of People's Deputies.[14]

Rediscovering the nation's history

It is in exploring their past that the Buryats are now bursting into activity. This involves first of all Buddhism and closer links with Mongolia. Even the official institutions are beginning to change. For years the Buryat monastery at Ivolga, re-opened after the Second World War, has been a leader in the 'Buddhists for Peace' movement, which holds Soviet propaganda-type conferences with representatives of Buddhist organisations from all over Asia. But these have become less concerned with condemning imperialism and more involved with religious questions. In 1989 thirty young Buddhists from the USSR, mostly Buryats, went to Ulaan-Baatar to study to become monks, and there were many more who wished to go. The current revival of Buddhism has resulted in closer ties with other Buddhist peoples of the USSR, especially the Kalmyks. There is already a Buddhist temple headed by a Buryat lama in Elista, capital of the Kalmyk ASSR, and in 1990 a Buddhist monastery is to be built there.

One of the signs of the rediscovery of the Buddhist past is the huge popularity of Tibetan medicine, of which the practitioners are mainly lamas. There is also a Centre of Eastern Medicine in Ulan-Ude. The emphasis in Tibetan medicine on ecological relations between plants, on the homoeopathic balance and individual psychology of the patient, has clearly struck a chord of sympathy with the Buryats and even Russians.

However, timidity reigns in public even here. So far publications have stressed the positive value for health of many of the Tibetan practices, and commentators have compared it favourably to the cult of 'psycho-healing' (often by television) now sweeping the USSR. But the roots of Tibetan medicine *in religion* are still often passed over in the most absurd way. For example, Buryat delegates to the 'round table' explained how fortunate they were to be able to lead the country in the study of Tibetan medicine because of the presence in the republic of the 'manuscript collection of folk knowledge of the Eastern people, the Ganjur-Danjur'. No one mentioned that the Ganjur is the Tibetan Buddhist equivalent of the Bible and that the Danjur is the vast collection of commentaries on it.[15] So thoroughly was knowledge of the Buryat cultural heritage erased during the Stalin-Brezhnev periods that it is quite possible that many young Buryats do not know this elementary fact.

For this reason the historical articles now being published must have enormous effect. These range from straightforward accounts of the Buryats who were guides to the Russian explorers of Central Asia and Mongolia in the nineteenth century to the more sensitive subject of Zhamsaran (Piotr) Badmayev, the Aga Buryat who was both a Christian and a doctor of Tibetan medicine at the tsarist court. For decades Badmayev was reviled as the charlatan doctor of 'odious types'. But recently his name has been rehabilitated, and his grandson has written a widely-published memoire of him.[16] This describes not only the many unfashionable patients in need tended by Badmayev himself but also how his wife and Buryat lama students carried on his work in Leningrad until 1937–38 when they were arrested. Despite the danger of such activity, Badmayev's family and descendants continued to pass on the recipes for Tibetan medicine and to collect them into a book. Newspaper accounts of other prominent Buryats unjustly arrested in the 1930s are now occasionally published, and readers are asked to contribute photographs and memoirs to the Museum of the History of Buryatiya. But as yet there is no complete account of the Burnatskom period, and it is worth noting that the publicity given to Badmayev originated in Leningrad, not in Ulan-Ude.

An article about the late 1930s is interesting in that it enables us to see just how far *glasnost'* has progressed in relation to Buryat nationalism of the past.[17] The author, a Buryat agent of 'Smersh', went into Mongolia on foot, in a variety of ingenious disguises entirely suitable for a thriller, with the aim of unmasking Mongolians acting as undercover agents for the Japanese. The point is, however, that these Mongolians were followers of De Wang – namely, Prince Demchukdongrub, the nationalist leader of the Inner Mongolian movement for independence from the Chinese. It is true that De Wang, having obtained no support from the Soviet-dominated Mongolian People's Republic, was forced unwillingly to accept Japanese patronage against overwhelming Chinese forces. But the Buryat author has little sympathy for him. The article calls him a 'Japanese puppet', assumes that his followers were working for the Japanese, and says not a word about the Inner Mongolian struggle for independence. We are forced to conclude that current Buryat nationalist stirrings stop short at wider Mongolian sympathies, or at least that they have not yet succeeded in pushing *glasnost'* to allow a radical re-analysis of this period.

Nevertheless, the old stereotype of the pre-revolutionary Buryats as primitive illiterates is at last being discredited. All aspects of the earlier *culture* (if not political history), from the use of the Mongolian script in the 1920s to the didactic teachings of the monasteries, can now be mentioned with pride, and a little caution.

Major issues related to the nationalities in the Buryat ASSR

Undoubtedly the most important current issue is the Buryat language. By the mid-1980s Buryat lobbying had succeeded in having the Buryat language reinstated in all schools, at least as a taught subject if not the medium of instruction. But still many young Buryats in the cities do not know their own language, or else have a much impaired command of it. To help in this situation the newspaper *Pravda Buryatii* started in early 1989 to publish an innocuous little column of Buryat conversational phrases, vocabulary and so on. This aroused an amazing degree of controversy. Many Buryats wrote in to thank the newspaper and to request the re-publication of Buryat grammars and dictionaries (which are still not available). But Russians wrote to complain about the 'ideological group' behind the column and to ask why they were being 'compelled' to learn a language of such limited usefulness. Other Russians responded that they had lived in Buryatiya for years and wished to have the possibility of learning the language of the native people. Behind all of this is the suggestion that Buryat should become the state language. This was officially criticised as showing disregard for the Russian majority, but it nevertheless re-emerges disguised in Marxist forms, such as linking it to the ethnic division of labour. One Buryat 'veteran of labour' wrote to say that since the agricultural livestock-breeding part of the economy is dominated by Buryats and the trade and services part staffed mainly by Russians, the time has come when all Russians should learn Buryat in order to improve economic results.[18]

Many contemporary problems in the Buryat region have little or no ethnic dimension. The difficulties with the new leasing system in agriculture, the dreadful living conditions in many rural areas, the huge rise in crime, bad sanitary conditions and epidemics in certain regions, the alcohol and drugs problem (marijuana grows wild in the region), the future of *neperspektivnyye* ('without prospects') villages, the low morale of the police and their alienation from the population, all apparently apply to Russians and Buryats alike.

More surprising, perhaps, is that, as far as it is possible to tell, ecological issues are also rarely seen as a 'national' problem. There is no doubt that the impurity of Lake Baikal and the River Selenga is important in local and national politics. The problems have been caused in the main by the cellulose industry, and effluents from Ulan-Ude and particularly from Severo-Baikal'sk. The Buryats might understandably identify the pollution with Russian incomers. But all the evidence is that it is Siberian Russians, not Buryats, who are most vocal on this issue. The writer Valentin Rasputin is famous for his publicity over many years on behalf of the purity of sacred Lake Baikal. By 1989 the 'Baikal Fund' was the focus of benefit concerts in Moscow by rock groups and experimental dance companies. It is also Russians who have suffered most from the consequences of pollution. Most of the lakeside dwellers are Russian, and the town of Severo-Baikal'sk, which suffered an epidemic earlier this year due to insanitary polluted conditions, is also predominantly Russian. Voluntary work days on behalf of the 'Baikal Fund' near Ulan-Ude are organised by Russians at least as often as by Buryats and are patchily attended.

A multi-disciplinary scientific study on 'Man and his Habitat Round Lake Baikal' is being proposed for the 1990s. This looks as though it will be at the leading edge scientifically combining environmental work with geography, experimental medicine, ethnography, economics and new subjects such as 'ethnic ecology' and 'eco-pedagogics'.[19] The point to note here is that this is a *regional* as opposed to an ethnic initiative, and the scientists' nationality seems to be irrelevant.

Nationalist activities and national organisations

It is now possible for Buryats to state openly that the division of the original Buryat ASSR was a 'mistake'. There have been calls published in the newspapers, from Buryat intellectuals and others, for the name 'Mongol' to be reinserted in the name for the republic and for the ASSR to be recombined with the two Buryat autonomous okrugs in Irkutsk and Chita oblasts. They say that the native terms '*aimak*' and '*somon*' for '*raion*' and '*selo*', used in Mongolia but abandoned in Buryatiya, should be reinstated. All of this is discussed in the same breath with the state of the Buryat language, young people's knowledge of their history, and the obliteration in the Stalin period of cultural links with Mongolia.[20] In other words, this move, although it is certainly interpreted by its opponents as 'nationalist', is really culturally rather than politically focused.

The evidence is that the government of the ASSR has at best only taken note of these protests. Its present line is that there should be 'wider relations' with the two okrugs; unification is not mentioned. The question is *not* attached to discussion of regional economic self-accounting (*khozraschet*). Indeed, the Party criticises the Buryat intelligentsia for giving insufficient help in solving the social, economic and ecological problems this will involve.[21] In the face of Russian accusations of nationalism, the Buryat response tends to be that 'national consciousness' is not the same as nationalism and that it is the former they want.

In the past two years numerous 'informal' clubs, societies and cultural centres have arisen in the Buryat ASSR. There are more than 100 of these in Ulan-Ude. They are local and spontaneous, based on streets or districts or even on young people of a block of flats. Here, as in many other parts of the Soviet Union pro-reform groups are opposed by ones with a conservative-military orientation.

Buryatiya has its own section of the People's Front for the Assistance of Perestroika (NFCP) and of the Baikal Fund and other ecological groups. The first of these is regarded with some suspicion by the authorities as 'ideologically undirected', permeated by demagogy, and having insufficient participation by people in leadership positions. A specifically Buryat group is the 'Geser Society', named after the famous epic, which aims to promote the Buryat language and 'consolidate the Buryat nation'. Unofficial Buddhist circles exist and are in vogue, as at the beginning of the century, in metropolitan intellectual circles. As against all of these there has been a growth of youth clubs, with both Buryat and Russian names, which engage in military-patriotic training. They are led as a rule by former 'soldier-internationalists' (usually a term for veterans of the war in Afghanistan).

All of the above seem to be 'informal' (that is, not established by the authorities) and possibly rather incoherent. There is one new initiative, however, which is well planned and set up with watertight academic and legal underpinning. This is the projected Centre of Buryat Culture.[22] It has as its aims the 'multi-faceted renaissance of Buryat national traditions with the purpose of creating a harmonic Buryat socialist culture, equal in value among the cultures of the USSR'. The basis for this is to be the 'mass creative appropriation of the historical past'. The contributions of shamanism and Buddhism, mythology, epic poetry and architecture are all mentioned. The centre is to be independent and to finance itself with donations. Clearly, direct foreign links will be encouraged. It is interesting that these specifically include Buryats living outside the USSR, whose existence has hardly been acknowledged till now. The Centre will have its own publishing section and it will provide courses in Buryat and in the Mongol script. Furthermore, it will also offer psychotherapeutic counselling for people involved in personal and ethnic disputes.

CONCLUSIONS

There is a pattern in Buryatiya, a political timidity combined with cultural resurgence, which may be repeated among several other peoples of the USSR. When generations of Soviet-educated youth have been instructed that their past glimmers backwards only into dark tribalism, and when the heroic propaganda picture of the Russian 'first teacher' is still alive and well, when past economic prosperity is denied and labelled 'feudal exploitation', when earlier Buryat political leaders are only gingerly brought out one by one and half dusted down, we need not be surprised at the timidity, or lack of imagination about a 'national' political alternative. The majority of Buryats today are still rural, and, furthermore, many town-dwellers think of themselves as a rural people, partly because that is all they were taught about their past. They look around and see the sheer, barren hardness of the present farming life, and this is what they mistakenly still identify as 'ours'; the city is 'theirs'. So, for some young urban people, the emphasis on being Buryat involves a frightening descent or estrangement from all that is progressive and successful. Increasingly alliance with an independent Mongolia is coming to seem an alternative, but because of Soviet administrative and language policies this issue undoubtedly divides the Buryats.

It is entirely rational therefore for the Buryat intelligentsia to concentrate on the recovery of the *cultured* past for the Buryat people as a whole. Unless this is done, unless in fact the aims of the Centre of Buryat Culture are achieved, there will be no basis for a national political movement, and the Buryats will remain merely the divided recipients of the 'reform from above'. It is entirely possible that such a coherent movement will never happen. As mentioned above, the basis for a regional alignment also exists, joining both Siberian Russians and Buryats in problems which concern them both, above all the environment and the economy.

NOTES

1. K. M. Gerasimova, *Lamaizm i natsional'no-kolonial'naya politika tsarizma*

v zabaikalye v XIX i nachale XX vekov (Ulan-Ude, Buryat Filial of the Academy of Sciences 1957).

2. *Pravda Buryatii* 31st Aug. 1989, p. 2.
3. Caroline Humphrey *Karl Marx Collective: Economy, Religion and Society in a Siberian Collective Farm* (Cambridge, Cambridge University Press 1983).
4. *Pravda Buryatii* 10 Sept. 1989, p. 2.
5. Ibid.
6. The Komsomol newspaper *Molodezh Buryatii* (Youth of Buryatiya) has been publishing articles highly critical of the Party and in its turn has been given an old-style dressing-down by the Obkom leadership, which at the same time castigates itself for a weakening in control over Komsomol activities.
7. G. E. Smith 'Gorbachev's greatest challenge: perestroika and the national question' *Political Geography Quarterly* 8 (1) 1989, pp. 7–20.
8. The First Secretary, A. M. Belyakov, a Russian, has been in power since 1984.
9. *Pravda* 18 June 1988, p. 2.
10. In the years 1986–9 it is reported that 386 *nomenklatura* Party officials were sacked, either because they were unable to fulfil their duties correctly or because they were 'compromised' (*Pravda Buryatii* 10 Sept., p. 2).
11. *Pravda Buryatii* 27 Aug. 1989, p. 2.
12. *Pravda Buryatii* 20 Sept. 1989, p. 2.
13. *Pravda Buryatii* 16 June 1989, p. 1.
14. O. Glebov and J. Crowfoot *The Soviet Empire: Its Nations Speak Out* (Chur and London: Harwood Academic Publishers 1989), pp. 93–101.
15. 'Iz sokrovishch drevnikh znanii' *Pravda Buryatii* 17 Sept. 1989, p. 3.
16. B. Gusev 'Badmayevy: legendy i fakty', *Nedelya* 15, 1988.
17. Ts. Tsyrendorzhiyev 'Po sledam shpionov' *Pravda Buryatii* 1 Aug. 1989, p. 4.
18. *Pravda Buryatii* 12 Sept. 1989. p. 1.
19. I. S. Urbanayeva and G. V. Manzanova 'Man and his habitat around Lake Baikal: past, present and future of the anthropological complex in Lake Baikal region' Programme for International Studies, Ulan–Ude: Buryat Research Centre USSR Academy of Sciences Siberian Department 1989.
20. See, e.g., articles in *Pravda Buryatii* on 31 Aug. 1989 and 1 Sept. 1989, and *Pravda* 20 Feb. 1989.
21. *Pravda Buryatii* 10 Sept. 1989, p. 2.
22. A copy of the project for the statutes of this centre was kindly made available to me by John Massey-Stewart.

CHAPTER NINETEEN

Yakut

Piers Vitebsky

BACKGROUND

The Yakut inhabit an area of north-eastern Siberia roughly the size of India. In 1989 they numbered 382,000. Apart from the Buryat, they are the only one of the thirty or so native peoples in Siberia and the Soviet Far East who number more than a few thousand. The origin of the Yakut is much debated. Their language is Turkic but with strong Mongol influence, and they are thought to have migrated northwards from around Lake Baikal in the Middle Ages, driven out, according to their own legends, by the Buryat. Unlike the larger Turkophone groups in Central Asia, from whom their language is now quite distant, the Yakut have been untouched by Muslim influence. The name 'Yakut' is a Russian corruption, through Evenk, of their own name 'Sakha'.

The Yakut brought with them a southern Siberian economy based on horses and cattle. Given the extreme climatic conditions of this mountainous Arctic and sub-Arctic region (with winter temperatures frequently as low as minus 70°C), they settled along the meadows of the middle Lena and the lower Vilyui and Aldan rivers, which provided suitable grazing. This contrasted with the hunting and reindeer-herding economies of the earlier, much smaller populations, mainly Even (Lamut), Evenk (Tungus) and Yukagir, who were absorbed or displaced into the uplands. Partly out of ecological necessity, the Yakut were influenced in turn by these peoples and adopted local traits, in the far north even including reindeer herding.[1] The Yakut thus came to occupy the centre of a world in which they dominated the smaller peoples in peripheral regions, not long before they themselves were to become gradually marginalised by the Russians.

The rich tradition of Yakut historical legends depicts a society of violent warfare and cattle raiding between patrilineal lineages under leaders called *toion* (itself a Mongol word). The greatest of these was Tygyn, who in the early seventeenth century conquered numerous other clans to form a chiefdom.[2] However, Tygyn failed to dominate his own clansmen and finally lost his power with the arrival of the Russians. The Russians came in quest of fur and established a fort at Yakutsk in 1632. Despite several uprisings the *toions* were subdued, permanent hostages taken and the population made subject to the tsar's fur tax (*yasak*). Yakutsk became the centre of the Russian population in eastern Siberia[3] and provided the main staging post for further Russian conquests towards the Pacific, which they reached with astonishing speed by 1641 – that is, before they had reached Kiev or the site of Leningrad. Though Russians encouraged some agriculture, they adopted many techniques of survival from the Yakut. Wealthy Yakut employed poor Russians. There was frequent intermarriage, and so few were the Russians that, unlike elsewhere in Siberia, they often adopted the Yakut language and forgot their own.

From an estimated 28,500 at contact[4] the Yakut had reached 226,000 by the first census of 1897. From the mid-seventeenth to the early nineteenth centuries, they were almost the only group in north-eastern Siberia apart from the Russians to increase in numbers.[5] They also became excellent traders. By the late eighteenth century, when the forests had been largely stripped of furs, the Yakut migrated increasingly to outlying areas, where they continued to displace or absorb smaller groups. But by the mid-nineteenth century the Yakut were declining under the burdens of disease, bad diet and poor housing,[6] caused by a progressive over-use of resources which was compounded by the gold rush of the 1850s.

The region's lawlessness was exacerbated by the exile there during the nineteenth century of criminals and convicts. But there were also political exiles, who included Decembrists, Populists, Social Democrats and Polish nationalists, writers such as Chernyshevskii and Korolenko and revolutionaries such as Yaroslavskii, Ordzhonikidze and Petrovskii. A Cyrillic Yakut alphabet was developed early in the nineteenth century and has since been progressively refined. Towards the end of the century a Yakut intelligentsia was receiving education in Tomsk and elsewhere and, influenced by exiles, was seeking ways to amalgamate socialism with their own cultural heritage. They also flirted with *oblastnichestvo*, the idea of an independent Siberia of which Yakutiya would have formed only a part. Yakut newspapers appeared by the early twentieth century and an indigenous nationalist 'Society of Yakuts' was founded in 1906 and suppressed soon after. The young Yakut intelligentsia of this period was later to be described in a Soviet work as 'by their class affiliation . . . inclined to the toyon camp, and . . . infected with nationalism'.[7]

THE SOVIET PERIOD: PROBLEMS OF RECONCILING SOCIALISM WITH NATIONALISM

The struggle to establish Soviet power in Yakutiya was long-drawn-out. The White officers, Kolchak and Pepelyaev, were active in the area, the latter until 1923. A linguist called Novgorodov, who had produced a modified Yakut alphabet based on the international phonetic script, founded a cultural society called Sakha aymakh (the Yakut Nation) and a federalist party, which hoped to rule under the anticipated state of autonomy. Support for the society among the Yakut intelligentsia was widespread, and membership in November 1917 stood at 1,198.[8] Bolshevik support by contrast was much lower, with membership standing at 30 in 1919 and 353 in 1921,[9] these figures including only a handful of Yakuts.[10] This was due largely to the Bolsheviks' uncompromising stand on the national question. In 1918, Yakut nationalists and socialist revolutionaries formed their own national soviet, in defiance of Petrograd and Irkutsk, whereupon a Red Army detachment came from Irkutsk and imposed Soviet power in Yakutiya, an imposition which was itself short-lived.[11]

The relationship between autonomy and nationalism was already problematic for the Bolsheviks. It was discussed, for example, at a meeting of the Siberian Bureau of the CPSU Central Committee in 1921, well before the final defeat of Pepelyaev. Here opinion was split. Whereas some argued that the granting of autonomy was required by Soviet nationality policy, others countered that it would not raise revolutionary spirit among Yakut workers and would leave the region open to seizure by Japan and America.[12] In 1922, however, Yakutiya was constituted an Autonomous Soviet Socialist Republic (ASSR). Various forms of nationalism, such as 'Pan-Turkism', an ideal which looked ultimately to Turkey, remained widespread among the intelligentsia. These were eliminated only progressively, for example, with the disbanding on Moscow's orders in 1928 of the 'Yakut Nation' society and the dismissal of the Yakutsk Obkom (Regional Party Committee). In 1930–31, substantial outlying areas of the republic were assigned to indigenous non-Yakut minorities such as the Even as subordinate autonomous regions (*raion*). But with a hardening of the ethnic climate in the later 1930s, these raions were abolished and the Yakuts themselves subjected to severe conformist pressure.

The task facing the new Soviet administration was daunting. The Yakut population had reached a dire state. In 1925–26 a medical survey[13] found widespread respiratory diseases, parasitoses, ulcers and blindness. In a large sample, child mortality was 61 per cent and smallpox rampant, over 35 per cent had tuberculosis in clinically apparent form and 45 per cent trachoma. The investigators considered only 14 per cent of the population to be adequately clothed in winter.[14] Collectivisation and social reconstruction were begun against the background of both this and the prolonged civil war. The emphasis was on collective farms (*kolkhoz*) rather than state farms (*sovkhoz*),[15] but *kolkhozes* were both small and few and by 1930 encompassed only 13 per cent of all holdings. There were difficulties in striking a balance between forcing the pace, which provoked incidents, and going slowly by adapting the process to local economic and socio-political conditions.[16] Whereas numbers of horses and cattle rose sharply during this period, wealthier reindeer herders destroyed around half the reindeer in Yakutiya, partly to avoid being labelled as *kulaks*, or rich farmers.[17] After 1930, the pace of collectivisation was intensified.

Yakutiya is endowed with exceptional mineral wealth, as well as vast forests. Already in 1922, the granting of autonomy by Moscow had been linked to the struggling young Soviet state's need for Yakutiya's natural resources, especially gold.[18] Development of the Aldan fields was intensified, and during the 1920s they were producing almost a quarter of the gold in the USSR.[19] Since the end of the Second World War, exploitation of these resources has greatly accelerated. Western Yakutiya now supplies most of the USSR's diamonds. There is natural gas on the River Vilyui, and coal and iron ore at Neryungri, forming the focus of the South Yakutian Territorial Production Complex which has close trade links to Japan. This is served by the Baykal–Amur Magistral (BAM) railway, described in the 1970s as the 'project of the century', now nearing completion and with an arm beginning to reach northwards to Yakutsk. Apart from this, Yakutiya has few roads and much transport is by light aircraft. The main highway is the River Lena, which at its delta joins the Arctic Ocean's Northern Sea Route along which ships run under icebreaker escort between Murmansk and the Far East.

These difficulties of transport make the region vulnerable. In an otherwise steady growth since the first census in 1897, the number of Yakuts dropped slightly between 1926 and 1939, from 234,000 to 233,000 (some versions give a bigger drop). While some writers attribute this to children of mixed marriages calling themselves Russian,[20] another explanation is that, in addition to purges of the late 1930s, troop movements associated with the Japanese invasion of China in 1936 jammed the trans-Siberian railway, causing widespread famine in the hinterland.[21]

The extraction of timber and minerals has caused an in-migration which has increased throughout the Soviet period. This has involved both free labour and prisoners. From the late 1930s until the early 1950s, Yakutiya experienced a revival on an enormous scale of its traditional role as a place of exile and punishment, especially around the River Kolyma, where the Far Eastern Construction Agency (*Dal'stroy*) was given absolute authority over north-eastern Yakutiya and adjoining territories and ran numerous labour camps. The in-migration of free labour has increased especially since the 1960s with the growth of large-scale development projects such as the BAM railway. Immigrants from European parts of the USSR are attracted by a combination of idealism (conquering the virgin landscape, contributing to their country's economic development) and a system of bonuses (*nadbavki*) and privileges for working in the North. The effect has been to create large Russian enclaves with a high turnover but an overall rate of increase. The republic's population of 287,300 in 1926 included 236,000 Yakuts, whereas in the 1979 census they numbered 314,000 out of a total population of 851,800, thus forming a considerably lower proportion. Many of the immigrants live in industrial centres, so that the republic also shows an accelerating overall shift from rural to urban settlement.

The struggle for collectivisation and related forms involved opposing not only '*kulaks*' but also the key figures of the shaman (spirit medium) and the *toion* (chief). Shamanism and 'toionism' (*toionatstvo*) have throughout the Soviet period been associated with 'bourgeois nationalism'. But because the roles of shaman and *toion* were intimately intertwined with Yakut culture and were legitimated in the tradition of epic poetry, they have been adapted to contemporary purposes in a way which perhaps failed ever to resolve the balance between national culture and Bolshevism.

The career of Platon Oiunskii, now considered the key figure in Yakut cultural history, epitomised this. He was the first President of the Soviet Republic of Yakutiya. But he was also a consummate singer of the traditional epic called *olonkho*, who transcribed it from the oral tradition and developed it as a literary form. The pseudonym 'Oiunskii' is derived from the Yakut word for shaman (*oiun*), and in one of his major poetic works, *The Red Shaman*, the central character is a shaman – perhaps representing Oiunskii himself – who defends his people against exploitative *toions* and predicts a radiant future for them. Where shamanic images had earlier been used by Kulakovskii (a distinguished Yakut ethnographer and writer) in his poem *The Shaman's Dream* to predict the destruction of the Yakut people under Soviet rule and to urge resistance to the last man, Oiunskii called Kulakovskii's poem the work of a 'raving nationalist and typical advocate of the struggle against the Russians'.[22] Though he had already been attacked in 1930 by young radicals, Oiunskii none the less became President of the republic's Union of Writers in 1935. But the purges of the late 1930s liquidated not only the remaining confederalists,[23] but also many prominent Yakuts who had fought to set up Soviet power, such as Oiunskii himself and the First Secretary of the republic's Communist Party, M. A. Ammosov. Despite their efforts on behalf of the Revolution, Oiunskii and others like him were now accused of being too attached to Yakut culture.

In 1944 a book appeared by a Yakut historian[24] which restored the positions of Kulakovskii and two other discredited Yakut writers, Neustroev and Sofronov. These were now called progressive 'enlighteners', on the grounds that their nationalism had opposed the oppression of tsarism. This book seems to have gone unnoticed in Moscow until

1951, when it was denounced in *Pravda* in an article which generally criticised the use in Yakut literature of archaic images to discuss modern realities.[25] This was followed in 1952 by a decree of the Yakutsk Obkom 'On bourgeois-nationalist distortions in the illumination of the history of Yakut literature'. This stated that pre-revolutionary Yakut literature had called on the Yakuts to adopt a confrontational attitude towards the Russians, that Sofronov and Neustroev had taken part in anti-soviet plots and White banditism, that Kulakovskii had supported Pepelyaev and Kolchak, and that all three had reflected the interests of the toionate and the rising Yakut bourgeoisie and *kulak* class.[26]

Many of these writers were rehabilitated after Stalin's death in 1953. The harsh tone of the 1952 decree was softened by a revised decree of 1962, which, however, still endorsed the former decree's stand on 'the struggle against survivals of nationalist attitudes' which had 'played a well-known positive role'.[27] In 1959 a collection of articles was dedicated to Oiunskii on what would have been his sixty-fifth birthday, followed by the rapid growth of his cult as a national hero. He was hailed as a founder of Yakut socialist realism,[28] and the national theatre in Yakutsk was named in his honour. During this period, the distinction between sovietisation and Russianisation remained problematic. Yakut resentment against Russians (and other equivalent European immigrants) was matched by a Russian tendency to brand Yakuts as primitive. It is known that fighting broke out in Yakutsk in 1979, and the Ukrainian Christian exile Vyacheslav Chornovil, who reports this, was so intimidated by the atmosphere of violence and mutual insult throughout his stay in the area that he petitioned the authorities to change his place of exile.[29] During the 1970s there were already signs of a growing confidence in Yakut identity. For instance, it became not uncommon for children to be given Yakut names, many of them dating from the old epic tradition, instead of the usual Russian (and thus ultimately Christian) names. For example, girls were named Nyurguyana, Sardana, Sargilana or Tuiara, and boys Nyurgun, Sarial or Timir. An extreme form of this, rather than to incorporate such names into the Russian format of name, patronymic and surname, is simply to adopt a single Yakut name, as was done in the pre-Russian period. An example of this is the writer Tumarcha,[30] who is a member of the editorial committee of the journal of the Yakut Writers' Union, *Polyarnaya Zvezda* (Polar Star).

THE GORBACHEV PERIOD: NATIONAL CONSCIOUSNESS AND THE SHIFT TOWARDS ENVIRONMENTALISM AND INCREASED AUTONOMY

Yakutiya is not a union (*soyuznaya*) republic, like the territories of most of the peoples in this volume, but only an autonomous republic. Despite its designation, an autonomous republic is a lower territorial category and has less real 'autonomy' than a union republic. As indeed does the whole of Siberia, Yakutiya lies within the Russian Federation (RSFSR). The RSFSR acts effectively as an encompassing union republic except that it is very much larger and is centred on the heartland of the Russian people, who clearly dominate it. Given that Yakutiya has less room for manoeuvre than do the union republics, modern forms of ethnic radicalism have been slower to develop here in response to the possibilities offered by Gorbachev's accession to power. The First Secretary, Yu. N. Prokop'ev, is a Yakut who has studied literature and has been in the post since 1982. He was a speaker at the 27th Congress of the CPSU in early 1986, and in 1988 was praised in *Pravda* for economic performance in work on the Yakut section of the BAM railway, as well as for introducing *glasnost'* into Party work. Prokop'ev now argues for greater autonomy from Moscow and urges that the status of Yakutiya should be raised from an autonomous republic to a union republic. At the same time, however, he is emphatic in his speeches that this should not be seen as anti-Russian or indeed as ethnically based, but rather as a matter of regional devolution and self-determination.

In these arguments he is in tune with Moscow's commitment to decentralisation and appears to be supported by his administration. However, it will be shown below that other figures in Yakut public life – for example, some writers – argue for a more radical, ethnically based approach to autonomy. This radicalism does not, however, appear to have been closely reflected in the elections of People's Deputies in 1989. The deputies elected for Yakutiya were V. P. Larionov, Director of the Institute for Physico-Technical Problems of the North; S. V. Boikov, a metal-working foreman; M. A. Micheev, a building foreman in the South Yakutian coalfields; and P. D. Osipov, a village Party Secretary.[31] The contrast is apparent when one considers that several areas inhabited by small native minorities elsewhere in the RSFSR, even if numerically dominated by Russian and other immigrants, have elected militant native writers and environmentalists as their People's Deputies.

However, there is a considerable spirit of reform in the air. The repudiation of Stalinism under Gorbachev is inevitably linked to a favourable reassessment of the Yakut national question and to a call for the unqualified completion of the rehabilitation of those who were killed. As the Yakut writer Tumarcha put it in his letter to the Moscow-based magazine for northerners, *Severnye Prostory* (Northern Open Spaces), 3,000 people were arrested in Yakutiya, 'principled, open, conscientious' people caught by the accusation of nationalism, a 'bogey-man' which 'literally paralysed the local intelligentsia and bound it hand and foot'.[32] In 1988 an article entitled 'A Worthy Memorial to the Victims of Stalinist Repression in Yakutiya' appeared in the newspaper *Molodezh Yakutii* (Youth of Yakutiya),[33] written by a man whose father had been arrested during this period. Readers' replies included one from a man who had himself been arrested and had been the only one of his group of companions to have survived;[34] he confirmed that he had known the father of the author of the article as an upright man and called for the establishment of a museum dedicated to such victims. Another reader writing in the same issue referred to an earlier biographical dictionary of those who had died for the establishment of Soviet power in Yakutiya and urged the publication of a similar volume for those who had died in the 1930s to 1950s. Thus the patriotism and ideological rectitude of the latter are being equated to those of the former.

In 1989 the Yakutsk Obkom completed the work, left unfinished in 1962, of rescinding the 1951 decree referred to above. An editorial commentary in *Polyarnaya Zvezda*,[35] appropriately sub-titled in large, bold type 'An Important Decision', explains that the 1962 decree had corrected some serious mistakes in the first decree which were characteristic of the period of personality cult and had thus started the process of healing the ideological situation in the republic. But the insistence, in the 1962 correction, on the struggle against nationalist attitudes had brought about a nihilistic attitude towards the Yakut cultural heritage. The editorial remarks that the denial of the Yakut literary heritage had been particularly prominent around the recent 100th anniversary of Kulakovskii's birth, when many were still being accused of idealising him. Universal human values, it says, must not be replaced by those 'surrogates' of the class approach which lead to the condemnation of particular authors. The time has come for a fresh, unprejudiced look at their biographies, especially when a new three-volume history of Yakut literature is under preparation, in which every author must find his proper place. The article states that of the twenty-seven writers who were purged, twenty have been rehabilitated, and concludes 'The cases of the rest are being examined'.[36] New editions of these writers have either appeared or are due to appear. In the same vein, a completely revised and updated version is being prepared of Pekarskii's monumental three-volume Yakut dictionary.[37]

The rehabilitation of such material is closely bound up with the question of language and schooling. In the town of Yakutsk in 1988 only two out of fourteen middle schools were teaching in the Yakut medium, and there are frequent complaints that the Yakut youth are losing their language to Russian. In one newspaper discussion, a teacher wrote in highlighting the problems of switching from Yakut to Russian textbooks for advanced subjects, and urging that schools throughout the republic should teach from the beginning in the Russian medium, with Yakut as a subject.[38] This accords with a widespread notion that Russian is the only 'cultured' medium, but this assumption is now opposed by many. In the same discussion, a Yakut who studied in the Russian medium wrote that she now feels ashamed to know so little of her own language and culture. Yakut schoolchildren, she said, know more about the central regions of Russia or about foreign countries than about their own, while Russians are often very dismissive of Yakut language and culture. The point is frequently made that cultural 'internationalism' must not be at the price of Yakut: when the Oiunskii Theatre Company took a production of Brecht to Leningrad, the many Yakut students living there had to use the headphones for a Russian translation, 'as indeed did I', reports the President of the Yakut Writers' Union 'it was in our native language'.[39]

In the countryside, the use of Yakut is widespread, and village schools are Yakut-medium. In outlying areas the situation is complex but also favourable to Yakut. Yakut serves as lingua franca among many minority indigenous peoples;[40] while for the far north-east, an area of early Russian pioneer settlement, Vakhtin reports that the old role of Russian as lingua franca is in some places being superseded by Yakut as this is brought in by a new wave of professional migrants.[41]

Wider problems of modernisation are related to loss of local language and culture, and to a pride in the Yakut past. The writer who was ashamed of not knowing her own culture also wrote that the Yakut people have many positive qualities, such as respect for the elderly, which, she says, must not be lost. Another argument is that the Yakut should be proud because they are unique in the world for having introduced horse- and cattle-herding into the harshest conditions of what is in fact the coldest region of the Arctic.[42] Russians should not regard this pride as a threat since the Yakut supplied and guided early Russian expeditions, which would not have survived without them. How then can they be accused of nationalism?[43]

This discussion takes place against a background of the increasing development of natural resources and the accompanying immigration of Russian labour. At the June 1989 session of People's Deputies, Yakutiya's V. P. Larionov stated that his republic's social facilities had been outpaced by industrial development and by population instability and were among the poorest in the RSFSR. While Yakutiya's population has grown over the past twenty years from 664,000 to well over 1 million, according to Larinov over 1 million people have entered the republic during that period and up to 1 million have left.[44] Since most Yakuts live inside the republic (314,000 out of 328,000 in 1979), few of those entering and leaving can have been Yakuts.

The industry which attracts this population has also fuelled a Yakut variant of the environmentalism which is now so potent a rallying point throughout the USSR and which frequently relates ethnic culture to nature and landscape.[45] Bones of contention include the whole approach to the mining of gold, diamonds and other minerals; timber felling; and a hydroelectric scheme near Mirnyi on the River Vilyui, which it is claimed has already rendered the river undrinkable, as well as further similar schemes projected for the rivers Lena and Yana. Such projects are generally sponsored by central ministries and have led to demands that the republic should be compensated for loss of land and forest. This is a very recent concept in Siberian development since, according to classical Marxist theory, natural resources have no value while they lie awaiting use and gain value only in proportion to the effort put into extracting them. Since extraction is organised by central ministries and departments based in Moscow, even with safeguards this formula inevitably tends to vest profits with the centre rather than with the republic.[46]

Earlier, Tokarev and Gurvich[47] could write from their base in the Institute of Ethnography in Moscow: 'Before the advent of the Soviet regime the very rich forest reserves of Yakutiya were hardly touched. The timber rotted where it stood, or else was destroyed by forest fire.' Now a Yakut author remarks with irony that, while the world heard during those years that the whole of Mendeleev's table of elements was to be found in the minerals of Yakutiya, little was heard about social or ecological problems:

Today my republic reminds me of a huge ship, laden with treasure and boarded by assorted departmental pirates. As they shovel diamonds, tin, gold, coal and mica feverishly into chests, they cast their predatory eyes yet further at the piles of timber, which like a giant float keep this ship from sinking. If they ever reach the timber, then the ship will go down once and for all.[48]

Another author, in an article entitled 'Man lives by nature'[49] writes that southern examples of development do not take account of special northern conditions and that in their concern only with their own products, the gold and diamond agencies are breaking the laws of nature. Though the concept of 'nature' seems European, an implicit or explicit strand of this kind of argument is that traditional 'ethnic wisdom' (narodnaya mudrost') is more respectful of nature. Since time immemorial, writes the author, the Yakut have believed that one must respect the silence of the forest, not pollute nature and not wound the earth. The world and man's soul are both made up of three corresponding elements. In polluting nature, he says, we pollute our own flesh and blood. Rather, we should protect the northern land just like our own body and soul.

This kind of association between Green thinking and ethnic consciousness is growing rapidly. To the old problems of the relationship between socialism and the development of indigenous culture has been added a new awareness of the Yakut republic's role in the USSR as a valuable supplier of raw materials both for internal consumption and for sale abroad in exchange for foreign currency. Those who argue for a respect for nature and traditional culture tend to reject development projects altogether: the dams should not be built, even the Amur-Yakutsk Magistral railway is tainted in advance as a branch of BAM, now widely admitted to be a white elephant and ironically dubbed 'the project of the stagnation [*zastoi*, that is, of the Brezhnev period]'.

The republic's administration, on the other hand, tends to support such developments but has started to argue for much greater control of them by the republic itself. At the September 1989 Plenum of the Central Committee of the CPSU on nationalities policy, the Yakut First Secretary Prokop'ev applauded Gorbachev's support for increased rights for the union republics, but complained that not enough had been said about the autonomous republics (ASSR). He urged that certain rights of union republics should be delegated to some ASSRs, on fixed conditions and for a certain period, especially within the Russian Federation (RSFSR). The ASSR would then have rights to oppose and even halt actions of ministries and departments of the Russian Federation and even of the USSR. The main emphasis of Prokop'ev's speech was on the need for the Yakut republic to control exploitation of the natural resources which constitute the republic's main sources of income, in order to ensure that a larger share of profits – including those in foreign currency – from these went, not to central ministries and departments, but into the republic's own exchequer.[50] At the heart of this is fair pricing, related to the principle of cost-accounting (*khozraschet*) or balancing one's books, on which the economy must now be based at every level. 'Price-setting, and consequently deductions in our budget,' said one official, 'depend on the centre. That's their monopoly and it's closed to us. What's the value of gold? – we don't know.'[51]

Such remarks imply a re-negotiation of the relationship between the republic and the centre. In the Yakut press, officials speak unambiguously about the need, not merely to acquire some of the rights of a union republic, but to become one. A recent Sociological Association poll conducted in Yakutiya found a substantial overall majority for this and even high support among local Russians. At the same time, officials still emphasise that they aim not at a division of peoples, but at their unification under equal rights (*ravnopravie*) and self-determination (*samoupravlenie*), terms which are part of official reformist discourse in Moscow. In fact, since the seventeenth century the Yakut have developed a deep, if ambivalent, involvement and accommodation with Russians and Russianness. Bilingualism is widespread, with 60 per cent of Yakuts claiming a knowledge of Russian. Mixed marriages, the majority between Yakuts and Russians, now account for 19 per cent of all unions: in this, Yakutiya comes fourth out of the Russian Federation's sixteen ASSRs and is expected to rise higher in this table.[52] Popov distinguishes three zones:[53] the Yakut rural heartland, where the few in-marrying outsiders are generally assimilated; Yakutsk and the industrial centres, where Russians equal or outnumber Yakut; and outlying areas where Yakut mix with smaller local peoples and the situation is complex.[54]

However, other evidence suggests that tension between Yakut and Russian remains. A liberal intellectual movement called the National Front (*Narodnyi Front*) is apparently subject to splits along ethnic lines. There are also said to be Yakut nationalist groups, either with an old-fashioned bourgeois style and an orientation towards Japan (supposedly enjoying sympathy among the older generation) or a shadowy, modern radical liberation movement which may have some support among the young. Whatever the reality, the latter kind is feared by some Russians. It is not clear how far such groups were involved in the 1979 disturbances or in those which occurred in Yakutsk University in June 1986. There a number of grievances were aired by Yakut students (Russian racial arrogance, the fact that very few Russians learn Yakut) and the affair was given a programme on Moscow television.[55] It is also said that the problem was fuelled by environmental concerns related to the rapid industrialisation of Yakutiya. In his 1989 speech, Prokop'ev still felt obliged to emphasise that, contrary to the impression given at the time in the Central Committee of the Party and in the central press, these disturbances were caused by an immature minority, quite unrepresentative of the majority who were tied to the Russian people by centuries of friendship.[56]

Yet the Yakut seem set to remain distinct. Despite wide knowledge of Russian, only 5 per cent claim Russian as a first language. In a sample of Yakut–Russian marriages in the Yakutsk passport office, Yakut nationality was chosen by 78 per cent of children with Yakut fathers and even by 14 per cent with Russian fathers.[57] Stories of mixed marriages are prominent where the offspring have assimilated to Yakut culture – for example, the numerous descendants over five generations of a Russian called Gotovtsev;[58] I also heard of the grandson of a Russian political exile who became a singer of *olonkho*. Even while applauding 'internationalism', Popov affirms that all-Yakut marriages are necessary for cultural continuity and the growth of the Yakut population.[59]

The rise of mixed marriages, confidently projected to continue, can only increase the authorities' desire that local demands for greater autonomy should take a regional form, rather than an ethnic one which would leave many people ambiguously placed. To be successful, this will need both to guarantee the development of the Yakut language and culture and to find a role for local Russians which does not amount to Russification of the rest. The continuing history of ethnic disturbances suggests that this will not be easy, and it may be that the balance between the ethnic and the regional interpretations of autonomy will correspond closely to that between the nativist and the developmentalist attitudes towards the environment. Certainly, it seems inevitable that the pressures towards greater local autonomy will increase, strengthening the demand for a change in Yakutiya's status to a union republic. Though this would leave some problems unresolved, there is now a feeling in the region that this would be in the spirit of the times and would give some sense of political evolution.

CONCLUSION AND FUTURE PROSPECTS

The Yakut appear historically as regionally powerful newcomers, dominating several smaller ethnic groups over a huge territory before themselves becoming dominated by the even more recently arrived Russians. With the Russians, they have engaged in a relationship which has been partly colonial, partly symbiotic and has turned to their demographic disadvantage only since the Second World War. The exploitation of natural resources, in the form of fur, was the main motive for Russian colonisation; in the form of minerals, it is now becoming the main rationale for greater Yakut autonomy. The economic reforms accompanying *perestroika* strongly encourage this desire. Thus earlier arguments in terms of national language and culture have now acquired a harder economic edge which will perhaps make them more cogent in negotiations with the centre. With the railway scheduled to come to Yakutsk and the possibility that foreign ships may soon use the Northern Sea Route,[60] Yakutsk is likely to be flooded with immigrants from the European part of the country, so that Yakut national feelings will require sensitive handling.

Yakut cultural identity has proved persistent and has frequently been associated with an ambivalent attitude to the Revolution. The rehabilitation of key cultural figures has thus been extremely important. As elsewhere in the USSR, the way forward now seems to lie in devising an acceptable way of distinguishing 'national development' and 'self-determination' from 'nationalism'. Though the republic is considered a border zone in the military sense (namely, along the Arctic Ocean), it is not so culturally. Within Siberia the Yakut have no relations across an international border, like the Buryat in Mongolia or even the 1,500-odd Siberian Eskimo in Alaska and beyond. They are too numerous and too locally dominant to use the growing international 'Fourth World' connections of the Eskimo and other small northern peoples, including their own minorities within the Yakut republic itself. Since there has never been a Muslim influence, today's Islamic militancy in the rest of the Turkic world renders the earlier Pan-Turkism obsolete. Though there is potential for increased foreign trade (such as with Japan), ethnically the Yakut are isolated and their identity will thus need to be sustained from their own inner resources. The Russians (and the Soviet state) cannot withdraw from Siberia even to the extent that they can from some of the union republics. Under the increasing current emphasis on territorial rights, the Yakuts' strongest card, in exchange for ethnic freedoms, is to stress their role as custodians of a vital part of the USSR's Siberian treasure-house.

NOTES

1. I. S. Gurvich *Kul'tura severnykh yakutov-olenevodov: k voprosu o pozdnikh etapakh formirovaniya yakutskogo naroda* (Moscow, Nauka 1977).
2. A. P. Okladnikov *Yakutia Before its Incorporation into the Russian State* H. N. Michael (ed.) (Montreal–McGill-Queen's [Arctic Institute of North America: Anthropology of the North: Translations from Russian Sources, vol. 8] 1970).
3. D. B. Shimkin and E. M. Shimkin 'Population Dynamics in Northeastern Siberia, 1650/1700 to 1970' *The Musk-Ox* (Saskatoon, Canada) no. 16 (1975), pp. 7–23 (p. 12).
4. B. O. Dolgikh 'Rodovoi i plemennoi sostav narodov Sibiri v xvii v' *Trudy Instituta Etnografii imeni N. N. Miklukho-Maklaya*, new series, vol. 55 (1960), pp. 615–21.
5. Shimkin and Shimkin 'Population Dynamics' p. 12.
6. R. Maak *Vilyuyskii okrug: Yakutskoi oblasti*, chast' 3 (St Petersburg, Typografiya i khromolitografiya A. Transhellya 1887).
7. S. A. Tokarev and I. S. Gurvich 'The Yakuts' in M. G. Levin and L. P. Potapov (eds), *The Peoples of Siberia* (Chicago University Press 1964) (Russian original 1956), pp. 243–304 (p. 287).
8. V. A. Demidov *Oktyabr'i natsional'nyi vopros* (Novosibirsk, Nauka 1978), p. 98.
9. G. A. Ammosov *Yakutskaya oblastnaya organizatsiya KPSS v shifrakh, 1919–1977* (Yakutsk 1979), p. 15.
10. B. Chichlo 'Histoire de la formation des territoires autonomes chez les peuples turco-mongoles de Sibérie' *Cahiers du monde russe et soviétique* XXVIII (3–4) (1987), pp. 361–402 (p. 372).
11. Chichlo, 'Histoire de la formation des territoires autonomes', pp. 365–66.
12. I. A. Argunov *Sotsial'noe razvitie yakutskogo naroda: istoriko-sotsiologicheskoe issledovanie obraza zhizni* (Novosibirsk, Nauka 1985).
13. S. E. Shreiber 'Mediko-sanitarnoe obsledovanie naseleniya vilyuyskogo i olekminskogo okrugov' *Materialy kommissii po izucheniyu Yakutskoi ASSR*, vyp.9 (Leningrad, AN SSSR 1931).
14. Ibid., pp. 147–8 and 365, cited in Argunov *Sotsial'noe razvitie yakutskogo naroda* p. 262.
15. Z. V. Gogolev *Sotsial'no-ekonomicheskoe razvitie Yakutii (1917–iyun' 1941 gg)* (Novosibirsk, Nauka 1972), pp. 189–90.
16. Ibid., pp. 192–95.
17. Ibid., p. 211.
18. Chichlo, 'Histoire de la formation des territoires autonomes', p. 372.
19. V. Antipin, Z. V. Gogolev, F. I. Golovnykh and Yu. A. Polyakov (eds) *Istoriya Yakutskoi ASSR* vol. 3, Sovetskaya Yakutiya (Moscow, Izdatel'stvo AN SSSR, 1963), pp. 131–35.
20. Gogolev, *Sotsial'no-ekonomicheskoe razvitie Yakutii*, p. 248.

21. Shimkin and Shimkin, 'Population Dynamics', p. 17.
22. P. A. Oiunskii 'Yakutskii yazyk i puti yego razvitiya' in *Russko-yakutskii terminologicheskiy slovar'* (Moscow 1935), p. 688, cited in Demidov, *Okryabr'i natsional'nyi vopras*, p. 286.
23. Chichlo *'Histoire de la formation des territoires autonomes'*, p. 372.
24. G. P. Basharin *Tri yakutskikh realista-prosvetitelya* (Yakutsk 1944).
25. 'Za pravil'noe osveshchenie istorii yakutskoi literatury' *Pravda* 10 Dec. 1951.
26. 'Postanovlenie byuro yakutskogo obkoma KPSS ot 10 maya 1989 g: vazhnoe reshenie' *Polyarnaya Zvezda* 1989:4, pp. 126–28 (p. 127).
27. Ibid.
28. E.g., V. A. Semenov *Tvorchestvo P. A. Oiunskog o i stanovlenie sotsialist-icheskogo realizma v yakutskoi sovetskoi literature* (Novosibirsk, Nauka 1980).
29. Racial tensions in Yakutia *Soviet Analyst* 24 (1980), pp. 6–8.
30. Tumarcha, letter headed 'Sprosi khozyaina', written to editors of *Severnye Prostory* 1989:3, p. 2.
31. *Pravda* 1 June 1989, p. 5.
32. Tumarcha, op. cit.
33. K. Turalysov 'Dostoinuyu pamyat' zhertvam stalinskikh represii v Yakutii' *Molodezh Yakutii* 16 July 1988.
34. *Molodezh Yakutii* 2 Aug. 1988, p. 1.
35. 'Postanovleniye . . .', op. cit.
36. Ibid, p. 128.
37. E. K. Pekarskii *Slovar' yakutskogo yazyka* (Moscow, AN SSSR), 3 vols, 1907–30.
38. *Sotsialisticheskaya Yakutiya* 23 Aug. 1988.
39. S. P. Danilov 'Perestroika i literatura' *Polyarnaya Zvezda* 1988:6, pp. 95–105 (p. 101).
40. P. Vitebsky, field-notes.
41. N. B. Vakhtin 'The Yukaghir Language in Sociolinguistic Perspective', to appear in *Lingua posnaniensis*.
42. Tumarcha, op. cit.
43. Ibid.
44. *Pravda* 3 June 1989, p. 4.
45. P. Vitebsky 'Landscape and Self-determination among the Eveny: the Political Environment of Siberian Reindeer Herders Today' in D. Parkin and L. Croll (eds) *Cultural Understandings of the Environment* (London, Routledge, forthcoming).
46. P. Vitebsky 'Gas, Environmentalism and Native Anxieties in the Soviet Arctic: the Case of Yamal Peninsula' *Polar Record* 26 (156) (1990), pp. 19–26 (pp. 23–24).
47. Tokarev and Gurvich 'The Yakuts', p. 288.
48. Tumarcha, op. cit.
49. I. Danilov 'Chelovek zhivet prirodoi' *Polyarnaya Zvezda* 1989:3, pp. 108–9.
50. *Pravda* 21 Sept. 1989, p. 3. That this echoes a widespread mood among the autonomous republics is shown by some of the speeches translated in O. Glebov and J. Crowfoot (eds) *The Soviet Empire: Its Nations Speak Out* (Chur [Switzerland]: Harwood [Soviet Studies, vol. 1], 1989).

51. 'V perspektiv – khozraschet' *Polyarnaya Zvezda* 1989: 6, pp. 96–99 (p. 98).
52. B. N. Popov, *Sotsialisticheskie preobrazovaniya semeino-brachnykh otnoshenii v Yakutii* (Novosibirsk, Nauka 1987), pp. 275–77.
53. Ibid., pp. 281–82.
54. Cf. Vakhtin 'The Yukaghir Language'.
55. A. Sheehy 'Racial Disturbances in Yakutsk' *Radio Liberty Research* RL 251/86 (1986), pp. 1–5.
56. *Pravda* 21 Sept. 1989, p. 3.
57. Popov *Sotsialisticheskie preobrazovaniya*, pp. 291–93.
58. Cited in Popov, *Sotsialisticheskie preobrazovaniya*, p. 271.
59. Ibid., p. 278.
60. See Gorbachev's speech reprinted in Pravda, 2 Oct. 1987 and translated in part by T. Armstrong 'Soviet Proposals for the Arctic: a Policy Declaration by Mr Gorbachev' *Polar Record* 24(148), 1988, pp. 68–69.

PART VI

THE DIASPORA NATIONALITIES

There are a number of nationalities whose members are scattered throughout the Soviet Union and who have become physically separated from their alleged or 'historical' homeland. The most notable cases include the Crimean Tatars, Jews, Volga Germans, Poles, Meskhetians and Greeks. Denied the benefits of territorial-administrative status and thus a level of institutional support provided for the union republic-based nationalities, the diaspora nationalities have had most to fear over their cultural and linguistic preservation and sense of national identities. Their diaspora status has thus meant that they have not been able to wield the institutional power to organise and protect national cultures in ways available to the union republic nationalities. While the goal of diaspora movements is similar in that their demands involve the right to resettlement, for some this means leaving the Soviet Union, whereas for others it entails both the right to resettlement and the creation or recreation of their homelands within the USSR's borders.

Gorbachev's policy of openness has enabled some diaspora demands to be accommodated. A major international exodus of diaspora peoples has occurred, particularly of Jews and Volga Germans. The reformist leadership, however, has been less forthcoming towards those demanding territorial-administrative accommodation within a reconstituted federal system. The most publicised case is that of the Crimean Tatars. Along with several other nationalities, they were deported during the Second World War and resettled in the east for essentially geostrategic reasons. But in contrast to most of the deported nationalities whose right to resettle in recreated territorial homelands was instituted after Stalin's death, these rights were not extended to the Crimean Tatars. Since Gorbachev came to power some resettlement has been permitted, although not the recreation of a Crimean Tatar Autonomous Republic.

CHAPTER TWENTY

Crimean Tatars

Edward J. Lazzerini

BACKGROUND

Among the many ethnic groups inhabiting the Soviet Union today, most are numerically small (usually well below 1 million members) and have played roles in the evolving Soviet experience consistent with their size. For reasons that defy convincing analysis but that have much to do with episodes of extraordinary assault upon the core cultural identifiers of particular groups, a very few have adopted a posture of collective resistance that would be striking even for much larger communities. The Davids confronting the Goliaths are seldom numerous in any society, but the Soviet Union has had its share of remarkable men and women over the past seven decades who have risked much to voice objections to official policy. One ethnic minority, perhaps above all others in that country, has for more than thirty years stood out for its persistent and often vociferous challenge to conditions affecting it particularly if not uniquely. That minority are the Crimean Tatars.

Ethnically and linguistically related to the Turkic family of peoples broadly dispersed across the Eurasian continent from the Mediterranean to the Pacific, the Crimean Tatars entered the historical record as 'Tatars' in the aftermath of the Mongol conquest of the Crimean Peninsula and surrounding territory in the mid-thirteenth century. For the next 200 years these Tatars lived among and assimilated with other immigrant Turkic peoples, and were governed by representatives of the Khans of the Golden Horde residing in Sarai, on the lower course of the Volga River, all the while shaping the socio-economic, cultural and political features of an independent polity. By the 1440s, they had succeeded in establishing their first state, the Crimean Khanate, under the leadership of Haci Giray, scion of one of the major clans providing the military-political elite of the territory. The dynasty that Haci Giray created would rule the Khanate until its collapse under Russian assault in 1783. A regional power until the mid-eighteenth century, the Khanate drew legitimacy and strength from proclaimed links to the steppe heritage of Genghis Khan and from alliance with the Ottoman empire.

The combination of internal decline and shifts in the balance of power in the greater Eastern European/steppe region by the beginning of the eighteenth century undermined the Khanate's pivotal role internationally and lessened its capacity to defend against external threats. The most dangerous challenge came increasingly from a reformed and expansive Russia looking to resolve a long-standing problem along its southern frontier. Four invasions of the Crimean Peninsula by Russian troops between 1771 and 1782 led to the Khanate's demise and its territory's annexation.

Under the tsars, the Crimea experienced a chequered fate. As a consequence of several extraordinary waves of out-migration punctuating the century following annexation, the Tatar presence in the peninsula declined by at least one-half, and its percentage of the total population fell to 35.1 according to the census of 1897. Overall the promised benefits of colonialism remained mostly unfulfilled, while the negative consequences – economic exploitation, social discrimination and cultural imperialism – weighed heavily on the local native population that stayed behind.

During the final decades of the *ancien régime*, many Crimean Tatars participated in the liberalising and revolutionary events overtaking the Russian empire as a whole, with some joining All-Union political and social organisations, and others forging more limited but highly nationalist (Crimean Tatar) associations. But also, as Muslims, they were caught up in the web of dilemmas and tensions resulting from the challenges of modernism. These, in many ways, had been crucial in generating a cultural and intellectual revival from the 1880s onward, spearheaded by and most identified with Ismail Bey Gasprinskii. A Crimean Tatar, Gasprinskii nevertheless propagandised a reform programme (*jadidism*) that spoke to all the empire's Turco-Muslim peoples, seeking their full integration into modern life through educational, linguistic and economic reform rooted in a fundamental shift in world-view. If aspects of his programme met with sometimes fierce resistance from imperial agents and more conservative elements within his own cultural milieu, or were eventually treated with disdain by more radical advocates of change, the dynamic spirit of Crimean society and the existence of a modern-thinking intelligentsia by the fateful year 1917 owed much to his efforts. In the long run, the failure to maintain this process – or rather its disruption by the political evolution of the Soviet state – proved a tragic loss for the Crimean Tatars.

THE CRIMEAN TATARS IN THE SOVIET PERIOD

By the approach of 1917, anti-tsarist opinion had spread widely among Crimean Tatars, as had the feeling that Russian influence – whether political, economic or cultural – emanating from central institutions was a major obstacle to fulfilment of Tatar national aspirations. During that tumultuous year in the destiny of the Russian empire, those aspirations turned increasingly radical as the definition of 'nationalist' moved from demands for cultural autonomy emphasising freedom, equality, brotherhood and justice, to claims for territorial autonomy within a federalist system, and finally to insistence on independence.

The evolution of Tatar sentiment, however, was bound to conflict fundamentally with centrist assumptions that guided virtually every contemporary Russian political ideology, especially, it turns out, Bolshevism. Ambivalent at best regarding self-determination and national autonomy when those matters were first treated comprehensively in 1913, Bolshevism gradually revealed itself to be antithetical to Tatar hopes through a succession of statements – some public, others confidential – delivered largely by Stalin between 1917 and 1921. Even as the Bolsheviks proclaimed the virtues of self-determination abroad as an antidote to other imperialisms, they were busy fabricating enough caveats to deny such proclamations any effective play domestically. And when Bolshevik troops occupied the Crimea for the third time in October 1920, bringing a certain end to the Civil War for that territory and its people, the possibility of real Tatar independence was foreclosed. The Cheka arrived immediately, led by Bela Kun, who turned that already notorious instrument of Bolshevik power to the task of eliminating all local opposition to the new regime. How many native inhabitants – both Tatars and others – perished within the next half year may never be known, but their number must be counted in the tens of thousands.

Still, sharpened by the inflexible policies of local Bolsheviks who showed every sign of insensitivity to the Tatar population, opposition continued. Troubled by the failure to pacify the Crimea fully, Moscow sent the Volga Tatar Mir Said Sultan Galiev on an inspection tour early in 1921. Sultan Galiev would soon make a name for himself – and an enemy of Stalin – by enunciating a theory of 'national communism' that would have, if implemented, shifted the balance of power and socialist development from the Russian centre of the new Soviet society to the non-Russian borderlands. From the report he submitted based on his Crimean observations, a report that was highly critical of local Bolshevik practice, one can see early evidence of the direction of his thinking. For the Crimea the impact was immediate: a shift in Bolshevik tactics (if not long-term goals) whereby the cooperation rather than antagonism of the Tatars was sought. The most important consequence of the new tactic, and one that continues to haunt the relationship between the Crimean Tatars and the Soviet system, was the decree of 18 October 1921 that created the Crimean Autonomous Soviet Socialist Republic (Crimean ASSR) within the jurisdiction of the Russian republic.

The period from 1921 to 1928 is commonly viewed by Crimean Tatars as a 'golden age' within their Soviet experience, in part because of easy positive comparisons with later decades that brought extraordinary Stalinist repression, but also because the heart of the 1920s witnessed genuine efforts to build within the autonomous administrative framework a new Soviet society in the Crimea while enhancing and ensuring its Tatar character. There have been tantalising suggestions that, in order to win over the Tatars, the Bolsheviks went especially far in conceding autonomy in cultural, economic and even political affairs, but these have proved impossible to corroborate. In any event, it is by now clear that the nationalist interests of the Tatars stood in such sharp contrast to the centralising thrust of the Bolsheviks that, Stalinism aside, the independence of the Crimea had to be narrowly circumscribed over the longer haul. For a while, however, the exigencies of state development and economic recovery following years of war, revolution, and civil strife, as well as the uncertainty and confusion engendered by the ideological and experimental nature of Soviet development, provided the conditions within which *korenizatsiya* (nativisation) could briefly thrive and local national or Communist leaders, like Veli Ibrahimov, could restrain the demands of the centre.

In the Crimea, *korenizatsiya* meant Tatarisation, despite the decided numerical inferiority of Tatars (179,094) to other ethnic groups inhabiting the peninsula (706,757), according to the 1926 census. Until the spring of 1928, Tatar leaders were allowed to encourage not merely the preservation but also the enhancement of Tatar culture, and to assert Tatar identity. This was accomplished through the recognition of Tatar as the official language of the republic along with Russian; the inclusion of Tatars in all levels of republican government; the re-establishment and expansion of republican schools wherein the language of instruction was Tatar; the creation of cultural institutions (museums, theatres, libraries, reading rooms) and centres for scholarship (including the Oriental Institute, for the study of Tatar language and literature, added in 1925 to Tavrida University); and the publication of books, newspapers and journals that provided vehicles not only for discussion of current cultural issues but also examination of the full range of historical themes.

For a brief period, then, CPSU policy coincided with Tatar ethnic aspirations to give substance to the claim of local autonomy. By the end of the 1920s, however, Stalin's rise to pre-eminence had the consequence of generating a relentless and often deadly campaign against 'nationalist deviations' among minorities throughout the country. Indigenous leaders, only recently the shapers of local policy, now found themselves the objects of criticism and condemnation; and most became victims of the purging process for which the Stalinist era is infamous. Thus, Veli Ibrahimov, who served as chairman of the Crimean Central Committee and of the Crimean Council of People's Commissars, was accused of an assortment of nationalist crimes as well as subversion of the collectivisation drive, and fell from grace along with a host of other Tatars now suspect in their loyalty to Moscow. In the push for political and economic centralisation, *korenizatsiya* became an inevitable casualty, associated fatally with the worst features of localism imaginable. The 'golden age' of the Crimean ASSR was not only over, but was also smeared as a time of *veliibrahimovshchina* (the 'Veli Ibrahimov years').

With an end to the policy of *korenizatsiya*, Tatar culture began to suffer blows against it through all the remaining years of peace before the outbreak of the Second World War. Sovietisation, often little more than a code word for Russification, became the goal for a new era that would produce new Soviet men and women immune to the seduction of nationalism. Achieving that goal required not only purging Tatar society of 'wrong-thinking' members but also eradicating, or at least severely curtailing, the institutions and practices that might continue to produce such people. Almost all mosques and clerically controlled schools were closed, the Cyrillic alphabet was 'adopted' for the Tatar language after it had been Latinised in 1928, the number of journals and newspapers in Tatar was reduced, the faculty of the Oriental Institute at Tavrida University was thoroughly 'weeded out', and virtually the gamut of pre-revolutionary Tatar literature was proscribed. And the past began to be rewritten in appropriate fashion, a process epitomised, perhaps, by the condemnation of Ismail Bey Gasprinskii as a 'bourgeois nationalist' that appeared at length in a path-defining study that Liutsian Klimovich, a specialist in anti-Islamic polemics, produced in 1936.[1]

The intervention of the Second World War in Soviet life is well documented in all its horrors and costs. Between September and 30 November 1941, only three months after the initial German invasion of the USSR, divisions under General Manstein captured the entire Crimean Peninsula. For the next two and a half years, the Nazis occupied the territory and ran an administration that to some degree took advantage of strong Tatar resentments toward the Soviet system while for all practical purposes keeping tight control over the local population and evincing the typical ideological disdain for the indigenous peoples as *Untermenschen*. The Tatar response to the German presence was as varied and contradictory as elsewhere in occupied Soviet Union, and included resistance through regular army and partisan units as well as collaboration for nationalist and other reasons.

What proved unusual, although utterly consistent with the spirit of Stalinism, was the policy pursued by Soviet authorities upon reoccupation of the Crimea. During the night of 17–18 May 1944, units of the NKVD systematically rounded up virtually the entire Crimean Tatar population, herded it into cattle-trucks and train cars, and transported it with almost no humane provision to a primarily Central Asian exile. Charges of collaboration and treason were levelled as justification. The deportation was devastating: Tatar sources, long as *samizdat* but more recently in open publications, have always insisted that nearly half of those making this fateful journey (about 195,000 out of more than 423,000 living in the Crimea following the German occupation), died before reaching their destination. Those who survived would be joined later by others demobilised from the Red Army at the war's end. All would be faced with a 'special settlement' (*spetsposelenie*) regime that would remain in place until the mid-1950s. Its primary features, all punitive, were: (1) denial of the right to move about freely – no further than 5 kilometres – even in the republic of habitation; (2) restrictions on the right to live in major cities; (3) prohibition against involvement in agricultural activity, the traditional livelihood for most Tatars; (4) the requirement of reporting personally to the local NKVD office every other week; and (5) exclusion from active military service.

Even more critical, perhaps, was the series of measures designed to eradicate Crimean Tatar identity. All historical, cultural and linguistic traces of a Tatar presence in the peninsular homeland were removed, even to the point of razing villages and levelling cemeteries. Another reassessment of Tatar history was undertaken, resulting in extraordinary silence about most of the past before the late nineteenth century, save for tendentious paeans on the progressive significance of the Crimea's annexation to the Russian empire in 1783. For the twentieth century, the focus was inevitably on the blessings of the October Revolution and the alleged treachery of the Tatars not only during the dark hours of the Great Patriotic War but even before, during the early decades of Sovietisation. As if to seal the drive to make of the Tatars a non-people, the Crimean ASSR was abolished on 30 June 1945 (although the Act was not announced until 28 June 1946), and its territory transformed into the Crimean oblast of the Russian republic (later transferred to the Ukrainian republic on 19 February 1954). Moreover, the name Tatar, without its Crimean attributive, would serve henceforth as the only identifier recognised officially. In consequence, no 'Crimean' Tatars existed any longer in the USSR, no 'Crimean' Tatar language needed to be studied, taught or published in, and no 'Crimean' Tatar culture in general required public sustenance. Since numbers always tell some tale, 'Crimean' Tatar ceased to be a statistical category, above all in national censuses.

For nearly a decade, the exiled Tatars suffered under the special settlement restrictions, living initially in primitive conditions before barracks were constructed and bearing the many burdens of discrimination encouraged by official propaganda. A few of the restrictions were lifted in 1954 for those who could prove that they had been loyal during the war by service in the Red Army or with partisan units. This concession, never explained publicly, is consistent with numerous measures whose adoption in the first years after Stalin's death in January 1953 were surely designed to bolster national support for an uncertain and anxious new leadership and minimise any outbursts of popular discontent. What had been applied to a few initially was extended by decree to all Crimean Tatars on 28 April 1956. Since this document was never published, however, the right to move freely about the USSR that it restored – Tatars were reissued with internal passports – was largely ineffective, given the nation-wide perception of the Tatars and their 'crimes'. Moreover, the decree insisted anew that 'the property of the Crimean Tatars confiscated at the time of their deportation will not be returned, and they do not have the right to return to the Crimea'.[2] Together these two restrictions would become the increasing focus of Tatar grievance, especially once some among them decided to make a public issue of their plight.

The window of opportunity was cracked by the unfolding process of de-Stalinisation that, even if he was not necessarily its author, Krushchev made the palpable theme of his regime. In a speech at a closed session of the Twentieth Congress of the CPSU in February 1956, the Party Chairman noted that 'mass deportations from their native places of whole nations, together with all Communists and Komsomol members ... are rude violations of the basic Leninist principles of the nationality policy of the Soviet state'. Ironically but shrewdly, this appeal to 'Leninist principles' would be seized upon by Tatar activists and made a unifying thread for their long struggle against the injustices meted out to their people.

But the immediate inspiration for the emergence of a Crimean Tatar movement were similar remarks by A.F. Gorkin, Secretary of the Presidium of the Supreme Soviet, published in *Izvestiya* on 12 February 1957, and a law of the same month that, while exculpating most of the peoples deported during the Second World War, failed to do so for the Tatars and the Volga Germans.[3] Dismayed yet convinced that the authorities had erred, the Tatars embarked upon a potentially dangerous campaign of public relations involving two tactics that became hallmarks of their efforts: mass petitioning, and group lobbying of officials and their offices in Moscow. The first such petition, with over 6,000 signatures, was addressed to the Supreme Soviet in June 1957; it would be followed during the next several years by others, culminating in deliverance of one to the 22nd Party Congress in October 1961, with over 25,000 names affixed. Full rehabilitation and the right to return to the Crimea were constant themes. What the Tatars received, however, were cultural tokens: a newspaper (*Lenin Bayrag'y*) in their native tongue, appearing thrice weekly since 1 May 1957 under the auspices and supervision of Uzbek party and state authorities; an ensemble (*Kaitarma*) to perform traditional Tatar music and dance; and optional classes in the Crimean Tatar language available to children in a small number of primary schools throughout the Uzbek SSR. The Tatars were not appeased.

While the authorities responded slowly to the Tatar's expanding public activity, when they did it was to use intimidation and the judicial process as means to shatter the movement's cohesion and isolate its leadership. Thus, in 1962 the first quasi-formal group spawned by the movement – the League of Crimean Tatar Youth, in Tashkent – was immediately crushed and activists such as Shevket Abduramanov, Enver Seferov and Mustafa Dzhemilev were arrested and tried.

Despite this reaction, persistent and systematic lobbying and the formation of initiative groups throughout Tatar society produced important developments during the second half of the 1960s and into the 1970s. On the one hand, the authorities grudgingly agreed to several meetings between Tatar representatives and high-ranking Party and state leaders, including one held in June 1967 with then KGB head, Yuri Andropov. At the latter meeting, Andropov is said to have promised that an announcement would be forthcoming rehabilitating the Tatars and setting the stage for measures to facilitate their return to the Crimea. In fact, on 5 September the Presidium of the Supreme Soviet issued two decrees. The first officially exculpated the Tatars of any collective crimes, but said nothing about a return to the homeland, arguably wishful thinking since the Tatars continued to be denied their Crimean identity. The second, however, confirmed the Tatars' right to 'live in any territory of the Soviet Union, in compliance with labour legislation and the passport regime'. On their basis, over the next several years, upwards of 100,000 Tatars sought to move to the Crimea, only to be prevented from resettling in their homeland by bureaucratic resistance and arbitrariness, as well as police harassment and brutality. As one Tatar source declared, the second of the 1967 edicts was nothing more than a 'veiled instrument for the eviction from the Crimea of Crimean Tatars who had returned to the homeland'.[4]

At the same time, initial steps were taken to link the particular grievances of the Tatars with the more universal ones of the Soviet human rights movement. Instrumental in furthering this tactic was an appeal to Moscow members of the Writers' Union in 1966 that drew the support of Aleksei Kosterin, an old writer, and through him, Petr Grigorenko, a retired general; equally significant was the work of Mustafa Dzhemilev in 1969 as a founding member of the Initiative Group for the Defence of Civil Rights in the USSR. From these developments the Tatars were encouraged to broaden their appeal not only within their own country but also, more importantly, abroad, particularly to the United Nations and other international organisations.

From the late 1960s to early 1980s, the Tatars continued their struggle, particularly of trying to register for resettlement in the Crimea, which now was presumably their right. Soviet authorities, however, persisted in obstructing their manoeuvres at every turn, utilising as much as possible low-visibility tactics that bore the aura of legalism. Thus, in order to prevent an anticipated large influx of Tatars into the Crimea, residence permits, never required previously, were hastily provided to all current inhabitants; unseen pressure was placed on the managers of enterprises in the Crimea not to hire Tatars; notary publics were instructed not to approve the purchase of property or homes if the purchaser was a Tatar; and workers were ordered not to provide electrical or water services to dwellings of unregistered Tatars.

Complex rules for official recruitment were enacted in the spring of 1968 that made the process of obtaining permission to resettle arduous and so limiting as to render the results insignificant. Ten years later, a resolution of the Council of Ministers ('On Additional Measures for Strengthening Passport Regulations in the Crimea'), attacked the problem from a different angle by making it easier for state officials to evict and deport passport violators; and an Uzbek republican edict that same year required emigrants to obtain a certificate from the local militia attesting that work and housing were available in the area to which they wished to move. Although figures are not precise, by 1980 perhaps between 4,000 and 5,000 families had arrived in the Crimea by way of the organisational levy (*orgnabor*), while only a few hundred families had managed to obtain residence permits otherwise.[5] Of unregistered Tatars, less than a hundred remained.

In early March 1984, barely a year before Mikhail Gorbachev's selection as Party Secretary, a document identified as 'Declaration – 1984' was sent with 240 signatures to the Politburo of the Central Committee of the CPSU by members of the Crimean Tatar community in Krasnodar krai. It summed up in carefully worded and effective fashion the history of the 'Crimean Tatar problem', the 'incredible torments and losses', the 'daily humiliation and insults from . . . local agencies', and the 'self-sacrifice' of this small people as a result of the failure of the Soviet authorities to honour the constitutional guarantees and the earlier Leninist instructions regarding the rights of national minorities. 'The party must boldly correct the errors that have been committed,' its authors admonished. Nothing less than 'genuine rehabilitation, . . . restoration of the good name and national dignity of our people, . . . [and] its right to live in its homeland – in the Crimea' would suffice.[6] Would a new leadership offer realistic hope that these long-fought for goals would be achieved? Would the finally recognised general crisis in the Soviet system provide a new kind of opportunity for even a small minority such as the Crimean Tatars?

THE CRIMEAN TATARS SINCE GORBACHEV'S ACCESSION TO POWER

On 20 March 1988, three years into the Gorbachev era, various wire services reported the following events:

– Some 2,000 Crimean Tatars marched through the city of Simferopol as part of a three-hour rally. Shouting slogans, the demonstrators demanded a return to their historic homeland and a restoration of their national autonomy;

– About 1,000 Crimean Tatars attended two separate meetings held for nearly four hours each in the Uzbek town of Bekabad. Banners were raised declaring 'Crimea – Homeland of the Crimean Tatars, Not Only a Resort,' and 'Democracy and *Glasnost*', Even for Crimean Tatars';

– Outside the Lenin Library in Moscow, eighteen Crimean Tatars demonstrated in favour of the right to return to their homeland. Carrying portraits of Lenin and Gorbachev, they unfurled a banner recalling the former's decree creating an Autonomous Tatar Republic in Crimea in 1921.

By the standards that Crimean Tatars have established over the past twenty-five years, these public demonstrations would not rank among the more dramatic or substantial. Yet, in that single day's actions the observer should be struck by the array of references – some undisguised, some symbolic – to what is most important to many members of this ethnic minority. The geographical settings that provide the back-drop for these particular public events are a useful case in point. Simferopol, once known by its Tatar name Ak Meshchit, is second only to Bakhchisarai in the homeland as a site of historic significance to the Crimean Tatars. Yet today one would be hard put to discover there much evidence of that significance, let alone many Tatar inhabitants. Symbolic of the entire Crimean Peninsula, with few of its native people in residence, Simferopol is a city to which its people wish the right to return.

Bekabad has been a place for Tatars by edict since 1944, a residence for displaced persons whom the managers of Soviet nationalities policy under Stalin uprooted for reasons yet veiled. Crimean Tatars live in Bekabad, as they mostly still do in Uzbek, Kazakh and Tajik places, but, congenial as it may be, the city is not a Tatar abode, not part of *ana yurt* (the homeland) steeped in ancestral memory. For many it remains a caravanserai on the long road home, a temporary residence where one lives and struggles now for the Tatar that one is and would be.

Moscow is the cradle of Russian (in the ethnic sense) culture, incubator of much Soviet history, and fortress of national authority. If the city serves as capital and symbol of the socialist motherland, it does so ambivalently for Crimean Tatars. From that imperial seat, since the birth of the Soviet state, have emanated insistent Communist Party voices, all too frequently redolent of Great Russian chauvinism and always dictating not only what the Tatars should do but also what they should be. To that imperious seat, since the first post-Stalin thaw in the mid-1950s, have trekked uncounted heralds of popular protest, bearing petitions signed at times by tens of thousands, setting up camp outside

331

Party and government offices, and speaking as one small but cohesive, vigorous and persistent voice for justice and cultural autonomy.

As we are reminded, however, many in the Soviet Union continue to believe and act as if 'small minorities do not have the right to strike or demonstrate'. Leaving aside whether large minorities have this right, it remains true that despite *glasnost'* and *perestroika*, under which we have witnessed truly remarkable public expressions of ethnic aspirations by Soviet standards, what is permissible remains officially limited, with constraints set not by social consensus openly reached but by authority that typically relinquishes little of its presumed right to control others except when compelled to do so by the pressure of circumstance or people. Herein lies, of course, one of the fundamental features of the Soviet experience, and one that the Crimean Tatars have long understood and sought to turn against the system that has denied them so much. In fairness to the new Party leadership, the liberalisation of Soviet society that it has wrought, for purposes that are still arguable, has made an extraordinary difference by dissipating a good deal of the residual Stalinist mentality that once permeated the USSR and crippled public discourse. One obvious consequence, for which there is often dramatically daily evidence, is the more broadly based spirit of public challenge continually stretching the bounds of the permissible and, to a significant degree, forcing the regime to adjust its own policies and goals. But what has this meant for the Crimean Tatars?

Heartened by the emergence of Gorbachev and his campaigns for *glasnost'*, *perestroika* and the democratisation of Soviet society, they continue to pursue the traditional tactics of organised petition and demonstration that have, despite setbacks, disappointments and official retribution, worked remarkably well for them for two and a half decades. Increasingly, it seems, Gorbachev has become the last best hope for the final resolution of their grievances, as several petitions addressed to him personally and numerous other documents, particularly since early 1987, reveal clearly. The overall tenor of the Gorbachev experiment has been understandably encouraging, as has the leniency accorded Mustafa Dzhemilev (in the manner shown earlier to Andrei Sakharov) in January of that year upon his release from Magadan at the end of his sixth term in prison. By the end of May one could discern a renewed upsurge of Tatar activism that included at least one new aspect: appeal for redress of Tatar religious grievances, accompanied by open acknowledgement of Tatar identification with Islam and the linkage of return to the homeland with restoring and safeguarding confessional rights.[7]

A significant juncture was reached towards the end of June when at a meeting with Petr Demichev, non-voting member of the Politburo, Tatar spokespersons were promised resolution of their problems in a month's time! Having learned that official promises are seldom what they seem, the Tatars refused to wait passively. On 6 July, about thirty people demonstrated in Red Square, but were handled with surprising indulgence. After carrying out their protest near Lenin's mausoleum for about forty-five minutes, five of their number met again with Demichev, who reiterated his promise and claimed that an entire section (*otdel*) of the Central Committee of the Party was working on the matter. In fact, three days later, although the act was not officially announced until 23 July, a special nine-man commission chaired by Andrei Gromyko and including five Politburo members would be created, the first such official body we know of to investigate minority complaints. Within several months, official working commissions were constituted in Uzbekistan, Tadzhikistan, the Russian republic and Ukraine to support the work of Gromyko's group and involve those republics within which most of the Tatars dwelled.

Attempting to hold Demichev to his word, the Tatars proclaimed 26 July as a deadline, and organised demonstrations in numerous locations, including Moscow, throughout the month. On 25 July, in the midst of a three-day sit-in near the Kremlin, activists announced a major demonstration for the following day. What ensued was an unprecedented, tension-filled, twenty-three-hour gathering in Red Square that broke up only when Gromyko agreed to meet with demonstrators and discuss their grievances. Though reluctant to deal with a man so clearly associated with decades of repressive policies, a delegation spoke with Gromyko for two and a half hours the next day. From the Tatar perspective the results were unsatisfying, as Gromyko adopted an 'elder brother' and patronising tone.

In the months that followed, Gromyko's commission went through a 'fact-finding' phase that included on-the-spot investigations by a working group despatched to Uzbekistan from 29 July until 5 August. Headed by V. I. Bessarabov, member of the CPSU Central Committee, the group visited Tatars living in five districts of the republic. Radio Tashkent, to the surprise of few, reported that all those spoken with declared that they had everything they needed 'for productively working, resting, participating in public life, and fulfilling their constitutional rights'.[8] Despite *glasnost'*, this kind of reporting – denial of the problem even as words and actions belie such denial – remains all too common in defence of official opinion. Insistence that Tatar activism is detrimental to fulfilment of group aspirations, charges that activists speak only for a small extremist element among the Tatars and are guilty of breaching the public order, of slander, provocation, parasitism, egotism, hooliganism and worse, of having Fascist or neo-Fascist links, all betray a continuing tactic to discredit the movement in the eyes of the population at large and avoid accommodating the real wishes of the Tatars themselves.

Other tactics, however, inform the state's approach to dealing with Tatar demands, and they are revealed in numerous pronouncements and acts, especially the three reports issued by the Gromyko Commission on 15 October and 4 February 1987, and 9 June 1988. In the cumulative documentation, three issues dominate: (1) discrimination against

Crimean Tatars in housing, employment and education; (2) promotion of Tatar culture; and (3) regulation of residence in the Crimea and other health-resort areas of the country. For the first, if we ignore opinion that such discrimination never existed, the official position is that relevant authorities (national and local) 'have lifted all restrictions on the rights of Crimean Tatars in various ways and guarantee their complete equality with other Soviet citizens in all matters, including the choice of place of residence, work, and study'.[9] As if to justify the discrimination that did (not) exist in the past, one is reminded that at least some Tatars (but members of no other ethnic group?) collaborated with the Nazis, and that the Tatars have historically been troublesome to the Slavic peoples (as far back as the Mongol era). Besides, as one Muscovite put it, 'what is done is done' and ought to be forgotten.[10]

For the second, one has witnessed both a general loosening of cultural restrictions, as has occurred for most Soviet ethnic groups of late, as well as official commitment to broadening state support to rectify particular Tatar problems. Noting the following should suffice to emphasise the changes that are taking place. First, courses teaching the Tatar language are being instituted in more and more schools in Uzbekistan and the Ukraine, including the Crimea itself.[11] Given the dearth of qualified instructors, these projects are being supported by expansion of teacher training programmes, including the opening of a Crimean Tatar faculty at Simferopol State University.[12] Moreover, textbooks, virtually non-existent save for those produced before the Second World War and long out of print, have been compiled in Tashkent and, more significantly, Kiev.[13] The Tatars themselves have long fought to preserve their native tongue and have used their newspaper (*Lenin Bayrag'y*) and literary journal (*Yildiz*) towards this end in many ways, one of which has been to serialise a Tatar–Russian dictionary and introduce a new column in *Lenin Bayrag'y* entitled 'Students' Page' (*Talebeler Saifesi*);[14] Second, radio and television programming in Crimean Tatar is being expanded in number and content in Uzbekistan and introduced in Tadzhikistan;[15] Third, a new newspaper in Crimean Tatar (*Dostluk*) is appearing as a weekly supplement to *Krymskaya pravda*, and at least one non-Tatar newspaper (*Zarya kommunizma*, appearing in the Dzhankoy region of the Crimea) has begun to publish untranslated excerpts from *Lenin Bayrag'y*;[16] Fourth, treatment of the Crimean Tatar past by Tatars increasingly includes previously 'blank' periods (for example, the late imperial decades and the 1920s), new themes (such as the richness of Tatar culture, including music and art, as well as literature), as well as persons formerly anathematised by CPSU fiat. The list of rehabilitated Tatar cultural figures continues to lengthen, but the most significant entry is the great nineteenth-century reformer, Ismail Bey Gasprinskii; Fifth, 'Crimean Tatar' has become a recognised ethnic identifier for the first time since 1946 with its insertion in the list of nationalities for the census conducted in the period 12–19 January 1989, and its inclusion as a separate entry in *Sovetskaya entsiklopediya* published that same year.[17]

Important as these developments are, one should avoid euphoria and recognise, as the Tatars do themselves, that cultural concessions not only serve as distractions from the deeper issues confronting them but also allow the authorities to 'look good' in the face of Tatar pressure and buy time, hoping that public support for the Tatars will remain minimal and the passage of time will weaken Tatar resolve. The hurried publication (May 1988) in large numbers (50,000 copies) of a collectively produced little book entitled *Krym: proshloe i nastoyashchee* reveals the extent to which piecemeal concessions possess a tactical dimension. For one thing, none of the contributors is a Crimean Tatar; for another, the critical period from 1860 to the October Revolution is glossed over. Moreover, the purpose for this book is clearly to support the current official line, with its emphasis on the place (the Crimea) and not its dominant native population (the Tatars), its insistence again and again on the multi-ethnic character of the territory since ancient times, and its equation of Tatar nationalism with Fascist collaboration during the war.[18]

This brings us to the third, and, by all accounts, the most intractable point of dispute between Soviet authorities and the Crimean Tatars: the latter's right to return to the Crimea *en masse* and their demand for restoration of autonomous status for their homeland. These have become of almost primal concern for the Tatars, hardening, not diminishing, with the passage of time and generations, yet the official response has been virtually unyielding on both issues. As spokesman for the Special Commission established to deal with Tatar affairs, Gromyko was true to his sobriquet 'Mr Nyet'. The call for national autonomy, rejected time and again over the past thirty years, has once more been dismissed as unreasonable and impossible to grant. (In the word of the Commission's third report, the present territorial boundaries are 'sealed' in the Soviet Constitution.)[19] The demographic character of the peninsula, never favourable to the Tatars in this century (only 19.4 per cent at the time of deportation), is startlingly less so today (0.8 per cent), a fact that is at the centre of justifications for the state's position.[20] Moreover, property rights, jobs, housing and all the other considerations of daily life, it is argued, defy just redistribution to accommodate a massive return of Tatars.

Faced with unrelenting Tatar pressure and defiance of regulations by tens of thousands of their number seeking to resettle in the homeland, in part given new impetus by the calls for *glasnost'*, *perestroika* and democratisation, the state has had to address the question of resettlement or risk jeopardising some of the key features of the Gorbachev era. Fearful that acceding to these ultimate Tatar demands would produce undesirable effects in other ethnically contested areas, let alone cause problems within the Crimea itself with the population currently ensconced there, the regime clearly wishes to tread cautiously along a narrow ridge between choices. Keeping distribution to a minimum, retaining control over all important processes at work within Soviet society, setting the tone and direction for social behaviour from the top: these are agenda that the new leadership, still influenced by the experiences and mentality of the old, find continually critical, even if attenuated by its interests in openness and reform.

Thus, with regard to the matter of resettlement, we have witnessed the authorities gingerly formulate and implement a policy over the past two years that seeks to defuse the issue by establishing a mechanism for permitting some Tatars to return to the Crimea. On 4 August 1987, the chief editor of Novosti News Agency, Valentin Felin, was quoted as saying that 'perhaps 5,000 Tatars would be permitted to resettle' as a test of the concept's feasibility.[21] The first report of the Gromyko Commission, however, was less encouraging, limiting its response to a call for 'more precisely defin[ing]' the existing regulations on residence in the Crimea and other health resort areas of the country.[22] This was followed by an unpublished decision of the USSR Council of Ministers (24 December) which 'temporarily' halted the granting of residence permits for fourteen regions and cities in the Crimea and for eleven in Krasnodar, effectively excluding new settlement of Tatars from half the peninsula and, from the Tatar perspective, its two most meaningful urban centres: Bakhchisarai and Simferopol.[23]

On 4 February 1988, the second Gromyko report, apparently in keeping with the decision of the Council of Ministers, announced without detail that the procedure for residence registration in all resort areas, including the Crimea, were now 'more clearly defined'. Simultaneously it called for the removal of 'unjustified obstacles to their [the Tatars'] change of residence'.[24] *Pravda vostoka* reported on 6 March that Gromyko's Commission decided to allow approved Tatars to return to the Crimea. Permission would be granted mainly to those who had a good work record and recommendations from official institutions. Resettlement, 'as conditions are created', would be primarily in the northern steppe region, not in resort areas along the Black Sea coast.[25] Incredibly, the first announced group to be permitted resettlement under the new procedure comprised only nine men and their families, although 300 families were projected to be involved by the end of 1988.[26]

These insignificant numbers clearly will do little to augment the Tatar population in their homeland, which according to the most recent estimate, is about 41,500.[27] As a result, a stalemate currently continues between the Tatars wanting to resettle and the authorities intent on maintaining restrictive policies. Especially telling is the effective conclusion, more in the form of a warning, of the Gromyko Commission's final report, where it is asserted that this was the extent of its compromise.

Within the past year, however, the refusal of the Tatars to accept the concessions granted is equally apparent. Demonstrations and petitions remain major aspects of their agenda; in response to the brutal treatment of about 5,000 demonstrators in Tashkent on 26 June 1988, the staff of *Lenin Bayrag'y* (twenty-two of its twenty-five members) undertook an immediate political strike; Mustafa Dzhemilev announced the creation of a Crimean Tatar National Movement Organisation on 2 May 1989, while information about the establishment of at least nine associations in the Crimea and Krasnodar has filtered abroad;[28] and, reflecting the recent public assertion of Islam's central position among the Tatars, pressure is building for the establishment of an official Muslim Religious Board for the Crimea and a religious teaching institution in Simferopol.

If anything, the keys to Tatar success in the past – the remarkable cohesion, steadfastness and resilience of their community, the flexibility of its tactics and adherence to simple principles of action that prize struggle within the framework of Soviet and international law and eschewal of all forms of violence – are even more likely to reap desired results under the current conditions of the Gorbachev era than under former ones. Whether cultural concessions granted piecemeal will assuage Tatar appetites remains to be seen; they will not, I suspect, prove a substitute for the one demand that has always been at the heart of the movement: return to the homeland for all who desire it. 'Let no one think,' wrote a Tatar poet not long ago, 'that the Crimean Tatar people is a flock of sheep which cares not where it grazes so long as it has its fill.'[29]

NOTES

1. L. Klimovich *Islam v tsarskoi Rossii* (Moscow 1936), chap. VII.
2. Ann Sheehy *The Crimean Tatars and Volga Germans: Soviet Treatment of Two National Minorities* (London 1971), p. 12.
3. Necip Abdülhamitoglu *Türksüz Kirim: Yüzbinlerin Sürgünü* (Istanbul 1974), pp. 135–36.
4. 'Declaration – 1984' in Edward Allworth (ed.) *Tatars of the Crimea: Their Struggle for Survival* (Durham NC, Duke University Press 1988), p. 225.
5. Ibid., p. 226.
6. Ibid., pp. 226, 228.
7. See the letter from Server Seutov, identified as the 'official religious representative of the Muslim believers of the Crimean Tatar Nation' in *The Central Asian Newsletter* 5–6 (Dec. 1988), p. 4.
8. CMD from Munich, 6 Aug. 1987.
9. Reuters in English from Moscow, 9 June 1988; 'Soobshchenie gosudarstvennoi komissii' *Izvestiya* 10 June 1988.

10. *Izvestiya* 1 Aug. 1987, cited in *The Central Asian Newsletter* VI (6) (Dec. 1987), p. 4.

11. See the following: TASS in English from Kiev, 25 Aug. 1988; 'Milletleraga Münasebet ve Milliy Til' *Lenin Bayrag'y* 49 (27 April 1989), p. 4' 'V TsK Kompartii Ukrainy' *Pravda Ukrainy* 5 Jan. 1989, p. 1, reporting a resolution of the Central Committee of the Ukrainian CP on inter-ethnic relations in the republic.

12. On the problems of teacher training, see M. Medzhitov 'K'rymtatar Tilinin Iak'yn Keledzhegi' *Lenin Bayrag'y* 147 (17 Dec. 1988), p. 4.

13. The most valuable texts are *Ana Tili* (treating phonetics and morphology), *Ana Tilinde* (a reader drawing upon classical and contemporary Tatar writers), and *K'rymtatardzha-Ruscha Lug'at* (a Crimean Tatar–Russian dictionary), all appearing in Kiev in 1988.

14. Portions of the dictionary appeared irregularly for several years through the mid-1980s; the column commenced on 1 May 1989.

15. For Uzbekistan, see the expanded programming as listed in *Lenin Bayrag'h;* for Tadzhikistan, see TASS in Russian from Dushanbe, 11 Jan. 1989, and TASS in Russian from Kulyab (Tadzhikistan), 18 Feb. 1989.

16. Pronina, 'Dostluk – znachit druzhba' *Pravda Ukrainy*, 19 April 1989, p. 4; Iu. Kandymov 'K'rymda Ana Tilimizde Gazeta Chyk'yp Bashlady' *Lenin Bayrag'y* 81 13 July 1989), p 4.

17. 'Tatar or Crimean Tatar?' *The Crimean Review* IV (1) (June 1989), p. 12; *Sovetskaya entsiklopediya* (Moscow, Narody mira 1989).

18. For critical reviews, see I.I. Krupnik in *Sovetskaya etnografiya*, 5 (Sept.–Oct. 1988), pp. 157–60 (reprinted in *Lenin Bayrag'y*, 146 (15Dec. 1988), p. 4; and E. Umerov and E. Amit, 'Rekord pospeshnosti' *Literaturnaya gazeta* 9 Nov. 1988.

19. 'Soobshchenie gosudarstvennoi komissii' *Izvestiya* 10 June 1988.

20. Novosti Press Agency, 24 May 1988.

21. AP from Frankfurt, 4 Aug. 1987.

22. TASS in English from Moscow, 15 Oct. 1987; 'Zasedanie gosudarstvennoi komissii' *Pravda* 16 Oct. 1987.

23. AFP from Moscow, 7 Feb. 1988.

24. AP from Moscow, 4 Feb. 1988.

25. AP from Moscow, 12 March 1988.

26. 'V goskomtrude Uzbekskoi SSR i respublikanskoi rabochei komissii predstabitelei krymskikh tatar' *Pravda vostoka* 30 April 1988.

27. TASS from Moscow, 16 May 1989.

28. The strike was reported by the Centre for Democracy in the USSR, 5 July 1988; the new national organisation was announced in 'Mustafa Dzhemilev's Latest Message' *The Crimean Review* IV (1) (June 1989), p. 8; on the associations, see *Central Asia and Caucasus Chronicle* VIII (2) (May 1989), pp. 9–10.

29. Reuters from Bakhchisarai, 24 Aug. 1987, quoting the poet Yazydzhiev.

CHAPTER TWENTY-ONE

Jews

Yoram Gorlizki

Had the Soviet ethnic minorities in the late inter-war period sought an affirmatory model of Lenin's integrationist prophecies for the nationalities,[1] they might well have turned to the example of the Jews. By the late 1930s, the Jews were educationally the most mobile, geographically the most urban and linguistically one of the most Russified of the non-Russian nationalities. It seemed, as Lenin had predicted, that once the artificial and discriminatory caste status imposed by the tsars had been erased, the Jews would be carried by their vaunted 'internationalism' towards inevitable assimilation.

Nevertheless, it was, paradoxically, the very rapidity and seeming success of this assimilation which provoked the new, Soviet mix of governmental restrictions and social resentment that was to impede the former's further development. Furthermore, sparked off, originally, by the Holocaust, but driven by a number of other factors, there was a conspicuous rise in the national self-awareness of the Jews in the post-war period. Although this came to be partially reflected in the emigration movement of the 1970s, it has only been under the Gorbachev administration that the contours of Jewish ethnic consciousness have been given their fullest range of expression.

However much the present changes might represent a return to the Jewish historical community, Soviet Jewry is structurally and geographically much transformed from what it was in 1917, and in order to grasp the distance travelled in the intervening period, we would do as well to delve, albeit briefly, into the circumstances under which Russian Jewry entered the Soviet fold.

BACKGROUND

It was with the Partitions of Poland in the latter third of the eighteenth century that Imperial Russia acquired the vast majority of its Jews.

The years of tsarist rule which followed saw many reforms and reactions, but two trends in particular stand out. The first of these was the marked deterioration of the Jewish economy. Jewish industry, drastically under-capitalized and largely focused on consumer goods (clothing and textiles), was fettered by the slow and uneven growth of the internal market and undercut by the rise of large-scale, non-Jewish manufacturing. Moreover, the many Jews formerly engaged as independent commercial intermediaries, creditors and tax collectors, were marginalised by the introduction of trade barriers and by the expansion of modern financial institutions. By the end of the nineteenth century the Jewish population had leapt to over 5 million, and numerous official reports recount that much of it had been proletarianised or reduced to petty hawking and peddling, and thrown into a poverty and destitution only partly alleviated by the extensive network of relief.[2]

The second feature of note was the much troubled relation between the Jews and the tsarist state. Imperial Russia never fully partook in the emancipation of Jewry which had occurred across the rest of Europe from the 1780s onwards. As much a consequence of the uniqueness of its 'Jewish problem' (that is, of integrating Russian Jewry, unparalleled in size and social composition, into an agrarian and economically under-developed society), and of its inherently bureaucratic response to the social unrest which threatened to flow from it, as it was of the supposedly virulent anti-Semitism at its higher reaches,[3] the empire retained a system of civil disabilities which cumulatively subjected the Jews to over 1,400 specific legal provisions and thousands of lesser rules.[4] The central pillar of this edifice of 'bureaucratic Judaeophobia' was the establishment of the Pale of Settlement, which by law confined the residence and movement of the overwhelming majority of Jews to the western borders of the empire; but many other significant rules existed as well, and the social and spatial separations which they entailed together acted to prevent the Jews from admission into full citizenship.[5]

It was in response to the especially severe 'May Laws' of 1882, and to the outbreak of anti-Jewish pogroms which had led up to them, that the Jews began to take their fate into their own hands. By the First World War nearly a third had emigrated, mostly to the United States. Others, meanwhile, were drawn into domestic and Zionist politics, with a particularly high incidence of Jews in the socialist and liberal movements. In reaction to the growing partisan pressures around them some of the exclusively Jewish groups began to display increasingly nationalist leanings. After 1901, the platform of the most important Jewish party, the Bund, was significantly to depart from that of their one-time allies, the Bolsheviks, for the former began to insist not only on the equal civil freedoms which the Jews had been denied as individuals, but also on collective national rights, such as cultural and linguistic autonomy for the Jews. Lenin's retort, that the preservation of national culture would merely service the caste status which had so far separated the Jews from their host environment, was later to prove decisive.[6]

THE JEWS AS PART OF SOVIET LIFE

In April 1917 the Provisional government legislated to free the Jews from their caste coordinates.[7] True to his word, Lenin did not go back on these newly won freedoms when the Bolsheviks swept to power in October. The price to be exacted for this, however, was a coordinated crackdown on independent Jewish national institutions of virtually any description. The Bund and the Jewish communal councils (the *kahals*) were disbanded, while the Zionist parties and the religious institutions, which proved the most resistant to change, were targeted in a series of intensive campaigns.[8] In this task the regime was assisted, even prompted, by the new Jewish section of the Party, the *Evsektsiya*.[9] But however much the Party may have turned to its *Evsektsii* to carry out the campaigns of the 1920s, its need for them was strictly provisional. Owing to their lack of a compact historical territory, the Jews did not qualify as a *nation* in the eyes of the regime.[10] The vain attempts to settle the Jews in common areas, such as the Jewish Autonomous Province first set up in Birobidzhan in 1928, only ended in failure. In true dialectical style, the *Evsektsiya* sowed the seeds of its own destruction by helping to create the conditions under which it was no longer needed. In not belonging to the class of territorial institutions that had become the only legitimate form of national Communist organisations, it was dispensed with in January 1930.[11]

These cultural and political upheavals were accompanied by shifts in the occupational structure of the Jews. War Communism and the pogroms of 1919–21 had seen the undoing of the Jewish economy in the old Pale of Settlement.[12] The number of Jewish merchants, owners of enterprises (including artisans) and 'persons without a defined occupation' fell dramatically, as Jewish workers were rapidly drawn into the nationalised economy. With the majority entering the state's new industrial plants, the proportion of labourers among Jews doubled between 1926 and 1939 (rising from 15.1 per cent to 30.5 per cent). Moreover, their cultural emphasis on learning fitted the Jews well to the requirements of the flourishing administrative and technical arms of the state. Consequently, the percentage of white-collar workers in the Jewish population swelled from 10 per cent in 1897 to 29 per cent in 1926 and 40 per cent in 1939.[13]

There were spatial corollaries too, of this conscription of the Jews into the Soviet modernisation programme. First, the already high percentage of urbanised Jews rose even further, and this was accompanied by the migration of Jews from the small market towns (the *shtetlakh*) to the larger cities.[14] And second, after the abrogation of the Pale there was a sizeable drift of Jews eastwards, with some 400,000 having moved towards the interior by 1939.[15]

These demographic and spatial trends were further enhanced by the Second World War and its after-effects. Centres of traditional Jewish life to the west were the worst hit by the ravages of the Holocaust. The Jewish population of the areas gained under the Molotov–Ribbentrop Pact was cut from 1.8 million to 220,000. In the 'old' Ukraine losses amounted to nearly half the pre-war population.[16] By contrast, the Jews of the interior, who were generally more assimilated, were spared the worst excess of the war, and their relative proportion consequently grew. Thus the social balance of Soviet Jewry swung further away from the so-called 'westerners' (*zapadniki*), who were relatively prone to ethnic particularism, and towards the more integrated and sovietised 'heartlanders'. By the late 1970s the latter accounted for nearly three quarters of Soviet Jewry.[17] And this process was geographically reflected in the further nation-wide dispersal of the Jews. By 1979 only just over a third dwelled in the Ukraine, nearly two-fifths in the RSFSR, 12 per cent in the southern republics, 7 per cent in Belorussia and 4 per cent in Moldavia.[18]

After the war, the Jews had become so heavily urbanised as to be described as the only fully urban Soviet ethnic group.[19] What migration there was, had become intra-urban rather than rural–urban, as the Jews came further to be concentrated in the largest cities, republican capitals and centres of higher education.[20] Their location in the cities was purportedly to provide further impetus to the modernisation of Soviet Jewry and to their acculturation and integration into Soviet society.

These trends towards assimilation were, however, significantly offset by the upsurge of Jewish national consciousness after the Second World War. This was caused, in part, by the ripples sent off by the newly established state of Israel in 1948, and by the effects of the movement eastwards of the war-wearied and more traditional Jews from the west. There were other reasons as well, however, for the growth in ethnic consciousness, and these we can directly ascribe to the Soviet state's treatment of the Jews. In the first place, and most strikingly, there was the trauma of the 'Black Years' of 1948–53. The specifically Jewish tragedies of the war[21] produced a profound sense of shock in much of Soviet Jewry and, by contrast to the official silences in the mainstream media, prompted a certain literary introversion among many Soviet Jewish writers.

However, such concerns were soon pegged on to the nail of 'bourgeois nationalism', and as the pitch of these attacks rose, many Jewish writers and cultural activists were arrested, and what Jewish cultural production that had survived the 1930s was eliminated. This campaign to neutralise Jewish national feeling was then superseded by the related, but separate, infamous offensive against 'rootless cosmopolitanism' which peaked early in 1949, and which was aimed more at the *assimilated* Jewish intelligentsia by decrying, rather, their *lack* of 'Soviet' sentiments.[22] The Jews, it seemed, 'were to be damned for remaining separate and damned for not'.[23] The press was heavy with accusations of anti-patriotism, obsequiousness to the West and 'alienation from Russian culture'. Over 80 per cent of those attacked more than three times in the press were Jews.[24] Four years later the exposure of the 'Doctors' Plot' was apparently designed to lead to a show trial and, possibly, to the mass deportation of Jews.[25] Although they were reprieved by Stalin's sudden death, these experiences were to damage irrevocably the image thus far cultivated by the regime of unhindered Jewish assimilation.

The second factor which contributed to a renewed Jewish self-awareness was the appearance of anti-Semitism in the print media from the early 1970s. Located on the fringes of the anti-Zionism campaign which followed the Six Day War, it often fused with popular misconceptions of the Jewish 'conspiracy' to cause great unease among many Soviet Jews. While the ostensible purpose of the campaign was to insulate the loyal and compliant corpus of Soviet Jewry from 'Zionist' elements at home and abroad, the effect was often the reverse. Certain writers and publicists trawled a wider net, using Zionism and Jewishness interchangeably, to the point where it was difficult in the popular mind to distinguish the one from the other.[26] Thus official anti-Semitism contributed to the marginalisation and self-identification of Jews as in some sense a separate category.

Growing discriminatory pressures in education and employment were the third, and possibly the major, factor behind the emerging estrangement of Soviet Jewry. From the late 1930s, Jewish representation in positions of high visibility (such as politics) and in the foreign and security services had been slashed. This tended to drive the Jews further in the direction of the relatively secluded backwaters of academic research and the professions. In 1959, the proportion of Jews who had completed at least half a programme of higher education was over four times that of the rest of the urban population.[27] But the Khrushchev education boom aroused professional career expectations that his successors were hard put to satisfy, thus increasing the competition for jobs traditionally held by Jews. With quotas tacitly organised along national lines, the Jews suffered from the lack of a representative apparatus to safeguard their interests. When combined with the effects of local active discrimination, this meant that the marked relative and absolute fall in Jewish students in the 1970s far exceeded the comparative decline of Jews in the age cohort from which students are chosen.[28] With nearly three-fifths of Soviet Jews loosely defined as 'a professional work force',[29] and the Jews variously over-represented among scientists, doctors, lawyers, journalists and the literary intelligentsia by factors of between five and ten,[30] this squeeze was likely to lead to a not inconsiderable escalation of middle-class ethnic consciousness among the Jews.

With varying degrees of influence and immediacy, these three factors helped set out the foundations for the demands which, seen in another light, were perhaps the most extreme form of 'exit' from the post-Stalin 'social contract' – namely, the demands to leave the USSR, to emigrate.[31] The appeal of winning international trading concessions and of ridding itself of unassimilable traditional and frustrated professional elements meant that these demands unexpectedly met with official Soviet approval in the early 1970s. Over the next ten years, until the final demise of *détente*, a quarter of a million Jews left the Soviet Union, the bulk heading for Israel but a growing proportion 'opting out' for the USA.

When taken in conjunction with the past effects of war and of boundary changes, the emigration of the 1970s and the various 'modern' demographic patterns exhibited by the Jews, such as low fertility and high rates of mixed marriage, have caused the Soviet Jewish population to shrink dramatically: from a high of 5.2 million at the turn of the century to a frayed and ageing 1.4 million in 1989. Moreover, the emigration markedly depleted the community of Jewish national content, the remaining active elements being subject to a wave of intense repression in the early 1980s. At the other end of the spectrum stood a Jewish sub-group that continued to strive for maximum integration and to attain those means of prestige still available to them. In the late 1970s, Jews still comprised the highest per capita membership of the Communist Party and, after the Russians, they accounted for a higher absolute number of 'scientific workers' than any other national group.[32] In between the nationalist wing, and the still successful portion of super-assimilated Jewry, were the so-called 'silent majority' – who returned to the status quo ante, adapted to conditions as best they could, and lowered their sights in a manner not unprecedented in Russian or, indeed, in Soviet, Jewish history.

GORBACHEV AND THE JEWS

The rebirth of a Jewish national movement in the 1970s, and the associated phenomena of Jewish dissidence and emigration, directed much media attention in the West to the plight of Soviet Jewry. Under Gorbachev, this former focus of overseas concern has been somewhat overshadowed by wider developments. By September 1987 all the veteran Prisoners of Zion, Anatolyi Sharanskii and Iosif Begun among them, had been released, and most have since left for Israel. The upsurge of national feeling in the Transcaucasus, the Baltic republics and elsewhere has further served to eclipse the Jewish issue from foreign view. Meanwhile, domestically, the Jews do not command a high priority on the official political agenda. Indeed, it is difficult to speak with confidence of a specific government *policy* towards the Jews. What government pronouncements there have been have centred more on the Jews as a member of the 'non-indigenous nationalities', a group whose profile has shot up under Gorbachev. Even here, however, as we shall see, concessions have been primarily cultural rather than political.

Nevertheless, Soviet Jewry continues to capture attention disproportionate to that which its percentage of the population would appear to warrant. This is, first, because emigration and cultural rights remain a live issue for international Jewry. Although less adversarial than they once were, Jewish and human rights lobbies abroad have acted to bring pressure to bear either on their own governments or directly on the Soviet regime.[33] The second reason is the high cultural and socio-economic profile of the Jews within the USSR. The Jews are highly concentrated in intelligentsia positions, and this is especially so in Leningrad and Moscow where, after the Russians, they constitute the largest nationality.[34] Furthermore, in common with other periods of transition and uncertainty in Russia, anti-Semitism has re-emerged under Gorbachev as an issue of great political resonance in wider internal debates.[35]

Glasnost' and anti-Semitism

Glasnost' has facilitated the acceptance of diversity in Soviet society and the recognition of conflict in its national relations, and this has had a tangible Jewish dimension. Originating in the broader and instrumentalist intention of exploring national complexities and airing their pent-up grievances,[36] there has been a gradual restoration of a Jewish presence in the Soviet media. After years of submitting to the exclusive dogma of assimilationism, whereby Jewishness was depicted as incidental, and Jewish achievements and history were belittled, there has been a notable rise of Jewish-related themes, and of Jewish names (where Russian-sounding pseudonyms had been used before), in the press. Following five decades of silence or distortion, the 'Jewish question' has once again resurfaced as an issue of importance in Soviet public affairs.[37]

Although the emergence of the 'Jewish question' is an inevitable accompaniment to the loosened and unfolding dynamics of a more liberal public sphere, it has also been prompted by two, more specific, political currents. The first of these relates to the growth of the anti-Semitic informal associations. The most noteworthy of such groups, *Pamyat'*, was flung into prominence in December 1985 after the reading at one of its meetings of the classic anti-Semitic text, 'The Protocols of the Elders of Zion'. Displaying certain affinities with movements from the turn of the century, *Pamyat'* has peddled the notion of a 'Jewish world conspiracy' and of a 'Zionist-Masonic plot', to which it allocates the blame for a number of contemporary Soviet ills.[38] Despite various ructions, the radical wing of the organisation was found sufficiently disturbing to arouse criticism in the press, as of the spring of 1987.[39] At first rather muted, the attacks were stepped up after the publicity given *Pamyat'* by the meeting of its leaders with Boris Yeltsin on 6 May 1987. For over two months there appeared a flurry of articles in the newspapers which condemned the organisation and its links with anti-Semitism in terms unseen in the Soviet Union for decades.[40] Although subsequent invectives have differed in their emphases, and some pieces have chosen to defend certain strands in *Pamyat'*, there has since March 1987 been an almost regular stream of articles on popular anti-Semitism, and their tone has been on occasion extremely hostile to it.[41]

The severity of this reaction to *Pamyat'* seems to have been prompted by the spread of its influence to branch and sister organisations in other cities,[42] and by an anxiety that its ideas might strike a vein of 'social anti-Semitism' previously nourished by the official anti-Zionist campaigns of the 1970s.[43] The campaigns of that period, prompted in high-circulation books and journals,[44] stressed the conspiratorial form and global intention of international Zionism in a manner which now appeared uncomfortably familiar. In order to discredit this line, a number of authoritative articles have, from the beginning of 1987, striven to reassert the orthodox critique of Zionism as a form of bourgeois Jewish nationalism, and to return to the classical position, that Zionism is a junior and not a senior partner in international imperialism.[45]

Pamyat's extreme anti-Semitism has a complex relationship with, secondly, the surrogate role played by anti-Semitism in mainstream debates over politics and history;[46] initially triggered off by a literary controversy in 1986, the anti-Semitic aspects of the debate have become increasingly widespread and more overtly political.[47] The most controversial manifestation of this was the publication of Nina Andreyeva's infamous letter-cum-article in *Sovetskaya Rossiya* of 13 March 1988. Widely considered a manifesto for the conservative opposition to *perestroika*,[48] the article simmered with anti-Semitic innuendo. It surreptitiously tied Soviet Jewish writers to overseas allegiances, scathingly linked 'refusenikism' with 'cosmopolitanism', and adopted plainly Stalinist categories such as the 'counter-revolutionary nations' with barely concealed anti-Jewish intent.[49] Although foiled by the comprehensive retort in *Pravda* three weeks later, the anti-Semitic (as well as other) leanings of the Andreyeva 'counter-offensive' have continued to find echoes in the conservative press.[50] A favoured tactic has been to divert opprobrium away from Stalin and the economic and political structures shaped under him, and on to Jewish figures, whose original names are on occasion 'unmasked'.[51]

Andreyeva's reference to the 'cosmopolitan tendency' and, implicitly, to the attacks of the late Stalin period on the assimilated Jewish intelligentsia ran utterly counter to the complete exoneration of this group simultaneously taking place in other parts of the media. In particular, Gorbachev's confirmation in November 1987 that the 'Doctors' plot' had been a fabrication gave the most authoritative of signals to a number of personal recollections of the case that appeared the following year.[52] Equally, after many years of petitioning, a front-page announcement of *Pravda* on 27 January 1989 finally publicised both the rehabilitation of the Jewish Anti-Fascist Committee (which had been dissolved in the 'Black Years') and the posthumous restoration of eight of their number to Communist Party membership.[53]

These officially sanctioned openings have led to initiatives in culture and the arts which extend beyond what might be conceived of as 'expedient' to the state. Vassily Grossman's long suppressed novel 'Zhizn' i Sud'ba', for example, which was serialised in *Oktyabr'* in early 1988, used anti-Semitism as a thread which ran through the war and post-war periods and through which the Soviet and Nazi systems were implicitly compared.[54] Other, completely candid, accounts of the Jewish Holocaust, and of anti-Semitism and anti-Jewish discrimination within the Soviet framework, have followed suit.[55]

In short, therefore, *glasnost'* has brought the Jewish question into the open, and this has had two major effects. First, hidden undercurrents of anti-Semitism have been raised to the surface and dealt with explicitly. In view of Soviet and Russian history, this must be considered a sign of health. Second, and this has come more slowly, it is now more common to find *positive* (as opposed to a defence against negative) descriptions of a distinct Jewish identity and traditions in the media.[56] This is especially important since it has been the pervasive ignorance of Jewish matters, borne out of the long-term denial of Jewish culture and history in the Soviet Union, that has given anti-Semitism such fertile ground on which to breed.

Jewish Issues

Important as has been the general elevation of the 'Jewish question' in public affairs, it needs to be separated from the various direct expressions of Jewish ethnic consciousness which have been generated 'from below'. A most obvious manifestation of this has been the organisation of Jewish meetings and demonstrations. Originally conducted in private apartments, such meetings have gradually moved out into the open. On the 26 April 1987, after the adverse publicity in the West given to the violent break-up of a 'refusenik'[57] rally that February, the two largest gatherings of Jews in many years were held, without the intervention of the authorities, in commemoration of Jewish resistance in the war.[58] A similar meeting a year later was the first to gain official permission, and since then a number of demonstrations on a variety of themes, and attracting ever larger numbers, have taken place.[59] By equal measure this progress has not been unimpeded. For example, the applications to demonstrate against contemporary anti-Semitism in September 1987 were not only rejected, but were also attended by a host of nasty attacks in the press.[60] Other events, particularly refusenik demonstrations, usually on a smaller scale, continue to be forcefully disbanded, and their participants subject to arrest.[61]

While these events might collectively be considered manifestations of a 'Jewish national movement' such a label conceals a significant heterogeneity of interests and issues. Even before the rebirth of the movement in the 1970s, core activists had long been afflicted by divisions between the Hebraists and the Yiddishists, the Zionists and the non-Zionists, the 'establishment' and the non-establishment Jews, and these differences persist to this day. This has been reflected in the diverse if not always mutually exclusive or contradictory nature of the issues involved.

The first such issue, which has won broad support among the movement as a whole, has been the remembrance of the Jewish past. This has been marked by commemorative meetings, the opening of museums, the introduction of study courses and by appeals that Jewish national monuments be erected.[62] Second, and with the active support of a smaller Jewish constituency, there have been calls for a relaxation of the conditions under which the Jewish religion is practised. These demands have been partly satisfied by the establishment of a Jewish seminary in Leningrad, of limited kosher facilities in Moscow, and by the transfer of 10,000 Jewish texts into the Soviet Union in the summer of 1988.[63] Although most estimates put the number of religious believers at less than 5 per cent of the Jewish population, the Holy Days have reportedly seen increasing throngs at the synagogues.[64]

A third issue, and one of the most divisive, is that of language. While the expanded teaching facilities[65] and the improved overall fortunes of the Yiddish press institutions (the journal *Soviet Heymland* and the newspaper *Birobidzhaner Shtern*), have helped counterbalance the long-term relative underproduction of materials in Yiddish, other groups, and especially the religious and Zionist ones, have tended to associate Yiddish with the antiquated culture of the nineteenth century, and to posit Hebrew instead as the linguistic basis of the Jewish renaissance. However, although there has been some movement on the latter front,[66] it is a measure of the linguistic acculturation of the Jews that many activists would prefer resources intended for Jewish consumption to be funnelled into the Russian rather than the Jewish languages, since Russian is now the mother tongue of the vast majority of Soviet Jews.[67] Early sign of such a development was the introduction in 1985 of an annual almanac of selected translations into Russian from *Sovetish Heymland*.[68]

The pursuit of each of these causes received a considerable boost from the reappraisal at the 19th Party Conference of cultural policy towards the non-indigenous nationalities.[69] Following the conference, a Jewish Academy was set up in Moscow and supplied with premises, a grant from the Academy of Sciences, and accommodation for some of its forty full-time and 100 part-time students; a Soviet Committee for the Preservation of Jewish Historical Monuments and Documents was established; and several experimental Jewish newspapers and broadsheets were brought out in Russian.[70] The conference resolution also added momentum to the many established and fledgeling Jewish ensembles and theatre companies in the USSR.[71] Its greatest impact, however, was to approve the 'creation of seats of national culture', thereby giving legitimacy to the Jewish clubs and societies which had, and have since, sprouted around the country.[72] The growth of these associations culminated in the 'festival of Jewish culture' in February 1989 which coincided with the opening of the showpiece Solomon Mikhoels Centre in Moscow.[73]

These developments have not been free of their doubts and ambiguities, however. Despite the fanfare at its opening, the Mikhoels centre has been ridden with bureaucratic resistance, to the extent that its foreign funding organisation at one point threatened to pull out of the scheme.[74] Moreover, the many years of suppression have left a narrow and somewhat inauthentic artistic and cultural basis to cope with such a hidden and unexpected boom in demand. In addition, some of the societies are organisationally linked to 'establishment' Jewish personalities and institutions, and there has been friction between them and their newly legitimised colleagues, some of whom were formerly their adversaries.[75] Nevertheless, there have been indications of certain forms of cooperation emerging, and none better nor, possibly, more politically significant, than the first All-Union meeting of cultural groups in Riga in May 1989, organised by the Moscow-based Jewish Cultural Association and attended by 180 delegates representing forty clubs and associations from all over the Soviet Union.[76]

The most controversial and internationally the best-known of the issues for which Soviet Jews have campaigned is that of emigration. After reaching a high point of 51,000 in 1979, the number of Jews leaving the USSR slumped as dramatically as it had grown ten years earlier, falling to 1,000 to 2,000 per annum in the mid-1980s. It seemed as if the maverick phenomenon had come to an end. Two years into the Gorbachev administration, however, amidst an improved international climate, the pace of Jewish emigration picked up again, soaring from 914 in 1986 to 8,155 in 1987, 18,961 in 1988 and an estimated 50,000 in 1989.[77]

Nevertheless, despite their virtue of codifying the procedure for emigration,[78] the new laws which have accompanied this escalation have not touched on the central issue: namely, that emigration does not exist as a *right* in the Soviet Union. This means that the rates of emigration remain theoretically liable to sharp vicissitudes, dependent in large measures on the particular receptiveness of the regime to internal and, especially, to external pressures. This essential *uncertainty* might lead some Jews to take advantage of the opportunities while they appear to last. In order to counteract this tendency, the authorities have made a point of wooing former 'refuseniks',[79] and they have eased conditions for short-term travel to Israel, hence removing some of the incentive from permanent emigration. Other, negative feedback processes, also appear to work in their favour. Over three-quarters of the Gorbachev Jewish emigrants, including the vast majority of 'refuseniks', have preferred the United States over Israel, but both the American Jewish community and the State Department have intimated that they will be unable to meet the long-term absorption costs of the projected influx.[80] Were the possibility of entering the USA to be significantly reduced, however, it is likely that the number of Soviet Jews seeking emigration would also fall.[81]

This raises the central point that the prime considerations leading to the present wave of emigration appear to be not cultural or religious but rather social and economic.[82] A major factor, first, is the unavailability of suitable employment opportunities, especially for the sizeable proportion of educated, middle-class Jews who fear for their careers, and for those of their children.[83] It is true that the Jews have been spared the purges of the national *apparat* which have afflicted the union republic nationalities; that the creative intelligentsia, which has a high proportion of Jews, has profited from the liberalisation of *glasnost*'[84] and that Jews are supposedly concentrated in the co-operative movement, which has also fared well under Gorbachev.[85] Nevertheless, the new bond of science and production, and the demand for skilled Jewish labour anticipated under *uskorenie* (economic acceleration), has clearly not materialised.[86] Moreover, the importance of ethnic criteria in determining the central allocation of prized placements in education and the economy does not appear to have been significantly eroded, and this is to the detriment of the Jews, who have no formal means of representation at this focal point of inter-national competition.[87] As for local active discrimination, where change is especially difficult to monitor, there are initial signs of improvements, though some institutions long blocked to the Jews appear to remain so.[88] Patterns of recruitment are notoriously slow to emerge, but veiled references in the liberal sections of the press to the continued presence of 'bureaucratism' and 'Lysenkoism' in the research institutions suggest that the build-up of restive anxieties among middle-class Jews, so evident in the 1970s, is yet to be relieved.[89]

A second factor prompting the desire to emigrate is the fear that in case of future instability, the ensuing strife might turn into violence against the traditional scapegoat, the Jews. Although there have so far been only relatively minor and isolated incidents of 'physical' anti-Semitism, such as the desecration of tombstones and the daubing of synagogues, the precedent of recent inter-ethnic violence elsewhere in the Soviet Union does not bode well.[90] Equally important is the *perception* of anti-Semitism, as was demonstrated at the time of the thousandth anniversary of Christian Rus' in June 1988, when 'pogroms' were widely anticipated by Jews in the south-west suburbs of Moscow.[91] Be it in the form of reality or expectation, the spectre of anti-Semitic violence may have a powerful transformatory effect.[92]

CONCLUSION

In order to survey the realities of change for Soviet Jewry we must take one look ahead and one behind. Setting aside the many uncertainties which might dictate future rates of emigration, the larger perspective is that emigration will merely add to the demographic decline in Soviet Jewry already caused by low fertility and high rates of intermarriage.[93] The basic political determinants for the Jews, such as the lack of a national administrative apparatus,[94] and the retention of the internal passport system through which the notion of Jewish nationality takes on its official meaning, are unlikely to be much altered. There appears to be, furthermore, little chance of a political solution to the general economic problem of the overproduction of graduates, which has hit the Jews, with their exceptionally high proportion of professionals, with particular severity. In addition, the rise of *Pamyat'* and of similar groups portends a possible escalation in popular and explicit anti-Semitism, and this has engendered a measure of panic in certain Jewish quarters.[95] Meanwhile, if it continues, the international *rapprochement* with the United States, and the looming contacts with Israel, suggests that overseas pressures in favour of the rights of Soviet Jewry are likely to carry more weight.

Taking a retrospective view, there is a widely held consensus that much has changed with Soviet Jewry since Gorbachev came to power.[96] For better or for worse, anti-Semitism and the 'Jewish question' have emerged as fully fledged elements of Soviet public life. There is now greater cultural freedom as regards national historical aware-ness, religious practice and the Jewish languages. Dozens of Jewish associations have been set up, and there have been hints of an organised Jewish national life taking shape. Although these associations remain in constant and unresolved tension with the so-called 'silent majority' of Jews, the seemingly shifting composition and purpose of the national core of Soviet Jewry does reflect some renewed hope of securing rights and a Jewish future *within* the Soviet Union, as opposed to outside it. And it also prompts us at last to move our attention away from the initiatives of the State, and towards the demands that the State, in its wisdom, might, or might not, be willing or able to meet.

ACKNOWLEDGEMENTS

I would like to thank Yaacov Ro'i for his useful comments on an earlier draft of this chapter, and Howard Spier and the staff at the Institute of Jewish Affairs in London for their assistance in researching it, though none other than the author should be held responsible for the views expressed.

NOTES

1. See Walker Connor *The Marxist Question in Leninist Theory and Strategy* (Princeton, NJ, Princeton University Press 1984), pp. 37, 42n. For the later recognition in Soviet theory of the durability of national identities, see Gail Lapidus 'Ethnonationalism and political stability: the Soviet case' *World Politics* 36 (4) (1984) pp. 562 ff.
2. L. Greenberg *The Jews in Russia* (New Haven, CT, Yale University Press 1965) 1, Chap. 12; Z.Y. Gitelman *Jewish Nationality and Soviet Politics* (NJ, Princeton University Press 1972), pp. 19–22.
3. For an excellent discussion of this, see H. Rogger *Jewish Policies and Right-Wing Politics in Imperial Russia* (London, Macmillan 1986), esp. chaps 1, 2 and 4.
4. Ibid., pp. 25 and 106.
5. For selected translations of these provisions, see P.R. Mendes-Flohr and J. Reinharz *The Jew in the Modern World* (Oxford, Oxford University Press 1980), pp. 303–9.
6. For the text of Bund's all-important resolutions at its fourth convention, and of Lenin's response to them, refer to *ibid.*, pp. 340–41 and 344–46.
7. Text in *ibid.*, p. 349.
8. Gitelman *Jewish Nationality and Soviet Politics*, chaps IV and V; and L. Kochan (ed.) *The Jews in Soviet Russia since 1917*, 3rd edn (Oxford, Oxford University Press 1978), esp. chaps 6 and 8.
9. Gitelman *Jewish Nationality and Soviet Politics*, chaps III ff.
10. See, e.g., J.V. Stalin 'Marxism and the national question' in Stalin *Works* vol. 2 (1907–13) (London, Lawrence & Wishart 1953), p 307, 312–13 and 344–45.
11. Gitelman *Jewish Nationality and Soviet Politics*, pp. 472–75.
12. A. Nove and J.A. Newth 'The Jewish population: demographic trends and occupational patterns' in L. Kochan *The Jews in Soviet Russia*, p. 138.
13. M. Altshuler *Soviet Jewry since the Second World War* (Westport, CT, Greenwood Press 1987), pp. 9–11.
14. Altshuler *Soviet Jewry* pp. 56; and Gitelman *Jewish Nationality and Soviet Politics*, p. 17.

15. At a rate of an estimated 20,000 per annum from 1923 to 1926, and 30,000 per annum between 1926 and 1939. See Nove and Newth 'The Jewish population' pp. 139 and 143. By 1939, 37% of Soviet Jewry lived outside the former Pale (Altshuler, *Soviet Jewry* p. 5).

16. *Ibid.*, pp. 147–49.

17. See T. Friedgut 'Soviet Jewry: the silent majority' *Soviet Jewish Affairs* (henceforth *SJA*) 10 (2) (Summer 1980), p. 5.

18. Altshuler, *Soviet Jewry* p. 62. This is to be compared to the figures for 1939: 50.8% in the Ukraine, 31.4% in the RSFSR, 5% in the southern republics, and 12.4% in Belorussia (B. Pinkus, *The Soviet Government and the Jews 1948–1967* (Cambridge, Cambridge University Press 1984), pp. 26–7.

19. Altshuler, *Soviet Jewry*, p. 229. According to the censuses, 87% of Jews were urban dwellers in 1939, 95.3% in 1959, 97.9% in 1970 and 98.5% in 1979 (*ibid.*, p. 65; and Pinkus, *The Soviet Government and the Jews* p. 28).

20. *Ibid.*, pp. 66, 71 and 230.

21. While the tragedies of the Second World War were far from confined to the Jews, the particularity and purpose with which they were singled out by the Nazis is given testimony to by the fact that in the Soviet areas the proportionate losses inflicted on them were four times greater than those suffered by the rest of the population (Nove and Newth 'The Jewish population', p. 149).

22. Pinkus, *The Soviet Government and the Jews*, chap. 4, esp. pp. 152 and 163.

23. *Ibid.*, p. 5.

24. Pinkus, *The Soviet Government and the Jews*, p. 159.

25. Y. Rapoport 'Vospominaniya o "Dele Vrachei"' *Druzhba Narodov* 4 (1988), p. 225; V. Grossman 'Vse Techet' *Oktyabr'* 6 (1989), p. 38 (translated in English as *Forever Flowing*, (London, Collins Harvill 1988); and B. Pinkus, *The Jews of the Soviet Union* (Cambridge, Cambridge University Press 1988), p. 180.

26. V. Zaslavsky and R.J. Brym *Soviet Jewish Emigration and Soviet Nationality Policy* (New York, St Martin's Press 1983) pp. 20–1.

27. Altshuler *Soviet Jewry*, pp. 108 and 232.

28. Altshuler *Soviet Jewry*, pp. 112, 118–19 and 127. See also *Human Rights and the Helsinki Accords* (London, Institute of Jewish Affairs 1985), pp. 23–6.

29. I.e., in receipt of higher, incomplete higher or a secondary vocational education. This is critical since, unlike the situation in the West, state education in the Soviet Union virtually guarantees later employment in a similar field. (Altshuler *Soviet Jewry*, pp. 143, 152 and 233).

30. L. Hirszowich 'Gorbachev's *perestroika* and the Jews' *IJA Research Report* (May 1987), p. 3.

31. G. Lapidus 'State and society: toward the emergence of civil society in the Soviet Union' in S. Bialer (ed.) *Inside Gorbachev's Russia* (Boulder, CO, Westview Press 1989) pp. 127 and 129.

32. Altshuler *Soviet Jewry*, pp. 163 and 210.

33. Witness, for example, the audience granted to representatives of the World Jewish Congress by senior Soviet officials such as Foreign Minister

Shevardnadze and the then Central Committee Secretaries Yakovlev and Dobrynin (*New York Times*, 31 March 1987, p. 14; and *BBC Summary of World Broadcasts* (henceforth *SWB*) SU/0385(i) 15 Feb. 1989). The issue of the right to leave has, often with direct or slightly disguised reference to the Jewish question, figured highly in international exchanges and informal agreements, as it did in advance of the 1987 superpower summit; in Gorbachev's speech to the UN on 7 Dec. 1988; and at the Vienna Follow-up meeting at the Conference on Security and Cooperation in Europe (E. Litvinoff *Insight: Soviet Jews* July 1988, p. 8; *Concluding Document of the Vienna Meeting of the CSCE Participating States* 17 Jan. 1989, pp. 36–41; and *Izvestiya* 26 Jan. 1989. p. 4).

34. *Argumenty i Fakty* 23, 4–10 June 1988, p. 6; *SJA* 18 p. 15. In 1970, in Moscow, one in eight *Kandidaty* were Jews, as were one in five *Doktory Nauk* (Doctors of Science) (Altshuler, *Soviet Jewry*, pp. 88 and 167).

35. See, e.g., S. Rogov and V. Nosenko 'Zachem "Korrektirobat'" Lenina' *Sovetskaya Kul'tura* 31 May 1989, p. 3.

36. See, e.g., '"Vernost" Bratstvu Narodov' *Pravda* 14 Aug. 1986, p. 1; I. Dedkov 'Vmeste Vchera' *Kommunist* 8 (1988), pp. 19–27.

37. J. Wishnevsky 'Some good news for Soviet Jews' *Radio Liberty Research Bulletin* (henceforth *RLRB*) 121/87, 23 March 1987; and 'A little more *Glasnost'* for Soviet Jews' *RLRB* 100/88, 16 March 1988.

38. H. Spier 'Anti-Semitism unchained' *Research Report no. 3* (London, Institute of Jewish Affairs 1987), p. 5. See also *Sovetskaya Rossiya* 17 July 1987, p. 3; and *Ogonek* 23, 4–11 June 1988, pp. 6–7.

39. A. Cherkizov 'Demokratiya – Ne Raspushchennost', *Sovetskaya Kul'tura* 31 March 1987, p. 3.

40. See esp. articles by E. Lesoto *Komsomolskaya Pravda* 22 May 1987, p. 3, and A. Cherkizov *Sovetskaya Kul'tura*, 18 June 1987, p. 3. Also, the pieces in *Ogonek* (no. 21, 23–30 May 1987). *Izvestiya* (3 June 1987) and *Vechernaya Moskva* (15 June 1987).

41. E.g., *Sovetskaya Kul'tura* 3 Oct. 1987, p. 6; *Komsomolskaya Pravda* 19 Dec. 1987, p. 3; and *Izvestiya* 27 Feb. 1988, p. 5. For two articles which attempted to present a positive, less extreme, side to *Pamyat'*, see: *Sovetskaya Rossiya* 31 Jan. 1988, p. 4; and *Pravda* 1 Feb. 1988, p. 4.

42. E.g., *Pamyat'* and 'Patriot' in Leningrad, 'Otechestvo' in Sverdlovsk, 'Soboryanie' in Irkutsk, and a sizeable branch of *Pamyat'* in Novosibirsk (see *Sovetskaya Kul'tura* 18 April, pp. 3–4, and 18 June 1987, p. 3); *Ogonek* no. 9, 26 Feb.–5 March 1989, pp. 28–31; *Literaturnaya Gazeta* 5 July 1989, p. 11).

43. Although some publications have tried to make the most of the *pre*-Soviet roots of *Pamyat'* (e.g., *Izvestiya* 3 June 1987, p. 3, and *Komsomolskaya Pravda* 19 Dec. 1987, p. 3), there has also been an increasing willingness to concede the recent *Soviet* sources of contemporary anti-Semitism – e.g. *Sovetskaya Kul'tura* 9 Feb. 1989, p. 6; and see the interview with V.I. Tumarkin of the Central Committee apparatus in *Jews and Jewish Topics in Soviet and East European Publications* Centre for Research and Documentation of East European Jewry at the Hebrew University, 7 (Summer 1988), p. 71.

44. Much of this material was brought out under the auspices of the *Molodaya Gvardiya* publishing house in Moscow. Its authors included Yuri Ivanov

(1969), Lev Korneev (1982), Vladimir Begun (1974 1977 and 1979), Valery Emelyanov (1977) and Evgeni Evseev (1978). The most renowned of the journals were *Molodaya Gvardiya, Moskva* and Safronov's *Ogonek* before its volte-face under the new editorship of Vitalyi Korotich in 1986.

45. E.g. Dadiani et al. 'O Nekotorykh Voprosakh . . .' *Voprosy Istorii KPSS* 1 (Jan. 1987), pp. 74–7.

46. The strict separation of *Pamyat'* from the nationalist writers which has been proposed by some commentators (e.g., *Pravda* 1 Feb. 1988, p. 4) has been contested by others; e.g., *Izvestiya*, 27 Feb. 1988, p. 5; and see V. Rasputin *Nash Sovremennik*, 1 (1988), pp. 169–72.

47. See V. Astaf'ev 'Pechal'nyi Detektiv' *Oktyabr'* 1 (1986), and V. Belov 'Vse Vperedi' *Nash Sovremennik* 6–7 (1986). For the responses: V. Lakshin, *Izvestiya* 4 Dec. 1986, p. 3, and N. Eidelman in *samizdat* (reprinted in *Jews and Jewish Topics*, 5 (Summer 1987), pp. 32–50; and the counter in V. Gorbachev *Melodaya Gvardiya* 3 (1987), esp. p. 171. For the increasing politicisation of the debate, refer to Ligachëv's speech at the *Sovetskaya Kul'tura* offices (*Sovetskaya Kul'tura* 7 July 1987, p. 2).

48. S. Bialer 'The changing soviet political system' in S. Bialer (ed.) *Inside Gorbachev's Russia* (Boulder, CO, Westview Press 1989), pp. 203–8.

49. One version of the original 'letter', discovered by the Italian paper '*L'Unita*', contained the chilling remark that 'on careful scrutiny . . . the majority of [Soviet Jews] display Zionist teeth. The Jews of our country have become a nationality apart.' See K. Devlin *RLRB* RL 215/88, 1 June 1988.

50. E.g., in the journals *Nash Sovremennik, Molodaya Gvardiya* and *Moskva*, and in the regional newspaper *Vologodskii Komsomolets*.

51. N. Gul'binskii *Ogonek* 23, 3–10 June 1989, pp. 23–4. For specific examples, see V. Kozhinov *Druzhba Narodov* 1, 1988, p. 181; I. Sein *Molodaya Gvardiya* 4, 1988, p. 278; V. Belov *Pravda* 15 April 1988, p. 3; and V. Pikul' *Nash Sovremennik* 2, 1989, p. 189. Conversely, for a dual denunciation of the Soviet system and its association with Jewish personalities, see A. Kuz'min *Nash Sovremennik* 3, 1988, p. 155 and pp. 157–58.

52. Y. Rapoport *Druzhba Narodov*, 5 (1988), pp. 222–45; D. Gai *Moscow News* 4, 7 Feb. 1988, p. 16; N. Rapoport *Yunost'* 4 (1988), pp. 76–81.

53. See also K. Simonov *Znamya* 4 (1988) esp. pp. 83–95; and M. Geizer *Literaturnaya Gazeta* 6 (1989) p. 8.

54. *Oktyabr'*, 1–4 (1988) and the addendum in 9 (1988), pp. 205–7. Also, see *Ogonek* 40, 3–10 Oct. 1987, pp. 19–23; *Izvestiya* 25 June 1988, p. 3; *Pravda* 4 July 1988, p. 4; *Literaturnaya Gazeta* 34 (1988), p. 5. The book's main character, the vilified Jewish physicist Viktor Shtrum was partly based on the real figure Lev Davidovitch Landau. See *Ogonek* 3, 16–23 Jan. 1988, pp. 13–15; and *Moscow News*, 5, 31 Jan. 1988, p. 10.

55. E.g., the path-breaking article by S. Rogov and V. Nosenko 'Chto skazal "A" i chto skazal "B"' *Sovetskaya Kul'tura*, 9 Feb. 1989, p. 6 (translation in *SJA* 18 (3), pp. 46–55); *Izvestiya* 19 April 1988, p. 5; and *Literaturnaya Gazeta*, 41 (1988), . 15.

56. See B. Berman *Moscow News*, 10, 7 March 1988, p. 3. Questions of Jewish identity have particularly been captured on stage, with Jewish plays put on at the Arts, the Studio and the Heritage theatres in Moscow – N.

Velekhova *Literaturnaya Gazeta* 11, 11 March 1987, p. 8; O. Martynenko
Moscow News, 2, 19 Jan. 1988, p. 11; and *SJA* 19, 1 (1989), p. 94; and
Jewish themes have also appeared on central television – *SJA* 18, 1,
pp. 98–99 (20 Aug. and 4 Sept.). Nevertheless, for an important attack at
the Secretariat of the RSFSR Writers' Union on the *inadequate* coverage
of Jewish literary matters, see *Literaturnaya Rossiya* 16 Dec. 1988, p. 6.

57. The 'refuseniks' are Jews who have submitted applications for emigration
which have been rejected by the authorities. At their height in 1986
there were approximately 11,000 refuseniks in the Soviet Union, who
had waited an average of nine years for permission to leave, and who
accounted for about 0.7% of the Jewish population there. The renewed
emigration of 1987 significantly cut this number, although the present
size of the refusenik community in the Soviet Union is a matter of some
controversy; see M. Altshuler 'Who are the "Refuseniks"? a statistical
and demographic analysis' *SJA* 18 (1) (Spring 1988), pp. 3–15.

58. Four hundred Jews in Leningrad and 250 at the *Vostryakovo* in Moscow;
Daily Telegraph 27 April 1987, p. 26; and *Jews in the USSR* 16 (6) 30
April 1987.

59. *SJA* 18 3 (Winter 1988), p. 97. Also, the demonstrations of 300 in Vilnius
on 8 July 1988 calling for the erection of a memorial to the ghetto; of 500
at the *Vostryakovo* in Moscow on 25 Sept. commemorating Babi Yar; of
500 in Leningrad on the 50th anniversary of *Kristallnacht* and a thousand
at the Jewish cemetery of the same city on 30 April 1989 to mark the
Holocaust (*SJA* 19 1 (Spring 1989), pp. 93–5; *Jews in the USSR* 18 (9)
4 May 1989, p. 1).

60. See A. Torpusman and V. Fulmakht 'Contemporary anti-Semitism and
the Jewish national movement in the USSR' *Jews and Jewish Topics . . .*,
7 (Summer 1988), pp. 60–8; and *Vechernaya Moskva* 7 Sept. 1987, and
Izvestiya, 19 Sept. 1987.

61. See, e.g., *SJA* 18 (3), pp. 96 and 98; and *Jews in the USSR* 16 (21), 11 June
1987; 16 (39), 22 Oct. 1987; 18 (7), 4 April 1989; 18 (11), 1 June 1989;
The Times, 26 Sept. 1988, p. 10. For early signs of a possible softening
of attitudes towards the refusenik demonstrations, see *Moscow News* 9,
26 Feb. 1989, p. 6.

62. See note 60. Also, the private library and museum opened in Moscow in
September 1987 and January 1988 respectively; the plans for a Lithuanian
museum of Jewish culture and for a memorial to the victims of the
Holocaust announced on 2 December 1987; see *Jerusalem Post Magazine*
16 Sept. 1988, pp. 9–11; *SJA* 18 (2), p. 96, and 18 (3), pp. 33 and 97.

63. *Jewish Press* (New York), 24 June 1988; *Jewish Chronicle* (henceforth *JC*),
10 March 1989, p. 5; *SJA* 18 (1), pp. 98–9 and 101.

64. E.g. *Jews in the USSR* 17 (36), 29 Sept. 1988, and 17 (38), 13 Oct. 1988.

65. L. Hirszowicz 'Breaking the mould: the changing face of Jewish culture
under Gorbachev' *SJA* 18 (3) (Winter 1988), pp. 36 and 39–40. Also, see
JC 24 March 1989, p. 3; and *SJA* 19 (1), pp. 94–5.

66. For example, the first convention of the Union of Hebrew Teachers on
18 September 1988 – *Focus Soviet Jewry* (Tel-Aviv) 2 (10), p. 2.

67. According to the 1979 census less than 20% of Jews declared Yiddish
as their second or native tongue, as opposed to the 97% with Russian
(Altshuler *Soviet Jewry*, pp. 182 and 185). The number of Hebrew

speakers is far lower than either, and though no figures are available, it is probably in the region of a few thousand.

68. *God za Godom* (Moscow, *Sovetskii pisatel'*, 1985, 1986, 1987 and 1988), in editions of 30,000.
69. 'O Mezhnatsional'nikh Otnosheniyakh' *Pravda* 5 July 1988, p. 3.
70. SJA 19 (1), p. 96, and 19 (2) (forthcoming); *Forward* (New York 13 Jan. 1989; *SWB* SU/0358, 14 Jan. 1989; *JC* 24 Feb. 1989. p. 3; *Jews in the USSR* 18 (5) 2 March 1989, pp. 1–2 and 18 (10) 18 May 1989, p. 4; *From Soviet Sources* (London, Institute of Jewish Affairs, July 1989), p. 3.
71. Theatres in Moscow, Vilnius and Kaunas and ensembles in Kiev, Chernovtsy, Kherson and Kishinev (interview with Gennadi Eistrakh of *Soviet Heymland* on 18 July 1988; and L. Hirszowicz 'Breaking the mould: the changing face of Jewish culture under Gorbachev' *Soviet Jewish Affairs* 18 (3) (Winter 1988), pp. 37–8).
72. E.g. in the Baltic republics (Vilnius, Riga and Tallinn), the Ukraine (Lvov and Kiev), Minsk, Ufa, Tashkent and Moscow (Hirszowicz, 'Breaking the mould', p. 38).
73. *Jewish Herald International* (London) 10 Feb. 1988, p. 1; *Jews in the USSR* 18 (4), 16 Feb. 1988; and *JC* 31 March 1989, p. 28.
74. *JC* 9 June 1989, p. 52; for the reconciliation, see *Jews in the USSR* 18 (12), 22 June 1989, p. 3.
75. E.g., in the combined involvement of affiliates of the Anti-Zionist Committee with refusenik sympathisers in the Shalom Society for Jewish Culture, which is attached to the Shalom Theatre. Of the other clubs and centres, the Mikhoels is connected to the Jewish Musical Chamber Theatre; the Baltic associations are linked to their respective republican Cultural Funds, while others have either been started from scratch or have become part of existing local, non-Jewish cultural networks (I. Leibler *JC* 31 March 1989, p. 28; L. Hirszowicz, 'Breaking the mould', pp. 32–3, 38 and 41; see also *Pravda* 12 Nov. 1988, p. 6). Jewish activists have also complained of the hand of 'establishment' Jews, such as Viktor Magidson, in the running of a new Jewish newspaper printed by *Izvestiya* (*Jews in the USSR* 18 (10), 18 May 1989, p. 4).
76. *SWB* SU/0465, 24 May 1989; *Jews in the USSR* 18 (11) 1 June 1989, p. 3; at the time of writing a further All-Union Congress was scheduled to take place in Moscow in December 1989 (*JC* 15 Sept. 1989).
77. *SJA* 17 (2), p. 94; 18 (2), p. 96; 19 (2) (forthcoming). The last statistic is based on the figures released by the *Jewish Telegraphic Agency, Jews in the USSR* and *Focus Soviet Jewry* (Tel-Aviv); also see *JC* 15 Sept. 1989, p. 8.
78. The Addendum to the Law on Emigration of January 1987 introduced a new clarity to the emigration procedure but also formalised the denial of exit visas on the grounds of insufficient kinship and the possession of state secrets (F.J. Feldbrugge 'The new Soviet Law on Emigration' *SJA* 17 (1) (Spring 1987), pp. 14–16 and 17–18; and *SJA* 18 (1) p. 97 (11 July). More recently, there has been talk of a draft law which would define the parameters of the secrecy clause; *Index on Censorship*, 17 (9) (Oct. 1988), p. 29; *Moscow News* 9, 26 Feb. 1989, p. 6; and M. Tavbory 'The Vienna CSCE Concluding Document: some general and Jewish perspectives' *SJA* 19 (1) (Spring 1989), pp. 10–12.

79. E.g. R.A. Kuznetsov of OVIR relates that 334 persons who received permission to leave in 1987, eventually decided not to avail themselves of the opportunity (*Argumenty i Fakty* 22, 23 May – 3 June 1988, p. 8; see also 'Soviet authorities seek to induce Jews not to emigrate' *RLRB* 185/87, 14 May 1987).

80. M. Altshuler, *Soviet Jewry* (1988), p. 14; *JC* 6 Jan. 1989, p. 3; 20 Jan. 1989, p. 2 and 15 Sept. 1989, p. 2; and 'Soviet Jews to the US – the tide turns' *Jerusalem Post* 16 June 1989.

81. E. Litvinoff *Insight: Soviet Jewry* July 1988, p. 5; *JC* 22 Sept. 1989, p. 4.

82. Hence the Vice-President of the World Jewish Congress, Isi Leibler, points out that it is not the '*national* obligation [of international Jewry] to contribute materially to the transfer of Jews from one diaspora to another, especially when most of these Jews (as is their right) drop out on the Jewish people as well as on Israel' (emphasis in the original), *JC* 31 March 1989, p. 28.

83. According to Altshuler's statistics, two-thirds of the refuseniks in 1987 were specialists in technology and science; Altshuler, 'Who are the "Refuseniks"?' (1988), pp. 12–13, and *Soviet Jewry* (1987) pp. 143 and 171).

84. Ibid., p. 170; L. Hirszowich *Gorbachev's Perestroika and the Jews* IJA Research Report no. 1 (1987), p. 3.

85. See, e.g. *Ogonek* 16, 16–23 April 1988, p. 5.

86. Ryzhkov *Pravda*, 4 March 1986, p. 2; Hirszowicz, *Gorbachev's Perest-roika* (1987), p. 3.

87. Altshuler, *op. cit.*, p. 127.

88. Personal interviews with Moscow Jews on 18 and 19 July 1988; I.J. Leibler *The Jerusalem Post* 25 Oct. 1987, p. 8; I. Beizer *Jews and Jewish Topics* . . . 5 (Summer 1987), pp. 54–5; and Torpusman and Fulmakht 'Contemporary anti-Semitism', p. 67.

89. M. Frank-Kamenetskii 'Mekhanizmy Tormozheniya v Nauke' in Yu. Afanasiev *Inovo ne Dano* (Moscow, *Progress* 1988), p. 640; and V. Goldanskii *Sovetskaya Kul'tura*, 28 May 1988, p. 3.

90. E.g., *Jews in the USSR* 17 (15) 21 April 1988; 17 (20) 26 May 1988; 17 (26) 7 July 1988; *SJA* 19 (1) pp. 93–4 (7 July and 9–10 Aug.); Torpusman and Fulmakht, 'Contemporary anti-Semitism', p. 61. The exception is the murder, probably for anti-Semitic reasons, of Naum Nemchenko in Sept. 1987 (*ibid.*,p. 68).

91. Interviews with Moscow Jews on 18 and 19 July 1988. It was as a result of these fears that local Jews contacted the KGB, and D. Vasil'ev, the leader of *Pamyat'*, was subsequently warned (*Argumenty i Fakty*, 23, 4–11 June 1988, p. 7.)

92. E.g., letter in *Pravda* 12 May 1989, p. 3; Torpusman and Fulmakht 'Contemporary anti-Semitism' p. 64; *JC* 7 April 1989.

93. Altshuler, *Soviet Jewry* (1987), p. 50.

94. Even the more radical proposals so far have limited themselves to 'non-bureaucratic' solutions such as Jewish cultural autonomy or Jewish representation on the Supreme Soviet. See e.g., G. Popov '*Pamyat*' i "*Pamyat*"' *Znamya* 1 (Jan. 1988), p. 200; *JC* 15 Sept. 1988, p. 8.

95. Apart from rumours of pogroms in Moscow, there has also been a threat

that inter-communal violence in the outlying republics to the south, where it is harder for the authorities to keep control, might take on an anti-Semitic colouring (e.g., *Jerusalem Post* 1 Sept. 1989, p. 4).

96. Compare, for example, a leading Western expert's depressingly bleak account of Soviet Jewry in 1980, in which he wrote of a 'final divorce between Jewish citizens and the Soviet system', and his cautiously optimistic treatment of the subject eight years later, where he spoke of 'significant numbers of people who believe that some form of Jewish existence is possible, and desirable, in the Soviet Union': Z. Gitelman 'Moscow and Soviet Jews: a parting of the ways' *Problems of Communism* 29 (1) (Jan. – Feb. 1980), p. 34; and Z. Gitelman 'Gorbachev's reforms and the future of Soviet Jewry' *SJA* 18 (2) (Summer 1988), pp. 14–15.

APPENDIX 1: TERRITORIAL AND ETHNIC CLAIMS IN TH

TRANSCAUCASIA

ERRATUM

In the final stages of the book's production an earlier version
of the map showing territorial and ethnic claims in the Soviet
Union was wrongly inserted as Appendix 1.
The correct version is printed overleaf.
p. 72 Line 7. Should read 62,500 square kilometres.

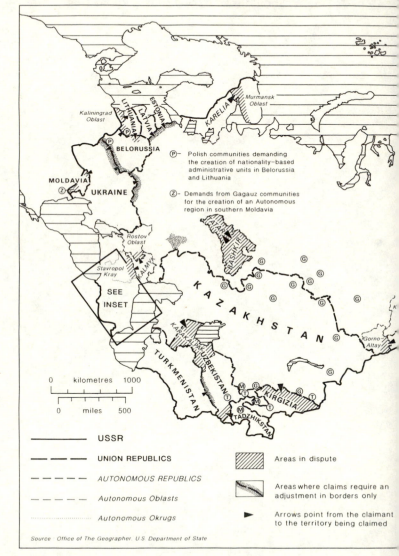

P – Polish communities demanding
the creation of nationality–based
administrative units in Belorussia
and Lithuania

Z – Demands from Gagauz communities
for the creation of an Autonomous
region in southern Moldavia

0   kilometres   1000

0   miles   500

——————— USSR

– – – – – UNION REPUBLICS

– · – · – · – AUTONOMOUS REPUBLICS

– – – – – Autonomous Oblasts

················ Autonomous Okrugs

Areas in dispute

Areas where claims require an
adjustment in borders only

► Arrows point from the claimant
to the territory being claimed

Source : Office of The Geographer, U.S. Department of State

THE SOVIET UNION

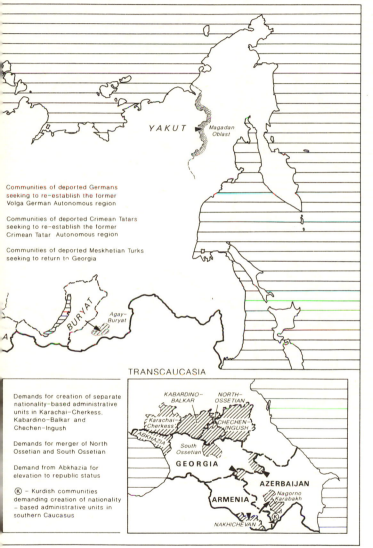

YAKUT

Magadan
Oblast

Communities of deported Germans
seeking to re-establish the former
Volga German Autonomous region

Communities of deported Crimean Tatars
seeking to re-establish the former
Crimean Tatar Autonomous region

Communities of deported Meskhetian Turks
seeking to return to Georgia

BURYAT

Agay-
Buryat

TRANSCAUCASIA

Demands for creation of separate
nationality-based administrative
units in Karachai-Cherkess,
Kabardino-Balkar and
Chechen-Ingush

Demands for merger of North
Ossetian and South Ossetian

Demand from Abkhazia for
elevation to republic status

Ⓚ - Kurdish communities
demanding creation of nationality
- based administrative units in
southern Caucasus

KABARDINO-
BALKAR

NORTH-
OSSETIAN

Karachai-
Cherkess

CHECHEN-
INGUSH

ABKHAZIA

South
Ossetian

GEORGIA

AZERBAIJAN

ARMENIA

Nagorno
Karabakh

Ⓚ

NAKHICHEVAN

Comparative tables for the major nationalities

Table no.

1. Populations of the major nationalities of the USSR, 1959–89

2. Republic populations, total and urban, 1979 and 1989

3. Nationality composition of the union republics, 1959–79

4. Proportion of the major nationalities declaring their nationality language as their native tongue, 1959, 1979 and 1989

5. Proportion of the major nationalities declaring a knowledge of Russian as a second language, 1970, 1979 and 1989

6. Social structure by nationality, 1959 and 1979

7. Students in higher education by union republic, 1970–71 and 1986–87

8. Personal income distribution by union republic, 1988

9. Births, deaths and natural increase by union republic, 1960–87

Table 1   Populations of the major nationalities of the USSR, 1959–89[1]

	Population (000s)			Population (000s)	
			Increase		*Increase*
	1959	*1979*	*1959–79 (%)*	*1989*	*1979–89 (%)*
Russians	114,114	137,397	20.4	145,071	5.6
Estonians	989	1,020	3.2	1,027	0.7
Latvians	1,400	1,439	2.8	1,459	1.4
Lithuanians	2,326	2,851	22.6	3,068	7.6
Ukrainians	37,253	42,347	13.7	44,135	4.2
Belorussians	7,913	9,463	19.5	10,304	6.0
Moldavians	2,214	2,968	34.0	3,355	13.0
Armenians	2,787	4,151	48.9	4,627	11.5
Azerbaijanis	2,940	5,477	86.3	6,791	24.0
Georgians	2,692	3,571	32.7	3,983	11.6
Kazakhs	3,622	6,556	81.0	8,137	24.1
Uzbeks	6,015	12,456	107.1	16,686	34.0
Turkmens	1,002	2,028	102.5	2,718	34.0
Tadzhiks	1,397	2,898	107.4	4,216	45.5
Kirgiz	969	1,906	96.8	2,530	32.8
Tatars[2]	4,968	6,317	26.0	6,645	–
Chuvash	1,470	1,751	50.7	839	5.0
Bashkirs	989	1,371	68.2	1,449	5.7
Mordovians	1,285	1,192	30.3	1,153	−3.2
Chechens	419	756	80.9	958	26.8
Udmurts	625	714	67.2	746	4.6
Mari	504	622	49.3	670	7.8
Ossetians	413	542	55.2	597	10.3
Buryats	253	353	58.6	421	19.6
Yakut	233	328	95.7	382	16.5
Germans	1,620	1,936	19.5	2,035	5.1
Jews	2,268	1,761	−22.4	1,376	−21.8
Poles	1,380	1,151	−16.6	1,126	−2.2

1 Includes all nationalities with populations of 500,000 or more at the time of the 1989 census, together with the Buryat and Yakut.

2 Both the 1959 and 1979 figures include the Crimean Tatars, whereas the 1989 census records them as a separate nationality. According to that census, there are 268,739 Crimean Tatars.

Sources: Tsentral'noe Statisticheskoe Upravlenie pri Sovete Ministrov SSSR *Itogi Vsesoyuznoi Perepisi 1970 Naseleniya goda* (Moscow, Statistika 1973) vol. IV, p.144; Tsentral'noe Statisticheskoe Upravlenie SSSR *Naselenie SSSR. Po Vsesoyuznoi Perepisi Naseleniya 1979 goda* (Moscow, Izdatel'stvo Politicheskoi Literatury 1980), pp. 23–6; Gosudarstvennyi Kommitet SSSR Po Statistike Soobshchaet *Natsional'nyi Sostav Naseleniya*, (Moscow, forthcoming), Vol. 11, pp. 3–4.

Table 2   Republic populations, total and urban, 1979 and 1989

	1979			1989		
	Total (000s)	Urban (000s)	% urban	Total (000s)	Urban (000s)	% urban
Russian republic	137,551	95,374	69	147,386	108,419	74
Estonia	1,466	1,022	70	1,573	1,127	71
Latvia	2,521	1,726	68	2,681	1,907	71
Lithuania	3,398	2,062	61	3,690	2,509	68
Ukraine	49,755	30,512	61	51,704	34,591	67
Belorussia	9,560	5,263	55	10,200	6,676	65
Moldavia	3,947	1,551	39	4,341	2,037	47
Armenia	3,031	1,993	66	3,283	2,225	68
Azerbaijan	6,028	3,200	53	7,029	3,785	54
Georgia	5,015	2,601	52	5,449	3,033	56
Kazakhstan	14,685	7,920	54	16,538	9,465	57
Uzbekistan	15,391	6,348	41	19,906	8,106	41
Turkmenistan	2,759	1,323	48	3,534	1,603	45
Tadzhikistan	3,801	1,325	35	5,112	1,667	33
Kirgizia	3,529	1,366	39	4,291	1,641	38
Tatar ASSR	3,436	2,172	63	3,640	2,658	73
Buryat ASSR	901	512	57	1,042	641	62
Yakut ASSR	839	514	61	1,081	721	67
USSR total	262,436	163,586	62	286,717	188,791	66

Sources: Tsentral'noe Statisticheskoe Upravlenie SSSR, *Naselenie SSSR, Po Vsesoyuznoi Perepisi Naseleniya 1979 goda* (Moscow, Izdatel'stvo Politicheskoi Literatury 1980), pp. 4–11; *Izvestiya* 28 April 1989; Pravda 29 April 1989.

Table 3 Nationality composition of the union republics, 1959–79

| | 1959 | | | | 1979 | | | |
	Total (000s)	Percentage Indigenous	Russian	Other	Total (000s)	Percentage Indigenous	Russian	Other
Russian republic	117,534	88.3	88.3	16.7	130,079	82.8	82.8	17.2
Estonia	1,197	74.6	20.1	5.3	1,464	64.7	27.9	7.4
Latvia	2,093	62.0	26.6	11.4	2,503	53.7	32.8	13.5
Lithuania	2,711	79.3	8.5	12.2	3,391	80.0	8.9	11.1
Ukraine	41,869	76.8	16.9	6.3	49,609	73.6	21.1	5.3
Belorussia	8,056	81.1	8.2	10.7	9,532	79.4	11.9	8.7
Moldavia	2,885	65.4	10.1	24.4	3,950	63.9	12.8	23.3
Armenia	1,763	88.0	3.2	8.8	3,037	89.7	2.3	8.0
Azerbaijan	3,698	67.5	13.6	18.9	6,027	78.1	7.9	14.0
Georgia	4,044	54.3	10.1	25.6	5,015	68.8	7.4	23.8
Kazakhstan	9,295	30.0	42.7	27.3	14,684	36.0	40.8	23.2
Uzbekistan	8,119	62.1	13.5	24.4	15,789	68.7	10.8	20.5
Turkmenistan	1,516	60.9	17.3	21.8	2,765	68.4	12.6	19.0
Tadzhikistan	1,981	53.1	13.3	13.6	3,806	58.8	10.4	30.8
Kirgizia	3,523	47.9	25.9	26.2	3,523	47.9	25.9	26.2

Sources: Tsentral'noe Statisticheskoe Upravlenie pri Sovete Ministrov SSSR *Itogi Vsesoyuznoi Perepisi Naseleniya 1970 goda* (Moscow, Statistika, 1973) vol. IV, p. 144; Tsentral'noe Statisticheskoe Upravlenie SSSR, *Naselenie SSSR. Po Vsesoyuznoi Perepisi Naseleniya 1979 goda* (Moscow, Izdatel'stvo Politicheskoi Literatury 1980) pp. 27–30.

Table 4 Proportion of the major nationalities declaring their nationality language as their native tongue, 1959, 1979 and 1989

	1959					1979			1989
	Total	Urban	Residing in own nationality republic	Residing outside nationality republic	Total	Urban	Residing in own nationality republic	Residing outside nationality republic	Total
Russians	99.8	99.9	100.0	99.3	99.8	99.4	100.0	99.9	99.8
Estonians	95.2	93.1	99.3	56.6	95.3	93.4	99.0	33.3	95.5
Latvians	95.1	93.1	98.4	53.2	95.0	93.3	97.8	55.3	94.8
Lithuanians	97.8	96.6	99.2	80.3	97.9	97.4	97.9	63.9	97.7
Ukrainians	87.7	77.2	93.5	51.2	82.8	73.7	89.1	43.8	81.1
Belorussians	84.2	63.5	93.2	41.9	74.2	59.1	83.5	36.8	70.9
Moldavians	95.2	78.4	98.2	77.7	93.2	81.3	96.5	74.3	91.6
Armenians	89.9	84.4	99.2	78.1	90.7	87.6	99.4	73.9	91.6
Azerbaijanis	97.5	96.4	98.1	95.1	97.9	96.2	98.7	92.7	97.6
Georgians	98.6	96.8	99.5	73.4	98.3	96.9	99.4	67.3	98.2
Kazakhs	98.4	96.7	99.2	95.6	97.5	97.1	98.6	92.8	97.0
Uzbeks	98.4	96.7	98.6	97.4	98.5	96.1	98.8	96.9	98.3
Turkmens	98.9	97.3	99.5	92.0	98.7	97.0	99.2	90.4	98.5
Tadzhiks	98.1	96.4	99.3	94.6	97.8	95.9	99.3	92.8	97.7
Kirgiz	98.7	97.4	99.7	92.3	97.9	97.3	99.6	84.8	97.8
Tatars	92.0	87.5	98.9	89.3	85.9	81.0	97.9	81.8	83.2
Chuvash	90.8	71.2	97.5	83.2	81.7	64.7	89.8	73.4	76.5
Bashkirs	61.9	73.3	57.6	75.1	67.0	72.8	64.4	72.6	72.3
Mordovians	78.1	52.2	97.3	70.9	72.6	55.1	94.3	63.9	67.0
Chechens	98.8	97.0	99.7	97.8	98.6	96.3	99.7	94.0	98.0
Udmurts	89.1	69.7	93.2	75.9	76.5	60.6	82.3	64.4	69.6
Mari	95.1	75.8	97.8	91.6	86.7	72.3	83.7	79.9	80.8
Ossetians	89.1	82.0	98.0	73.1	88.2	84.2	92.3	75.8	87.0

Table 4—Contd.

	1959				1979				1989
	Total	Urban	Residing in own nationality republic	Residing outside nationality republic	Total	Urban	Residing in own nationality republic	Residing outside nationality republic	Total
Buryats	94.9	81.5	97.3	84.9	90.2	78.8	93.1	86.0	86.3
Yakut	97.5	90.7	98.2	82.8	95.3	86.1	96.4	72.3	93.8
Germans	75.0	66.3	–	–	57.0	48.5	–	–	48.7
Jews	21.5	21.0	–	–	14.2	12.3	–	–	11.1
Poles	45.2	38.6	–	–	29.1	27.8	–	–	30.4
Crimean Tatars	–	–	–	–	–	–	–	–	92.5

Sources: Tsentral'noe Statisticheskoe Upravlenie pri Sovete Ministrov SSSR *Itogi Vsesoyuznoi Perepisi Naseleniya 1970 goda* (Moscow, Statistika 1973) vol. IV, p.144; Tsentral'noe Statisticheskoe Upravlenie SSSR *Naselenie SSSR. Po Vsesoyuznoi Perepisi Naseleniya 1979 goda* (Moscow, Izdatel'stvo Politicheskoi Literatury 1980); Gosudarstvennyi Komitet SSSR Po Statistike Soobshchaet, *Natsional'nyi Sostav Naseleniya* (Moscow, forthcoming), Vol. 11, pp. 3–5.

Table 5   Proportion of the major nationalities declaring a knowledge of Russian as a second language, 1970, 1979 and 1989 (percentages)

	1970	1979	1989
Russians	0.1	0.1	0.1
Estonians	29.0	24.2	33.8
Latvians	45.2	56.7	64.4
Lithuanians	35.9	52.1	37.9
Ukrainians	36.3	49.8	56.2
Belorussians	49.0	57.0	54.7
Moldavians	36.1	47.4	53.8
Armenians	30.1	38.6	47.1
Azerbaijanis	16.6	29.5	34.4
Georgians	21.3	26.7	33.1
Kazakhs	41.8	52.3	60.4
Uzbeks	14.5	49.3	23.8
Turkmens	15.4	25.4	27.8
Tadzhiks	15.4	29.6	27.7
Kirgiz	19.1	29.4	35.2
Tatars	62.5	68.9	70.8
Chuvash	58.4	64.8	65.1
Bashkirs	53.3	64.9	71.8
Mordovians	65.7	65.5	62.5
Chechens	66.7	76.0	74.0
Udmurts	63.3	64.4	61.3
Mari	62.4	69.9	68.8
Ossetians	58.6	64.9	68.9
Buryats	66.7	71.9	72.0
Yakut	41.7	55.6	64.9
Germans	59.6	51.7	45.0
Jews	16.3	13.7	10.1
Poles	37.0	44.7	43.9
Crimean Tatars	–	–	76.0

Sources: Tsentral'noe Statisticheskoe Upravlenie SSSR *Naselenie SSSR. Po Vsesoyuznoi Perepisi Naseleniya 1979 goda* (Moscow, Izdatel'stvo Politicheskoi Literatury 1980), pp. 23–6; Gosudarstvennyi Komitet SSSR Po Statistike Soobshchaet, *Natsional'nyi Sostav Naseleniya* (Moscow, forthcoming), Vol. 11, pp. 3–5.

Table 6 Social structure by nationality, 1959 and 1979 (percentages)

	1959			1979		
	Workers	*White-collar workers*	*Collective farm workers*	*Workers*	*White-collar workers*	*Collective farm workers*
Russians	54	22	24	63	31	6
Estonians	51	22	27	57	32	10
Latvians	46	19	35	58	28	14
Lithuanians	34	14	52	56	27	17
Ukrainians	34	13	52	56	23	22
Belorussians	31	12	57	59	23	18
Moldavians	13	4	83	54	15	31
Armenians	40	22	40	62	31	7
Azerbaijanis	34	15	51	58	23	19
Georgians	22	23	54	49	32	19
Kazakhs	43	16	40	64	28	8
Uzbeks	27	8	65	50	18	32
Turkmens	22	9	69	39	16	45
Tadzhiks	18	8	74	55	15	30
Kirgiz	22	8	70	56	20	24

Source: Yu. Arutunyan et al. *Sotsial'no-Kul'turnyi oblik Sovetskikh Natsii (Po materialam etnosotsiologicheskogo issledovaniya)* (Moscow, Nauka 1986), p. 55.

Table 7   Students in higher education by union republic, 1970–71 and 1986–87 (per 10,000 population)

	1970–71	1986–87
Russian republic	204	200
Estonia	161	151
Latvia	171	164
Lithuania	180	178
Ukraine	170	166
Belorussia	154	179
Moldavia	124	126
Armenia	214	160
Azerbaijan	191	155
Georgia	189	163
Kazakhstan	151	169
Uzbekistan	192	153
Turkmenistan	131	117
Tadzhikistan	149	115
Kirgizia	162	141
USSR total	188	181

Source: Gosudarstvennyi komitet SSSR po Statistike *Narodnoe Khozyaistvo SSSR za 70 let* (Moscow, Finansy i statistika 1987), p. 550.

Table 8 Personal income distribution by union republic, 1988
(percentage monthly earnings in roubles)

	Less than 75	75–100	100–150	150–200	Over 200
Russian republic	6.3	13.1	34.0	24.6	22.0
Estonia	3.9	9.0	28.0	25.5	33.6
Latvia	3.2	9.5	31.8	27.2	28.3
Lithuania	3.6	10.7	34.6	27.1	24.0
Ukraine	8.1	16.8	38.5	22.4	14.2
Belorussia	5.0	12.9	36.8	25.8	19.5
Moldavia	13.0	19.8	37.3	18.9	11.0
Armenia	18.1	21.5	34.7	16.2	9.5
Azerbaijan	33.3	22.2	27.3	10.9	6.3
Georgia	16.3	17.4	31.6	18.1	16.6
Kazakhstan	15.9	19.3	33.7	18.1	13.0
Uzbekistan	44.7	23.9	22.2	6.4	2.8
Turkmenistan	36.6	23.0	25.8	9.4	5.2
Tadzhikistan	58.6	20.7	15.5	3.8	1.4
Kirgizia	37.1	23.1	26.0	9.2	4.6
USSR	12.6	15.7	33.3	21.2	17.2

Source: A Kovalev Kto i pochemu za chertoi bednosti, *Ekonomicheskaya gazeta* 25, 1989, p. 11.

Table 9   Births, deaths and natural increase by union republic, 1960–87
(per thousand population)

	1960			1987		
	Births	Deaths	Natural increase	Births	Deaths	Natural increase
Russian republic	23.2	7.4	15.8	17.1	10.5	6.6
Estonia	16.6	10.5	6.1	16.0	11.7	4.3
Latvia	16.7	10.0	6.7	15.8	12.1	3.7
Lithuania	22.5	7.8	14.7	16.2	10.1	6.1
Ukraine	20.5	6.9	11.4	14.8	13.6	3.4
Belorussia	24.4	6.6	17.8	16.1	9.9	6.2
Moldavia	29.3	6.4	22.9	21.8	9.6	12.2
Armenia	40.1	6.8	33.3	22.9	5.7	17.2
Azerbaijan	42.6	6.7	35.9	26.9	6.7	20.2
Georgia	24.7	6.5	18.2	17.9	8.8	9.1
Kazakhstan	37.2	6.6	30.6	25.5	7.5	18.0
Uzbekistan	39.8	6.0	33.8	37.0	6.9	30.1
Turkmenistan	42.2	6.5	35.9	37.2	7.9	29.3
Tadzhikistan	33.5	5.1	28.4	41.8	6.9	34.9
Kirgizia	36.9	6.1	30.8	32.6	7.3	25.3
USSR	24.9	7.1	17.8	19.8	9.9	9.9

Source: Gosudarstvennyi Komitet SSSR po Statistike. *Narodnoe khozyaistvo SSSR v 1987g. Statisticheskii Ezhegodnik* (Moscow, Finansy i statistika 1988), pp. 354–55.

Select Bibliographic Guide to Further Reading in the English Language

GENERAL

Besancon, A. 'The Nationalities Issue in the USSR' *Survey* vol. 30 (4), (1989), pp. 113–30.

Bialer, S. (ed) *Politics, Society and Nationality inside Gorbachev's Russia* (Boulder, Westview Press 1989).

Connor, W. *The National Question in Marxist-Leninist Theory and Strategy* (Princeton, NJ, Princeton University Press 1984).

Carrere d'Encausse, H. *Decline of Empire: the Soviet Socialist Republics in Revolt* (New York, Newsweek Books 1979).

Gellner, E. 'Ethnicity and Faith in Eastern Europe' *Daedalus* vol. 119 (1), 1990, pp. 279–94.

Gleason, G. *Federalism and Nationalism. The Struggle for Republican Rights in the USSR* (Westview Press, 1990).

Goble, P. 'Ethnic Politics in the USSR *Problems of Communism*, vol. 38 (1989), pp. 1–14.

Karklins, E. *Ethnic Relations in the USSR: the Perspective from Below* (Boston, Allen & Unwin 1986).

Katz Z. (ed.) *Handbook of Major Soviet Nationalities* (New York, Free Press 1975).

Kozlov, V. *The Peoples of the Soviet Union* The Second World Series (London, Hutchinson 1988).

Lapidus, G. 'Gorbachev's Nationalities Problem' *Foreign Affairs* (autumn 1989), pp. 92–108.

McAuley, M. 'Nationalism and the Soviet Multi-Ethnic State' in N. Harding (ed.) *The State in Socialist Society* (London, Macmillan 1984).

Motyl, A. *Will the Non-Russians Rebel? State, Ethnicity and Stability in the USSR* (Ithaca, NY, and London, Cornell University Press 1987).

Nahaylo, B. and Swoboda, V. *Soviet Disunion: A History of the Nationalities Problem in the USSR* (London, Hamish Hamilton, 1990).

Shanin, T. 'Ethnicity in the Soviet Union: Analytical Perceptions and Political Strategies' *Comparative Studies in Society and History* vol. 31, (1989), pp. 409–24.

Smith, G. 'Gorbachev's Greatest Challenge: Perestroika and the National Question' *Political Geography Quarterly*, vol. 8(1), (1989), pp. 7–20.

RUSSIANS

Allworth, E. (ed.) *Ethnic Russia in the USSR: the Dilemma of Dominance* (New York, Pergamon 1980).

Carter, S. *Russian Nationalism: Yesterday, Today and Tomorrow* (London, Pinter, 1990).

Dunlop, J. *The Faces of Contemporary Russian Nationalism* (Princeton, NJ, Princeton University Press 1983).

Hosking, G. *Beyond Socialist Realism: Soviet Fiction since Ivan Denisovich* (London, Granada 1980).

Szporluk, R. 'Dilemmas of Russian Nationalism' *Problems of Communism* 38(4), (1989), pp. 15–35.

Yanov, A. *The Russian Challenge* (Oxford, Basil Blackwell 1987).

BALTIC REPUBLICS

Allworth, E. (ed.) *Nationality Group Survival in Multi-Ethnic States: Shifting Support Patterns in the Soviet Baltic Region* (New York, Praeger 1977).

Dreifelds, J. 'Latvian National Rebirth' *Problems of Communism* vol. 38 (1989), pp. 77–94.

Misiunas, R. and Taagepera, R. *The Baltic States: Years of Dependence, 1940–1980* (Berkeley, University of California Press 1983).

Parming, T. and Jarvesoo, E. *A Case Study of a Soviet Republic: the Estonian SSR* (Boulder, CO, Westview Press 1978).

Remeikis, T. *Opposition to Soviet rule in Lithuania, 1945–1980* (Chicago, Institute of Lithuanian Studies Press 1980).

Smith, G. 'The Nationalities Problem in the Soviet Baltic Republics of Estonia, Latvia and Lithuania' *Acta Baltica* vol. 21, (1982), pp. 143–77.

Vardys, V. S. *The Catholic Church, Dissent and Nationality in Soviet Lithuania* (Boulder, CO/New York, East European Quarterly-Columbia University Press 1978).

Vardys, V. S. 'Lithuanian National Politics' *Problems of Communism* vol. 38 (1989), pp. 53–76.

Von Rauch, G. *The Baltic States: the Years of Independence, 1917–1940* (London, C. Hurst & Co. 1974).

SOUTH-WESTERN BORDERLANDS

Bacon, W. M. *Behind Closed Doors: Secret Papers on the Failure of the Romanian–Soviet Negotiations, 1931–1932* (Stanford, CA. 1979).

Bruchis, M. *Nations–Nationalities–People: a Study of the Nationalities Policy of the Communist Party in Soviet Moldavia* (New York, Columbia University Press 1984).

Guthier, S. 'The Belorussians: National Identification and Assimilation, 1897–1970' *Soviet Studies* vol. 29(1), (Jan. 1977) pp. 37–61, and vol. 29(2) (April 1977), pp. 270–83.

Krawchenko, B. (ed.) *Ukraine after Shelest* (Edmonton, Canadian Institute of Ukrainian Studies, University of Alberta 1983).

Krawchenko, B. *Social Change and National Consciousness in Twentieth-Century Ukraine* (London, Macmillan 1985).

Lewytzkyj, B. *Politics and Society in Soviet Ukraine 1953–1980* (Edmonton, Canadian Institute of Ukrainian Studies, University of Alberta, 1984).

Popovici, A. *The Political Status of Bessarabia* (Washington, DC, Randsdell 1931).

Vakar, N. *Belorussia: the Making of a Nation* (Cambridge, MA, Harvard University Press 1956).

TRANSCAUCASIA

Allen, W. *A History of the Georgian People* (New York, Barnes & Noble 1971).

Dragadze, T. 'The Armenian–Azerbaijani Conflict:Structure and Sentiment' *Third World Quarterly* vol. 11(1) (1989).

Lang, D. M. *A Modern History of Georgia* (New York, Grove Press 1962).

Lang, D. M. *The Armenians: a People in Exile* (London, Unwin Hyman 1988).

Jones, S. 'The Establishment of Soviet Power in Transcaucasia: the Case of Georgia 1921–1928' *Soviet Studies* vol. 40 (4) (Oct. 1982).

Matossian, M. K. *The Impact of Soviet Policies on Armenia* (Leiden, E. J. Brill 1962).

Parsons, R. 'National Integration in Soviet Georgia', *Soviet Studies* vol. 34 (4) (Oct. 1982).

Suny, R. G. *The Making of the Modern Georgian Nation* (London, Tauris 1989).

Suny, R. G. (ed.) *Transcaucasia, Nationalism and Social Change*, (Michigan Slavic Publications, University of Michigan 1983).

Swietochowski, T. *Russian Azerbaijan 1905–1920: the Shaping of National Identity in a Muslim Community* (Cambridge, Cambridge University Press).

Walker, C. J. *Armenia: the Survival of a Nation* (London, Croom Helm 1980).

MUSLIM CENTRAL ASIA

Akiner, S. *Islamic Peoples of the Soviet Union* (London, Kegan Paul International 1983).

Allworth, E. (ed.) *The Nationality Question in Soviet Central Asia* (New York, Praeger 1973).

Bennigsen, A. and Wimbush, A. S. *Muslims of the Soviet Empire: a Guide* (London, C. Hurst & Co. 1986).

Benson, L. and Svanberg, I. (eds) *The Kazaks of China: Essays on an Ethnic Minority* Acta Universitatis Upsaliensis: Studia Mulitiethnica Upsaliensia, 5 (Uppsala, Almqvist & Wiksell International 1988).

Hambly, G. *et al. Central Asia* (London, Weidenfeld & Nicolson 1969).

Hatto, A. T. *The Memorial Feast for Kokotoy-Khan* (Oxford, Oxford University Press 1977).

Krader, L. and Wayne, I. *The Kazakhs: a Background Study for Psychological Warfare* Human Resources Research Office, Technical Report 23 (Washington, DC 1955).

Lubin, N. *Labour and Nationality in Soviet Central Asia* (Princeton N.J., Princeton University Press 1984).

McCagg, W. O. and Silver, B. (eds) *Soviet Asian Ethnic Frontiers* (New York and Oxford, Pergamon 1979).

Olcott, M. B. *The Kazakhs* (Stanford, CA, Hoover Institution Press 1987).

Omurkulov, K. *Kirghizia* (Moscow, Novosti 1987).

Rakowska-Harmstone, T. *Russia and Nationalism in Central Asia: the Case of Tadzhikistan* (Baltimore, MD, Johns Hopkins University Press 1970).

Rywkin, M. *Moscow's Muslim Challenge: Soviet Central Asia* (New York and London, Hurst, 1982).

Rumer, B. *Soviet Central Asia: 'A Tragic Experiment'* (Boston, Unwin Hyman 1989).

Saray, M. *The Turkmen in the Age of Imperialism: a Study of the Turkmen People and their Incorporation into the Russian Empire* (Ankara, Turkish Historical Society Printing House 1989).

Wheeler, G. *The Modern History of Soviet Central Asia*, (New York, Praeger 1964).

NON-RUSSIANS OF THE RUSSIAN REPUBLIC

Armstrong, T. *Russian Settlement in the North* (Cambridge, Cambridge University Press 1965).

Bawden, C. *Shamans, Lamas and Evangelicals* (London, Routledge & Kegan Paul 1985).

Humphrey, C. *Karl Marx Collective: Economy, Society and Religion in a Siberian Collective Farm* (Cambridge, Cambridge University Press 1983).

Jochelson, W. 'The Yakut' *American Museum of Natural History, Anthropological Papers* vol. 33, Pt. 2 (1933), pp. 35–225.

Rorlich, A–A. *The Volga Tatars: the Profile of a People in National Resilience* (Stanford, CA, Hoover Institution Press, Stanford University 1986).

Tokarev, S. A. and Gurvich, I. S. 'The Yakuts' in M. Levin and L. Potapov (eds) *The Peoples of Siberia* (Chicago, Chicago University Press 1964), pp. 243–304.

Wood, A. and French, A. (eds) *The Development of Siberia: People and Resources* (London, Macmillan 1989).

DIASPORA NATIONALITIES

Allworth, E. (ed.) *Tatars of the Crimea: Their Struggle for Survival* (Durham, NC, Duke University Press 1988).

Fisher, A. *The Crimean Tatars* (Stanford, CA, Hoover Institution Press, 1978).

Freedman, I. (ed.) *Soviet Jewry in the 1980s* (Durham, NC, Duke University Press 1989).

Gitelman, Z. *A Century of Ambivalence* (New York, Schocken Books 1988).

Koch, F. C. *The Volga Germans in Russia and the Americas from 1763 to the Present* (Pennsylvania, Pennsylvania University Press 1977).

Kochan, L. (ed.) *The Jews in Soviet Russia since 1917* 3rd ed (Oxford, Oxford University Press 1978).

Kreindler, I. 'The Soviet Deported Nationalities: a Summary and an Update' *Soviet Studies* vol. 38, no. 3 (1986), pp. 387–405.

Pinkus, B. *The Soviet Government and the Jews 1948–1967* (Cambridge, Cambridge University Press 1984).

Sheehy, A. *The Crimean Tatars and Volga Germans: Soviet Treatment of Two National Minorities* (London, Minority Rights Group Report no. 6, 1971).

Wimbush S. E. and Wixman, R. 'The Meskhetian Turks: a New voice in Soviet Central Asia' *Canadian Slavonic Studies* no. 2–3 (1975).

Index